T0332235

Cost Estimation Techniques for Web Projects

Emilia Mendes
University of Auckland, New Zealand

IGI PUBLISHING
Hershey • New York

Acquisition Editor:	Kristin Klinger
Senior Managing Editor:	Jennifer Neidig
Managing Editor:	Sara Reed
Development Editor:	Kristin Roth
Typesetter:	Amanda Appicello
Cover Design:	Lisa Tosheff
Printed at:	Yurchak Printing Inc.

Published in the United States of America by
IGI Publishing (an imprint of IGI Global)
701 E. Chocolate Avenue
Hershey PA 17033
Tel: 717-533-8845
Fax: 717-533-8661
E-mail: cust@igi-pub.com
Web site: http://www.igi-pub.com

and in the United Kingdom by
IGI Publishing (an imprint of IGI Global)
3 Henrietta Street
Covent Garden
London WC2E 8LU
Tel: 44 20 7240 0856
Fax: 44 20 7379 0609
Web site: http://www.eurospanonline.com

Copyright © 2008 by IGI Global. All rights reserved. No part of this book may be reproduced in any form or
by any means, electronic or mechanical, including photocopying, without written permission from the publisher.

Product or company names used in this book are for identification purposes only. Inclusion of the names of
the products or companies does not indicate a claim of ownership by IGI Global of the trademark or registered
trademark.

Library of Congress Cataloging-in-Publication Data

Mendes, Emilia.
 Estimation techniques for web projects / Emilia Mendes.
 p. cm.
 Summary: "This book provides a step-by-step methodology to improving cost estimation practices for Web
projects. Utilizing such techniques as stepwise regression modeling, case-base reasoning, classification and
regression trees, and expert opinion, it is a powerful tool for scholars, researchers, and practitioners in the areas
of Web development, Web engineering, project management, and software engineering"--Provided by publisher.
 Includes bibliographical references and index.
 ISBN 978-1-59904-135-3 (hardcover) -- ISBN 978-1-59904-137-7 (ebook)
 1. Web site development industry--Costs. 2. Web site development--Costs. 3. Web site development--Man-
agement. I. Title.
 HD9696.82.A2M46 2008
 006.7068'1--dc22
                          2007022426

British Cataloguing in Publication Data
A Cataloguing in Publication record for this book is available from the British Library.

All work contributed to this book is new, previously-unpublished material. The views expressed in this book are
those of the authors, but not necessarily of the publisher.

Cost Estimation Techniques for Web Projects

Table of Contents

Preface

A cornerstone of Web project management is sound effort estimation, which is the process by which a person, group of people, tool, model, or a combination of these predicts the amount of effort needed to accomplish a given task. The importance of having realistic effort estimates at an early stage in a project's life cycle is widely recognised by Web project managers and developers since accurate estimates are paramount to manage resources effectively, and to considerably increase the probability that projects will be finished on time and within budget.

However, recent findings showed that numerous Web projects worldwide are still not finished within time and budget, and one of the main reasons for that is the use of poor project management practices, which includes poor effort estimation (Ginige, 2002).

Given that the field of Web effort estimation is relatively new, with its first paper published only in 2000 (Mendes, Counsell, & Mosley, 2000), it would not be surprising that research findings in this field may not have reached industry widely.

Effort estimation, also known as cost estimation, is a necessary part of an effective process, whether this process is Web authoring, design, testing, or development as a whole. An effort estimation process involves the following steps (Fenton & Pfleeger, 1987).

1. The identification of factors perceived to influence effort (e.g., size measures, cost drivers) and the type of relationship they have with effort

2. The gathering of past project data using as basis the factors identified in Step 1. If gathering a Web company's own data is not possible, this phase can in-

volve the use of large cross-company data sets with data on numerous diverse projects.

3. The use of one or several effort estimation techniques to be applied to estimate effort for new projects. The effort estimates generated by these techniques can also be adjusted using expert opinion.

4. The assessment of how effective the prediction technique is

It is important that all these steps are followed; otherwise, the effort estimates obtained may not be as useful as they should.

Another important point is that effort prediction is generally based on the following.

• Knowledge of previous similar projects and applications managed by an organisation. This means that data from past projects may be essential in helping organisations estimate effort for new projects.

• Other project and application characteristics that are believed to be related to effort. Examples of project characteristics are the size of the development team, its experience with working on similar projects, and the number of different programming languages being used in a project. An example of an application characteristic is the size of the problem to be developed, which may encompass different attributes such as the total number of new Web pages, total number of images, number of features that were reused, and so forth.

The objective of this book is therefore to provide Web companies, researchers, and students with the necessary knowledge on Web effort and cost estimation. It includes step-by-step guidelines on how to use and compare several effort estimation techniques, which may considerably help companies improve their current effort estimation practices, and help researchers and students understand the process that needs to be carried out to estimate development effort.

The effort estimation techniques that are detailed in this book are those that have been to date the three mostly used effort estimation techniques in the Web effort estimation literature, namely, stepwise regression, case-based reasoning, and classification and regression trees (CART).

Throughout this book, we take the view that the use of past data on finished Web projects can be extremely useful and necessary to help obtain accurate effort estimates for new Web projects and also to help Web companies understand how they currently estimate effort for their new projects.

All chapters are self-contained, and whenever applicable, the chapters present a literature review of previous studies on the topic being explained in order to ensure that readers are familiarised with what has been previously published in the literature.

We also present detailed chapters on principles of statistics and empirical studies to provide readers with additional knowledge not only useful for Web effort and cost estimation, but also useful within the context of Web engineering.

It is important to note that despite Web effort estimation being one of the main components of project management, there are at least two other components also related to effort estimation that can indirectly benefit from the use of more sound estimating processes. These two other components are project productivity and development processes. Once a Web company identifies important factors that have a bearing on effort and gathers data on past projects, it is also possible to identify current productivity trends between projects and also between developers, and to assess if differences in development processes have any effect on the effort estimates proposed and learn how to improve processes. Therefore, a change to a more systematic way of estimating effort can also drive a company to improve its productivity and current development processes, which is always a positive outcome.

Purpose

The purpose of this book is to introduce practitioners, lecturers, researchers, and students to Web effort estimation concepts and detailed case studies. Our objective is to provide detailed knowledge on Web effort estimation, step-by-step guidelines on how to use particular effort estimation techniques to estimate effort for new projects, and lessons on how to compare the effort estimates provided by these techniques, which may also include comparison with other benchmarking effort estimates.

The motivation for this book was threefold. First, our experience in dealing with Web companies to improve their effort estimates showed that companies would like to know how to use different effort estimation techniques and how to compare these techniques; however, the literature available was either too brief or unavailable. Second, our experience teaching Web effort estimation to postgraduate students showed that the books that were completely devoted to the topic of effort estimation were all applied to conventional software development projects, which are very different from Web projects (see Chapter 1 for a detailed discussion). Third, our experience in giving tutorials on Web effort estimation to Web engineering researchers also showed the need for a single place where all the necessary information was available. There are several papers on Web effort estimation available, and also a book chapter; however, none details the processes that are used by different techniques to obtain effort estimates. Papers may compare different techniques, however each technique is presented very briefly and readers have to look for complementary literature to understand in detail and learn how to use these techniques.

Target Audience

The target audience of this book comprises Web project managers and developers, Web engineering and software engineering students, and Web and software researchers. This book does not assume readers are familiar with either effort estimation concepts or any of the effort estimation techniques described, or statistical principles.

Outline

The book is organised into 11 chapters, each briefly described as follows.

Chapter I introduces terminology related to hypertext, since this is the model the Web is based upon, then provides an overview of differences between Web and software development with respect to their development processes, technologies, quality factors, and measures. Finally it discusses the differences between Web cost estimation and software cost estimation.

Chapter II introduces the concepts related to Web effort estimation and effort estimation techniques. These concepts are later used in further chapters.

Chapter III describes the process to be used to assess the accuracy of an effort technique or model. This process is called cross-validation. In parallel with conducting a cross-validation, prediction accuracy measures are also obtained and aggregated. Examples of accuracy measures are the mean magnitude of relative error (MMRE), the median magnitude of relative error (MdMRE), the magnitude of relative error (MRE), and the prediction at Level l (Pred[25]).

Chapter IV presents a literature survey of size measures (attributes) that have been published within the last 14 years and classifies the surveyed measures according to a proposed taxonomy. In addition, this chapter also discusses ways in which Web companies can devise their own size measures.

Chapter V presents a case study where a real effort prediction model based on data from completed industrial Web projects is constructed step by step using a statistical technique called regression analysis.

Chapter VI presents a case study that details step by step how to obtain effort estimations using real data from completed industrial Web projects using a machine learning technique called case-based reasoning.

Chapter VII presents a case study where a real effort prediction model based on data from completed industrial Web projects is constructed step by step using a machine learning technique called CART.

Chapter VIII details the use of statistical significance tests to compare different effort estimation techniques and models.

Chapter IX provides suggestions believed to help improve effort estimation practices that can be of benefit to Web companies, in particular, small Web development companies. The discussion also includes suggestions on how to improve project management practices as means to improving effort estimates.

Chapter X provides an introduction to parts of statistics that are frequently used when dealing with data for effort estimation. The concepts presented here are in no way exhaustive since statistics comprises a very large body of knowledge where entire books are devoted to specific topics. The parts that are the focus of this chapter are those that are necessary to use when building effort estimation models, and also when comparing different effort estimation techniques.

Chapter XI discusses the need for empirical investigations in Web engineering, which is motivated by the very definition of engineering. It describes the three main types of empirical investigations: surveys, case studies, and formal experiments. Although all three types of empirical investigations are presented, formal experiments are detailed further since they are the most difficult type of investigation to plan.

References

Fenton, N. E., & Pfleeger, S. L. (1997). *Software metrics: A rigorous and practical approach* (2nd ed.). Boston: PWS Publishing Company.

Ginige, A. (2002, July). Workshop on Web engineering. Web engineering: Managing the complexity of Web systems development. *Proceedings of the 14th International Conference on Software Engineering and Knowledge Engineering* (pp. 72-729).

Mendes, E., Counsell, S., & Mosley, N. (2000, June). Measurement and effort prediction of Web applications. *Proceedings of 2nd ICSE Workshop on Web Engineering* (pp. 57-74).

Acknowledgments

I would like to take this opportunity to thank all those who directly or indirectly have influenced my career as an academic and by doing so have contributed to the creation of this book.

First, I thank Wendy Hall, who was the first to suggest that software measurement was a topic she believed I would be enthusiastic about.

I also thank Steve Counsell, a great friend with whom I had the great opportunity to collaborate with, and who gave me one of his own books on statistics.

I thank Barbara Kitchenham, who has been a remarkable mentor and a role model, from whom I always have learned so much and to whom I will be forever indebted.

I would also like to thank all the colleagues and friends with whom I had the opportunity to collaborate on publications on the topic of software or Web effort estimation, namely, Steve Counsell, Rachel Fewster, Chris Lokan, Chris Triggs, and Ian Watson.

Finally, my deepest gratitude goes to my husband for his constant help and infinite support, and for bringing light into my life.

Emilia Mendes
May 2007

Section I

Web Cost Estimation Principles

This section provides the motivation for Web cost estimation, introduces principles and techniques that can be used to estimate costs, and discusses how to size a Web application.

Chapter I

What is Different about Web and Software Projects?

Abstract

The objective of this chapter is threefold. First is to introduce new terminology that relates specifically to hypertext, the model the Web is based upon. Second, it provides an overview of differences between Web and software development with respect to their development processes, technologies, quality factors, and measures. Third, it discusses the differences between Web effort estimation and software effort estimation.

Introduction

The Web was originally conceived in 1989 as an environment for the sharing of information (e.g., research reports, databases, user manuals) with geographically

Copyright © 2008, IGI Global. Copying or distributing in print or electronic forms without written permission of IGI Global is prohibited.

dispersed individuals. The information itself was stored on different remote servers and was retrieved by means of a single user interface (Web browser). The information consisted primarily of text documents interlinked using a hypertext metaphor (Offutt, 2002).

Since its inception, the Web has morphed into an environment used as a carrier for the deployment of many different types of applications. Such applications range from small-scale information-dissemination-like applications, typically developed by writers and artists, to large-scale commercial, enterprise-planning and -scheduling, collaborative-work applications, developed by multidisciplinary teams of people with diverse skills and backgrounds using cutting-edge technologies (Gellersen & Gaedke, 1997; Ginige & Murugesan, 2001; Offutt, 2002). Many of the Web applications currently in use are fully functional systems that provide business-to-customer and business-to-business e-commerce, and numerous services to numerous users (Offutt).

The massive increased use of the Web to provide a carrier platform for commercial applications has been motivated by several key factors, such as the following:

- The possible increase of an organisation's competitive position
- The opportunity for small organisations to project a corporate presence in the same way as larger organisations (Taylor, McWilliam, Forsyth, & Wade, 2002)
- Industries such as travel and hospitality, manufacturing, banking, education, and government utilising Web-based applications to improve and increase their operations (Ginige & Murugesan, 2001)
- The development of corporate intranet Web applications for use within the boundaries an organisation

The seemingly insatiable appetite for Web applications reaching into areas of communication and commerce makes it one of the leading and most important branches of the software industry to date (Offutt, 2002).

The World Wide Web (or simply Web) is the best known example of hypertext. The concept of hypertext was described by Conklin (1987, p. 1) as follows (see Figure 1): "windows on the screen are associated with objects in a database, and links are provided between these objects, both graphically (as labelled tokens) and in the database (as pointers)."

A collection of objects stored in a database is typically called a hyperdocument. When the objects are pure text, the hyperdocument is called hypertext; otherwise, objects that also include graphics, digitised speech, audio recordings, pictures, animation, film clips, and so forth are generally referred to as hypermedia, though these terms are often used interchangeably. Hypertext can also be described as a web of

Copyright © 2008, IGI Global. Copying or distributing in print or electronic forms without written permission of IGI Global is prohibited.

Figure 1. The concept of hypertext (Adapted from Conklin, 1987)

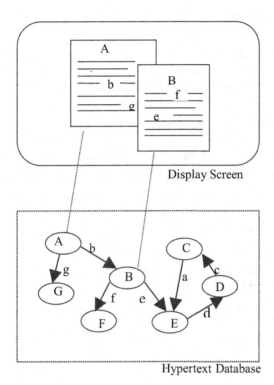

chunked information interrelated by hyperlinks. The origin or destination of a link is an anchor. Anchors can be words, sentences, areas of an image, and so on.

To date, the development of Web applications is in general ad hoc, resulting in poor-quality applications that are difficult to maintain (Murugesan & Deshpande, 2002) and projects that are not finished on time or within budget. The main reasons for such problems can be attested to an unsuitable design and development process, as well as poor project management practices (Ginige, 2002).

A survey on Web-based projects, published by the Cutter Consortium in 2000, revealed a number of problems with large outsourced Web-based projects (Ginige, 2002):

- 84% of surveyed delivered projects did not meet business needs
- 53% of surveyed delivered projects did not provide the required functionality

Copyright © 2008, IGI Global. Copying or distributing in print or electronic forms without written permission of IGI Global is prohibited.

- 79% of surveyed projects presented schedule delays
- 63% of surveyed projects exceeded their budget

As both our reliance and requirements for larger and more complex Web applications increase, so too does the need for methodologies, standards, and best-practice guidelines to help organisations develop applications that are delivered on time and within budget, and are high quality and easy to maintain (Lee & Shirani, 2004; Ricca & Tonella, 2001; Taylor et al., 2002). To develop such applications, Web development teams need to use sound methodologies, systematic techniques, quality assurance, rigorous disciplined and repeatable processes, better tools, and baselines.

Web engineering aims to meet such needs head on (Ginige & Murugesan, 2001).

The term Web engineering was first published in 1996 in a conference paper by Gellersen, Wicke, and Gaedke (1997). Since then, this term has been cited in numerous publications, and activities devoted to discussing Web engineering are constantly taking place (e.g., workshops, conference tracks, entire conferences).

Murugesan and Deshpande (2001) describe Web engineering as "the use of scientific, engineering, and management principles and systematic approaches with the aim of successfully developing, deploying and maintaining high quality Web-based systems and applications."

It should be noted that this is a similar definition used to describe software engineering; however, these disciplines differ in many ways, and the differences will be explored in more depth in the next section.

Differences between Web Applications and Conventional Software

The main focus of this section is to discuss and highlight the differences between Web and conventional software applications. However, it is first important to define what exactly we mean by a Web application.

Web Hypermedia, Web Software, and Web Application

The Web literature uses numerous synonyms for a Web application, such as Web site, Web system, and Internet application. The Institute of Electrical and Electronics Engineers (IEEE, 2003) defines the term Web site as a "collection of logically connected Web pages managed as a single entity."

Copyright © 2008, IGI Global. Copying or distributing in print or electronic forms without written permission of IGI Global is prohibited.

However, using the terms Web site and Web application interchangeably does not allow one to distinguish between a Web pages' physical storage and a live business application. For this reason, we consider that they are not similar.

In addition, we can distinguish Web applications into three different categories as first suggested by Christodoulou, Zafiris, and Papatheodorou (2000).

- *Web hypermedia application:* An application characterised by the authoring of information using nodes (chunks of information), links (relations between nodes), anchors, access structures (for navigation), and delivery over the Web. These applications are often called static Web applications as Web pages and links are not generated on the fly. Technologies commonly used for developing such applications are HTML (hypertext markup language), XML (extensible markup language), JavaScript, and multimedia. In addition, typical developers are writers, artists, and organisations who wish to publish information on the Web and/or CD-ROMs without the need to know programming languages such as Java. These applications have unlimited potential in areas such as software engineering, literature, education, and training.
- *Web software application:* An application that often implements a conventional business domain and uses the Web's infrastructure for execution. Typical applications include legacy information systems such as databases, booking systems, knowledge bases, and so forth. Many e-commerce applications fall into this category. Typically they employ development technologies (e.g., DCOM, ActiveX, etc.), database systems, and development solutions (e.g., J2EE). Developers are in general young programmers fresh from a computer science or software engineering degree course, managed by a few more senior staff.
- *Web application:* An application delivered over the Web that combines characteristics of both Web hypermedia and Web software applications

Differences between Web and Software Development

Web and software development differ in a number of areas, more of which will be discussed later. However, of these, three key areas provide the greatest differences and affect the entire Web-software development and maintenance processes. These areas encompass the people involved in the development of these applications, the intrinsic characteristics of the applications, and the audience for which they are developed.

The development of conventional software remains largely dominated by IT professionals as a sound knowledge of programming, database design, and project

Copyright © 2008, IGI Global. Copying or distributing in print or electronic forms without written permission of IGI Global is prohibited.

management is necessary. In contrast, Web development encompasses a much wider variety of developers, such as amateurs with no programming skills, graphics designers, writers, database experts, and IT professionals, to name but a few. This is possible as Web pages can be created by anyone without the necessity for programming knowledge (Brereton, Budgen, & Hamilton, 1998).

Web applications by default use communications technology and have multiplatform accessibility. In addition, since they employ a hypermedia paradigm, they are nonsequential by nature, using hyperlinks to interrelate Web pages and other documents. Therefore, navigation and pluralistic design become important aspects to take into account when developing Web applications in general. Finally, the multitude of technologies available for developing Web applications means that developers can build a full spectrum of applications, from a static simple Web application using HTML to a fully fledged distributed e-commerce application (Taylor et al., 2002). Conventional software can be developed using several programming languages running on a specific platform, components off the shelf (COTS), and so forth. It can also use communications technology to connect to and use a database system. However, the speed of implementing new technology is faster for Web development relative to conventional software development.

Web applications are aimed at wide-ranging groups of users. Such groups may be known ahead of time (e.g., applications available within the boundaries of an intranet). However, it is more often the case that Web applications are devised for an unknown group of users, making the development of aesthetically pleasing applications more challenging (Deshpande & Hansen, 2001). In contrast, conventional software applications are generally developed for a known user group (e.g., department, organisation, clients), making the explicit identification of target users and specific functional and nonfunctional requirements an easier task.

For the purpose of discussion, we have grouped the differences between Web and software development into seven areas, which are as follows:

1. Application characteristics and availability
2. Technology and architecture
3. Quality drivers
4. Information structuring, design, and maintenance
5. Disciplines and people involved in development
6. Stakeholders
7. Legal, social, and ethical issues

Copyright © 2008, IGI Global. Copying or distributing in print or electronic forms without written permission of IGI Global is prohibited.

Application Characteristics and Availability

Web Creation: Web applications are created by integrating numerous distinct elements, such as fine-grained components (e.g., DCOM, OLE, ActiveX); interpreted scripting languages; COTS (e.g. customised applications, library components, third-party products); multimedia files (e.g., audio, video, 3-D objects); HTML, SGML (standard generalized markup language), and XML files; graphical images; and databases (Deshpande & Hansen, 2001; Offutt, 2002; Reifer, 2000).

Components may be integrated in many different ways and present different quality attributes. In addition, their source code may be proprietary or unavailable, and may reside on and/or be executed from different remote computers (Offutt, 2002).

Conventional software creation: In contrast, conventional software applications can also be developed using a wide palate of components (e.g., COTS) and are generally developed using conventional programming languages such as C++, Java, Visual Basic, and Delphi. These applications may also use multimedia files, graphical images, and databases.

Web platforms: Web applications are in general platform independent (although there are exceptions, e.g., OLE, ActiveX), and Web browsers in general provide a similar user interface and functionality, freeing users from the chore of having to relearn (Deshpande & Hansen, 2001).

Conventional software platforms: Unlike Web applications, modern software products are mainly still highly monolithic and platform dependant: limited in use by the underlying hardware configuration and the operating system used on the target platform (Deshpande & Hansen, 2001). There are in addition programming languages on the market (e.g., Java, cross compilers) that are intentionally cross-platform or allow the conversion of one application to run on one or more different platforms (e.g., Borland CBuilder/Delphi for Windows and Linux).

Web navigation: Uniquely different from conventional software, Web applications employ the navigation of navigational structures with the use of a hypermedia paradigm, where content is structured and presented using anchors and hyperlinks. Navigational structures may also be customised, providing a dynamic adaptation of content structure that may include atomic hypermedia components and different presentation styles (Fraternali & Paolini, 2000).

Conventional software navigation: Despite numerous attempts by the hypermedia community to develop conventional applications using a hypermedia-style

Copyright © 2008, IGI Global. Copying or distributing in print or electronic forms without written permission of IGI Global is prohibited.

interface, the majority of conventional software applications do not use this paradigm.

Web availability: Stakeholders use the Web with an expectation that all applications will be fully operational throughout the year (24/7, 365 days a year), suggesting that any downtime, no matter how short, can be detrimental (Offutt, 2002) to both the user and the organisation that owns and runs the application (e.g., online banking).

Conventional software availability: Except in a relatively few application domains (e.g., security, safety critical, military, and banking), clients using conventional software applications do not expect their applications to be available 24/7, 365 days a year.

Technology and Architecture

Web development technology: Web applications are developed using a wide range of diverse technologies such as the many-flavoured Java solutions available (Java servlets, Enterprise JavaBeans, applets, and JavaServer pages), HTML, JavaScript, XML, UML, databases, and much more. In addition, there is an ever increasing use of third-party components and middleware, saving an organisation's valuable resources in that it does not have to reinvent the wheel. Since Web technology is a dynamic area that changes quickly, some authors suggest it may be difficult for developers and organisations to keep in step with the technology currently available and to decide on the best choice of technology for a given type of application (Offutt, 2002).

Conventional software technology: The principle technology used to develop conventional software applications are mostly object-oriented-based languages, relational databases, and CASE tools (Reifer, 2000). The speed with which new programming technologies are proposed is considerably slower than that for Web applications. For example, one of the most recent developments in software development might be the use of on-the-fly compilers. In this instance, productivity is reduced by the removal of the need to first make and then link an application. However, there is still a requirement for a person to write the code. This comes with the advent of the WYSIWYG ("what you see is what you get") HTML editor used to build Web applications, which removed the need for any HTML programming experience at all.

Web architecture: Web applications can utilise a whole stream of diverse configurations, ranging from typical solutions developed using a simple client-server architecture (two tier), represented by Web browsers on the client's computer connecting to a remote Web server hosting the Web application, to more sophisticated configurations such as three-tier or even *n*-tier architecture

Copyright © 2008, IGI Global. Copying or distributing in print or electronic forms without written permission of IGI Global is prohibited.

(Offutt, 2002). The servers and clients embodied within these more complex architectures are representative of computers that may have different operating systems, and software and hardware configurations, and may be connected to each other using different network settings and bandwidth.

The introduction of multitier architecture was motivated by limitations of the two-tier model (e.g., implementation of an application's business logic on the client machine and an increased network load as data processing is only executed on the client machine). For multitier architectures, the business logic is moved to a separate server (middle tier), which is now used to service client requests for data and functionality. The middle tier then requests and sends data to and from a (usually) separate database server (data tier). In addition, the type of networks used by the various stakeholders may also be unknown, so assumptions have to be made while developing these applications (Deshpande & Hansen, 2001).

Finally, the infrastructure used to deliver Web applications means these applications are inherently distributed as their content pages can reside on any number of Web servers distributed across the Internet.

Conventional software architecture: Conventional software applications run either in isolation on a client's machine (a centralised system), or in general use a two-tier architecture whenever applications intend to use data from database systems running on a separate server (distributed). In addition, the type of networks used by the stakeholders is usually known in advance since most conventional software applications are limited to specific places and organisations (Deshpande & Hansen, 2001).

Quality Drivers

Web applications: Web companies that operate their businesses using the Web rely heavily on providing applications and services of high quality so that customers return to do repeat business. As such, these companies only see a return on investment if customers' needs have been satisfied. In addition, customers who use the Web for obtaining services have little or no loyalty to the company with which they do business with (for example, a client wishing to purchase socks online, on finding the cheapest e-store for his or her purchase, may not necessarily return to that store if the Web site is difficult to navigate or the price is no longer competitive with other e-stores, found with only a few simple keystrokes and clicks through a search engine). This also suggests that new companies providing Web applications of an even higher quality will most likely displace customers from previously established busi-

Copyright © 2008, IGI Global. Copying or distributing in print or electronic forms without written permission of IGI Global is prohibited.

nesses. Furthermore, it can be asserted that quality is a principal factor that will bring repeated business, and for this reason, quality is often considered higher in priority than getting delivery on time to market, with the mantra "later and better" as the mission statement for Web companies who wish to remain competitive (Offutt, 2002).

The dominant quality criteria for Web companies are as follows (Offutt, 2002).

Reliability: Applications that work well, do not crash, and provide the correct data and data processing

Usability: A characteristic of applications that are simple to use. If a customer wants to use a Web application to purchase a product online, the application should be as simple to use as the process of physically purchasing that product in a real shop. Many existing Web applications present poor usability despite an extensive range of Web usability guidelines that have been published to date. An application with poor usability will be quickly replaced by another more usable application as soon as its existence becomes known to the target audience (Offutt, 2002).

Security: A characteristic of applications where the handling of customer data and other information is done securely such that problems (e.g., financial loss, legal consequences, loss of credibility) can be avoided (Offutt, 2002)

Conventional software: Within the context of conventional software development, software contractors are often paid for their delivered applications regardless of their quality. Return on investment is immediate. Ironically, they are also often paid for fixing defects in the delivered application, where these failures principally exist because of a lack of thorough testing. This knock-on effect suggests that the customer paying for the development may end up paying at least twice the initial bid before the application is fully functional. For conventional software, time to market takes priority over quality as it can be more lucrative to deliver applications with hidden defects sooner than go for the high-quality applications to be delivered later. For these companies, the "sooner but worse" rule applies (Offutt, 2002).

Another popular mechanism employed by software companies is to fix defects and make the updated version into a new release, which is then resold to customers, bringing in additional revenue.

Copyright © 2008, IGI Global. Copying or distributing in print or electronic forms without written permission of IGI Global is prohibited.

Information Structuring, Design, and Maintenance

Web applications structuring: Web applications present structured and unstructured content, which may be distributed over multiple sites and use many different systems (e.g., database systems, file systems, multimedia storage devices; Fraternali & Paolini, 2000). In addition, the design of a Web application, unlike that of conventional software applications, includes the organisation of content into navigational structures by means of anchors and hyperlinks. These structures are created to provide users with easily navigable Web applications. Well-designed applications should allow for suitable navigation structures (Deshpande et al., 2002) as well as the structuring of content, which should take into account efficiency and reliable management (Deshpande & Hansen, 2001).

Conventional software structuring: Conventional software presents structured content (although help files many times also have unstructured content), which may also be distributed generally using a two-tier architecture when a database system is used to store the data. In addition, the design of a conventional software application generally uses a conventional methodology of a specific paradigm (e.g., object orientation, aspect orientation), and does not include the organisation of content into navigational structures by means of anchors and hyperlinks.

Application file formats: Another difference between Web and conventional applications is that Web applications often contain a variety of specific file formats for multimedia content (e.g., graphics, sound, and animation). These files must be thoroughly integrated into the configuration management system, and their maintenance routines also need to be organised as it is likely these will also differ from the maintenance routine used for simple text-based documents (Brereton et al., 1998).

Conventional software formats: Conventional software applications present structured content that use flat file or database systems. The structuring of such content has been addressed over the years by software engineering, so the methods employed within this discipline for information structuring and design are well known by IT professionals (Deshpande & Hansen, 2001).

Web application maintenance: For the maintenance cycle of applications, Web applications are updated frequently and without the need for specific releases, updates, and patches, and have maintenance cycles of days or even hours (Offutt, 2002). In addition, their content and functionality may also change significantly from one moment to another, and so the concept of project completion may seem unsuitable in such circumstances. Some organisations also allow non-information-systems experts to develop and modify Web ap-

Copyright © 2008, IGI Global. Copying or distributing in print or electronic forms without written permission of IGI Global is prohibited.

plications. In environments such as these, it is often necessary to provide an overall management structure for the delivery and modification of applications to avoid confusion (Standing, 2002).

Conventional software maintenance: The maintenance cycle for conventional software applications adheres to a more rigorous process. Upon a product's release, software organisations usually initiate a cycle whereby a list of requested changes, adjustments, or improvements (either from customers or from its own development team) is prepared over a set period of time, and later incorporated as a specific version or release for distribution to all customers simultaneously. This cycle can be as short as a week and as long as several years. It requires more planning as it often entails other, possibly expensive, activities such as marketing, sales, product shipping, and occasionally personal installation at a customer's site (Ginige & Murugesan, 2001; Offutt, 2002). This cycle has become more transparent over the years as online automated updates using Web technology come into play.

Disciplines and People Involved in Development

Web application development teams: To develop large and complex Web applications, a team of people with a wide range of skills and expertise in different areas is required. These areas reflect distinct disciplines such as software engineering (development methodologies, project management, tools), hypermedia engineering (linking, navigation), requirements engineering, usability engineering, information engineering, graphics design, and network management (performance measurement and tuning; Deshpande et al., 2002; Ginige, 2002; Ginige & Murugesan, 2001).

Conventional software development teams: Building a conventional software application involves contributions from a smaller number of disciplines than those used for developing Web applications. These may include software engineering, requirements engineering, and usability engineering.

Web application people: For the people involved in development, the Web provides a broad spectrum of different types of Web applications, varying in quality, size, complexity, and technology. This variation is also applicable to the range of skills presented by those involved in Web development projects. Web applications can be created by artists and writers using simple HTML code or more likely one of the many commercially available Web authoring tools (e.g., Macromedia Dreamweaver, Microsoft Frontpage), making the authoring process transparent to those with no prior programming experience (Standing, 2002). However, Web applications can also be very large and complex, requiring teams of people with diverse skills and experience. Such

Copyright © 2008, IGI Global. Copying or distributing in print or electronic forms without written permission of IGI Global is prohibited.

teams consist of Web designers and programmers, graphic designers, librarians, database designers, project managers, network security experts, and usability experts (Offutt, 2002).

Again for large and complex sites, Web designers and programmers are necessary to implement the application's functionality using the necessary programming languages and technology. In particular, they must decide on the application's architecture and the choice of technologies applicable for their goal, and must also design the application taking into account its documents and links (Deshpande & Hansen, 2001). Graphic designers, usability experts, and librarians provide applications pleasing to the eye, easy to navigate, and that provide good search mechanisms to obtain the required information. It is often the case that where this type of expertise is required, it is outsourced on a project-by-project basis.

In addition, large Web applications most likely use database systems for data storage, making it important to have a team member with expertise in database design and with the use of a suitable query language, such as structured query language (SQL), to build the necessary query scripts required for data manipulation.

Project managers are responsible for managing the project in a timely manner and allocating resources such that applications are developed on time, within budget, and with high quality. Finally, network security experts provide solutions for various security aspects (Ginige, 2002).

Conventional software people: For the development of conventional software applications, the field remains dominated by IT professionals, where a sound knowledge of programming, database design, and project management is fundamental.

Stakeholders

Web applications: Web applications can be developed for use within the boundaries of a single organisation (intranet) or a number of participating organisations (extranets), or for use by any person anywhere in the world. This implies that stakeholders may come from a wide range of intersecting groups, some clearly identified (e.g., employees within an organisation) while others remain unknown (Deshpande & Hansen, 2001; Deshpande et al., 2002; Offutt, 2002; Standing, 2002). As a direct consequence, Web developers are regularly faced with the challenge of developing applications for unknown users, whose expectations (requirements) and behaviour patterns are also unknown at development time (Deshpande & Hansen). In this case, new approaches and guidelines must be

Copyright © 2008, IGI Global. Copying or distributing in print or electronic forms without written permission of IGI Global is prohibited.

devised to better understand prospective needs of these clients such that quality requirements can be determined beforehand and as a prelude to delivering
high-quality applications (Deshpande et al.).

Another issue is that whenever the target client group is unknown, it also becomes
more difficult to provide aesthetically pleasing user interfaces, an important factor
necessary to enable a Web company to successfully stand out from the competition
(Deshpande & Hansen, 2001). In addition, some stakeholders may reside locally,
or in another state, province, or country. Those who reside overseas may present
different social and linguistic backgrounds as well different cultural demands and
sensitivity. The challenge, therefore, of developing successful applications increases
as a consequence of an increase in the number of factors that can influence the success of an application (Deshpande & Hansen; Standing, 2002).

Finally, whenever the stakeholders are unknown, it becomes difficult to estimate the
number of users that will use the service, so applications should ideally be developed
so they can grow to meet demand, and as such should be scalable (Offutt, 2002).

Conventional software: For conventional software applications, it is usual for
stakeholders to be explicitly identified prior to development. These stakeholders often represent groups confined within the boundaries of departments,
divisions, or organisations (Deshpande & Hansen, 2001).

Legal, Social, and Ethical Issues

Web applications: As a distributed environment, the Web enables a vast amount of
structured (e.g., database records) and unstructured (e.g., text, images, audio)
content to be readily available to a multitude of users worldwide, and this is
often cited as one of the best advantages of using the Web. However, this environment is open to abuse for the purpose of dishonest actions, such as copying
content from Web applications without acknowledging the source, distributing
information about customers without their consent, infringing copyright and
intellectual property rights, and even, in some instances, stealing a person's
identity (Deshpande & Hansen, 2001). The consequences that follow from the
unlawful use of the Web are that Web companies, customers, entities (e.g., the
World Wide Web Consortium, W3C), and government agencies must apply a
similar paradigm to the Web as those applied to publishing, where legal, social,
and ethical issues are taken into consideration (Deshpande et al., 2002).

Copyright © 2008, IGI Global. Copying or distributing in print or electronic forms without written permission
of IGI Global is prohibited.

Table 1. Web-based vs. traditional approaches to development

	Web-Based Approach	Conventional Software Approach
Application Characteristics and Availability	Integration of numerous distinct components (e.g., fine-grained, interpreted scripting languages; COTS; multimedia files; HTML, SGML, and XML files; databases; graphical images) and distributed, cross-platform applications, and structuring of content using navigational structures with hyperlinks. Availability throughout the whole year (24/7/365).	Integration of distinct components (e.g., COTS, databases, graphical images) and monolithic single-platform applications Except for a few application domains, no need for availability 24/7/365.
Technology and Architecture	Variety of Java solutions (Java servlets, Enterprise JavaBeans, applets, and JavaServer Pages), HTML, JavaScript, XML, UML, databases, third-party components and middleware, and so forth. Architecture comprises two-tier to n-tier clients and servers with different network settings and bandwidth, sometimes unknown.	Object-oriented languages, relational databases, and CASE tools. One- to two-tier architecture with network settings and bandwidth that are likely to be known in advance.
Quality Drivers	Quality is considered of higher priority than time to market. Main quality drivers are reliability, usability, and security.	Time to market takes priority over quality. Main quality driver is time to market.
Information Structuring, Design, and Maintenance	Structured and unstructured content, use of hyperlinks to build navigational structures. Maintenance cycles are frequent without specific releases. Maintenance cycles of days or even hours.	Structured content, with seldom use of hyperlinks. Maintenance cycles are done via specific releases. Maintenance cycles ranging from a week to several years.
Disciplines and People Involved in Development	Disciplines are software engineering, hypermedia engineering, requirements engineering, usability engineering, information engineering, graphics design, and network management. People are Web designers and programmers, graphic designers, librarians, database designers, project managers, network security experts, usability experts, artists, and writers.	Disciplines are software engineering, requirements engineering, and usability engineering. People are IT professionals with knowledge of programming, database design, and project management.
Stakeholders	Wide range of groups, known and unknown, residing locally or overseas.	Generally groups confined within the boundaries of departments, divisions, or organizations.
Legal, Social, and Ethical Issues	Content can be easily copied and distributed without permission or acknowledgement of copyright and intellectual property rights. Applications should take into account all groups of users including disabled people.	Content can also be copied infringing privacy, copyright, and IP (Internet protocol) issues, albeit to a smaller extent.

Copyright © 2008, IGI Global. Copying or distributing in print or electronic forms without written permission of IGI Global is prohibited.

Issues referring to the accessibility offered by Web applications should also take into account user groups such as that of disabled people (Deshpande & Hansen, 2001).

Conventional software: Conventional software applications also share a similar fate as that of Web applications although to a smaller extent since these applications are not so readily available for such a large community of users.

Table 1 summarises the differences between Web-based and conventional development contexts.

As we have seen, there are a number of differences between Web and conventional software application development. However, these two engineering fields also share a number of similarities that become more self-evident when we focus on the development of large-scale complex applications. Both need quality assurance mechanisms, development methodologies, tools, processes, techniques for requirements elicitation, and effective testing and maintenance methods and tools (Deshpande et al., 2002).

What Differentiates Web Effort Estimation from Software Effort Estimation?

Within the context of software and Web development, effort estimation, also known as cost estimation (or "costimation"), represents the attainment of an estimated effort for a new project to be developed. Such an effort estimate can be obtained via expert opinion and/or the use of explicit models (e.g., generic equations generated using statistical regression analysis and machine-learning algorithms), built from past project data. The challenge here is to obtain realistic effort estimates, that is, estimates that are close in value to the actual effort it will take to complete the new project.

Currently, there are numerous factors as to why effort estimates lack accuracy. However, within the context of Web development, those that seem to occur the most are highlighted as the following.

- Project managers who lack suitable or relevant experience with projects using the in-house development environment, technologies, and programming languages

Copyright © 2008, IGI Global. Copying or distributing in print or electronic forms without written permission of IGI Global is prohibited.

- Development teams that lack suitable or relevant experience with projects using the in-house development environment, technologies, and programming languages
- Unclear user requirements (fluidic scope; Pressman, 1998)
- Users who frequently request changes
- Pressure for on-time deliverables despite the need to deliver quality applications, which often leads to the development of applications without a full and complete understanding of the application's requirements (Reifer, 2000)
- Company's poor process maturity
- Hype associated with a new technology, and the lack of a careful consideration of the merits of using the technology (e.g., Java)

A reliable effort estimate is fundamental to the successful management of both software and Web projects. Having realistic estimates at an early stage in a project's life cycle allows project managers and development organisations to manage resources effectively, and to prepare realistic project bids that are sensible and more likely to be successful.

For example, an effort estimate will help a project manager determine who to allocate to the project and when. Therefore, effort estimation (effort prediction) is a necessary part of an effective process, no matter if the process represents requirements gathering, design, or testing.

An objective effort estimation process (see Figure 2) involves the following steps.

- The use of empirical observation and/or experience to identify variables (measures) that are believed to influence the effort required to develop a new application. Examples of variables are the total number of new Web pages, total number of new images, developer's experience within the development environment, and maximum number of developers on a project. Note that the size of an application is a variable (set of variables) that is always considered important due to its strong relationship with effort.
- The formulation of hypotheses about the relationship between the selected variables and effort. Examples of hypotheses are the following statements: It seems that the greater the number of new static Web pages, the greater the amount of effort to develop a new application; it seems that larger teams will spend more time on developing an application compared to smaller teams.
- The gathering of data about past finished projects or even past development phases within the same project. The gathered data correspond to the variables

Copyright © 2008, IGI Global. Copying or distributing in print or electronic forms without written permission of IGI Global is prohibited.

believed to influence effort and effort itself. Note that if a company only uses past data from very successful projects, the effort estimate obtained for a new project may provide an estimated effort that is not typical of the company's situation. Here it may be useful (if there is enough available data) to compare predictions obtained using a subset of successful projects, a subset of less successful projects, and a subset containing both types of projects (each subset should have data on at least 12 projects, as per previous work in this area).

•   The use of historical data to build effort estimation models for use in predicting effort for new projects

•   The assessment of how effective (accurate) those effort estimation models are, that is, the assessment of their prediction accuracy

The prediction process illustrated in Figure 2 remains unchanged when applied to either Web or software effort estimation. However, despite sharing similar prediction processes, Web effort estimation differs from its software cousin for the following reasons:

•   There is no standard for sizing Web applications as Web companies vary widely with regard to the types of applications they develop and the technologies employed as part of this process. For example, some companies focus on the development of small, multimedia-rich, static Web applications,

Figure 2. General prediction process (Adapted from Fenton & Pfleeger, 1996)

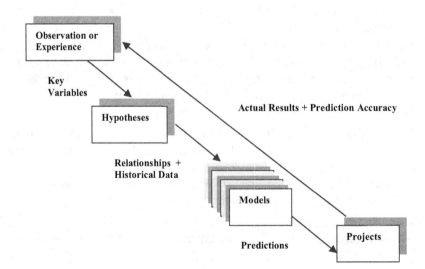

Copyright © 2008, IGI Global. Copying or distributing in print or electronic forms without written permission of IGI Global is prohibited.

where the development teams may argue it reasonable to measure application size as the total number of new Web pages and total number of new images. However, for those applications that will incorporate fewer static Web pages but will in addition incorporate a large number of complex scripts, databases, and conventional programming languages such as Java or C#, it becomes more difficult to determine which variable(s) should represent application size. Suggestions on how to size Web applications have been made by both practitioners and researchers, and will be detailed in Chapter 4. In relation to conventional software, size is often measured using function points (e.g., IFPUG, COSMIC-FFP), and less often using lines of code.

- Numerous Web companies are too small to provide a stable environment from which they can develop and maintain their applications. Successful projects rely entirely on having experienced individuals, and the general lack of overall structure and control lead to the production of similar projects that can vary widely in their productivity and the application's quality. In such instances, success cannot be repeated as there is no understanding of the factors involved, and as such, effort estimate is tantamount to a guesstimate. This scenario is also common to software companies; however, software companies have at their disposal a range of literature in effort estimation and project management that has been accumulated over the past 20 to 30 years, a stark contrast to the development of Web applications in such a new field.

- Small Web companies may use technologies that differ widely from project to project due to frequently bidding for contracts in domains where they have little or no previous experience, and for which they require the use of a different set of technologies. In this instance, the added learning curve to implement the required technology makes it difficult to utilise data on past projects in an attempt to estimate effort for new Web projects.

- Except for the Tukutuku database (Mendes, Mosley, & Counsell, 2003), there are practically no existing benchmark databases that can be used to obtain and then compare Web effort estimates and to benchmark Web projects' productivity. This contrasts directly with conventional software development, for which there are several known benchmark databases available (e.g., ISBSG, Laturi) to which software companies regularly contribute data on finished projects and from which they are able to calculate productivity baselines and effort estimates.

- Web development differs substantially from traditional software development approaches. As such, variables (e.g., size variables) and effort models that have been proposed for software cannot be readily reused for Web projects.

- Despite the proposal of numerous Web development methodologies, there is no single, unifying methodology that entirely captures all the intricacies of Web development projects and project management. Most of the methodolo-

Copyright © 2008, IGI Global. Copying or distributing in print or electronic forms without written permission of IGI Global is prohibited.

gies proposed have not been readily assimilated by practitioners as they lack simplicity and appear to be too academic (Barry & Lang, 2001). Without the full understanding of what characterises Web development projects, it is difficult to determine factors that are influential upon developing projects within time and budget.

One of the aims of researchers in the field of Web engineering is to provide the means for practitioners to objectively estimate effort for their projects and to improve their current practices. Even though there are no standard size measures or development methodologies, currently it is not impossible for Web companies to measure effort objectively. The chapters that follow aim to help companies pursue this objective.

Conclusion

This chapter outlines the distinctions between Web and software applications, and discusses differences between Web and conventional software development. These have been summarised below:

Application Characteristics and Availability

- Web applications are distributed, are cross-platform, integrate numerous distinct components, and contain content that is structured using navigational structures with hyperlinks. In addition, they are expected to be always available (24/7/365) to the client.
- Traditional software applications are generally monolithic and single platform, and can integrate distinct components. Except for a few application domains, these applications are not required to be available 24/7/365.

Technology and Architecture

- Web applications use a variety of Java solutions, HTML, JavaScript, XML, UML, databases, third-party components and middleware, and so forth. In terms of their architecture, they use anything from a two-tier to an n-tier solution, with different network settings and bandwidth. Network settings and bandwidth are unknown in advance.

Copyright © 2008, IGI Global. Copying or distributing in print or electronic forms without written permission of IGI Global is prohibited.

- Traditional software applications use object-oriented languages, relational databases, and CASE tools. In terms of their architecture, they typically use a one- or two-tier architecture, and network settings and bandwidth are likely to be known in advance.

Quality Drivers

- Web companies in general take the view that the delivery of a quality product should be given a higher priority than time to market. In addition, the main quality drivers for these companies are reliability, usability, and security.
- Traditional software applications take the view that time to market should take priority over the delivery of a quality product, and as such, this becomes their core quality driver.

Information Structuring, Design, and Maintenance

- Web applications use content that is both structured and unstructured, in addition to navigational structures built using hyperlinks. Maintenance cycles are frequent and without specific releases, with updates ranging from an hour to several months.
- Traditional software applications use content that is structured and seldom employ hyperlinks (except on help pages). Their maintenance cycles are carried out via specific releases and can range from a week to several years.

Disciplines and People Involved in Development

- The disciplines related to Web development are software engineering, hypermedia engineering, requirements engineering, usability engineering, information engineering, graphics design, and network management. In addition, the people involved in Web development are Web designers and programmers, graphic designers, librarians, database designers, project managers, network security experts, usability experts, artists, and writers.
- The disciplines related to traditional software development are software engineering, requirements engineering, and usability engineering. Generally, the people involved in software development are IT professionals with knowledge of programming, database design, and project management.

Copyright © 2008, IGI Global. Copying or distributing in print or electronic forms without written permission of IGI Global is prohibited.

Stakeholders

- Within the context of Web development, stakeholders represent a wide range of groups, known and unknown, residing locally or overseas.

- Conversely, within the context of traditional software development, stakeholders are generally groups confined within the boundaries of departments, divisions, or organisations.

Legal, Social, and Ethical Issues

- Within the context of Web development, content can be easily copied and distributed without permission or acknowledgement of copyright and intellectual property rights. In addition, applications should take into account all groups of users including the disabled.

- Within the context of traditional software development, content can be copied and in so doing infringe privacy, copyright, and IP issues, albeit to a smaller extent when compared to Web-based environments.

Finally, this chapter also discussed the differences between Web and software effort estimation. These are due to the nonexistence of standard size measures to be used to size any type of Web application; many development companies are too small to look into the use of organised development processes, measures, and measurement. This suggests that their effort estimates are no better than an educated guess. The diversity of new technologies and languages used to develop Web applications may sometimes make it prohibitive to learn from the experience of past projects, and there are no existing benchmarking databases of Web projects (except for the Tukutuku database) for the creation of effort models and for benchmarking productivity within and across companies.

References

Barry, C., & Lang, M. (2001). A survey of multimedia and Web development techniques and methodology usage. *IEEE Multimedia, 8*(2), 52-60.

Brereton, P., Budgen, D., & Hamilton, G. (1998). Hypertext: The next maintenance mountain. *Computer, 31*(12), 49-55.

Copyright © 2008, IGI Global. Copying or distributing in print or electronic forms without written permission of IGI Global is prohibited.

Christodoulou, S. P., Zafiris, P. A., & Papatheodorou, T. S. (2000). WWW2000: The developer's view and a practitioner's approach to Web engineering. *Proceedings of the 2nd ICSE Workshop on Web Engineering* (pp. 75-92).

Conklin, J. (1987). Hypertext: An introduction and survey. *Computer, 20*(9), 17-41.

Deshpande, Y., & Hansen, S. (2001). Web engineering: Creating a discipline among disciplines. *IEEE Multimedia, 8*(2), 82-87.

Deshpande, Y., Murugesan, S., Ginige, A., Hansen, S., Schwabe, D., Gaedke, M., et al. (2002). Web engineering. *Journal of Web Engineering, 1*(1), 3-17.

Fenton, N. E., & Pfleeger, S. L. (1997). *Software metrics: A rigorous and practical approach* (2nd ed.). Boston: PWS Publishing Company.

Fraternali, P., & Paolini, P. (2000). Model-driven development of Web applications: The AutoWeb system. *ACM Transactions on Information Systems, 18*(4), 1-35.

Gellersen, H., & Gaedke, M. (1999). Object-oriented Web application development. *IEEE Internet Computing, 3*(1), 60-68.

Gellersen, H., Wicke, R., & Gaedke, M. (1997). WebComposition: An object-oriented support system for the Web engineering lifecycle. *Journal of Computer Networks and ISDN Systems, 29*(8-13), 865-1553.

Ginige, A. (2002, July). Workshop on Web engineering. Web engineering: Managing the complexity of Web systems development. *Proceedings of the 14th International Conference on Software Engineering and Knowledge Engineering* (pp. 72-729).

Ginige, A., & Murugesan, S. (2001). Web engineering: An introduction. *IEEE Multimedia, 8*(1), 14-18.

Institute of Electrical and Electronics Engineers (IEEE). (2003). *Recommended practice for the Internet Web site engineering, Web site management, and Web site life cycle.* Author.

Lee, S. C., & Shirani, A. I. (2004). A component based methodology for Web application development. *Journal of Systems and Software, 71*(1-2), 177-187.

Mendes, E., Mosley, N., & Counsell, S. (2003). Investigating early Web size measures for Web costimation. *Proceedings EASE 2003 Conference.*

Murugesan, S., & Deshpande, Y. (2001). *Lecture notes in computer science: Vol. 2016. Web engineering: Managing diversity and complexity of Web application development.* Heidelberg, Germany: Springer Verlag.

Murugesan, S., & Deshpande, Y. (2002). Meeting the challenges of Web application development: The Web engineering approach. *Proceedings of the 24th International Conference on Software Engineering* (pp. 687-688).

Copyright © 2008, IGI Global. Copying or distributing in print or electronic forms without written permission of IGI Global is prohibited.

Offutt, J. (2002). Quality attributes of Web software applications. *IEEE Software, 19*(2), 25-32.

Reifer, D. J. (2000). Web development: Estimating quick-to-market software. *IEEE Software, 17*(6), 57-64.

Ricca, F., & Tonella, P. (2001). Analysis and testing of Web applications. *Proceedings of the 23rd International Conference on Software Engineering* (pp. 25-34).

Standing, C. (2002). Methodologies for developing Web applications. *Information and Software Technology, 44*(3), 151-160.

Taylor, M. J., McWilliam, J., Forsyth, H., & Wade, S. (2002). Methodologies and Website development: A survey of practice. *Information and Software Technology, 44*(6), 381-391.

Copyright © 2008, IGI Global. Copying or distributing in print or electronic forms without written permission of IGI Global is prohibited.

Chapter II

Introduction to Web Cost Estimation

Abstract

Software effort models and effort estimates help project managers allocate resources, control costs, and schedule and improve current practices, which in theory should allow projects to be finished on time and within budget. In the context of Web development and maintenance, these issues are also crucial and very challenging given that Web projects have short schedules and a highly fluidic scope. Therefore, the objective of this chapter is to introduce the concepts related to Web effort estimation and effort estimation techniques. These concepts will be used in further chapters.

Introduction

As discussed in Chapter I, the Web is used as a delivery platform for numerous types of Web applications, ranging from complex e-commerce solutions with back-end

Copyright © 2008, IGI Global. Copying or distributing in print or electronic forms without written permission of IGI Global is prohibited.

databases to online personal static Web pages and blogs. With the sheer diversity of types of Web applications and technologies employed, there is an ever-growing number of Web companies bidding for as many Web projects as they can accommodate. As usual, in order to win the bid, companies are apt to estimate unrealistic schedules, leading to applications that are rarely developed on time and within budget.

It should be noted that cost and effort are often used interchangeably within the context of effort estimation (prediction) since effort is taken as the main component of project costs. However, given that project costs also take into account other factors such as contingency and profit (Kitchenham, Pickard, Linkman, & Jones, 2003), we will use the word *effort* and not *cost* throughout this chapter.

Overview of Effort Estimation Techniques

The purpose of estimating effort is to predict the amount of effort required to accomplish a given task based on the knowledge of previous similar projects and other project characteristics that are believed to be related to effort. Using the black box metaphor, project characteristics (independent variables) are the input, and effort (dependent variable) is the output we wish to predict (see Figure 1). For example, a given Web company may find that to predict the effort necessary to implement a new Web application, it will require the following input.

- Estimated number of new Web pages
- The number of functions and features (e.g., shopping cart) to be offered by the new Web application
- Total number of developers who will help develop the new Web application
- Developers' average number of years of experience with the development tools employed
- The choice of the main programming language used

Of these variables, the estimated number of new Web pages and the number of functions or features to be offered by the new Web application are size variables (measures). The other three—the total number of developers who will help develop the new Web application, the developers' average number of years of experience with the development tools employed, and the main programming language used—are not used to size the problem to be solved (Web application); rather, they are believed to influence the amount of effort necessary to develop a Web application, and in this

Copyright © 2008, IGI Global. Copying or distributing in print or electronic forms without written permission of IGI Global is prohibited.

Figure 1. Steps used to obtain an effort estimate

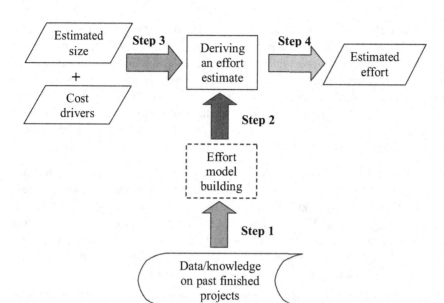

more abstract sense are still very much related to effort. Therefore, they are also considered input and jointly named cost drivers.

A task to be estimated can be as simple as developing a single function (e.g., creating a Web form with 10 fields) or as complex as developing a large e-commerce application. Regardless of the application type, in general the one consistent input (independent variable) believed to have the strongest influence on effort is size (i.e., the total number of Web pages), with cost drivers also playing an influential role.

In most cases, even when effort estimation is based on past experience, knowledge or data on past finished projects can be used to help estimate effort for new projects yet to start.

Several techniques for effort estimation have been proposed over the past 30 years in software engineering. These fall into three broad categories (Shepperd & Kadoda, 2001): expert-based effort estimation, algorithmic models, and artificial-intelligence techniques. Each category is described in the next sections.

Copyright © 2008, IGI Global. Copying or distributing in print or electronic forms without written permission of IGI Global is prohibited.

Expert-Based Effort Estimation

Expert-based effort estimation is the process of estimating effort by subjective means; it is often based on previous experience with developing and/or managing similar projects and is by far the most commonly used technique for Web effort estimation, with the attainment of accurate effort estimates being directly proportional to the competence and experience of the individuals involved (e.g., project manager, developer). Within the context of Web development, our experience suggests that expert-based effort estimates are obtained using one of the following mechanisms.

- An estimate that is based on a detailed effort breakdown that takes into account all of the lowest level parts of an application and the functional tasks necessary to develop this application. Each task attributed with effort estimates is repeatedly combined into higher level estimates until we finally obtain one estimate that is considered as the sum of all lower level estimate parts. This type of estimation is called bottom-up. Each estimate can be an educated guess or based on sound previous experience with similar projects.

- An estimate representing an overall process to be used to produce an application, as well as knowledge about the application to be developed, that is, the product. A total estimate is suggested and used to calculate estimates for the component parts (tasks): relative portions of the whole. This type of estimation is called top-down.

Estimates can be suggested by a project manager or by a group of people mixing project managers and developers, usually by means of a brainstorming session.

A survey of 32 Web companies in New Zealand conducted in 2004 (Mendes et al., 2005) showed that 32% companies prepared effort estimates during the requirements gathering phase, 62% prepared estimates during their design phase, and 6% did not have to provide any effort estimates to their customers since they were happy to pay for the development costs without the need for a quote.

Of the 32 companies surveyed, 38% did not refine their effort estimate, and 62% did refine their estimates but not often. For the companies surveyed, this indicates that the majority of companies' initial effort estimates were used as their final estimates, and work was adjusted to fit these initial quotes. These results corroborated those published in Jørgensen and Sjøberg (2001).

Sometimes Web companies gather data on effort for past Web projects believing these data are sufficient to help obtain accurate estimates for new projects. However, without understanding the factors that influence effort within the context of a specific company, effort data alone are unlikely to be sufficient to warrant successful results.

Copyright © 2008, IGI Global. Copying or distributing in print or electronic forms without written permission of IGI Global is prohibited.

The drawbacks of expert-based estimation can be identified as follows:

1. It is very difficult to quantify and to clearly determine the factors that have been used to derive an estimate, making it difficult to apply the same reasoning to other projects (repeatability).

2. When a company finally builds up its expertise with developing Web applications using a given set of technologies, other technologies appear and are rapidly adopted (mostly due to hype), thus leaving behind valuable knowledge that had been accumulated in the past.

3. Obtaining an effort estimate based on experience with past similar projects can be misleading when projects vary in their characteristics. For example, knowing that a Web application containing 10 new static HTML (hypertext markup language) documents and 10 new images with a development time of 40 person hours does not mean that a similar application developed by two people will also consume 40 person hours to complete the task. Two people may need additional time to communicate, and may also have different experience with using HTML. In addition, another application eight times its size is unlikely to take exactly eight times longer to complete. This suggests that experience alone is not enough to identify the underlying relationship between effort and size-cost drivers (e.g., linear or exponential).

4. Developers and project managers are known for providing optimistic effort estimates (DeMarco, 1982) for tasks that they have to carry out themselves. Optimistic estimates lead to underestimated effort with the direct consequence of projects being over budget and late.

To cope with underestimation, it is suggested that experts provide three different estimates (Vliet, 2000): an optimistic estimate o, a realistic estimate r, and a pessimistic estimate p. Based on a beta distribution, the estimated effort E is then calculated as:

$$E = (o + 4r + p) / 6. \tag{1}$$

This measure is likely to be better than a simple average of o and p; however, caution is still necessary.

Although there are problems related to using expert-based estimations, a few studies have reported that when used in combination with other less subjective techniques (e.g., algorithmic models), expert-based effort estimation can be an effective estimating tool (Gray, MacDonell, & Shepperd, 1999; Reifer, 2000).

Copyright © 2008, IGI Global. Copying or distributing in print or electronic forms without written permission of IGI Global is prohibited.

Expert-based effort estimation is a process that has not been objectively detailed, however it can still be represented in terms of the diagram presented in Figure 1, where the order of steps that take place to obtain an expert-based effort estimate are as follows.

a. An expert or group of developers implicitly looks at the estimated size and cost drivers related to a new project for which effort needs to be estimated (Step 3).

b. Based on the data obtained in the previous step, they remember or retrieve data and knowledge on past finished projects for which actual effort is known (Step 1).

c. Based on the data from the previous steps, they subjectively estimate effort for the new project (Step 4).

The order of steps used to obtain an expert-based effort corresponds to Steps 3, 1, and 4 in Figure 1. The knowledge regarding the characteristics of a new project is necessary to retrieve knowledge on finished similar projects, from either memory or a database. Once this knowledge is retrieved, effort can be estimated.

It is important to stress that within a context where estimates are obtained via expert-based opinion, deriving a good effort estimate is much more likely to occur when the previous knowledge or data about completed projects relate to projects that are very similar to the one having its effort estimated. Here we use the principle "similar problems have similar solutions." Note that for this assumption to be correct, we also need to guarantee that the productivity of the team working on the new project is similar to the productivity of the team(s) for the past similar projects.

The problems aforementioned related to expert-based effort estimation led to the proposal of other techniques for effort estimation. Such techniques are presented in the next sections.

Algorithmic Techniques

Algorithmic techniques are the most popular techniques described in the Web and software effort estimation literature. Such techniques attempt to build models that precisely represent the relationship between effort and one or more project characteristics via the use of algorithmic models. Such models assume that application size is the main contributor to effort; thus in any algorithmic model, the central project characteristic used is usually taken to be some notion of application size (e.g., the number of lines of source code, function points, number of Web pages, number of

Copyright © 2008, IGI Global. Copying or distributing in print or electronic forms without written permission of IGI Global is prohibited.

new images). The relationship between size and effort is often translated into an equation shown by equation 2, where a and b are constants, S is the estimated size of an application, and E is the estimated effort required to develop an application of size S.

$$E = aS^b. \tag{2}$$

In equation 2, when $b < 1$, we have economies of scale; that is, larger projects use less effort, comparatively, than smaller projects. The opposite situation $(b > 1)$ gives diseconomies of scale; that is, larger projects use more effort, comparatively, than smaller projects. When b is either more than or less than 1, the relationship between S and E is nonlinear. Conversely, when $b = 1$, the relationship is linear.

However, size alone is unlikely to be the only contributor to effort. Other project characteristics, such as the developer's programming experience, the tools used to implement an application, and maximum or average team size, are also believed to influence the amount of effort required to develop an application. As previously said, these variables are known in the literature as cost drivers. Therefore, an algorithmic model should include not only size but also the cost drivers believed to influence effort. Thus, effort is determined mainly by size, however its value can also be adjusted by taking into account cost drivers (see equation 3):

$$E = aS^b CostDrivers. \tag{3}$$

Different proposals have been made in an attempt to define the exact form such an algorithmic model should take. The most popular are presented next.

COCOMO

One of the first algorithmic models to be proposed in the literature was the constructive cost model (COCOMO; Boehm, 1981). COCOMO aimed to be a generic algorithmic model that could be applied by any organisation to estimate effort at three different stages in a software project's development life cycle: early on in the development life cycle, when requirements have not yet been fully specified (basic COCOMO); later in the cycle, once detailed requirements have been specified (intermediate COCOMO); and even later when the application's design has been finalised (advanced COCOMO). Each stage corresponds to a different model, and all three models take the same form (see equation 4):

$$EstimatedEffort = a\ EstSizeNewproj^b\ EAT, \tag{4}$$

Copyright © 2008, IGI Global. Copying or distributing in print or electronic forms without written permission of IGI Global is prohibited.

where the following statements apply

- *EstimatedEffort* is the estimated effort, measured in person months, to develop an application.

- *EstSizeNewproj* is the size of an application measured in thousands of delivered source instructions (KDSI).

- *a* and *b* are constants that are determined by the class of the project to be developed. The three possible classes are as follows:

  - *Organic:* The organic class incorporates small, uncomplicated software projects developed by teams that have a great amount of experience with similar projects, and where software requirements are not strict.

  - *Semidetached:* The semidetached class incorporates software projects that are halfway between small and easy, and large and complex. Development teams show a mix of experiences, and requirements also present a mix of strict and slightly vague requirements.

  - *Embedded*: The embedded class incorporates projects that must be developed within a context where there are rigid hardware, software, and operational restrictions.

- *EAF* is an effort adjustment factor, calculated from cost drivers (e.g., developers, experience, tools).

The COCOMO model makes it clear that size is the main component of an effort estimate. Constants *a* and *b*, and the adjustment factor *EAF*, all vary depending on the model used, and in the following ways.

Basic COCOMO uses a value *EAF* of 1; *a* and *b* differ depending on a project's class (see Table 1).

Intermediate COCOMO calculates *EAF* based on 15 cost drivers, grouped into four categories: product, computer, personnel, and project (see Table 2). Each cost driver is rated on a six-point ordinal scale ranging from *very low importance* to *extra high importance*. Each scale rating determines an effort multiplier, and the product of all 15 effort multipliers is taken as the *EAF*.

Advanced COCOMO uses the same 15 cost drivers as intermediate COCOMO, however they are all weighted according to each phase of the development life cycle; that is, each cost driver is broken down by development's phase (see example in Table 3). This model therefore enables the same cost driver to be rated differently depending on the development's phase. In addition, it views a software application as a composition of modules and subsystems, to which the intermediate COCOMO model is applied to.

Copyright © 2008, IGI Global. Copying or distributing in print or electronic forms without written permission of IGI Global is prohibited.

Table 1. Parameter values for basic and intermediate COCOMO

	Class	a	b
Basic	Organic	2.4	1.05
	Semidetached	3.0	1.12
	Embedded	3.6	1.20
Intermediate	Class	a	b
	Organic	3.2	1.05
	Semidetached	3.0	1.12
	Embedded	2.8	1.20

Table 2. Cost drivers used in intermediate and advanced COCOMO

	Cost Driver
Personnel	Analyst capability
	Applications experience
	Programmer capability
	Virtual machine experience
	Language experience
Project	Modern programming practices
	Software tools
	Development schedule
Product	Required software reliability
	Database size
	Product complexity
Computer	Execution time constraint
	Main storage constraint
	Virtual machine volatility
	Computer turnaround time

The four development phases used in the advanced COCOMO model are require-ments planning and product design (RPD), detailed design (DD), coding and unit test (CUT), and integration and test (IT). An overall project estimate is obtained by aggregating estimates obtained for subsystems, which themselves were obtained by combining estimates made for each module.

Copyright © 2008, IGI Global. Copying or distributing in print or electronic forms without written permission of IGI Global is prohibited.

Table 3. Example of rating in advanced COCOMO

Cost Driver	Rating	RPD	DD	CUT	IT
ACAP (Analyst Capability)	Very low	1.8	1.35	1.35	1.5
	Low	0.85	0.85	0.85	1.2
	Nominal	1	1	1	1
	High	0.75	0.9	0.9	0.85
	Very high	0.55	0.75	0.75	0.7

The original COCOMO model was radically improved 15 years later and was re-named the COCOMO II model, which incorporates knowledge of changes that have occurred in software development environments and practices over the previous 15 years (Boehm, 2000). COCOMO II is not detailed in this book, however, interested readers are referred to Boehm (2000) and Boehm et al. (2000).

The COCOMO model is an example of a general-purpose model, where it is assumed that it is not compulsory for ratings and parameters to be adjusted (calibrated) to specific companies in order for the model to be used effectively.

Despite the existence of general-purpose models, such as COCOMO, the effort estimation literature has numerous examples of specialised algorithmic models that were built using applied regression analysis techniques (Schofield, 1998) on data sets of past completed projects. Specialised and regression-based algorithmic models are most suitable to local circumstances, such as in-house analysis, as they are derived from past data that often represent projects from the company itself. Regression analysis, used to generate regression-based algorithmic models, provides a procedure for determining the best straight-line fit (see Figure 2) to a set of project data that represents the relationship between effort (response or dependent variable) and cost drivers (predictor or independent variables; Schofield).

Figure 2 shows, using real data on Web projects, an example of a regression line that describes the relationship between log(*Effort*) and log(*totalWebPages*). It should be noted that the original variables *Effort* and *totalWebPages* have been transformed using the natural logarithmic scale to comply more closely with the assumptions of the regression analysis techniques. Details on these assumptions and how to identify variables that need transformation are described in more depth in Chapter V. Further details on regression analysis techniques are provided in Chapter X.

The equation represented by the regression line in Figure 2 is as follows:

$$\log Effort = \log a + b \log totalWebPages, \tag{5}$$

Copyright © 2008, IGI Global. Copying or distributing in print or electronic forms without written permission of IGI Global is prohibited.

Figure 2. Example of a regression line

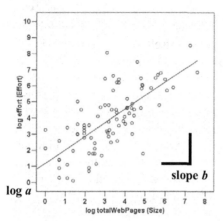

where $\log a$ is the point in which the regression line intercepts the Y-axis, now known simply as the intercept, and b represents the slope of the regression line, that is, its inclination, generically represented by the form:

$$y = mx + c. \tag{6}$$

Equation 5 shows a linear relationship between $\log(Effort)$ and $\log(totalWebPages)$. However, since the original variables were transformed before the regression technique was employed, this equation needs to be transformed back so that it uses the original variables. The resultant equation is:

$$Effort = a \; totalWebPabes^b. \tag{7}$$

Other examples of equations representing regression lines are given in equations 8 and 9:

$$EstimatedEffort = C + a_0 EstSizeNewproj + a_1 CD_1 + \ldots + a_n CD_n, \text{ and} \tag{8}$$

$$EstimatedEffort = C \; EstSizeNewproj^{a_0} \; CD_1^{a_1} \cdots CD_n^{a_n}, \tag{9}$$

Copyright © 2008, IGI Global. Copying or distributing in print or electronic forms without written permission of IGI Global is prohibited.

where C is the regression line's intercept, a constant denoting the initial estimated effort (assuming size and cost drivers to be zero), a_0 to a_n are constants derived from past data, and CD_1 to CD_n are cost drivers that have an impact on effort.

Regarding the regression analysis itself, two of the most widely used techniques are multiple regression (MR) and stepwise regression (SWR). The difference between these two techniques is that MR obtains a regression line using all the independent variables at the same time, whereas SWR is a technique that examines different combinations of independent variables, looking for the best grouping to explain the greatest amount of variation in effort. Both use least squares regression, where the regression line selected is the one that reflects the minimum values of the sum of the squared errors. Errors are calculated as the difference between actual and estimated effort and are known as residuals (Schofield, 1998).

In terms of the diagram presented in Figure 1, an algorithmic model uses constant scalar values based on past project data; however, for anyone wishing to use this model, the steps to use are 1, 2, 3, and 4.

A general-purpose algorithmic model tends to use Step 1 once, and use the values obtained for all its constants, estimated size, and cost drivers to derive effort estimates. It is common for such models to be used by companies without recalibration of values for the constants. Within the context of a specialised algorithmic model, Step 1 is used whenever it is necessary to recalibrate the model. This can occur after several new projects are finished and incorporated to the company's database of data on past finished projects. However, a company may also decide to recalibrate a model after every new project is finished, or to use the initial model for a longer time period. If the development team remains unchanged (and assumes that the team does not have an excessive learning curve for each new project) and new projects are similar to past projects, there is no pressing need to recalibrate an algorithmic model too often.

The sequence of steps (see Figure 1) is as follows.

a.   Past data is used to generate an algorithmic model (Step 1).

b.   An algorithmic model is built from past data obtained in Step 1 (Step 2).

c.   The model created in the previous step then receives, as input, values for the estimated size and cost drivers relative to the new project for which effort is to be estimated (Step 3).

d.   The model generates an estimated effort (Step 4).

The sequence described is different from that for expert opinion detailed at the start of the chapter.

Copyright © 2008, IGI Global. Copying or distributing in print or electronic forms without written permission of IGI Global is prohibited.

Artificial-Intelligence Techniques

Artificial-intelligence techniques have, in the last decade, been used as a comple-ment to, or as an alternative to, the previous two categories. Examples include fuzzy logic (Kumar, Krishna, & Satsangi, 1994), regression trees (Schroeder, Sjoquist, & Stephan, 1996), neural networks (Shepperd, Schofield, & Kitchenham, 1996), and case-based reasoning (CBR; Shepperd & Kadoda, 2001). We will cover case-based reasoning and classification and regression trees (CARTs) in more detail as these are currently the most popular machine-learning techniques employed for Web effort estimation. A useful summary of numerous machine-learning techniques can also be found in Gray and MacDonell (1997).

Case-Based Reasoning

CBR uses the assumption that similar problems provide similar solutions. It provides estimates by comparing the characteristics of the current project to be estimated against a library of historical information from completed projects with known effort (case base).

Using CBR involves (Angelis & Stamelos, 2000) the following.

1. Characterising a new project p, for which an estimate is required, with vari-ables (features) common to those completed projects stored in the case base. In terms of Web and software effort estimation, features represent size measures and cost drivers that have a bearing on effort. This means that if a Web com-pany has stored data on past projects where, for example, the data represent the features *effort*, *size*, *development team size*, and *tools used*, the data used as input to obtaining an effort estimate will also need to include these same features.

2. Use of this characterisation as a basis for finding similar (analogous) completed projects for which effort is known. This process can be achieved by measur-ing the distance between two projects at a time (project p and one finished project) based on the features' values for all features (k) characterising these projects. Each finished project is compared to project p, and the finished project presenting the shortest distance overall is the most similar project to project p. Although numerous techniques can be used to measure similarity, nearest-neighbour algorithms using the unweighted Euclidean distance measure have been the most widely used to date in Web and software engineering.

Copyright © 2008, IGI Global. Copying or distributing in print or electronic forms without written permission of IGI Global is prohibited.

3.   Generation of a predicted value of effort for project p based on the effort for those completed projects that are similar to p. The number of similar projects taken into account to obtain an effort estimate will depend on the size of the case base. For small case bases (e.g., up to 90 cases), typical values use the most similar finished project, or the two or three most similar finished projects (one, two, and three closest neighbours or analogues). For larger case bases, no conclusions have been reached regarding the best number of similar projects to use. The calculation of estimated effort is obtained using the same effort value as the closest neighbour, or the mean effort for two or more closest neighbours. This is the common choice in Web and software engineering.

Again, with reference to Figure 1, the sequence of steps used with CBR is as follows.

a.   The estimated size and cost drivers relating to a new project p are used as input to retrieve similar projects from the case base for which actual effort is known (Step 3).

b.   Using the data from the previous step, a suitable CBR tool retrieves similar projects to project p and ranks these similar projects in ascending order of similarity, that is, from most similar to least similar (Step 1).

c.   A suitable CBR tool calculates estimated effort for project p (Step 4).

The sequence just described is similar to that employed for expert opinion. The characteristics of a new project must be known in order to retrieve finished similar projects. Once similar projects are retrieved, effort can be estimated.

When using CBR, there are six parameters that need to be considered, which are as follows (Selby & Porter, 1998).

Feature Subset Selection

Feature subset selection involves determining the optimum subset of features that yields the most accurate estimation. Some existing CBR tools, for example, ANGEL (Shepperd & Kadoda, 2001), optionally offer this functionality using a brute-force algorithm, searching for all possible feature subsets. Other CBR tools (e.g., CBR-Works from tec:inno) have no such functionality, and therefore to obtain estimated effort, we must use all of the known features of a new project to retrieve the most similar finished projects.

Copyright © 2008, IGI Global. Copying or distributing in print or electronic forms without written permission of IGI Global is prohibited.

Similarity Measure

The similarity measure records the level of similarity between different cases. Several similarity measures have been proposed in the literature to date; the three most popular currently used in the Web and software engineering literature (Angelis & Stamelos, 2000; Mendes, Counsell, & Mosley, 2000; Selby & Porter, 1998) are the unweighted Euclidean distance, the weighted Euclidean distance, and the maximum distance. However, there are also other similarity measures available as presented in Angelis and Stamelos. Each of the three similarity measures aforementioned is described below.

Unweighted Euclidean distance: The unweighted Euclidean distance measures the Euclidean (straight-line) distance d between two cases, where each case has n features. The equation used to calculate the distance between two cases x and y is the following:

$$d(x, y) = \sqrt{\left|x_0 - y_0\right|^2 + \left|x_1 - y_1\right|^2 + \ldots + \left|x_{n-1} - y_{n-1}\right|^2 + \left|x_n - y_n\right|^2}, \qquad (10)$$

where x_0 to x_n represent features 0 to n of case x, and y_0 to y_n represent features 0 to n of case y.

This measure has a geometrical meaning as the shortest distance between two points in an n-dimensional Euclidean space (Angelis & Stamelos, 2000; see Figure 3).

Figure 3. Euclidean distance using two size features (n = 2)

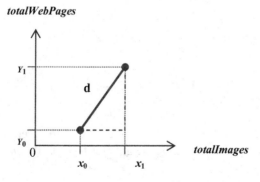

Copyright © 2008, IGI Global. Copying or distributing in print or electronic forms without written permission of IGI Global is prohibited.

Figure 3 illustrates the unweighted Euclidean distance by representing coordinates in a two-dimensional space; E2 as the number of features employed determines the number of dimensions, E*n*.

Project	*totalWebPages*	*totalImages*
1 (new)	100	20
2	350	12
3	220	25

Given the example above, the unweighted Euclidean distance between the new Project 1 and finished Project 2 would be calculated using the following equation:

$$d = \sqrt{|100-350|^2 + |20-12|^2} = 250.128. \tag{11}$$

The unweighted Euclidean distance between the new Project 1 and finished Project 3 would be calculated using the following equation:

$$d = \sqrt{|100-220|^2 + |20-25|^2} = 120.104. \tag{12}$$

Using the weighted Euclidean distance, the distance between Projects 1 and 3 is smaller than the distance between Projects 1 and 2; thus, Project 3 is more similar than Project 2 to Project 1.

Weighted Euclidean distance: The weighted Euclidean distance is used when features are given weights that reflect the relative importance of each feature. The weighted Euclidean distance measures the Euclidean distance d between two cases, where each case has n features and each feature has a weight w. The equation used to calculate the distance between two cases x and y is the following:

$$d(x,y) = \sqrt{w_0|x_0 - y_0|^2 + w_1|x_1 - y_1|^2 + \ldots + w_{n-1}|x_{n-1} - y_{n-1}|^2 + w_n|x_n - y_n|^2} \tag{13}$$

where x_0 to x_n represent features 0 to n of case x, y_0 to y_n represent features 0 to n of case y, and w_0 to w_n are the weights for features 0 to n.

Copyright © 2008, IGI Global. Copying or distributing in print or electronic forms without written permission of IGI Global is prohibited.

Maximum distance: The maximum distance computes the highest feature similarity, that is, the one to define the closest analogy. For two points (x_0, y_0) and (x_1, y_1), the maximum measure d is equivalent to the equation

$$d = \sqrt{\max((x_0 - y_0)^2, (x_1 - y_1)^2)}. \tag{14}$$

This effectively reduces the similarity measure down to a single feature, although this feature may differ for each retrieval episode. So, for a given new project P_{new}, the closest project in the case base will be the one that has at least one size feature with the most similar value to the same feature in project P_{new}.

Scaling

Scaling (also known as standardisation) represents the transformation of a feature's values according to a defined rule such that all features present values within the same range and as a consequence have the same degree of influence on the result (Angelis & Stamelos, 2000). A common method of scaling is to assign zero to the observed minimum value and one to the maximum observed value (Kadoda, Cartwright, Chen, & Shepperd, 2000), a strategy used by ANGEL and CBR-Works. Original feature values are normalised (between 0 and 1) by case-based reasoning tools to guarantee that they all influence the results in a similar fashion.

Number of Analogies

The number of analogies refers to the number of most similar cases that will be used to generate an effort estimate. With small sets of data, it is reasonable to consider only a small number of the most similar analogues (Angelis & Stamelos, 2000). Several studies in Web and software engineering have used only the closest case or analogue ($k = 1$) to obtain an estimated effort for a new project (Briand, El-Emam, Surmann, Wieczorek, & Maxwell, 1999; Mendes, Watson, Triggs, Mosley, & Counsell, 2002), while others have also used the two closest and the three closest analogues (Angelis & Stamelos; Jeffery, Ruhe, & Wieczorek, 2000, 2001; Mendes et al., 2000; Mendes, Mosley, & Counsell, 2001, 2003a, 2003b; Ruhe, Jeffery, & Wieczorek, 2003).

Copyright © 2008, IGI Global. Copying or distributing in print or electronic forms without written permission of IGI Global is prohibited.

Analogy Adaptation

Once the most similar cases have been selected, the next step is to identify how to generate (adapt) an effort estimate for project P_{new}. Choices of analogy adaptation techniques presented in the literature vary from the nearest neighbour (Briand et al., 1999; Jeffery et al., 2001), the mean of the closest analogues (Shepperd & Kadoda, 2001), the median of the closest analogues (Angelis & Stamelos, 2000), the inverse distance weighted mean, and inverse rank weighted mean (Kadoda et al., 2000), to illustrate just a few. The adaptations used to date for Web engineering are the nearest neighbour, mean of the closest analogues (Mendes et al., 2000; 2001), and the inverse rank weighted mean (Mendes, Mosley, & Counsell, 2002, 2003a, 2003b; Mendes, Watson, et al., 2002).

Each adaptation is explained below.

Nearest neighbour: For the estimated effort of P_{new}, this type of adaptation uses the same effort as its closest analogue.

Mean effort: For the estimated effort of P_{new}, this type of adaptation uses the average of its closest k analogues, when $k > 1$. This is a typical measure of central tendency, often used in the Web and software engineering literature. It treats all analogues as being equally important toward the outcome: the estimated effort.

Median effort: For the estimated effort of P_{new}, this type of adaptation uses the median of the closest k analogues, when $k > 2$. This is also a measure of central tendency, and has been used in the literature when the number of selected closest projects is greater than 2 (Angelis & Stamelos, 2000).

Inverse rank weighted mean: This type of adaptation allows higher ranked analogues to have more influence over the outcome than lower ones. For example, if we use three analogues, then the closest analogue (CA) would have weight 3, the second closest analogue (SC) would have weight 2, and the third closest analogue (LA) would have weight 1. The estimated effort would then be calculated as:

$$Inverse\ Rank\ Weighed\ Mean = \frac{3CA + 2SC + LA}{6}. \tag{15}$$

Adaptation Rules

Adaptation rules are used to adapt the estimated effort, according to a given criterion, such that it reflects the characteristics of the target project (new project) more closely.

Copyright © 2008, IGI Global. Copying or distributing in print or electronic forms without written permission of IGI Global is prohibited.

For example, in the context of effort prediction, the estimated effort to develop an application *a* would be adapted such that it would also take into consideration the size value of application *a*. The adaptation rule that has been employed to date in Web engineering is based on the linear size adjustment to the estimated effort (Mendes et al., 2003a, 2003b), obtained as follows:

- Once the most similar analogue in the case base has been retrieved, its effort value is adjusted and used as the effort estimate for the target project (new project).
- A linear extrapolation is performed along the dimension of a single measure, which is a size measure strongly correlated with effort. The linear size adjustment is calculated using the following equation:

$$Effort_{new\,Project} = \frac{Effort_{finished\,Project}}{Size_{finished\,Project}}\,Size_{new\,Project} \tag{16}$$

Project	*totalWebPages* (size)	*totalEffort* (effort)
Target (new)	100 (estimated value)	20 (estimated and adapted value)
Closest analogue	350 (actual value)	70 (actual value)

Given the example above, the estimated effort for the target project will be calculated as:

$$Effort_{new\,Project} = \frac{70}{350}\,100 = 20. \tag{17}$$

When we use more than one size measure as a feature, the equation changes to:

$$E_{est.P} = \frac{1}{q}\left(\sum_{q=1}^{q=x} \frac{E_{act}S_{est.q}}{S_{act.q}\big|_{>0}}\right), \tag{18}$$

where the following statements apply.

q is the number of size measures used as features.

Copyright © 2008, IGI Global. Copying or distributing in print or electronic forms without written permission of IGI Global is prohibited.

$E_{est.P}$ is the total effort estimated for the new Web project P.

E_{act} is the total effort for the closest analogue obtained from the case base.

$S_{est.q}$ is the estimated value for the size measure q, which is obtained from the client.

$S_{ast.q}$ is the actual value for the size measure q for the closest analogue obtained from the case base.

This type of adaptation assumes that all projects present similar productivity; however, it may not necessarily represent the Web development context of numerous Web companies worldwide.

Classification and Regression Trees

CARTs (Brieman, Friedman, Olshen, & Stone, 1984) use independent variables (predictors) to build binary trees, where each leaf node represents either a category to which an estimate belongs, or a value for an estimate. The former situation occurs with classification trees and the latter occurs with regression trees; that is, whenever predictors are categorical (e.g., yes or no), the tree is called a classification tree, and whenever predictors are numerical, the tree is called a regression tree.

In order to obtain an estimate, one has to traverse tree nodes from root to leaf by selecting the nodes that represent the category or value for the independent variables associated with the project to be estimated.

For example, assume we wish to obtain an effort estimate for a new Web project

Figure 4. Example of a regression tree for Web effort estimation

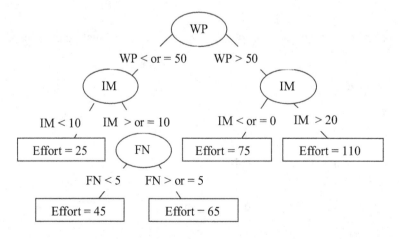

Copyright © 2008, IGI Global. Copying or distributing in print or electronic forms without written permission of IGI Global is prohibited.

using as its basis the simple regression tree structure presented in Figure 4. This regression tree was generated from data obtained from past completed Web applications, taking into account their existing values of effort and independent variables (e.g., new Web pages [WP], new images [IM], and new features or functions [FN]). The data used to build a CART model are called a learning sample, and once a tree has been built, it can be used to estimate effort for new projects. Assuming that the estimated values for WP, IM, and FN for a new Web project are 25, 15, and 3, respectively, we would obtain an estimated effort of 45 person hours after navigating the tree from its root down to leaf: Effort = 45.

If we now assume that the estimated values for WP, IM, and FN for a new Web project are 56, 34, and 22, respectively, we would obtain an estimated effort of 110 person hours after navigating the tree from its root down to leaf: Effort = 110.

A simple example of a classification tree for Web effort estimation is depicted in Figure 5. It uses the same variable names as that shown in Figure 4, however these variables are now all categorical, where possible categories (classes) are *Yes* and *No*. The effort estimate obtained using this classification tree is also categorical, where possible categories are *High effort* and *Low effort*.

A CART model constructs a binary tree by recursively partitioning the predictor space (set of all values or categories for the independent variables judged relevant) into subsets where the distribution of values or categories for the dependent variable (e.g.,

Figure 5. Example of a classification tree for Web effort estimation

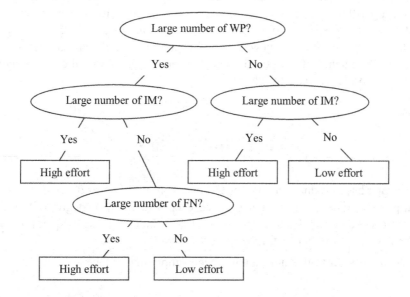

Copyright © 2008, IGI Global. Copying or distributing in print or electronic forms without written permission of IGI Global is prohibited.

effort) is successively more uniform. The partition (split) of a subset $S1$ is decided on the basis that the data in each of the descendant subsets should be "purer" than the data in $S1$. Thus, node "impurity" is directly related to the amount of different values or classes in a node; that is, the greater the mix of classes or values, the higher the node impurity. A pure node means that all the cases (e.g., Web projects) belong to the same class, or have the same value. The partition of subsets continues until a node contains only one class or value. Note that it is not necessarily the case that all the initial independent variables are used to build a CART model, rather only those variables that are related to the dependent variable are selected by the model. This means that a CART model can be used not only to produce a model that can be applicable for effort prediction, but also to obtain insight and understanding of the factors relevant to estimate a given dependent variable (more on CART and its use for Web effort estimation is also presented in Chapter VII).

The sequence of steps (see Figure 1) followed here are as follows:

a.   Past data are used to generate a CART model (Step 1).

b.   A CART model is built based on the past data obtained in the previous step (Step 2).

c.   The model created in Step 2 then receives, as input, values or categories for the estimated size and cost drivers relative to the new project for which effort is to be estimated (Step 3).

d.   The model generates a value or category for estimated effort (Step 4).

The sequence of steps described above corresponds to the same sequence used with the algorithmic techniques. In both situations, data are used to either build an equation that represents an effort model, or build a binary tree, which is later used to obtain effort estimates for new projects. This sequence of steps contrasts with the different sequence of steps used for expert opinion and CBR, where knowledge about a new project is used to select similar projects.

Which Technique to Use?

This chapter has introduced numerous techniques for obtaining effort estimates for a new project; all have been used in practice, each with a varying degree of success. Therefore, the question that is often asked is this: Which of the techniques provides the most accurate prediction for Web effort estimation?

To date, the answer to this question has been simply that it depends.

Copyright © 2008, IGI Global. Copying or distributing in print or electronic forms without written permission of IGI Global is prohibited.

Algorithmic and CART models have some advantages over CBR and expert opinion, such as the following:

- They allow users to see how a model derives its conclusions, an important factor for verification as well as theory building and understanding of the process being modeled (Gray & MacDonell, 1997).

- They often need to be specialised relative to the local environment in which they are used. This means that the estimations that are obtained take full advantage of using models that have been calibrated to local circumstances.

Despite these advantages, no convergence for which effort estimation technique has the best predictive power has yet been reached, even though comparative studies have been carried out over the past 17 years (e.g., Angelis & Stamelos, 2000; Briand et al., 1999; Briand, Langley, & Wieczorek, 2000; Finnie, Wittig, & Desharnais, 1997; Gray & MacDonell, 1997a, 1997b; Hughes, 1997; Jeffery et al., 2000, 2001; Kadoda et al., 2000; Kemerer, 1987; Mendes, Mosley, et al., 2002; Ruhe et al., 2003; Selby & Porter, 1998; Shepperd & Kadoda, 2001).

One justification is that these studies often use data sets with differing numbers of characteristics (e.g., number of outliers, amount of collinearity, number of variables, and number of projects) and different comparative designs. Note that an outlier is a value that is far from the others, and collinearity represents the existence of a linear relationship between two or more independent variables.

Shepperd and Kadoda (2001) presented evidence showing there is a relationship between the success of a particular technique and factors such as training set size (size of the subset used to derive a model), nature of the effort estimation function (e.g., continuous or discontinuous), and characteristics of the data set. They concluded that the best prediction technique that can work on any type of data set may be impossible to obtain. Note that a **continuous** function is one in which "small changes in the input produce small changes in the output" (http://e.wikipedia.org/wiki/Continuous_function). If small changes in the input "can produce a broken jump in the changes of the output, the function is said to be **discontinuous** (or to have a **discontinuity**)" (http://e.wikipedia.org/wiki/Continuous_function).

Stepwise regression, CART, and CBR have been applied to Web effort estimation, and have also had their prediction accuracy compared (see Mendes, Watson, et al., 2002). Mendes, Watson, et al. showed that stepwise regression provided the best results overall, and this trend has also been confirmed using a different data set of Web projects. However, the data sets employed in both studies presented a very strong linear relationship between size and cost drivers, and effort, and as such it comes as no surprise that, of the three techniques, stepwise regression presented the best prediction accuracy. These three techniques are also detailed later in Chapters

Copyright © 2008, IGI Global. Copying or distributing in print or electronic forms without written permission of IGI Global is prohibited.

5, 6, and 7, which also provide step-by-step examples of how to apply a particular technique for Web effort estimation based on the same data set of industrial Web projects.

Web Effort Estimation Survey

This section presents a survey of Web effort estimation models proposed in the literature. Each work is described and finally summarised in Tables 4 and 5.

First Study: Measurement and Effort Prediction for Web Applications

Mendes et al. (2000) investigated the use of case-based reasoning, linear regression, and stepwise regression techniques to estimate development effort for Web applications developed by experienced and inexperienced students. The case-based reasoning estimations were generated using a freeware tool, ANGEL, developed at the University of Bournemouth, United Kingdom. The most similar Web projects were retrieved using the unweighted Euclidean distance and the "leave one out" cross-validation process. Estimated effort was generated using either the closest analogue or the mean of two or three analogues. The two data sets (HEL and LEL) used collected data on Web applications developed by second-year computer science students from the University of Southampton, United Kingdom, and had 29 and 41 projects respectively. HEL represented data from students with high experience in Web development, whereas LEL had data from students inexperienced in Web development.

The size measures collected were page count (total number of HTML pages created from scratch), reused page count (total number of reused HTML pages), connectivity (total number of links in the application), compactness (Botafogo, Rivlin, & Shneiderman, 1992; measured using an ordinal scale from 1, no connections, to 5, totally connected, indicating the level of interconnectedness of an application), stratum (Botafogo et al.; measured using an ordinal scale from 1, no sequential navigation, to 5, complete sequential navigation, indicating how linear the application is), and structure (represents the topology of the application's backbone, being either sequential, hierarchical, or network). Prediction accuracy was measured using the mean magnitude of relative error (MMRE; Conte, Dunsmore, & Shen, 1986) and the median magnitude of relative error (MdMRE; Conte et al.). Results for the HEL group were statistically significantly better than those for the LEL group. In addition, case-based reasoning showed the best results overall.

Copyright © 2008, IGI Global. Copying or distributing in print or electronic forms without written permission of IGI Global is prohibited.

Second Study: Web Development: Estimating Quick-to-Market Software

Reifer (2000) proposed a Web effort estimation model, WEBMO, which is an extension of the COCOMO II model. The WEBMO model has nine cost drivers and a fixed effort power law instead of seven cost drivers and variable effort power law as used in the COCOMO II model. Size is measured in WebObjects, which is a single aggregated size measure calculated by applying Halstead's formula for volume.

The elements of the WebObjects measure are as follows:

- Number of building blocks (Active X, DCOM [distributed component object model], OLE [object linking and embedding], etc.)
- Number of components off the shelf (COTS; includes any wrapper code)
- Number of multimedia files, except graphics files (text, video, sound, etc.)
- Number of object or application points (Cowderoy, 2000) or others proposed (e.g., number of server data tables, number of client data tables)
- Number of XML (extensible markup language), SGML (standard generalized markup language), HTML, and query language lines (number of lines including links to data attributes)
- Number of Web components (applets, agents, etc.)
- Number of graphics files (templates, images, pictures, etc.)
- Number of scripts (visual language, audio, motion, etc.) and any other measures that companies find suitable

Reifer (2000) allegedly used data on 46 finished industrial Web projects and obtained predictions that are reported as being "repeatable and robust." However, no information is given regarding the data collection and no summary statistics for the data are presented.

Third Study: Web Metrics: Estimating Design and Authoring Effort

Mendes et al. (2001) investigated the prediction accuracy of top-down and bottom-up Web effort estimation models generated using linear and stepwise regression models. They employed one data set with data from 37 Web applications developed by honours and postgraduate computer science students from the University of Auckland, New Zealand. Gathered measures were organised into five categories.

Copyright © 2008, IGI Global. Copying or distributing in print or electronic forms without written permission of IGI Global is prohibited.

- Length size measures
- Reusability measures
- Complexity size measures
- Effort
- Confounding factors (factors that, if not controlled, could influence the validity of the evaluation)

In addition, measures were also associated with one of the following entities: Web application, Web page, media, and program. Effort prediction models were generated for each entity and prediction accuracy was measured using the MMRE measure. Results showed that the best predictions were obtained for the entity program based on nonreused program measures (code length and code comment length).

Fourth Study: Measurement, Prediction, and Risk Analysis for Web Applications

Fewster and Mendes (2001) investigated the use of a generalised linear model (GLM) for Web effort estimation and risk management. Generalised linear models provide a flexible regression framework for predictive modeling of effort since they permit nonlinear relationships between the response and predictor variables and in addition allow for a wide range of choices for the distribution of the response variable (e.g., effort).

Fewster and Mendes (2001) employed the same data set used in Mendes et al. (2001), however they reduced the number of size measures targeting only those measures related to the entity type Web application. The measures used were organised into five categories:

- Effort measures
- Structure measures
- Complexity measures
- Reuse measures
- Size measures

Finally, they did not use de-factor measures of prediction accuracy (e.g., MMRE, MdMRE) to assess the accuracy of their proposed model; instead, they used the model fit produced for the model as an accuracy measure. However, it should be

Copyright © 2008, IGI Global. Copying or distributing in print or electronic forms without written permission of IGI Global is prohibited.

noted that a model with a good fit to the data is not the same as a good prediction model.

Fifth Study: The Application of Case-Based Reasoning to Early Web Project Cost Estimation

Mendes, Mosley, et al. (2002) focused on the harvesting of size measures at different points in a Web application's development life cycle to estimate development effort, and their comparison was based on several prediction accuracy indicators. The rationale for using different measures harvested at different points was as follows.

Most work on Web effort estimation propose models based on late product size measures, such as the number of HTML pages, number of images, and so forth. However, for the successful management of software and Web projects, estimates are necessary throughout the whole development life cycle. Preliminary (early) effort estimates in particular are essential when bidding for a contract or when determining a project's feasibility in terms of cost-benefit analysis.

Mendes, Mosley, et al.'s (2002) aim was to investigate if there were any differences in accuracy between the effort predictors gathered at different points during the development life cycle. In addition, they also checked if these differences were statistically dissimilar. Their effort estimates were generated using the case-based reasoning technique, where different combinations of parameters were used: similarity measure, scaling, number of closest analogues, analogy adaptation, and feature subset selection. Their study was based on data from 25 Web applications developed by pairs of postgraduate computer science students from the University of Auckland, New Zealand. The measures of prediction accuracy employed were MMRE, MdMRE, prediction at 25% (Pred[25]), and boxplots of residuals. Contrary to the expected, their results showed that late measures presented similar estimation accuracy to early measures.

Sixth Study: A Comparison of Development Effort Estimation Techniques for Web Hypermedia Applications

Mendes, Watson, et al. (2002) present an in-depth comparison of Web effort estimation models, where they do the following.

1. Compare the prediction accuracy of three CBR techniques to estimate the effort to develop Web applications

Copyright © 2008, IGI Global. Copying or distributing in print or electronic forms without written permission of IGI Global is prohibited.

2.   Compare the prediction accuracy of the best CBR technique vs. three commonly used prediction models, specifically, multiple linear regression, stepwise regression, and regression trees

Mendes, Watson, et al. (2002) employed one data set of 37 Web applications developed by honours and postgraduate computer science students from the University of Auckland, New Zealand. The measures used in their study were the following.

- Page count (number of HTML or SHTML files used in the Web application)
- Media count (number of media files used in the Web application)
- Program count (number of JavaScript files and Java applets used in the Web application)
- Reused media count (number of reused or modified media files)
- Reused program count (number of reused or modified programs)
- Connectivity density (total number of internal links divided by page count)
- Total page complexity (average number of different types of media per Web page)
- Total effort (effort in person hours to design and author a Web application)

Note that the participants did not use external links to other Web hypermedia applications; that is, all the links pointed to pages within the original application only. Regarding the use of case-based reasoning, they employed several parameters, as follows:

- Three similarity measures (unweighted Euclidean, weighted Euclidean, and maximum)
- Three choices for the number of analogies (one, two, and three)
- Three choices for the analogy adaptation (mean, inverse rank weighted mean, and median)
- Two alternatives regarding the standardisation of the attributes (*Yes* for standardised and *No* for not standardised)

Prediction accuracy was measured using MMRE, MdMRE, Pred(25), and boxplots of residuals. Their results showed that different measures of prediction accuracy

Copyright © 2008, IGI Global. Copying or distributing in print or electronic forms without written permission of IGI Global is prohibited.

gave different results. MMRE and MdMRE showed better prediction accuracy for multiple regression models whereas boxplots showed better accuracy for CBR.

Seventh Study: Cost Estimation for Web Applications

Ruhe et al. (2003) employed the COBRA™ (cost estimation benchmarking and risk analysis) method to investigate if this method was adequate for estimating effort for Web applications. They used real project data on 12 Web projects, all developed by a small Web company in Sydney, Australia. COBRA is a registered trademark of the Fraunhofer Institute for Experimental Software Engineering (IESE), Germany, and is a method that aims to develop an effort estimation model that is to be built from a company-specific data set. It uses expert opinion and data on past projects to estimate development effort and risks for a new project. The size measure employed was WebObjects (Reifer, 2000), measured for each one of the 12 finished Web applications used in this study. The prediction accuracy obtained using CO-BRA™ was compared to that obtained using expert opinion and linear regression, all measured using MMRE and Pred(25). They found that COBRA provided the most accurate results.

Eighth Study: Do Adaptation Rules Improve Web Cost Estimation?

Mendes et al. (2003a) compared several methods of CBR-based effort estimation, investigating the use of adaptation rules as a contributing factor for better estimation accuracy. They used two data sets, where the difference between these data sets was a level of "messiness" each had. Messiness was evaluated by the number of outliers and the amount of collinearity (Shepperd & Kadoda, 2001) that each data set presented. The data set considered less messy than the other presented a continuous cost function, which also translated into a strong linear relationship between size and effort. However, the messiest data set presented a discontinuous cost function, where there was no linear or log-linear relationship between size and effort.

Both data sets represented data on Web applications developed by computer science students from the University of Auckland, New Zealand, and two types of adaptation were used: one with weights and another without weights (Mendes et al., 2003a). None of the adaptation rules gave better predictions for the messier data set; however, for the less messy data set, one type of adaptation rule (no weights) gave good prediction accuracy, measured using MMRE, Pred(25), and boxplots of absolute residuals.

Copyright © 2008, IGI Global. Copying or distributing in print or electronic forms without written permission of IGI Global is prohibited.

Ninth Study: Estimating the Design Effort of Web Applications

Baresi, Morasca, and Paolini (2003) investigated the relationship between a number of size measures, obtained from design artefacts that were created according to the W2000 methodology, and the total effort needed to design Web applications. Their size measures were organised into categories that are presented in more detail in Table 5. The categories employed were information model, navigation model, and presentation model. Their analysis identified some measures that appear to be related to the total design effort. In addition, they also carried out a finer grained analysis, studying which of the used measures had an impact on the design effort when using W2000. Their data set was comprised of 30 Web applications developed by computer science students from Politecnico di Milano, Italy.

Discussion

Table 4 summarises the studies that were presented in the survey literature, and provides us with means to identify a number of trends such as the following.

- The prediction technique used the most was linear regression.
- The measures of prediction accuracy employed the most were MMRE and Pred(25).
- The sizes of the data sets employed were small and not greater than 46 data points.

Size measures differed throughout studies, which indicate the lack of standards to sizing Web applications.

Using the survey literature previously described, we also investigated the type of Web applications that were used in those studies. Our rationale was that we believed earlier studies would have more static Web applications (Web hypermedia applications), and that more recent studies would show a use of more dynamic Web applications (Web software applications).

The classification of Web applications into Web hypermedia and Web software applications was proposed by Christodoulou, Zafiris, and Papatheodorou (2000). They define a Web hypermedia application as an unconventional application characterised by the authoring of information using nodes (chunks of information), links (relations between nodes), anchors, and access structures (for navigation), and its delivery over the Web. Technologies commonly used for developing such applications are

Copyright © 2008, IGI Global. Copying or distributing in print or electronic forms without written permission of IGI Global is prohibited.

Table 4. Summary of literature in Web effort estimation

Study	Type (case study, experiment, survey)	# Data Sets (# data points)	Participants (students, professionals)	Size Measures	Prediction Techniques	Best Technique(s)	Measure Prediction Accuracy
1st	Case study	2 (29 and 41)	second-year computer science students	Page count, reused page count, connectivity, compactness, stratum, structure	Case-based reasoning, linear regression, stepwise regression	Case-based reasoning for high-experience group	MMRE
2nd	Case study	1 (46)	Professionals	Web objects	WEBMO (parameters generated using linear regression)	-	Pred(n)
3rd	Case study	1 (37)	Honours and postgraduate computer science students	Length size, reusability, complexity, size	Linear regression, stepwise regression	Linear regression	MMRE
4th	Case study	1 (37)	Honours and postgraduate computer science students	Structure metrics, complexity metrics, reuse metrics, size metrics	Generalised linear model	-	Goodness of fit
5th	Case study	1 (25)	Honours and postgraduate computer science students	Requirements and design measures, application measures	Case-based reasoning	-	MMRE, MdMRE, Pred(25), boxplots of residuals
6th	Case study	1 (37)	Honours and postgraduate computer science students	Page count, media count, program count, reused media count, reused program count, connectivity density, total page complexity	Case-based reasoning, linear regression, stepwise regression, classification and regression trees	Linear/ stepwise regression or case-based reasoning (depends on the measure of accuracy employed)	MMRE, MdMRE, Pred(25), boxplots of residuals
7th	Case study	1 (12)	Professionals	Web objects	COBRA, expert opinion, linear regression	COBRA	MMRE, Pred(25), boxplots of residuals

Copyright © 2008, IGI Global. Copying or distributing in print or electronic forms without written permission of IGI Global is prohibited.

Table 4. continued

Study	Type (case study, experiment, survey	# Data Sets (# data points)	Participants (students, professionals)	Size Measures	Prediction Techniques	Best Technique(s)	Measure Prediction Accuracy
8th	Case study	2 (37 and 25)	Honours and postgraduate computer science students	Page count, media count, program count, reused media count (only one data set), reused program count (only one data set), connectivity density, total page complexity	Case-based reasoning	-	MMRE, Pred(25), boxplots of absolute residuals
9th	Experiment	1 (30)	Computer science students	Information model measures, navigation model measures, presentation model measures	Linear regression	-	-

HTML, JavaScript, and multimedia. In addition, typical developers are writers, artists, and organisations that wish to publish information on the Web and/or CD-ROMs without the need to use programming languages such as Java.

Conversely, Web software applications represent conventional software applications that depend on the Web or use the Web's infrastructure for execution. Typical applications include legacy information systems such as databases, booking systems, knowledge bases, and so forth. Many e-commerce applications fall into this category. Typically they employ technology such as COTS, and components such as DCOM, OLE, Active X, XML, PHP, dynamic HTML, databases, and development solutions such as J2EE. Developers are young programmers fresh from a computer science or software engineering degree program, managed by more senior staff.

Table 5 lists the types of Web applications used in each of the studies described in the literature review, and shows that, out of the nine papers described in this section, six (66%) have used data sets of Web hypermedia applications, and another two (22%) have used Web software applications.

Copyright © 2008, IGI Global. Copying or distributing in print or electronic forms without written permission of IGI Global is prohibited.

Table 5. Types of Web applications used in Web effort estimation studies

Study	Type of Web Application: Web Hypermedia or Web Software Application
1st	Web hypermedia applications
2nd	Not documented
3rd	Web hypermedia applications
4th	Web hypermedia applications
5th	Web hypermedia applications
6th	Web hypermedia applications
7th	Web software applications
8th	Web software applications
9th	Web hypermedia applications

Conclusion

Effort estimation enables companies to know beforehand and before implementing an application the amount of effort required to develop the application on time and within budget. To estimate effort, it is necessary to have knowledge of previous similar projects that have already been developed by the company, and also to understand the project variables that may affect effort prediction.

These variables represent an application's size (e.g., number of new Web pages and images, the number of functions or features, e.g., a shopping cart, to be offered by the new Web application) and also include other factors that may contribute to effort (e.g., total number of developers who will help develop the new Web application, developers' average number of years of experience with the development tools employed, main programming language used).

The mechanisms used to obtain an effort estimate are generally classified as the following.

Expert-based estimation: Expert-based effort estimation represents the process of estimating effort by subjective means, and is often based on previous experience with developing and/or managing similar projects. This is by far the most used technique for Web effort estimation.

Algorithmic-based estimation: Algorithmic-based effort estimation attempts to build models (equations) that precisely represent the relationship between effort and one or more project characteristics via the use of algorithmic models

Copyright © 2008, IGI Global. Copying or distributing in print or electronic forms without written permission of IGI Global is prohibited.

(statistical methods that are used to build equations). These techniques have been to date the most popular techniques used in the Web and software effort estimation literature.

Estimation using artificial-intelligence techniques: Finally, artificial-intelligence techniques also aim to obtain effort estimates, although not necessarily using a model, such as the ones created with algorithmic-based techniques. Artificial-intelligence techniques include fuzzy logic (Kumar et al., 1994), regression trees (Schroeder et al., 1996), neural networks (Shepperd et al., 1996), and case-based reasoning (Shepperd & Kadoda, 2001).

This chapter has detailed the use of case-based reasoning and regression trees, the two artificial-intelligence techniques that have been employed in the literature for Web effort estimation.

This chapter also presented a survey of previous work in Web effort estimation, and the main findings were as follows:

- The most widely used prediction technique is linear regression.
- The measures of prediction accuracy employed the most were MMRE and Pred(25).
- The data sets used in the studies were small, with no more than 46 projects.
- Size measures differed throughout the studies, which indicates the lack of standards to sizing Web applications.
- Out of the nine papers, six (66%) have used data sets of Web hypermedia applications, and another two (22%) have used data sets of Web software applications.

References

Angelis, L., & Stamelos, I. (2000). A simulation tool for efficient analogy based cost estimation. *Empirical Software Engineering, 5*, 35-68.

Baresi, L., Morasca, S., & Paolini, P. (2003, September). Estimating the design effort of Web applications. *Proceedings of the Ninth International Software Measures Symposium*, 62-72.

Boehm, B. (1981). *Software engineering economics*. Englewood Cliffs, NJ: Prentice-Hall.

Copyright © 2008, IGI Global. Copying or distributing in print or electronic forms without written permission of IGI Global is prohibited.

Boehm, B. (2000). *COCOMO II.* The University of Southern California. Retrieved January 2006 from http://sunset.usc.edu/research/COCOMOII/Docs/model-man.pdf

Bohem, B., Abts, C., Brown, A., Chulani, S., Clark, B., Horowitz, E., et al. (2000). *Software cost estimation with Cocomo II.* Pearson Publishers.

Botafogo, R., Rivlin, A. E., & Shneiderman, B. (1992). Structural analysis of hypertexts: Identifying hierarchies and useful measures. *ACM Transactions on Information Systems, 10*(2), 143-179.

Briand, L. C., El-Emam, K., Surmann, D., Wieczorek, I., & Maxwell, K. D. (1999). An assessment and comparison of common cost estimation modeling techniques. *Proceedings of ICSE 1999* (pp. 313-322).

Briand, L. C., Langley, T., & Wieczorek, I. (2000). A replicated assessment and comparison of common software cost modeling techniques. *Proceedings of ICSE 2000* (pp. 377-386).

Brieman, L., Friedman, J., Olshen, R., & Stone, C. (1984). *Classification and regression trees.* Belmont: Wadsworth.

Christodoulou, S. P., Zafiris, P. A., & Papatheodorou, T. S. (2000). WWW2000: The developer's view and a practitioner's approach to Web engineering. *Proceedings of the 2nd ICSE Workshop Web Engineering* (pp. 75-92).

Conte, S., Dunsmore, H., & Shen, V. (1986). *Software engineering metrics and models.* Menlo Park, CA: Benjamin/Cummings.

Cowderoy, A. J. C. (2000). Measures of size and complexity for Web-site content. *Proceedings of the 11th ESCOM Conference* (pp. 423-431).

DeMarco, T. (1982). *Controlling software projects: Management, measurement and estimation.* New York: Yourdon Press.

Fewster, R. M., & Mendes, E. (2001). Measurement, prediction and risk analysis for Web applications. *Proceedings of the IEEE METRICS Symposium* (pp. 338-348).

Finnie, G. R., Wittig, G. E., & Desharnais, J.-M. (1997). A comparison of software effort estimation techniques: Using function points with neural networks, case-based reasoning and regression models. *Journal of Systems and Software, 39*, 281-289.

Gray, A., & MacDonell, S. (1997a). Applications of fuzzy logic to software metric models for development effort estimation. *Proceedings of IEEE Annual Meeting of the North American Fuzzy Information Processing Society–NAFIPS* (pp. 394-399).

Gray, A. R., & MacDonell, S. G. (1997b). A comparison of model building techniques to develop predictive equations for software metrics. *Information and Software Technology, 39*, 425-437.

Copyright © 2008, IGI Global. Copying or distributing in print or electronic forms without written permission of IGI Global is prohibited.

Gray, R., MacDonell, S. G., & Shepperd, M. J. (1999). Factors systematically associated with errors in subjective estimates of software development effort: The stability of expert judgement. *Proceedings of the 6th IEEE Metrics Symposium* (pp. 216-226).

Hughes, R. T. (1997). *An empirical investigation into the estimation of software development effort.* Unpublished doctoral dissertation, Department of Computing, University of Brighton, Brighton, UK.

Jeffery, R., Ruhe, M., & Wieczorek, I. (2000). A comparative study of two software development cost modelling techniques using multi-organizational and company-specific data. *Information and Software Technology, 42,* 1009-1016.

Jeffery, R., Ruhe, M., & Wieczorek, I. (2001). Using public domain metrics to estimate software development effort. *Proceedings of the 7th IEEE Metrics Symposium* (pp. 16-27).

Jørgensen, M., & Sjøberg, D. (2001). Impact of effort estimates on software project work. *Information and Software Technology, 43,* 939-948.

Kadoda, G., Cartwright, M., Chen, L., & Shepperd, M. J. (2000). *Experiences using case-based reasoning to predict software project effort.* Proceedings of the EASE 2000 Conference, Keele, UK.

Kemerer, C. F. (1987). An empirical validation of software cost estimation models. *Communications of the ACM, 30*(5), 416-429.

Kitchenham, B. A., Pickard, L. M., Linkman, S., & Jones, P. (2003). Modelling software bidding risks. *IEEE Transactions on Software Engineering, 29*(6), 542-554.

Kok, P., Kitchenham, B. A., & Kirakowski, J. (1990). The MERMAID approach to software cost estimation. *Proceedings of the ESPRIT Annual Conference* (pp. 296-314).

Kumar, S., Krishna, B. A., & Satsangi, P. S. (1994). Fuzzy systems and neural networks in software engineering project management. *Journal of Applied Intelligence, 4,* 31-52.

Mendes, E., Counsell, S., & Mosley, N. (2000, June). Measurement and effort prediction of Web applications. *Proceedings of 2nd ICSE Workshop on Web Engineering* (pp. 57-74).

Mendes, E., Mosley, N., & Counsell, S. (2001). Web measures: Estimating design and authoring effort. *IEEE Multimedia, 8*(1), 50-57.

Mendes, E., Mosley, N., & Counsell, S. (2002). The application of case-based reasoning to early Web project cost estimation. *Proceedings of IEEE COMPSAC* (pp. 393-398).

Copyright © 2008, IGI Global. Copying or distributing in print or electronic forms without written permission of IGI Global is prohibited.

Mendes, E., Mosley, N., & Counsell, S. (2003a). Do adaptation rules improve Web cost estimation? *Proceedings of the ACM Hypertext Conference 2003* (pp. 173-183).

Mendes, E., Mosley, N., & Counsell, S. (2003b). A replicated assessment of the use of adaptation rules to improve Web cost estimation. *Proceedings of the ACM and IEEE International Symposium on Empirical Software Engineering* (pp. 100-109).

Mendes, E., Watson, I., Triggs, C., Mosley, N., & Counsell, S. (2002, June). A comparison of development effort estimation techniques for Web hypermedia applications. *Proceedings IEEE Metrics Symposium* (pp. 141-151).

Reifer, D. J. (2000). Web development: Estimating quick-to-market software. *IEEE Software, 17*(6), 57-64.

Ruhe, M., Jeffery, R., & Wieczorek, I. (2003). Cost estimation for Web applications. *Proceedings of ICSE 2003* (pp. 285-294).

Schofield, C. (1998). *An empirical investigation into software estimation by analogy.* Unpublished doctoral dissertation, Department of Computing, Bournemouth University, Bournemouth, UK.

Schroeder, L., Sjoquist, D., & Stephan, P. (1986). *Understanding regression analysis: An introductory guide* (No. 57). Newbury Park: Sage Publications.

Selby, R. W., & Porter, A. A. (1998). Learning from examples: Generation and evaluation of decision trees for software resource analysis. *IEEE Transactions on Software Engineering, 14*, 1743-1757.

Shepperd, M. J., & Kadoda, G. (2001). Using simulation to evaluate prediction techniques. *Proceedings of the IEEE 7th International Software Metrics Symposium* (pp. 349-358).

Shepperd, M. J., & Schofield, C. (1997). Estimating software project effort using analogies. *IEEE Transactions on Software Engineering, 23*(11), 736-743.

Shepperd, M. J., Schofield, C., & Kitchenham, B. (1996). Effort estimation using analogy. *Proceedings of ICSE-18* (pp. 170-178).

Vliet, H. V. (2000). *Software engineering: Principles and practice* (2nd ed.). New York: John Wiley & Sons.

Copyright © 2008, IGI Global. Copying or distributing in print or electronic forms without written permission of IGI Global is prohibited.

Chapter III

How Accurate is an Effort Model?

Abstract

Building effort models or using techniques to obtain a measure of estimated effort does not mean that the effort estimates obtained will be accurate. As such, it is also important and necessary to assess the estimation accuracy of the effort models or techniques under scrutiny. For this, we need to employ a process called cross-validation. Cross-validation means that part of the original data set is used to build an effort model, or is used by an effort estimation technique, leaving the remainder of the data set (data not used in the model-building process) to be used to validate the model or technique. In addition, in parallel with conducting cross-validation, prediction accuracy measures are also obtained. Examples of de facto accuracy measures are the mean magnitude of relative error (MMRE), the median magnitude of relative error (MdMRE), and prediction at 25% (Pred[25]).

Copyright © 2008, IGI Global. Copying or distributing in print or electronic forms without written permission of IGI Global is prohibited.

Introduction

As previously seen in Chapter II, effort estimation models and techniques aim to provide accurate effort predictions for new projects. In general, these models and techniques use data on past finished projects, which are then employed to obtain effort estimates for new projects. However, providing an effort estimate does not guarantee the estimate will be accurate, that is, close to the actual effort used to develop the new Web project.

To determine how good a model or technique is to estimate effort for new projects, we need to measure its predictive accuracy, which can be calculated using past finished projects for which actual effort is known.

Measuring the predictive accuracy of an effort estimation model m or technique t is a four-step process, described below and illustrated in Figure 1.

Step 1: Split the original data set into two subsets: validation and training. The validation set represents data on finished projects p_n to p_q that will be used to simulate a situation as if these projects were new. Each project p_n to p_q will have its effort estimated using the model m or technique t, and, given that we also know the project's actual effort, we are in a position to compare its actual effort to the estimated effort obtained using m or t, and therefore ultimately assess how far off the estimate is from the actual.

Step 2: Use the remaining projects (training subset) to build an effort estimation model m. There are estimation techniques that do not build an explicit model (e.g., case-based reasoning). If that is the case, then the training set becomes a database of past projects to be used by the effort technique t to estimate effort for p_n to p_q.

Step 3: Apply model m to each project p_n to p_q, and obtain estimated effort. Once estimated effort is obtained, accuracy statistics for each of these projects p_n to p_q can also be calculated. If the technique does not build a model, then this step comprises applying this technique t to each project p_n to p_q to obtain estimated effort, and once estimated effort is obtained, accuracy statistics for each of these projects can be calculated.

Step 4: Once estimated effort and accuracy statistics for p_n to p_q have been attained, aggregated accuracy statistics can be computed, which provide an overall assessment of the predictive accuracy of model m or technique t.

It is important to note that the subset of new projects (see Figure 1) comprises data on finished projects, for which actual effort is known. These data are used to simulate a situation where a Web company has a subset of new projects for which

Copyright © 2008, IGI Global. Copying or distributing in print or electronic forms without written permission of IGI Global is prohibited.

Figure 1. Overall process to measure prediction accuracy

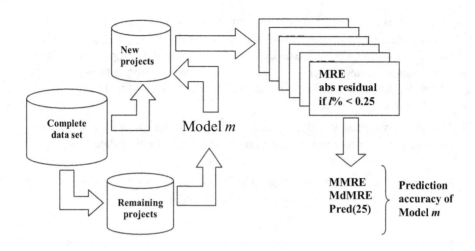

they wish to obtain estimated effort. A simulation allows us to compare effort estimates obtained using model m, or technique t, and the actual known effort used to develop these projects. This comparison will indicate how close the estimated effort is from the actual effort, and consequently, how accurate the effort model m or the technique t is.

This chapter begins by describing the most widely used accuracy statistics and how they are employed to measure the predictive accuracy of a model or technique. Later, we provide a detailed example using data on real industrial Web projects and a real effort model to obtain effort estimates and to measure this model's prediction accuracy.

Measuring Effort Prediction Accuracy

Project Prediction Accuracy Statistics

To date, the three most commonly used project effort prediction accuracy statistics are the following.

Copyright © 2008, IGI Global. Copying or distributing in print or electronic forms without written permission of IGI Global is prohibited.

- The magnitude of relative error (MRE; Kemerer, 1987)
- A measure that assesses if relative error associated with a project is not greater than l (Shepperd & Schofield, 1997). The value for l is generally set at 25% (or 0.25).
- Absolute residual, which is the absolute difference between actual and estimated effort

MRE is defined as:

$$MRE = \frac{|e - \hat{e}|}{e},$$

(1)

where e is the actual effort of a project in the validation set, and $\hat{e}$ is the estimated effort that was obtained using model m or technique t.

A project's prediction statistics are calculated for each project being simulated as a new project, and is later used to calculate accuracy statistics for model m. Thus, the project's prediction accuracy statistics are the basis for obtaining a model's prediction accuracy statistics.

Model Prediction Accuracy Statistics

The three measures of a model's prediction accuracy that are widely used are the following.

- The mean magnitude of relative error (MMRE; Shepperd, Schofield, & Kitchenham, 1996)
- The median magnitude of relative error (MdMRE; Myrtveit & Stensrud, 1999)
- The prediction at level n (Pred[n]; Shepperd & Schofield, 1997)

MMRE, MdMRE, and Pred(l) are taken as the de facto standard evaluation criteria to measure the predictive accuracy (power) of effort estimation models and techniques (Stensrud, Foss, Kitchenham, & Myrtveit, 2002). Suggestions have been made that a good prediction model or technique should have MMRE and MdMRE no greater than 0.25, and that Pred(25) should not be smaller than 75% (Conte, Dunsmore, & Shen, 1986).

Copyright © 2008, IGI Global. Copying or distributing in print or electronic forms without written permission of IGI Global is prohibited.

MMRE and MdMRE are the mean (arithmetic average) and median MRE for a set of projects, respectively.

MMRE is calculated as:

$$MMRE = \frac{1}{n}\sum_{i=1}^{i=n}\frac{|e_i - \hat{e}_i|}{e_i}. \tag{2}$$

Since the mean is calculated by taking into account the value of every estimated and actual effort from the validation set employed, the result may give a distorted assessment of a model's or technique's predictive power when there are extreme MREs. For example, taking into account the effort data provided below (see Table 1), we will show that the mean provides a partial interpretation of the prediction accuracy when based on MMRE.

All projects, except for P1, have MREs less than or equal to 0.25, thus indicating good accuracy per project. Without P1, the MMRE for the remaining 13 projects is 0.25, which suggests that the prediction model, or technique, also provides good prediction accuracy. However, when we calculate MMRE based on all 14 projects, its value changes to 0.30, which now does not indicate good prediction accuracy.

Table 1. Example project data

projID	toteffort	esteffort	MRE	MRE <= 0.25?
P1	2020	100	0.95	FALSE
P2	84.5	63.36	0.25	TRUE
P3	33.6	25.2	0.25	TRUE
P4	600	4.50	0.25	TRUE
P5	160	120	0.25	TRUE
P6	40	30	0.25	TRUE
P7	600	4.50	0.25	TRUE
P8	300	2.25	0.25	TRUE
P9	12	15	0.25	TRUE
P10	303.75	3.79	0.25	TRUE
P11	330	250	0.24	TRUE
P12	5	6.2	0.24	TRUE
P13	250	190	0.24	TRUE
P14	400	310	0.23	TRUE
			Pred(25)	93%

Copyright © 2008, IGI Global. Copying or distributing in print or electronic forms without written permission of IGI Global is prohibited.

This happened because P1 has a very large MRE (an extreme value that makes it an outlier); thus its use provides an overall result that has been distorted by a single value.

Whenever we anticipate that the MREs may have extreme values, we should also consider using the MdMRE, which is the median MRE. Unlike the mean, the median always represents the middle value v, given a distribution of values, and guarantees that there is the same number of values below v as above v.

In our example, the MdMRE is 0.25, calculated as the average of P7 and P8. The MdMRE is less sensitive to the existence of extreme MREs, and in this example suggests that the model's, or technique's, prediction accuracy is good. Because of the likeliness of obtaining extreme MREs, many studies report both MMRE and MdMRE.

The third accuracy measure often used is the prediction at level l, also known as Pred(l). This measure computes, given a validation set, the percentage of effort estimates that are within l% of their actual values. The choice of l often used is $l = 25$. Table 1 shows that, except for P1, all remaining projects have MREs less than or equal to 0.25; thus Pred(25) for this data set is 93%, which also indicates good prediction accuracy.

In addition to MMRE, MdMRE, and Pred(25), it is also suggested that boxplots of absolute residuals should be employed to assess a model's or technique's prediction accuracy.

Boxplots (see Figure 2) use the median, represented by the horizontal line in the middle of the box, as the central value for the distribution. The box's height is the interquartile range and contains 50% of the values. The vertical lines (whiskers) up or down from the edges contain observations that are less than 1.5 times the interquartile range. Outliers are taken as values greater than 1.5 times the height of the box. Values greater than 3 times a box's height are called extreme outliers (Kitchenham, MacDonell, Pickard, & Shepperd, 2001).

When upper and lower tails are approximately equal and the median is in the centre of the box, the distribution is symmetric. If the distribution is not symmetric, the relative lengths of the tails and the position of the median in the box indicate the nature of the skewness.

If the distribution of data is positively skewed (skewed right distribution), it means that there is a long right tail containing a few high values widely spread apart, and a small left tail where values are compactly crowded together. This is the distribution presented in Figure 2. Conversely, if the distribution of data is negatively skewed (skewed left distribution), it means that there is a long left tail containing a few low values widely spread apart, and a small right tail where values are compactly crowded together.

Copyright © 2008, IGI Global. Copying or distributing in print or electronic forms without written permission of IGI Global is prohibited.

Figure 2. Main components of a boxplot

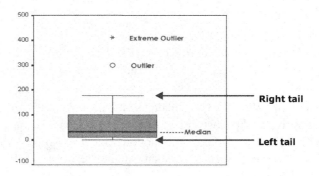

Figure 3. Boxplot of absolute residuals for project data in Table 1

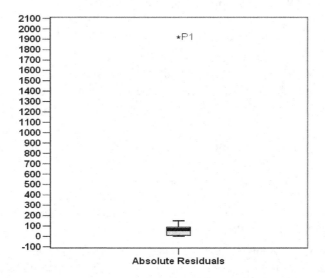

The length of the box relative to the length of the tails gives an indication of the shape of the distribution. Thus, a boxplot with a small box and long tails represents a very peaked distribution, meaning that 50% of the data points are all cluttered around the median. A boxplot with a long box represents a flatter distribution, where data points are scattered apart (Kitchenham et al., 2001).

Figure 3 shows that the distribution of data based on absolute residuals for the projects presented in Table 1 is positively skewed, and project P1 has an absolute residual that is so high that it is an outlier. The box's size is not very compact when compared to the tails, thus indicating a distribution closer to a flatter distribution.

Copyright © 2008, IGI Global. Copying or distributing in print or electronic forms without written permission of IGI Global is prohibited.

Cross-Validation

Figure 1 showed that whenever we wish to measure the prediction accuracy of a model m or technique t, we should split the complete data set into two subsets: one to build the model and another to use as "new" projects. This is done because if we build a model using a set of projects p_1 to p_n and then use part of these same projects as new projects, we would bias the results; that is, the subset of projects used to build a model has to be different from the subset of projects taken as new. The subset of projects used to build a model is called the training set, and the subset of projects used as new projects is the validation set.

The splitting of a data set into training and validation sets is also known as cross-validation. An n-fold cross-validation means the original data set is divided into n subsets of training and validation sets. Thus, 20-fold cross-validation represents the splitting of the complete data set into 20 different training and validation sets. When the validation set has only one project, cross-validation is called "leave-one-out" cross-validation.

Thus, to summarise, in order to calculate the predictive accuracy of a given effort estimation model m or technique t, based on a given data set of finished projects d, we do the following.

1. Divide the data set d into a training set tr and a validation set v. It is common to create training sets that include 66% of the projects from the complete data set, leaving 34% for the validation set.

2. Using tr, produce an effort estimation model m (if applicable). Even when a technique does not build a model, it still uses tr in order to obtain effort estimates for the projects in the validation set.

3. Using m or t, predict the effort for each of the projects in v, simulating new projects for which effort is unknown.

Once done, we will have for each project in v an estimated effort $\hat{e}$ calculated using the model m or technique t, and also the actual effort e that the project actually used. We are now able to calculate MRE and absolute residual for each project in the validation set v. The final step, once we have obtained the predictive power for each project, is to aggregate these values to obtain MMRE, MdMRE, and Pred(25) for v, which is taken to be the same for m or t. We can also use boxplots of absolute residuals to help understand the distribution of residuals values.

In principle, calculated MMREs and MdMREs with values up to 0.25, and Pred(25) at 75% or above, indicate good prediction models (Conte et al., 1986). However,

Copyright © 2008, IGI Global. Copying or distributing in print or electronic forms without written permission of IGI Global is prohibited.

each situation needs to be interpreted within its own context rather than taken from a dogmatic approach.

Detailed Example

The example described in this section uses data from Web projects from a single Web company and are projects taken from the Tukutuku database (Mendes, Mosley, & Counsell, 2003).

Table 2. Web project data from single company

Project ID	Total Effort (person hours)
1	62.5
2	58.16
3	178
4	72.3
5	91
6	13.1
7	8.15
8	37.3
9	11.45
10	20.2
11	16.15
12	25.15
13	7.15
14	26.14

Table 3. Summary statistics for total effort

Summary Statistics	Total Effort (person hours)
Mean	44.76
Median	25.64
Minimum	7.15
Maximum	178.00

Copyright © 2008, IGI Global. Copying or distributing in print or electronic forms without written permission of IGI Global is prohibited.

The total effort in person hours for the complete set of 14 projects is presented in Table 2, followed by their summary statistics in Table 3.

The Web projects in this example are relatively small, with effort values that range from 7.15 to 178 person hours. If we take a working week to last 40 hours, these applications should not have taken longer than a maximum of 5 weeks to develop. This may seem to be a short duration for projects; however, it is common practice amongst Web companies to have projects with very short duration.

The cross-validation we will employ is three-fold cross-validation, therefore three training and validation sets are used to obtain accuracy statistics. Each time we will use 10 projects in the training set and 4 projects in the validation set (71%:29% split). There is no standard as to how many training and validation sets should be used; however, it seems that the smallest number that has been employed in the literature is three.

The three training and validation sets are as follows.

Set 1	Training Set 1 {1,2,3,4,5,6,7,8,9,10}	Validation Set 1 {11,12,13,14}
Set 2	Training Set 2 {5,6,7,8,9,10,11,12,13,14}	Validation Set 2 {1,2,3,4}
Set 3	Training Set 3 {1,2,3,4,5,6, 11,12,13,14}	Validation Set 3 {7,8,9,10}

The three effort estimation models employed in our example were built using a technique called stepwise regression, which is detailed in Chapter V. For now, what is important to know is that three different effort models were created: one using the project data from Training Set 1 (Model 1), another using the project data from Training Set 2 (Model 2), and the third one using the project data from Training Set 3 (Model 3). Models 1, 2, and 3 are used to obtain estimated effort for the projects in the Validation Sets 1, 2, and 3, respectively. The results of the three-fold cross-validation are presented in Table 4.

We did not obtain consistent prediction accuracy across all three intermediate models, calculated using our validation sets. Both MMRE and MdMRE for Set 2 are clearly smaller than those for Sets 1 and 3. However, a situation such as this is very likely to occur whenever the data set is not entirely homogenous, suggesting that some projects may not be similar in their characteristics (e.g., size). It is important here to examine the overall prediction accuracy by aggregating the intermediate results obtained for each model, which are presented in Table 5. The overall MMRE for the effort estimation model was 0.49, suggesting poor prediction accuracy. Two projects have contributed to this MMRE: Projects 13 and 7, both of which provide MREs much larger than those of the remaining projects. As previously seen, any extreme MRE values will push the average MRE up. Without these two projects, the MMRE would have been 0.27.

Copyright © 2008, IGI Global. Copying or distributing in print or electronic forms without written permission of IGI Global is prohibited.

Table 4. Prediction accuracy statistics for Models 1, 2, and 3

	Project ID	Total Effort	Estimated Effort	MRE		MRE <= 0.25?	Absolute Residuals
Set 1	11	16.15	17.79		0.10	TRUE	1.64
	12	25.15	17.79		0.29	FALSE	7.35
	13	7.15	17.79		1.48	FALSE	10.64
	14	26.14	17.79		0.31	FALSE	8.34
				MMRE = 0.55		Pred(25) = 25%	
				MdMRE = 0.30			
	Project ID	Total Effort	Estimated Effort	MRE		MRE <= 0.25?	Absolute Residuals
Set 2	1	62.5	64.15		0.02	TRUE	1.65
	2	58.16	64.15		0.10	TRUE	5.99
	3	178	212.74		0.19	TRUE	34.74
	4	72.3	64.15		0.11	TRUE	8.15
				MMRE = 0.10		Pred(25) = 100%	
				MdMRE = 0.10			
	Project ID	Total Effort	Estimated Effort	MRE		MRE <= 0.25?	Absolute Residuals
Set 3	7	8.15	21.74		1.66	FALSE	13.59
	8	37.3	62.84		0.68	FALSE	25.54
	9	11.45	21.74		0.89	FALSE	10.29
	10	20.2	21.74		0.07	TRUE	1.54
				MMRE = 0.83		Pred(25) = 25%	
				MdMRE = 0.79			

A MdMRE of 0.24 means that half of the projects in the validation sets presented MREs smaller or equal to 0.24, and the other half presented MREs greater or equal to 0.24. Based on the MdMRE, the overall effort prediction accuracy for the model is good. The MdMRE is less likely to be vulnerable to extreme values since it is based on the median rather than the mean. As such, whenever there are wide discrepancies between MMRE and MdMRE, the MdMRE should take precedence.

The next accuracy statistic is Pred(25), which, for the effort model used in our example, is 50%. This indicates that half the projects in the validation sets pre-

Copyright © 2008, IGI Global. Copying or distributing in print or electronic forms without written permission of IGI Global is prohibited.

sented estimated effort within 25% of the actual effort. Given this information, we can conclude that all values above the median are greater than 0.25. Despite good MdMRE, what the Pred(25) also suggests is that using the current effort model, a company has a 50% chance of obtaining an effort estimate for a project that is within 25% of its actual effort.

Depending on the size of projects a Web company develops, a value of Pred(25) may not necessarily mean bad news. For example, looking at the summary statistics for the Web projects in our example (see Table 3), we have a median of about 26 person hours per project. Assuming an 8-hour working day, that effort would correspond to 3 full days and 2 hours on the fourth day. If a project with an estimated effort of 26 person hours is late by 35%, this would represent an extra day to complete the project, a time period unlikely to cause the client undue concern. Comparatively, on a project with estimated effort of 2,600 person hours (325 working days), a delay of 35% would represent a delay of nearly 114 days, now a more serious delay that could cost the developer more than just the time overspill.

It is important that Web companies that use prediction accuracy measures define their own acceptable boundaries since blindly applying what is suggested in the literature may be unrealistic.

The last accuracy measure we examine, within the context of the above example, is the absolute residual. In addition, we will also discuss what can be interpreted when using boxplots of absolute residuals.

Table 5. Aggregated prediction accuracy statistics

Set	Project ID	MRE	MRE <= 0.25?	Absolute Residuals	Total Effort
2	1	0.02	TRUE	1.65	62.5
3	10	0.07	TRUE	1.54	20.2
1	11	0.10	TRUE	1.64	16.15
2	2	0.10	TRUE	5.99	58.16
2	4	0.11	TRUE	8.15	72.3
2	3	0.19	TRUE	34.74	178
1	12	0.29	FALSE	7.35	25.15
1	14	0.31	FALSE	8.34	26.14
3	8	0.68	FALSE	25.54	37.3
3	9	0.89	FALSE	10.29	11.45
1	13	1.48	FALSE	10.64	7.15
3	7	1.66	FALSE	13.59	8.15
		MMRE = 0.49 MdMRE = 0.24	Pred(25) = 50%		

Copyright © 2008, IGI Global. Copying or distributing in print or electronic forms without written permission of IGI Global is prohibited.

The boxplots for the absolute residuals obtained for Models 1, 2, and 3, and for the aggregated model are presented in Figure 4. It is important to keep in mind that good prediction accuracy is directly related to how good the residuals are. The smaller the residuals, the better the indication that estimated and actual effort are similar. A residual of zero means that actual and estimated effort are the same; however, given two absolute residuals of 4 and 55, based on different validation sets and estimation models, we cannot assert that the model that leads to a residual of 4 is better than the model that leads to a residual of 55. Within this context, a residual of 4 for a project with an actual effort of 5 is not good at all. Conversely, a residual of 55 for a project with an actual effort of 5000 is excellent. This is the context presented in Figure 4. Thus, Figure 4 has to be interpreted by also taking into account the data presented in Table 5.

The first three boxplots (bp1, bp2, and bp3) display absolute residuals obtained using the three effort models built as part of our cross-validation. Thus, each boxplot presents a different version of what the results would be like given training and validation sets. At first, these boxplots suggest that the absolute residuals seem much better for bp1 and worse for bp2. Bp3 does not seem as good as bp1, but does score better than bp2. Let us look at each of these boxplots in detail in order to confirm or refute our initial supposition.

Bp1: Bp1's largest absolute residual is 10.64 person hours. This residual corresponds to a project for which actual effort is only 7.15 person hours, indicating a large difference between actual and estimated effort. In fact, the MRE for this project is 1.48, showing that there was an error of 148% in the estimation, relative to the project's actual effort. The other three absolute residuals contain estimation errors of 10%, 29%, and 31%, which are not bad overall. Table 4 shows that this model version obtained an MMRE of 0.55, MdMRE of 0.30, and Pred(25) of 25%. Overall, if a Web company were to decide on the usefulness of a new effort model based on the results of bp1, it would probably be skeptical regarding its adoption.

Bp2: Bp2's largest absolute residual is 34.74 person hours. This residual corresponds to a project with an actual effort of 178 person hours, indicating a small difference between actual and estimated effort. The project's MRE is 0.19, showing that there was an error of 19% in the estimation relative to the project's actual effort. The other three absolute residuals contain estimation errors of 2%, 10%, and 11%, which are excellent overall. Table 4 shows that this model gave an MMRE of 0.10, MdMRE of 0.10, and Pred(25) of 100%. Overall, a Web company using this effort model would find this prediction accuracy most satisfactory.

Bp3: Bp3's largest absolute residual is 13.59 person hours. This residual corresponds to a project for which actual effort is 8.15 person hours, indicating a

Copyright © 2008, IGI Global. Copying or distributing in print or electronic forms without written permission of IGI Global is prohibited.

very large difference between actual and estimated effort. The project's MRE is 1.66, showing an error of 166% in the estimation relative to the project's actual effort. The other three absolute residuals contain estimation errors of 7%, 68%, and 89%, which, except for the 7%, are not good at all. Table 4 shows that this model version obtained an MMRE of 0.83, MdMRE of 0.79, and Pred(25) of 25%.

Overall, of the three versions detailed above, bp3 clearly illustrates the worst performance. Another point to consider is the location of the median in a boxplot. The median for bp2 is the lowest overall, followed closely by bp1. Bp3 has a median much higher than the other two boxplots.

At first glance, it may seem that these three versions provide contradicting trends; however, this is not the case as it is very common for Web projects to present different characteristics, and, even within the same company, to be developed by different people, with different expertise, and different development environments. Therefore, it is more than possible that projects may not actually be too similar to one another, resulting in the project data set not being homogenous. Given these circumstances, it is not advisable to use a single training and validation set to decide on how good a prediction model is.

In our example above, the three different versions obtained were aggregated, thus providing an overall assessment of a model's prediction accuracy. The aggregated boxplot is also displayed in Figure 4. This boxplot presents two outliers, identified as Projects 3 and 8. Project 8 has been looked at while discussing bp2; Project 3 presents a residual of 25.54 for a project that has an actual effort of 37.3, thus an error of 68%. Projects 8, 9, 13, and 7 all presented poor estimation accuracy. Their

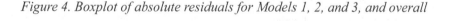

Figure 4. Boxplot of absolute residuals for Models 1, 2, and 3, and overall

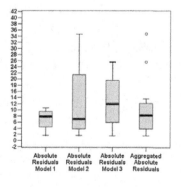

Copyright © 2008, IGI Global. Copying or distributing in print or electronic forms without written permission of IGI Global is prohibited.

poor estimation has influenced both the model's Pred(25) and its MMRE. The median absolute residual (8.24) represents a difference of 32% from the median actual effort (25.64). This figure is not as positive as the MdMRE; however, it may still be acceptable for a Web company.

Note that whenever boxplots of absolute residuals are used to compare effort estimation models, and knowing that all models used the same training and validation set, a residual of 4 for a given model *m1* will always be better than a residual of 55 for a given model *m2* as the context has changed.

Conclusion

This chapter has described de facto measures of prediction accuracy—MRE, MMRE, MdMRE, Pred(25), and absolute residuals—measured as part of a cross-validation process. This process entails splitting the original data set into training and validation sets. Once done, the training sets are used to obtain effort estimates for the projects in the validation set as if these projects were new. In parallel with conducting cross-validation, prediction accuracy measures are also obtained and used to measure the prediction accuracy of a model or technique under scrutiny.

The steps to be carried out with cross-validation were detailed, and an example using real data on Web projects was used to practically illustrate how such measures can be obtained and interpreted.

References

Conte, S., Dunsmore, H., & Shen, V. (1986). *Software engineering metrics and models.* Menlo Park, CA: Benjamin/Cummings.

Kemerer, C. F. (1987). An empirical validation of software cost estimation models. *Communications of the ACM, 30*(5), 416-429.

Kitchenham, B. A., MacDonell, S. G., Pickard, L. M., & Shepperd, M. J. (2001). What accuracy statistics really measure. *IEE Proceedings Software, 148*(3), 81-85.

Mendes, E., Mosley, N., & Counsell, S. (2003, September). Early Web size measures and effort prediction for Web costimation. *Proceedings of the IEEE Metrics Symposium* (pp. 8-29).

Copyright © 2008, IGI Global. Copying or distributing in print or electronic forms without written permission of IGI Global is prohibited.

Myrtveit, I., & Stensrud, E. (1999). A controlled experiment to assess the benefits of estimating with analogy and regression models. *IEEE Transactions on Software Engineering, 25*(4), 510-525.

Shepperd, M. J., & Schofield, C. (1997). Estimating software project effort using analogies. *IEEE Transactions on Software Engineering, 23*(11), 736-743.

Shepperd, M. J., Schofield, C., & Kitchenham, B. (1996). Effort estimation using analogy. *Proceedings of ICSE-18* (pp. 170-178).

Stensrud, E., Foss, T., Kitchenham, B. A., & Myrtveit, I. (2002). An empirical validation of the relationship between the magnitude of relative error and project size. *Proceedings of the IEEE 8th Metrics Symposium* (pp. 3-12).

Copyright © 2008, IGI Global. Copying or distributing in print or electronic forms without written permission of IGI Global is prohibited.

Chapter IV

Sizing Web Applications

Abstract

Surveying and classifying previous work in a particular field brings several benefits, which are to (a) help organise a given body of knowledge, (b) provide results that can help identify gaps that need to be filled, (c) provide a categorisation that can also be applied or adapted to other surveys, and (d) provide a classification and summary of results that may benefit practitioners and researchers who wish to carry out meta-analyses. This chapter presents a literature survey of size measures (attributes) that have been published since 1992 and classifies these measures according to a proposed taxonomy. We also discuss ways in which Web companies can devise their own size measures.

Introduction

Since 1992, several hypermedia and Web size measures have been proposed, motivated by the need to help the development (authoring) process of applications and

Copyright © 2008, IGI Global. Copying or distributing in print or electronic forms without written permission of IGI Global is prohibited.

for use in Web effort estimation. It is important that such a body of knowledge be structured and made available to give practitioners access to existing measures so they can assess whether or not the measures are applicable to their own environment; in addition, researchers may use this body of knowledge as a starting point to understand trends in Web size measures and measurement.

The literature to date has published two previous surveys on Web measures (Calero, Ruiz, & Piattini, 2004; DeMarco, 1982). However, neither of them has looked specifically into hypermedia and Web size measures, or measures for authoring and effort estimation. We briefly describe these two surveys in this chapter to inform readers. Each survey is briefly documented below.

First Survey

Dhyani, Ng, and Bhowmick (2001) classified 52 Web measures according to the following categories, which are also illustrated in Figure 1.

- Web graph properties: Set of measures that measure structural properties of Web applications and sites. Here, Web applications and sites are represented using a graph structure where Web pages denote nodes and hyperlinks denote directed edges. Measures are arranged into three types: centrality, global, and local.

- Web page significance: Set of measures used to rank Web pages in order to determine their relevance to keyword queries, and also measures the quality of Web pages, where quality in this context represents the relevance of a page characterised by how easy it is for that page to be reached within the hyperdocument's structure. Measures are arranged into two types: relevance and quality.

- Web page similarity: Set of measures that measure the level of connectedness between Web pages. Measures are arranged into two types: content and link.

- Web page search and retrieval: Set of measures used to measure the performance of Web search and retrieval services. Measures are arranged into two types: effectiveness and comparison.

- Usage characterisation: Measures users' behaviour with regard to the way they browse Web resources; these measures are used to provide feedback to improve the content, organisation, and presentation of Web applications.

- Information theoretic: Set of measures that measure attributes related to information needs (e.g., does this page provide useful content?), survivability, and the maintenance rate of Web pages.

Copyright © 2008, IGI Global. Copying or distributing in print or electronic forms without written permission of IGI Global is prohibited.

Figure 1. Web measures taxonomy (Adapted from Dhyani et al., 2001)

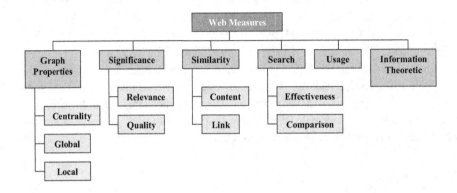

These measures are not geared toward a particular type of Web application or Web site (e.g., informational, e-commerce), and overall their objective is to provide feedback to be used to improve the quality and usefulness of applications and sites.

Second Survey

Calero et al. (2004) classified 385 measures from 40 studies according to a framework called the Web quality model (WQM). This framework is structured according to three orthogonal dimensions, described below.

- Web features: Features are organised into three perspectives: content, presentation, and navigation. Content relates to the content of a page, application, or site; presentation relates to the way in which the content is presented to its users. Finally, navigation relates to the way in which users browse (navigate) through an application.

- Web life-cycle processes: A collection of features organised into five perspectives: development process, operation process, maintenance process, project management process, and reuse program-management process. These life-cycle processes are a subset of those prescribed in the ISO 12207 (International Organisation for Standardization) standard.

- Web quality characteristics: A collection of features organised into six perspectives: functionality, reliability, usability, efficiency, portability, and maintainability; the perspectives are an extension to the ISO 9126 standard.

Copyright © 2008, IGI Global. Copying or distributing in print or electronic forms without written permission of IGI Global is prohibited.

In addition to the above classification, the authors also assess their surveyed measures according to a second set of criteria.

- Granularity level: Whether the measure's scope is a Web page or Web site
- Theoretical validation: Whether or not a measure has been validated theoretically
- Empirical validation: Whether or not a measure has been empirically validated
- Automated support: Whether or not there is a support tool that facilitates the automatic calculation of the measure

The focus of the survey was to gather data on measures proposed to measure the attributes of Web information systems, thus any measures outside this scope (e.g., process measures) were not included.

The measures' classification showed that most of the proposed measures were for an application's pr site's presentation, the operation process, and usability.

This chapter aims to complement the body of knowledge on Web measures by providing first a survey on hypermedia and Web size measures based on literature published since 1992. Second, it presents a taxonomy of size measures that helps classify this existing body of knowledge. Third, it discusses ways in which Web companies can devise their own size measures.

The remainder of this chapter is organised as follows:

- First, it introduces our taxonomy, explaining terms and definitions that are part of this classification.
- Second, it presents our literature review, which was based on 15 papers. Note that we only included in our review papers that proposed a new set of measures; that is, if two or more papers used the same set of size measures, we included only the first one published.
- Third, it applies the proposed taxonomy to classify each of the papers from our literature review.
- Fourth, it discusses the change in trends that have occurred in the area of hypermedia and Web measures within the last 14 years.
- Fifth, it details the necessary steps to be used by a Web company to derive its own size measures.
- Finally, we present its conclusions.

Copyright © 2008, IGI Global. Copying or distributing in print or electronic forms without written permission of IGI Global is prohibited.

Size Measures Taxonomy

A taxonomy represents a model that is used to classify and understand a body of knowledge. The classification used by our taxonomy was based on basic concepts of software measurement, and literature on software size measures and measurement (Briand & Wieczorek, 2002).

Our taxonomy uses nine different categories to be applied to each size measure identified in the literature. These nine categories are as follows.

Motivation: The motivation category describes the rationale for proposing a given size measure. Examples of motivation can be to help author hypermedia applications, or to estimate development effort.

Harvesting time: This category describes when in a Web project's development life cycle a measure should be acquired. Whenever a measure is meant to be acquired early on in a Web project's development life cycle, it is very likely that this measure will need to be estimated. Otherwise, in cases when the measure is meant to be obtained close to the delivery of an application, it may be directly measured. The main reason for using this category is to document whether a measure, when it was proposed, was aimed at being acquired early on or later on in the development life cycle. Therefore, this category can be simply identified using phrases such as early size measure or late size measure; however, a longer description can also be given whenever necessary (e.g., late size measure to be measured after the implementation is finished).

Measure foundation: The foundation category tells if the size measure is a problem-orientated measure or a solution-orientated measure (Briand & Wieczorek, 2002).

- *Problem-orientated measure:* A problem-orientated measure assumes that an application's size corresponds directly to the size of the problem to be solved in order to deliver a corresponding application. So, the greater the problem, the greater the size. In this context, the problem to be solved is denoted by the functionality of the application to be developed. Problem-orientated size measures generally take the form of surrogate measures of functionality. These measures can be extracted from the specification or design documents (e.g., use-case diagrams, data flow diagrams [DeMarco, 1982], or entity-relationship models [Mendes, Mosley, & Counsell, 2002]). An example of a common problem-oriented measure is function points, which aims to measure the size of an application in terms of the amount of functionality within the application as described by its proposed specification (1997).

Copyright © 2008, IGI Global. Copying or distributing in print or electronic forms without written permission of IGI Global is prohibited.

- *Solution-orientated measure:* In contrast, a solution-orientated measure assumes that an application's size corresponds to its actual delivered size. A frequently used size measure is lines of code (LOC), which measures the size of a given software implementation. This measure has been frequently criticised for its difficulty in being measured consistently (Jones, 1998) and for being a difficult measure to estimate early in a software's development life cycle. Finally, another source of criticism is that LOC is a measure that is highly dependent on the programming paradigm, language, and style employed (Briand & Wieczorek, 2002). Within the scope of Web development, an example of a solution-orientated measure would be the number of lines of code used in the server-side or client-side scripts, or the number of tags or lines of code in an HTML (hypertext markup language) file.

Class: The class category allows for the organisation of size measures into one of three possible classes: length, complexity, and functionality (Fenton & Pfleeger, 1997).

- *Length:* Measures the physical size of a hypermedia or Web application

- *Functionality:* Measures the functions supplied to the user by the application

- *Complexity:* Measures the structural complexity of an application, where the application's structure is represented by nodes (e.g., Web pages) that are interconnected using links (hyperlinks). The assumption behind complexity size measures is that by analysing the application's structure, the development (authoring) of an application can be improved by creating more comprehensible and easier-to-navigate structures. As a consequence, these improve an application's usability as they enable users to better traverse (navigate) the application. More comprehensible structures also reduce the disorientation caused by traversing a complex structure.

According to the descriptions given above, we can say that the foundation for both length and complexity measures is solution orientated, whereas the foundation for a functionality size measure is problem orientated.

Entity: The entity category represents the product with the size measure associated to it. Within the context of this chapter, there are eight different types of products, which are described below.

- *Web hypermedia application* (Christodoulou, Zafiris, & Papatheodorou, 2000): Represents an unconventional application characterised by the

Copyright © 2008, IGI Global. Copying or distributing in print or electronic forms without written permission of IGI Global is prohibited.

authoring of information using nodes (chunks of information), links (relations between nodes), anchors, access structures (for navigation), and its delivery over the Web. Technologies commonly used for developing such applications are HTML, XML (extensible markup language), JavaScript, and multimedia. In addition, typical developers are writers, artists, and organisations who wish to publish information on the Web and/or CD-ROM without the need to know programming languages such as Java. These applications have unlimited potential in areas such as software engineering, literature, education, and training.

- *Web software application* (Christodoulou et al., 2000)*:* Represents a conventional software application that relies on the Web or uses the Web's infrastructure for execution. Typical applications include legacy information systems such as databases, booking systems, knowledge bases, several e-commerce applications, and so forth. Typically they employ development technologies (e.g., DCOM [distributed component object model], ActiveX, etc.), database systems, and development solutions (e.g., J2EE). Developers are in general computer science or software engineering programmers, managed by project managers.

- *Web application:* Represents an application, delivered over the Web, that combines characteristics of both Web hypermedia and Web software applications

- *Hypertext application:* Represents an application where information is conveyed to the user using chunks of text (nodes) that are interrelated using anchors and links (Conklin, 1987). Anchors are words, sentences, areas of an image, and so forth that are the origin or destination of a link.

- *Hypermedia application:* Represents an application where information is conveyed to the user using nodes that include a mix of text, graphics, digitised speech, audio recordings, pictures, animation, film clips, and so forth that are interrelated using anchors and links (Conklin, 1987).

- *Media:* Represents a multimedia component, for example, graphic, audio, video, animation, photograph, or film clip

- *Program/script:* Represents code employed to add functionality to an application (e.g., Perl scripts, JavaScript).

- *Web application design model:* A conceptual representation of a Web application. Such representations are characterised by models, for example, a navigation model or presentation model, that represent an application in a higher level of abstraction, and that later on in the Web development life cycle are translated into an implementation of that Web application.

Copyright © 2008, IGI Global. Copying or distributing in print or electronic forms without written permission of IGI Global is prohibited.

Measurement scale type: To understand this category, it is first important to understand what measurement means. Measurement represents a process by which numbers or symbols are assigned to attributes (measures) of entities in the real world such that these entities can be described according to clearly defined rules. For example, in relation to an entity Person, the attributes (measures) height, weight, and gender are used as characteristics of Person. Each attribute (measure) can be measured using one of five different measurement scale types. Each scale type represents a set of characteristics associated with a measure that help interpret this measure and also determine what sort of manipulations can be applied to it. The five scale types are nominal, ordinal, interval, ratio, and absolute (Fenton & Pfleeger, 1997), and their descriptions are as follows.

- *Nominal:* Defines classes or categories, and places entities in a particular class or category based on the value of the attribute. Let us suppose we wish to measure the attribute *application type* for the entity Web application, and that the types of application considered are the following.

  - Academic
  - Corporate
  - E-commerce
  - E-trading
  - Educational
  - Entertainment
  - Multimedia presentation
  - News and information
  - Nonprofit
  - Online community or forum
  - Personal
  - Political
  - Promotional
  - Virtual marketplace (B2B, business to business)
  - Other

  Each Web application would then be placed within one of these classes, and we would choose the one that represents the attribute *application type*. Note that there is no notion of ordering between these classes. This means that even if we had used symbols or numbers from 1 to 15, they would not represent any notion of importance between the classes (e.g., an application identified by the number 14 is more important than an application identified by the number 4). The same also applies to symbols;

Copyright © 2008, IGI Global. Copying or distributing in print or electronic forms without written permission of IGI Global is prohibited.

that is, an application of type *news and information* is not more or less important than an application of type *personal* or *educational*.

- *Ordinal:* Augments the nominal scale with information about an ordering of classes or categories. This means that entities belong to classes that are ordered with respect to the attribute. Let us suppose we wish to measure the attribute *application structural complexity* for the entity Web application, and that structural complexity is measured using the following classes.

  - Very high
  - High
  - Average
  - Low
  - Very low

  Each Web application would then be placed within one of the classes that represent the attribute *application structural complexity*. Here there is a notion of ordering between the classes. This means that applications that belong to class Very High have greater structural complexity than those that belong to class High, and so on. Classes can be represented by numbers or symbols; however, it is important to note that even if we had used numbers (e.g., 1 to 5) to represent classes, these numbers would only represent ranking, so addition, subtraction, and other arithmetic operations have no meaning. In other words, it would make no sense to obtain the average or the standard deviation of an application's structural complexity.

- *Interval:* Augments the ordinal scale with information about the size of the intervals that separate the classes. Thus, the ranking between classes is preserved; however, now the interval between two classes is constant. For example, the difference between 20°C and 10°C is the same as the difference between 30°C and 20°C. However, it does not make sense to say that 20°C is twice as hot as 10°C because in the Celsius scale the 0°C temperature does not really mean complete absence of temperature. As a consequence, the amount of temperature that corresponds to 20°C is not twice the amount of temperature that corresponds to 10°C. Let us look at this example in more detail.

  Let us suppose that the real absence of temperature in the Celsius scale corresponded to 10 intervals down from where the fictitious 0°C is located (see Figure 2). This means that a temperature of 10°C in fact corresponds to an amount of temperature of 20 intervals (10 intervals from the real absence of temperature to 0°C, and another 10 intervals from 0°C to 10°C). Using the same rationale, a temperature of 20°C in

Copyright © 2008, IGI Global. Copying or distributing in print or electronic forms without written permission of IGI Global is prohibited.

Figure 2. Fictitious example using the Celsius scale

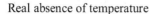
Real absence of temperature

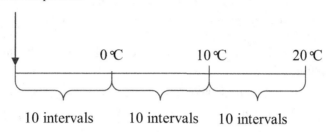

fact corresponds to an amount of temperature of 30 intervals (10 intervals from the real absence of temperature to 0°C, another 10 intervals from 0°C to 10°C, and finally another 10 intervals from 10°C to 20°C). Therefore, a temperature of 20°C (or 30 intervals) is not twice as hot as a temperature of 10°C (or 20 intervals) because 30 intervals do not represent 2 times 20 intervals.

Another example of an interval scale is relative time, for example, the number of calendar days since the start of a given Web project. The difference between two consecutive calendar days is always the same, but the start of a Web project does not represent an absence of calendar days. As previously stated, this measurement scale type does not have a natural zero representing the complete absence of a class. Therefore, addition and subtraction are acceptable operations between two classes, but not multiplication and division.

- *Ratio:* Preserves ordering, the size of intervals between classes, and ratios between classes. Here there is a natural zero representing the complete absence of a class. For example, people's heights and weights are typical ratio scale measures. It is meaningful to say that someone who has height of 180 cm is twice as tall as someone who has height of 90 cm, and this holds true regardless of whether height is being measured in centimeters, meters, or yards. As a consequence, all arithmetic operations are acceptable between two classes.

- *Absolute:* The measure always takes the form of the number of occurrences of x in the entity E. For example, to measure the size of a Web application using as a measure the number of new Web pages, we use an absolute scale since there is only one choice here, which is to count the

Copyright © 2008, IGI Global. Copying or distributing in print or electronic forms without written permission of IGI Global is prohibited.

number of new Web pages. This scale type is very often used to measure software and Web application attributes.

Computation: The computation category describes whether a size measure can be measured directly or indirectly (Fenton & Pfleeger, 1997). Indirect measurement means that the measure is computed based on other measures. Conversely, direct measurement means that the size measure does not rely on other measures in order to be obtained. For example, assume the three size measures presented below.

- *Page count:* Number of HTML or SHTML files
- *Connectivity:* Number of internal links, not including dynamically generated links
- *Connectivity density:* Computed as connectivity divided by page count

Page count and connectivity are both direct measures since they can be measured directly without depending on other measures. However, connectivity density is an indirect measure since in order to be computed, it uses the other two measures connectivity and page count.

Validation: The validation category describes whether a size measure has been validated. To be validated means that evidence has been gathered regarding the measure's usefulness to measure what it purports to measure. Validations can be carried out empirically, where generally data is used to provide evidence of a measure's usefulness, or theoretically, where the measurement principles associated with a proposed measure are checked to make sure that they are in line with the measurement theory that supports the definition of that measure.

Possible values for the validation category are that the measure is validated empirically, validated theoretically, both, and none. This is similar to one of the criteria suggested by Calero et al. (2004).

Model dependency: This category represents whether a size measure requires the use of a specific Web methodology or model in order to be measured. For example, as will be discussed later, Mangia and Paiano (2003) proposed size measures to estimate effort to develop Web applications that were modeled using the W2000 Web development methodology. This means that, unless a Web company has used the W2000 methodology to design and model their Web applications, it is unlikely that this company will find the size measures proposed by Mangia and Paiano useful for their own context. On the other hand, Mendes, Mosley, and Counsell (2003) have proposed size measures that are applicable to measure the size of any Web application, whether applications are designed using the W2000 methodology or not. The two possible values that this category takes are specific and Nonspecific.

Copyright © 2008, IGI Global. Copying or distributing in print or electronic forms without written permission of IGI Global is prohibited.

Now that we have presented our taxonomy, our next step is to describe previous work where hypermedia and Web size measures were proposed, which will later be used when we apply our taxonomy to classify hypermedia and Web size measures.

Literature Review of Hypermedia and Web Size Measures

This section presents a literature review of hypermedia and Web size measures proposed since 1992, which we describe in chronological order.

1992: Size Measures by Botafogo, Rivlin, and Shneiderman

Botafogo et al. (1992) proposed size measures based on the assumption that giving authors an idea of the complexity and cross-referencing of a hypertext application could help them to reduce undesired structural complexity and create applications that readers can traverse more easily. Thus, their measures were to be used to help identify problems with the hyperdocument being created. Their focus was on the application's (hyperdocument's) navigation rather than on its content. The two size measures we describe here are compactness and stratum:

- *Compactness:* Measures the level of cross-referencing of a hypertext application. A high compactness indicates that each node can easily reach any other node in the application (hyperdocument), suggesting a large amount of cross-referencing. Its value varies between 0 and 1, which correspond respectively to a completely disconnected and a completely connected application.

- *Stratum:* Measures to what degree the application (hyperdocument) is organised so that some nodes must be read before the others. Its value also varies between 0 and 1, which correspond respectively to an application (hyperdocument) with no imposed reading order and an application where reading is sequential; that is, it is a linear application.

1995: Size Measures by Yamada, Hong, and Sugita

Yamada et al. (1995) proposed size measures that can be used to identify authoring and maintenance problems with hypermedia applications.

Copyright © 2008, IGI Global. Copying or distributing in print or electronic forms without written permission of IGI Global is prohibited.

- *Interface shallowness:* Measures the cognitive load that an application imposes on users. It assumes that hypermedia applications are structured hierarchically, and that each level in the hierarchy corresponds to a cognitive layer. Thus, moving from one layer to another is equivalent to moving down in the hierarchy, and it is assumed to increase the cognitive load on users. In other words, the essential idea proposed by Yamada et al. (1995) is that the way in which nodes are linked can overload users cognitively if they have to keep moving back and forth from and to documents that are located in different layers. This approach suggests that hypermedia applications that preserve interface linearity are the ones that cognitively load the users the least.

- *Downward compactness:* Measures the compactness of links using as a starting point the root node; that is, it measures the structural complexity associated with reaching the nth node from the root.

- *Downward navigability:* Measures hypermedia navigability, where an easily navigable hypermedia application is taken as an application that complies with the following principles: (a) It has a shallow interface layer from the root to the nth node (light cognitive load) and (b) it is compact from the root (that is, it is structurally simple to reach the nth node from the root).

1995: Size Measures by Hatzimanikatis, Tsalidis, and Chistodoulakis

Hatzimanikatis et al. (1995) proposed application-based structure measures, that is, measures that can be computed using only the structure of the hypertext or hypermedia application (the hypertext or hypermedia graph). The two quality factors that these measures intended to measure were the readability and maintainability of hypertext or hypermedia applications. The structure measures they proposed are described below.

- *Path complexity:* Measures the number of different paths or cycles that can be found in an application (hyperdocument) when we take a hyperdocument to be a graph. The path complexity of a linear hyperdocument is minimal. Path complexity can be measured using compactness, stratum (Botafogo et al., 1992), cyclomatic complexity number (assuming that the hyperdocument can be compared to a program), or a measure of the data structure's complexity.

- *Tree impurity:* Measures the extent to which an application (taken as a graph) deviates from being structured as a tree, that is, hierarchically.

- *Modularity:* Measures if the nodes are self-contained and independent.

- *Individual node complexity:* Measures the complexity that a single node imposes on the overall structure.

Copyright © 2008, IGI Global. Copying or distributing in print or electronic forms without written permission of IGI Global is prohibited.

1996: Size Measures by Bray

Bray (1996) proposed three size measures to measure the size of Web applications. These measures are described below:

- *Page size:* Measured in three different ways:
    1. The sum of the space used (Kbytes) by the Web pages as part of a Web application (PS1)
    2. The sum of the number of words in the Web pages used as part of a Web application (PS2)
    3. The sum of the number of image references in the Web pages used as part of a Web application (PS3)
- *Outbound connection:* The number of links within a Web application that point to another Web application or site
- *Inbound connection:* The number of links from other Web applications pointing to a given Web application *w*

1997: Size Measures by Fletcher, MacDonell, and Wong

Fletcher et al. (1997) proposed size measures to predict effort to develop multimedia applications. Although this work targets multimedia applications, the strong similarities allow for the same assessment to be applied to hypermedia applications. They proposed seven measures, described below:

- *Media type:* Measures the number of graphics, audio clips, video clips, animations, and photographs that a multimedia application contains
- *Media source:* Measures if media is original or reused
- *Component duration:* Measures the duration of an animation, sound clip, or video
- *Number of objects* (including sounds)*:* Measures the number of objects on the screen for a given screen
- *Screen connectivity:* Measures the number of links between a screen and other screens
- *Screen events:* Measures the number of events on a screen
- *Actions per event:* Measures the average number of actions per event

Copyright © 2008, IGI Global. Copying or distributing in print or electronic forms without written permission of IGI Global is prohibited.

1998 and 2000: Size Measures by Cowderoy, Donaldson, and Jenkins (1998) and Cowderoy (2000)

Cowderoy et al. (1998) and Cowderoy (2000) proposed size measures to predict effort to develop Web applications. These measures were organised into four distinct categories: Web application, Web page, media, and program. The sets of measures related to each category are presented:

Web Application

- *Web pages:* Measures the number of Web pages in a Web application.
- *Home pages:* Measures the number of major entry points to a Web application.
- *Leaf nodes:* Measures the number of Web pages in a Web application without siblings.
- *Hidden nodes:* Measures the number of Web pages excluded from the main navigation buttons.
- *Depth:* Measures the number of Web pages on the second level that have siblings.
- *Application paragraph count:* Measures the number of page paragraphs (described later) for all Web pages in a Web application.
- *Delivered images:* Measures the number of unique images used by a Web application.
- *Audio files:* Measures the number of unique audio files used in a Web application.
- *Application movies:* Measures the number of page movies (described later) for all the Web pages in a Web application.
- *3-D objects:* Measures the number of files (including 3-D objects) used in a Web application.
- *Virtual worlds:* Measures the number of files (including virtual worlds) used in a Web application.
- *External hyperlinks:* Measures the number of unique URLs (uniform resource locators) in a Web application.
- *Navigational structures:* Measures the number of different navigational structures in a Web application. Here a navigational structure represents a path, that is, sequence of Web pages that can be traversed by a user.

Copyright © 2008, IGI Global. Copying or distributing in print or electronic forms without written permission of IGI Global is prohibited.

Web Page

- *Actions:* Measures the number of independent actions in a Web page by use of JavaScript, Active X, and so forth
- *Page paragraph count:* Measures the number of paragraphs in a Web page
- *Word count:* Measures the number of words in a Web page
- *Page movies:* Measures the number of movie files used in a Web page
- *Interconnectivity:* Measures the number of URLs in a Web page that link to other Web pages in the same Web application

Media

- *Image size (IS):* Measures the size of an image, computed as width × height
- *Image composites:* Measures the number of layers from which the final image was created
- *Language versions:* Measures the number of image versions that must be produced to accommodate different languages and/or different cultural priorities
- *Duration:* Measures the summed duration of all sequences within an audio file
- *Audio sequences:* Measures the number of sequences within an audio file
- *Imported images:* Measures the number of graphics images imported into an audio file

Program

- *Lines of source code:* Measures the number of lines of code in a program or script
- *McCabe cyclomatic complexity:* Measures the structural complexity of a program or script

1999, 2000, and 2001: Size Measures by Mendes, Hall, and Harrison (1999), Mendes, Counsell, and Mosley (2000), and Mendes, Mosley, and Counsell (2001)

Mendes et al. (1999, 2000, 2001) proposed size measures that were initially aimed to be used as predictors to estimate development effort for hypermedia applications

Copyright © 2008, IGI Global. Copying or distributing in print or electronic forms without written permission of IGI Global is prohibited.

(Mendes et al., 1999) that later were used to estimate development effort for Web applications (Mendes et al., 2000, 2001). They organised their measures into five distinct categories: hypermedia application, Web application, Web page, media, and program. The sets of measures, arranged per category, are presented below.

Hypermedia Application

- *Hyperdocument size:* Measures the number of files (e.g., HTML files) that a hypermedia application contains
- *Connectivity:* Measures the number of nondynamically generated links within a hypermedia application
- *Compactness:* Measures how interconnected the nodes of an application are
- *Stratum:* Measures to what degree the hypermedia application is organised for directed reading
- *Link generality:* Measures if the link applies to a single instance or to multiple instances. Instances can be anchors, nodes, or the entire application.

Web Application

- *Page count:* Measures the total number of HTML or SHTML files contained in a Web application
- *Media count:* Measures the total number of unique media files contained in a Web application. The media types include pictures, audio, video, movies, and so forth.
- *Program count:* Measures the total number of CGI scripts, JavaScript files, and Java applets contained in a Web application
- *Total page allocation:* Measures the total amount of space (Mbytes) allocated for all the HTML or SHTML pages contained in a Web application
- *Total media allocation:* Measures the total amount of space (Mbytes) allocated for all media files contained in a given Web application
- *Total code length:* Measures the total number of lines of code contained in all the programs that are part of a given Web application. Programs represent CGI scripts, JavaScript files, and Java applets contained in a Web application.
- *Reused media count:* Measures the total number of reused or modified media files contained in a given Web application.
- *Reused program count:* Measures the total number of reused or modified programs contained in a given Web application. Programs represent CGI scripts, JavaScript files, and Java applets contained in a Web application.

Copyright © 2008, IGI Global. Copying or distributing in print or electronic forms without written permission of IGI Global is prohibited.

- *Total reused media allocation:* Measures the total amount of space (Mbytes) allocated for all reused media files contained in a given Web application.

- *Total reused code length:* Measures the total number of lines of code for all reused programs that are contained in a given Web application. Programs represent CGI scripts, JavaScript files, and Java applets contained in a Web application.

- *Code comment length:* Measures the total number of comment lines in all the programs that are contained in a given Web application. Programs represent CGI scripts, JavaScript files, and Java applets contained in a Web application.

- *Reused code length:* Measures the total number of reused lines of code in all the programs that are contained in a given Web application. Programs represent CGI scripts, JavaScript files, and Java applets contained in a Web application.

- *Reused comment length:* Measures the total number of reused comment lines in all the programs that are contained in a given Web application. Programs represent CGI scripts, JavaScript files, and Java applets contained in a Web application.

- *Total page complexity:* Measures the average number of different types of media used, excluding text, contained in a given Web application

- *Connectivity:* Measures the total number of internal links, not including dynamically generated links, contained in a given Web application

- *Connectivity density:* Measures the average number of links per Web page for a given Web application. This measure is computed as connectivity divided by page count.

- *Cyclomatic complexity:* Measures the cyclomatic complexity of a given Web application. This measure is computed as (connectivity - page count) + 2.

Web Page

- *Page allocation:* Measures the total allocated space (Kbytes) of an HTML or SHTML file

- *Page complexity:* Measures the total number of different types of media used on a Web page, not including text

- *Graphic complexity:* Measures the total number of graphics media contained on a Web page

- *Audio complexity:* Measures the total number of audio media contained on a Web page

Copyright © 2008, IGI Global. Copying or distributing in print or electronic forms without written permission of IGI Global is prohibited.

- *Video complexity:* Measures the total number of video media contained on a Web page
- *Animation complexity:* Measures the total number of animations contained on a Web page
- *Scanned image complexity:* Measures the total number of scanned images contained on a Web page
- *Page linking complexity:* Measures the total number of links contained on a Web page

Media

- *Media duration:* Measures the total duration (minutes) of an audio, video, or animation clip
- *Media allocation:* Measures the total amount of space (Kbytes) used by a media file

Program

- *Program code length:* Measures the total number of lines of code in a program. Programs represent CGI scripts, JavaScript files, and Java applets contained in a Web application.

2000: Size Measures by Rollo

Rollo (2000) did not suggest any new size measures. However, he was the first, as far as we are aware, to investigate the issues of measuring the functionality of Web applications, specifically aiming at effort estimation, using numerous function-point analysis methods.

- *Functional size:* Measures the total number of function points associated with a Web application. Function points were measured using COSMIC-FFP, Mark II, and Albrecht (Rollo, 2000).

Later, other studies also employed the COSMIC full function-points method to size Web applications (Mendes et al., 2002; Umbers & Miles, 2004). These studies are not described here as the size measure employed is the same one used by Rollo.

Copyright © 2008, IGI Global. Copying or distributing in print or electronic forms without written permission of IGI Global is prohibited.

2000: Size Measures by Cleary

Cleary (2000) proposed size measures to be used as effort predictors to help esti-mate effort to develop Web applications. These measures were organised into three categories: Web hypermedia application, Web software application, and Web page. Each measure is detailed here:

Web Hypermedia Application

- *Nontextual elements:* Measures the total number of unique nontextual elements within a Web hypermedia application

- *Externally sourced elements:* Measures the total number of externally sourced elements. Being externally sourced means that such elements were not devel-oped by the project team responsible for developing the given Web hypermedia application. They can be developed within the same company by a different group of developers, or even developed by third party.

- *Customised infrastructure components:* Measures the total number of cus-tomised infrastructure components. Such components would not have been developed from scratch for the given Web hypermedia application but rather reused from elsewhere and adapted to the needs of this given application.

- *Total Web points:* Measures the total size of a Web hypermedia application in Web points. The Web points measure computes size by taking into account the complexity of the Web pages contained within an application. Complexity of a page is a function of the number of words this page contains, number of existing links, and number of nontextual elements. Once the complexity of a page is measured, it is used to compute the number of Web points for that page (Abrahao, Poels, & Pastor, 2004).

Web Software Application

- *Function points:* Measures the functionality of a Web software application using any existing function-points measurement method (e.g., IFPUG, Mark II, COSMIC)

Web Page

- *Nontextual elements page:* Measures the total number of nontextual elements contained in a Web page

Copyright © 2008, IGI Global. Copying or distributing in print or electronic forms without written permission of IGI Global is prohibited.

- *Words page:* Measures the total number of words contained in a Web page
- *Web points:* Measures the total length of a Web page. This measure uses an ordinal scale with scale points *low, medium,* and *high.* Each point is attributed a number of Web points, previously calibrated to a specific data set of Web projects data.
- *Number of links into a Web page:* Measures the total number of incoming links (internal or external links). Incoming links are links that point to a given Web page.
- *Number of links out of a Web page:* Measures the total number of outgoing links (internal or external links). Outgoing links are links that have their origin at the given Web page and destination elsewhere (other Web page within the same Web application or within another application).
- *Web page complexity:* Measures the complexity of a Web page based upon its number of words and combined number of incoming and outgoing links, plus the number of nontextual elements

2000: Size Measures by Reifer

Reifer (2000) proposed a single size measure to be used to estimate effort to develop Web applications.

- *Web objects:* Measures the total number of Web objects contained in a Web application using Halstead's equation for volume, tuned for Web applications. The equation is as follows:

$$V = N \log_2(n) = (N_1 + N_2) \log_2 (n_1 + n_2), \tag{1}$$

where the following apply.

N = number of total occurrences of operands and operators

n = number of distinct operands and operators

N_1 = total occurrences of operand estimator

N_2 = total occurrences of operator estimators

n_1 = number of unique operand estimator

n_2 = number of unique operator estimators

V = volume of work involved represented as Web objects

Copyright © 2008, IGI Global. Copying or distributing in print or electronic forms without written permission of IGI Global is prohibited.

Operands comprise the following measures:

- *Number of building blocks:* Measures the total number of components in a Web application. Examples of components are Active X, DCOM, and object linking and embedding (OLE).
- *Number of COTS:* Measures the total number of components off the shelf (COTS; including any wrapper code) contained in a Web application
- *Number of multimedia files:* Measures the total number of multimedia files, except graphics files, contained in a Web application
- *Number of object or application points* (Cowderoy, 2000; Cowderoy et al., 1998)*:* Measures the total number of object or application points contained in a Web application
- *Number of lines:* Measures the total number of XML, SGML (standard generalized markup language), HTML, and query language lines of code contained in a Web application
- *Number of Web components:* Measures the total number of applets, agents, and so forth contained in a Web application
- *Number of graphics files:* Measures the total number of templates, images, pictures, and so forth contained in a Web application
- *Number of scripts:* Measures the total number of scripts for visual language, audio, motion, and so forth contained in a Web application

2003: Size Measures by Mendes et al.

Mendes et al. (2003) proposed early size measures to be used to estimate, early on in the development life cycle, the effort necessary to develop Web applications.

Web Application

- *Web pages:* Measures the total number of *Web pages* contained in a Web application.
- *New Web pages:* Measures the total number of Web pages contained in a Web application that were created from scratch.
- *Customer Web pages:* Measures the total number of Web pages contained in a Web application that were provided by the customer.
- *Outsourced Web pages:* Measures the total number of outsourced Web pages contained in a Web application.

Copyright © 2008, IGI Global. Copying or distributing in print or electronic forms without written permission of IGI Global is prohibited.

- *Text pages:* Measures the total number of text pages (A4 size) that had to be typed.
- *Electronic text pages:* Measures the total number of reused text pages that are in electronic format.
- *Scanned text pages:* Measures the total number of reused text pages that had to be scanned using optical character recognition (OCR) technology.
- *New images:* Measures the total number of new images, photos, icons, and buttons created from scratch for a given Web application.
- *Electronic images:* Measures the total number of reused images or photos that are in electronic format.
- *Scanned images:* Measures the total number of reused images or photos that need to be scanned.
- *External images:* Measures the total number of images that were obtained from an image or photo library, or outsourced.
- *New animations:* Measures the total number of new animations (Flash, GIF, 3-D, etc.) that were created from scratch.
- *External animations:* Measures the total number of animations (Flash, GIF, 3-D, etc.) that were reused.
- *New audio:* Measures the total number of new audio or video clips that were created from scratch.
- *External audio:* Measures the total number of audio or video clips that are reused.
- *High FOTS:* Measures the total number of high-effort features off the shelf (FOTS) contained in a given Web application. Features off the shelf are features that have been reused as they are, without any adaptation. High effort represents the minimum number of hours necessary to develop a single function or feature by one experienced developer whose skill is considered high (above average). This number is currently set to 15 hours based on collected data from industrial Web projects.
- *High FOTSA:* Measures the total number of high-effort FOTS that were reused and adapted to local circumstances. High effort here represents the minimum number of hours required to adapt a single function or feature by one experienced developer whose skill is considered high (above average). This number is currently set to 4 hours based on collected data from industrial Web projects.
- *High new:* Measures the total number of new high-effort features or functionalities that were developed from scratch.
- *FOTS:* Measures the total number of low-effort FOTS contained in a Web application.

Copyright © 2008, IGI Global. Copying or distributing in print or electronic forms without written permission of IGI Global is prohibited.

- *FOTSA:* Measures the total number of low-effort FOTS that were adapted to local circumstances.
- *New:* Measures the total number of low-effort features or functionalities that were developed from scratch.

Examples of features and functionalities are listed here:

- Auction or bid utility
- Bulletin boards
- Discussion forums or newsgroups
- Chat rooms
- Database creation
- Database integration
- Other persistent storage integration (e.g., flat files)
- Credit card authorization
- Member log-in
- Online secure order form
- Charts
- File upload and download
- Traffic statistics
- Search engines
- User guest books
- Visitor statistics

2003: Size Measures by Mangia and Paiano

Mangia and Paiano (2003) proposed size measures to be used as effort predictors to estimate the effort required to develop Web applications that have been modeled according to the W2000 Web development methodology (Baresi, Morasca, & Paolini, 2003). These measures are presented using a single category: Web application.

Web Application

- *Macro:* Measures the total number of macro functions contained in a Web application that are required by the user

Copyright © 2008, IGI Global. Copying or distributing in print or electronic forms without written permission of IGI Global is prohibited.

- *DEI:* Measures the total number of input data for each operation
- *DEO:* Measures the total number of output data for each operation
- *Entities:* Measures the total number of information entities that model the database conceptually
- *AppLimit:* Measures the total application limit of each operation
- *LInteraction:* Measures the total level of interaction that various users of the application have with each operation
- *Compatibility:* Measures the total compatibility between each operation and an application's delivery devices
- *TypeNodes:* Measures the total number of types of nodes that constitute the navigational structure
- *Accessibility:* Measures the total number of accessibility associations and patterns of navigation between node types
- *NavCluster:* Measures the total number of navigation clusters
- *ClassVisibility:* Measures the total visibility that classes of users have over a Web application's navigational structure
- *DeviceVisibility:* Measures the total visibility that delivery devices have over a Web application's navigational structure

2003: Size Measures by Baresi et al.

Baresi et al. (2003) also proposed size measures to be used as predictors to help estimate the effort required to design Web applications designed according to the W2000 Web development methodology. Their size measures were organised according to the three different types of design models that result from using the W2000 methodology, which are information model, navigation model, and presentation model. These measures are detailed below.

Information Model

- *Entities:* Measures the total number of entities in the information model
- *Components:* Measures the total number of components in the information model
- *InfoSlots:* Measures the total number of slots in the information model
- *SlotsSACenter:* Measures the average number of slots per semantic association center

Copyright © 2008, IGI Global. Copying or distributing in print or electronic forms without written permission of IGI Global is prohibited.

- *SlotsCollCenter:* Measures the average number of slots per collection center in the information model
- *ComponentsEntity:* Measures the average number of components per entity
- *SlotsComponent:* Measures the average number of slots per component
- *SAssociations:* Measures the number of semantic associations in the information model
- *SACenters:* Measures the number of semantic association centers in the information model
- *Segments:* Measures the number of segments in the information model

Navigation Model

- *Nodes:* Measures the total number of nodes in the navigation model
- *NavSlots:* Measures the total number of slots in the navigation model
- *NodesCluster:* Measures the average number of nodes per cluster
- *SlotsNode:* Measures the average number of slots per node
- *NavLinks:* Measures the total number of links in the navigation model
- *Clusters:* Measures the total number of clusters in the navigation model

Presentation Model

- *Pages:* Measures the total number of pages in the presentation model
- *pUnits:* Measures the total number of publishing units in the presentation model
- *prLinks:* Measures the total number of links in the presentation model
- *Sections:* Measures the total number of sections in the presentation model

Application of Taxonomy to Surveyed Size Measures

This section discusses the literature review in light of the taxonomy previously proposed. In order to provide a more effective discussion, we present the detailed findings in Table 1, followed by Table 2, where a summary of the main findings from the literature review is shown. The literature review was based on 16 studies, where a total of 153 measures were proposed.

Copyright © 2008, IGI Global. Copying or distributing in print or electronic forms without written permission of IGI Global is prohibited.

The motivations of each study are also presented:

- 1992: Size Measures by Botafogo et al.

  Motivation: To help author hypermedia applications
- 1995: Size Measures by Yamada et al.

  Motivation: To give feedback on possible improvements that will lead to better authoring and maintenance of hypermedia applications
- 1995: Size Measures by Hatzimanikatis et al.

  Motivation: To measure the readability and maintainability of hypermedia applications
- 1996: Size Measures by Bray

  Motivation: To measure the size of Web applications
- 1997: Size Measures by Fletcher et al.

  Motivation: To estimate the effort necessary to develop multimedia applications
- 1998 and 2000: Size Measures by Cowderoy et al. (1998) and Cowderoy (2000)

  Motivation: To estimate the effort necessary to develop Web applications
- 1999, 2000, and 2001: Size Measures by Mendes et al.

  Motivation: To estimate the effort necessary to develop hypermedia applications and later Web applications
- 2000: Size Measures by Rollo

  Motivation: To estimate the effort necessary to develop Web applications
- 2000: Size Measures by Cleary

  Motivation: To estimate the effort necessary to develop Web applications
- 2000: Size Measures by Reifer

  Motivation: To estimate the effort necessary to develop Web applications
- 2003: Size Measures by Mendes et al.

  Motivation: To estimate the effort necessary to develop Web applications
- 2003: Size Measures by Mangia and Paiano

  Motivation: To estimate the effort necessary to develop Web applications modeled according to the W2000 Web development methodology
- 2003: Size measures by Baresi et al.

  Motivation: To estimate the effort necessary to develop Web applications modeled according to the W2000 Web development methodology

Copyright © 2008, IGI Global. Copying or distributing in print or electronic forms without written permission of IGI Global is prohibited.

Twelve studies (75%) proposed size measures to be used as effort predictors to estimate the necessary effort to develop applications. This suggests that, at least for these studies, which aimed to improve effort estimation, size measures should be harvested early in the development life cycle for use in estimating effort and costs. Out of the 129 measures proposed for effort estimation, 65 measures (50%) are early measures; however, of these, 32 measures can only be obtained after the Web application has been designed. These results therefore show that only 33 measures used for effort estimation (25.5%) can be gathered very early on in the development life cycle, even before a detailed requirements stage is completed. These 33 measures were proposed by only two studies (Mangia & Paiano, 2003; Mendes et al., 2003).

Most of the proposed measures are solution-orientated (72%) and length (65%) measures. Thirteen (64%) measures, out of a total of 19 functionality measures, measure functionality using some of the traditional function-points analysis methods proposed to be used with conventional software projects, and the remaining 6 base their measurement on a list of features and functions to be provided to customers at the start of the development (Mendes et al., 2003).

More than half of the proposed size measures (63%) relate to the entities Web application or Web application design model, which suggests that they are applicable to static as well as dynamic Web applications. Only 38 size measures (25%) are bottom-up measures, allowing for the measurement of parts of an application (e.g., Web page, media). The remaining size measures (75%) target the entire application, where the application can be represented as hypermedia (9.2%), Web hypermedia (2.6%), Web software (0.6%), or Web (41.8%), or represented as a conceptual abstraction using a Web design model (21%).

The majority of measures are measured on a ratio scale (90%)—not surprising given that most measures are solution orientated. This is also reflected in the number of measures that can be computed directly (76%) as opposed to indirectly (24%). A comparatively high number of measures has been proposed without empirical or theoretical validation (39%), which makes their corresponding studies "advocacy research." Empirical and/or theoretical validations are fundamental to building our scientific knowledge.

Despite the small number of size measures measured using either the nominal (2.6%) or ordinal scale (2.6%), researchers and practitioners alike should take care when applying these measures since their measures cannot be employed arithmetically without being in violation of the representational theory of measurement, a fundamental concept that is often ignored (Cleary, 2000; Reifer, 2000).

Copyright © 2008, IGI Global. Copying or distributing in print or electronic forms without written permission of IGI Global is prohibited.

Table 1. Taxonomy applied to all 153 measures

Measure	Harvesting Time	Measure Foundation	Class	Entity	Measurement Scale	Computation	Validation	Model Dependency
Botafogo et al.								
Compactness	Late	Solution orientated	Complexity	Hypermedia application	Ratio	Indirect	None	Nonspecific
Stratum	Late	Solution orientated	Complexity	Hypermedia application	Ratio	Indirect	None	Nonspecific
Yamada et al.								
Interface Shallowness	Late	Solution orientated	Complexity	Hypermedia application	Ratio	Indirect	Empirically	Nonspecific
Downward Compactness	Late	Solution orientated	Complexity	Hypermedia application	Ratio	Indirect	Empirically	Nonspecific
Downward Navigability	Late	Solution orientated	Complexity	Hypermedia application	Ratio	Indirect	Empirically	Nonspecific
Hatzimanikatis et al.								
Path Complexity	Late	Solution orientated	Complexity	Hypermedia application	Ratio	Indirect	None	Nonspecific
Tree Impurity	Late	Solution orientated	Complexity	Hypermedia application	Ratio	Indirect	None	Nonspecific
Modularity	Late	Solution orientated	Complexity	Hypermedia application	Nominal	Direct	None	Nonspecific
Individual Node Complexity	Late	Solution orientated	Complexity	Hypermedia application	Ratio	Indirect	None	Nonspecific
Bray								
Total Space Web Pages	Late	Solution orientated	Length	Web application	Absolute	Indirect	None	Nonspecific
Total Words Web pages	Late	Solution orientated	Length	Web application	Absolute	Indirect	None	Nonspecific
Total Images Web pages	Late	Solution orientated	Length	Web application	Absolute	Indirect	None	Nonspecific
Outbound Connection	Late	Solution orientated	Complexity	Web application	Ratio	Direct	None	Nonspecific
Inbound Connection	Late	Solution orientated	Complexity	Web application	Ratio	Direct	None	Nonspecific
Measure	**Harvesting Time**	**Measure Foundation**	**Class**	**Entity**	**Measurement Scale**	**Computation**	**Validation**	**Model Dependency**
Fletcher et al.								
Media Type	Late	Solution orientated	Length	Media	Nominal	Direct	Empirically	Nonspecific
Media Source	Late	Solution orientated	Length	Media	Nominal	Direct	Empirically	Nonspecific
Component Duration	Late	Solution orientated	Length	Media	Ratio	Direct	Empirically	Nonspecific
Number of Objects	Late	Solution orientated	Length	Web page	Absolute	Direct	Empirically	Nonspecific
Screen Connectivity	Late	Solution orientated	Complexity	Web page	Absolute	Direct	Empirically	Nonspecific
Screen Events	Late	Problem orientated	Functionality	Program/script	Absolute	Direct	Empirically	Nonspecific
Actions per Event	Late	Problem orientated	Functionality	Program/script	Absolute	Direct	Empirically	Nonspecific
Cowderoy et al.								
Web Pages	Late	Solution orientated	Length	Web application	Ratio	Direct	None	Nonspecific
Home Pages	Late	Solution orientated	Length	Web application	Ratio	Direct	None	Nonspecific
Leaf Nodes	Late	Solution orientated	Length	Web application	Ratio	Direct	None	Nonspecific

Copyright © 2008, IGI Global. Copying or distributing in print or electronic forms without written permission of IGI Global is prohibited.

Table 1. continued

Measure	Harvesting Time	Measure Foundation	Class	Entity	Measurement Scale	Computation	Validation	Model Dependency
Hidden Nodes	Late	Solution orientated	Length	Web application	Ratio	Direct	None	Nonspecific
Depth	Late	Solution orientated	Length	Web application	Ratio	Direct	None	Nonspecific
Application Paragraph Count	Late	Solution orientated	Length	Web application	Ratio	Indirect	None	Nonspecific
Delivered Images	Late	Solution orientated	Length	Web application	Ratio	Direct	None	Nonspecific
Audio Files	Late	Solution orientated	Length	Web application	Ratio	Direct	None	Nonspecific
Application Movies	Late	Solution orientated	Length	Web application	Ratio	Indirect	None	Nonspecific
3-D Objects	Late	Solution orientated	Length	Web application	Ratio	Direct	None	Nonspecific
Virtual Worlds	Late	Solution orientated	Length	Web application	Ratio	Direct	None	Nonspecific
External Hyperlinks	Late	Solution orientated	Complexity	Web application	Ratio	Direct	None	Nonspecific
Actions	Late	Problem orientated	Functionality	Web page	Ratio	Direct	None	Nonspecific
Page Paragraph Count	Late	Solution orientated	Length	Web page	Ratio	Direct	None	Nonspecific
Word Count	Late	Solution orientated	Length	Web page	Ratio	Direct	None	Nonspecific
Navigational Structures	Late	Solution orientated	Complexity	Web page	Ratio	Direct	None	Nonspecific
Page Movies	Late	Solution orientated	Complexity	Web page	Ratio	Direct	None	Nonspecific
Interconnectivity	Late	Solution orientated	Complexity	Web page	Ratio	Indirect	None	Nonspecific
Image Size	Late	Solution orientated	Length	Media	Ratio	Direct	None	Nonspecific
Image Composites	Late	Solution orientated	Length	Media	Ratio	Direct	None	Nonspecific
Language Versions	Late	Solution orientated	Length	Media	Ratio	Direct	None	Nonspecific
Duration	Late	Solution orientated	Length	Media	Ratio	Indirect	None	Nonspecific
Audio Sequences	Late	Solution orientated	Length	Media	Ratio	Direct	None	Nonspecific
Imported Images	Late	Solution orientated	Length	Media	Ratio	Direct	None	Nonspecific
Lines of Source Code	Late	Solution orientated	Length	Program/script	Ratio	Direct	None	Nonspecific
McCabe Cyclomatic Complexity	Late	Solution orientated	Length	Program/script	Ratio	Indirect	None	Nonspecific
Mendes et al.								
Hyperdocument Size	Late	Solution orientated	Length	Hypermedia application	Ratio	Direct	Both	Nonspecific
Connectivity	Late	Solution orientated	Complexity	Hypermedia application	Ratio	Direct	Both	Nonspecific
Compactness	Late	Solution orientated	Complexity	Hypermedia application	Ordinal	Direct	Both	Nonspecific
Stratum	Late	Solution orientated	Complexity	Hypermedia application	Ordinal	Direct	Both	Nonspecific
Link Generality	Late	Solution orientated	Complexity	Hypermedia application	Nominal	Direct	Both	Nonspecific

Copyright © 2008, IGI Global. Copying or distributing in print or electronic forms without written permission of IGI Global is prohibited.

Table 1. continued

Measure	Harvesting Time	Measure Foundation	Class	Entity	Measurement Scale	Computation	Validation	Model Dependency
Page Count	Late	Solution orientated	Length	Web application	Ratio	Direct	Empirically	Nonspecific
Media Count	Late	Solution orientated	Length	Web application	Ratio	Direct	Empirically	Nonspecific
Program Count	Late	Solution orientated	Length	Web application	Ratio	Direct	Empirically	Nonspecific
Total Page Allocation	Late	Solution orientated	Length	Web application	Ratio	Indirect	Empirically	Nonspecific
Total Media Allocation	Late	Solution orientated	Length	Web application	Ratio	Indirect	Empirically	Nonspecific
Total Code Length	Late	Solution orientated	Length	Web application	Ratio	Indirect	Empirically	Nonspecific
Reused Media Count	Late	Solution orientated	Length	Web application	Ratio	Direct	Empirically	Nonspecific
Reused Program Count	Late	Solution orientated	Length	Web application	Ratio	Direct	Empirically	Nonspecific
Total Reused Media Allocation	Late	Solution orientated	Length	Web application	Ratio	Indirect	Empirically	Nonspecific
Total Reused Code Length	Late	Solution orientated	Length	Web application	Ratio	Direct	Empirically	Nonspecific
Code Comment Length	Late	Solution orientated	Length	Web application	Ratio	Direct	Empirically	Nonspecific
Reused Code Length	Late	Solution orientated	Length	Web application	Ratio	Direct	Empirically	Nonspecific
Reused Comment Length	Late	Solution orientated	Length	Web application	Ratio	Direct	Empirically	Nonspecific
Total Page Complexity	Late	Solution orientated	Length	Web application	Ratio	Indirect	Empirically	Nonspecific
Connectivity	Late	Solution orientated	Complexity	Web application	Ratio	Indirect	Empirically	Nonspecific
Connectivity Density	Late	Solution orientated	Complexity	Web application	Ratio	Indirect	Empirically	Nonspecific
Cyclomatic Complexity	Late	Solution orientated	Complexity	Web application	Ratio	Indirect	Empirically	Nonspecific
Page Allocation	Late	Solution orientated	Length	Web page	Ratio	Direct	Empirically	Nonspecific
Page Complexity	Late	Solution orientated	Length	Web page	Ratio	Direct	Empirically	Nonspecific
Graphic Complexity	Late	Solution orientated	Length	Web page	Ratio	Direct	Empirically	Nonspecific
Audio Complexity	Late	Solution orientated	Length	Web page	Ratio	Direct	Empirically	Nonspecific
Video Complexity	Late	Solution orientated	Length	Web page	Ratio	Direct	Empirically	Nonspecific
Animation Complexity	Late	Solution orientated	Length	Web page	Ratio	Direct	Empirically	Nonspecific
Scanned Image Complexity	Late	Solution orientated	Length	Web page	Ratio	Direct	Empirically	Nonspecific
Page Linking Complexity	Late	Solution orientated	Complexity	Web page	Ratio	Direct	Empirically	Nonspecific
Media Duration	Late	Solution orientated	Length	Media	Ratio	Direct	Empirically	Nonspecific
Media Allocation	Late	Solution orientated	Length	Media	Ratio	Direct	Empirically	Nonspecific
Program Code Length	Late	Solution orientated	Length	Program/script	Ratio	Direct	Empirically	Nonspecific
Rollo								
Functional Size	Late	Problem orientated	Functionality	Web application	Ratio	Indirect	None	Nonspecific

Copyright © 2008, IGI Global. Copying or distributing in print or electronic forms without written permission of IGI Global is prohibited.

Table 1. continued

Cleary

Measure	Harvesting Time	Measure Foundation	Class	Entity	Measurement Scale	Computation	Validation	Model Dependency
Nontextual Elements	Late	Solution orientated	Length	Web hypermedia application	Ratio	Direct	Empirically	Nonspecific
Externally Sourced Elements	Late	Solution orientated	Length	Web hypermedia application	Ratio	Direct	Empirically	Nonspecific
Customised Infrastructure Components	Late	Solution orientated	Length	Web hypermedia application	Ratio	Direct	Empirically	Nonspecific
Total Web Points	Late	Solution orientated	Length	Web hypermedia application	Ratio	Indirect	Empirically	Nonspecific
Function Points	Late	Problem orientated	Functionality	Web software application	Ratio	Indirect	None	Nonspecific
Nontextual Elements Page	Late	Solution orientated	Length	Web page	Ratio	Direct	Empirically	Nonspecific
Words Page	Late	Solution orientated	Length	Web page	Ratio	Direct	Empirically	Nonspecific
Web Points	Late	Solution orientated	Length	Web page	Ordinal	Direct	Empirically	Nonspecific
Number of Links into a Web Page	Late	Solution orientated	Complexity	Web page	Ratio	Direct	Empirically	Nonspecific
Number of Links out of a Web Page	Late	Solution orientated	Complexity	Web page	Ratio	Direct	Empirically	Nonspecific
Web Page Complexity	Late	Solution orientated	Complexity	Web page	Ordinal	Direct	Empirically	Nonspecific

Reifer

Measure	Harvesting Time	Measure Foundation	Class	Entity	Measurement Scale	Computation	Validation	Model Dependency
Web Objects	Late	Solution orientated	Length	Web application	Ratio	Indirect	None	Nonspecific
Number of Building Blocks	Late	Solution orientated	Length	Web application	Ratio	Direct	None	Nonspecific
Number of Multimedia Files	Late	Solution orientated	Length	Web application	Ratio	Direct	None	Nonspecific
Number of Object or Application Points	Late	Problem orientated	Functionality	Web application	Ratio	Indirect	None	Nonspecific
Number of Lines	Late	Solution orientated	Length	Web application	Ratio	Direct	None	Nonspecific
Number of Web Components	Late	Solution orientated	Length	Web application	Ratio	Direct	None	Nonspecific
Number of Graphics Files	Late	Solution orientated	Length	Web application	Ratio	Direct	None	Nonspecific
Number of Scripts	Late	Solution orientated	Length	Web application	Ratio	Direct	None	Nonspecific

Mendes et al. (2003)

Measure	Harvesting Time	Measure Foundation	Class	Entity	Measurement Scale	Computation	Validation	Model Dependency
Web Pages	Early	Solution orientated	Length	Web application	Ratio	Indirect	Empirically	Nonspecific

Copyright © 2008, IGI Global. Copying or distributing in print or electronic forms without written permission of IGI Global is prohibited.

Table 1. continued

Measure	Harvesting Time	Measure Foundation	Class	Entity	Measurement Scale	Computation	Validation	Model Dependency
New Web Pages	Early	Solution orientated	Length	Web application	Ratio	Direct	Empirically	Nonspecific
Customer Web Pages	Early	Solution orientated	Length	Web application	Ratio	Direct	Empirically	Nonspecific
Outsourced Web Pages	Early	Solution orientated	Length	Web application	Ratio	Direct	Empirically	Nonspecific
Text Pages	Early	Solution orientated	Length	Web application	Ratio	Direct	Empirically	Nonspecific
Electronic Text Pages	Early	Solution orientated	Length	Web application	Ratio	Direct	Empirically	Nonspecific
Scanned Text Pages	Early	Solution orientated	Length	Web application	Ratio	Direct	Empirically	Nonspecific
New Images	Early	Solution orientated	Length	Web application	Ratio	Direct	Empirically	Nonspecific
Electronic Images	Early	Solution orientated	Length	Web application	Ratio	Direct	Empirically	Nonspecific
Scanned Images	Early	Solution orientated	Length	Web application	Ratio	Direct	Empirically	Nonspecific
External Images	Early	Solution orientated	Length	Web application	Ratio	Direct	Empirically	Nonspecific
New Animations	Early	Solution orientated	Length	Web application	Ratio	Direct	Empirically	Nonspecific
External Animations	Early	Solution orientated	Length	Web application	Ratio	Direct	Empirically	Nonspecific
New Audio	Early	Solution orientated	Length	Web application	Ratio	Direct	Empirically	Nonspecific
External Audio	Early	Solution orientated	Length	Web application	Ratio	Direct	Empirically	Nonspecific
High FOTS	Early	Problem orientated	Functionality	Web application	Ratio	Direct	Empirically	Nonspecific
High FOTSA	Early	Problem orientated	Functionality	Web application	Ratio	Direct	Empirically	Nonspecific
High New	Early	Problem orientated	Functionality	Web application	Ratio	Direct	Empirically	Nonspecific
FOTS	Early	Problem orientated	Functionality	Web application	Ratio	Direct	Empirically	Nonspecific
FOTSA	Early	Problem orientated	Functionality	Web application	Ratio	Direct	Empirically	Nonspecific
New	Early	Problem orientated	Functionality	Web application	Ratio	Direct	Empirically	Nonspecific
Measure	**Harvesting Time**	**Measure Foundation**	**Class**	**Entity**	**Measurement Scale**	**Computation**	**Validation**	**Model Dependency**
Mangia and Paiano								
Macro	Early	Problem orientated	Functionality	Web application design model	Ratio	Direct	None	Specific
DEI	Early	Problem orientated	Functionality	Web application design model	Ratio	Direct	None	Specific
DEO	Early	Problem orientated	Functionality	Web application design model	Ratio	Direct	None	Specific
Entities	Early	Problem orientated	Functionality	Web application design model	Ratio	Direct	None	Specific
AppLimit	Early	Problem orientated	Functionality	Web application design model	Ratio	Direct	None	Specific
LInteraction	Early	Problem orientated	Functionality	Web application design model	Ratio	Direct	None	Specific

Copyright © 2008, IGI Global. Copying or distributing in print or electronic forms without written permission of IGI Global is prohibited.

Table 1. continued

Measure	Harvesting Time	Measure Foundation	Class	Entity	Measurement Scale	Computation	Validation	Model Dependency
Compatibility	Early	Problem orientated	Functionality	Web application design model	Ratio	Direct	None	Specific
TypeNodes	Early	Problem orientated	Complexity	Web application design model	Ratio	Direct	None	Specific
Accessibility	Early	Problem orientated	Complexity	Web application design model	Ratio	Direct	None	Specific
NavCluster	Early	Problem orientated	Complexity	Web application design model	Ratio	Direct	None	Specific
ClassVisibility	Early	Problem orientated	Complexity	Web application design model	Ratio	Direct	None	Specific
DeviceVisibility	Early	Problem orientated	Complexity	Web application design model	Ratio	Direct	None	Specific
Baresi et al.								
Entities	Early	Problem orientated	Length	Web application design model	Ratio	Direct	Empirically	Specific
Components	Early	Problem orientated	Length	Web application design model	Ratio	Direct	Empirically	Specific
InfoSlots	Early	Problem orientated	Length	Web application design model	Ratio	Direct	Empirically	Specific
SlotsSACenter	Early	Problem orientated	Length	Web application design model	Ratio	Indirect	Empirically	Specific
SlotsCollCenter	Early	Problem orientated	Length	Web application design model	Ratio	Indirect	Empirically	Specific
ComponentsEntity	Early	Problem orientated	Length	Web application design model	Ratio	Indirect	Empirically	Specific
SlotsComponent	Early	Problem orientated	Length	Web application design model	Ratio	Indirect	Empirically	Specific
SAssociations	Early	Problem orientated	Complexity	Web application design model	Ratio	Direct	Empirically	Specific
SACenters	Early	Problem orientated	Length	Web application design model	Ratio	Direct	Empirically	Specific
Segments	Early	Problem orientated	Length	Web application design model	Ratio	Direct	Empirically	Specific
Nodes	Late	Problem orientated	Length	Web application design model	Ratio	Direct	Empirically	Specific

Copyright © 2008, IGI Global. Copying or distributing in print or electronic forms without written permission of IGI Global is prohibited.

Table 1. continued

NavSlots	Late	Problem orientated	Length	Web application design model	Ratio	Direct	Empirically	Specific
NodesCluster	Late	Problem orientated	Length	Web application design model	Ratio	Indirect	Empirically	Specific
SlotsNode	Late	Problem orientated	Length	Web application design model	Ratio	Indirect	Empirically	Specific
NavLinks	Late	Problem orientated	Complexity	Web application design model	Ratio	Direct	Empirically	Specific
Clusters	Late	Problem orientated	Length	Web application design model	Ratio	Direct	Empirically	Specific
Pages	Late	Problem orientated	Length	Web application design model	Ratio	Direct	Empirically	Specific
pUnits	Late	Problem orientated	Length	Web application design model	Ratio	Direct	Empirically	Specific
pwLinks	Late	Problem orientated	Complexity	Web application design model	Ratio	Direct	Empirically	Specific
Sections	Late	Problem orientated	Length	Web application design model	Ratio	Direct	Empirically	Specific

Copyright © 2008, IGI Global. Copying or distributing in print or electronic forms without written permission of IGI Global is prohibited.

Table 2. Summary of findings from the literature review

Category	Values	Studies	%
Motivation	Help author hypermedia applications	1	6.25%
	Give feedback on possible improvements that will lead to better authoring and maintenance of applications	1	6.25%
	Measure readability and maintainability of applications	1	6.25%
	Measure the size of Web applications	1	6.25%
	Estimate effort to develop multimedia applications	1	6.25%
	Estimate effort to develop Web applications	8	50%
	Estimate effort to develop hypermedia applications	1	6.25%
	Estimate effort to design Web applications modeled according to a specific methodology	2	12.5%
Category	**Values**	**Measures**	**%**
Harvesting Time	Early	53	35%
	Late	100	65%
Measure Foundation	Problem orientated	43	28%
	Solution orientated	110	72%
Class	Length	99	65%
	Functionality	19	12%
	Complexity	35	23%
Entity	Web software application	1	0.6%
	Web hypermedia application	4	2.6%
	Web application	64	41.8%
	Hypermedia application	14	9.2%
	Hypertext application	0	0%
	Web page	22	14.3%
	Media	11	7.2%
	Program/script	5	3.3%
	Web application design model	32	21%
Measurement Scale	Nominal	4	2.6%
	Ordinal	4	2.6%
	Interval	0	0%
	Ratio	138	90%
	Absolute	7	4.8%
Computation	Direct	117	76%
	Indirect	36	24%
Validation	Empirically	89	58%
	Theoretically	0	0%
	Both	5	3%
	None	59	39%

Copyright © 2008, IGI Global. Copying or distributing in print or electronic forms without written permission of IGI Global is prohibited.

Change in Trends

For the years 1992 to 1996, size was measured solely using complexity size measures. In 1997 came the first publication that demonstrated the use of hypermedia or multimedia size measures for effort estimation. From 1998 to 2000, more work was devoted to size measures applicable to effort estimation; three of these were by industry practitioners (Cleary, 2000; Cowderoy, 2000; Cowderoy et al., 1998; Reifer, 2000) who proposed measures and exemplified their use with very small data sets or development practices from just one single Web company. Regrettably, their findings may not be applicable to other Web companies' work and practices and cannot be considered an empirical validation, hampering the external and internal validity of their findings, respectively.

Except for Baresi et al. (2003), Mangia and Paiano (2003), and Mendes et al. (2003), all size measures proposed for effort estimation presented previously have been related to implemented Web applications, represented predominantly by solution-orientated size measures. Even when targeted at measuring functionality based on function-point analysis, researchers only considered the final Web application rather than requirements documentation generated using existing Web development methods. This makes their usefulness as early effort predictors questionable. Except for Rollo (2000), all literature that was described as part of our literature review employed at least one solution-orientated type of measure. This may be explained by the difficulty in using early size measures gathered at the start of a Web development life cycle.

Length and complexity measures are classes used respectively by 65% and 23% of the 153 size measures previously presented. Functionality was a class used by only 12% of the size measures. The small amount of previous work using functionality size measures may be explained by the fact that until recently, the highest volume of Web applications were developed using just static pages, written in HTML, with graphics and JavaScript. Therefore, both researchers and practitioners would have focused on size measures that were adequate for this type of Web application.

Recent work (Mendes et al., 2003; Reifer, 2000) showed that complexity size measures do not seem to be as important as functionality and length size measures. This may be due to the motivation behind the proposition of such measures. However, it may also point toward a change in the characteristics of Web applications developed in the past compared to those that are developed today. Many Web applications are presenting characteristics of dynamic applications, where pages are generated on the fly. This may suggest that looking at an application's structure, represented by its links, ceases to be as important as it was in the past. This also explains the gradual exclusion of complexity size measures from recent literature.

Copyright © 2008, IGI Global. Copying or distributing in print or electronic forms without written permission of IGI Global is prohibited.

Defining Your Own Size Measure

Different organisations use and sometimes propose size measures with different aims. If your organisation's aim is to improve the way effort is estimated for your Web projects, then this section may be of help. The first step would be to look at the size measures that have been proposed in the literature to assess whether or not they can be reused within the context of your own organisation.

Table 1 and the section presenting the literature review will provide the necessary details for you to decide what to reuse. It is also important to decide if the Web applications developed by your organisation can be measured using a single size measure, or if a combination of size measures will be a better choice. Previous work has provided size measures that reflect both situations. For example, Mendes et al. (2003) proposed a set of size measures that can be gathered at a project's bidding stage; Reifer (2000) proposed a single size measure that can be obtained once an application's implementation details have been defined. It may be necessary and useful for your organisation to use different size measures at different points in a Web application's development life cycle. An organisation may decide to initially use early size measures, such as those proposed by Mendes et al., and later to use Reifer's size measure once the Web application's physical design is complete. Another option is to use Mendes et al.'s measures very early on, followed by measures that can be gathered from a Web application's conceptual design (see Baresi et al., 2003; Mangia & Paiano, 2003), and finally to use Reifer's measure once the Web application's physical design has been documented.

The use of different sets of size measures at different stages of a Web application development life cycle is only applicable if late measures provide more precise effort estimates than early measures. One would assume that this should always be the case; however, some empirical studies have not corroborated this assumption (Mendes et al., 2002).

The choice of size measures is also related to how well-structured your current Web development processes are. For example, if you use an in-house or third-party development methodology, you can propose size measures that take into account all the deliverables produced using the Web development methodology. This may be a reasonable option, and is similar to the approach for proposing size measures used by Baresi et al. (2003). There are also other constraints that may need to be taken into account, such as the amount of time it may take to manually gather the necessary data. This may be a decisive point determining the number of size measures to use. Ideally, as many measures as possible should be automatically gathered to reduce the amount of error associated with the data, which can bias the results.

Copyright © 2008, IGI Global. Copying or distributing in print or electronic forms without written permission of IGI Global is prohibited.

Conclusion

This chapter presented a literature survey of hypermedia and Web size measures published since 1992, and classified them according to a proposed taxonomy. The main findings from the survey were the following:

- Most size measures were proposed to be used as predictors to help estimate the effort necessary to develop Web applications
- Most size measures proposed for effort estimation are harvested late in the Web development life cycle
- Most measures were solution orientated and measured length
- Most measures measured attributes of Web applications or Web application design models, and were measured directly using a ratio scale
- Close to half of the proposed measures were validated empirically; however, 39% were not validated at all

Regarding the change in trends observed from 1996 onward, the majority of size measures were geared toward Web applications rather than hypermedia applications, illustrating a shift in the focus not only from the research community but also by practitioners. Most size measures, except for those proposed between 1992 and 1996, were aimed at Web effort estimation.

References

Abrahao, S., Poels, G., & Pastor, O. (2004). Evaluating a functional size measurement method for Web applications: An empirical analysis. *Proceedings of the 10ᵗʰ International Symposium on Software Measures* (pp. 358-369).

Baresi, L., Morasca, S., & Paolini, P. (2003, September). Estimating the design effort of Web applications. *Proceedings of Ninth International Software Measures Symposium* (pp. 62-72).

Bevo, V., Lévesque, G., & Abran, A. (1999, September). *Application de la méthode FFP à partir d'une spécification selon la notation UML: Compte rendu des premiers essais d'application et questions.* International Workshop on Software Measurement (IWSM'99), Lac Supérieur, Canada.

Botafogo, R., Rivlin, A. E., & Shneiderman, B. (1992). Structural analysis of hypertexts: Identifying hierarchies and useful measures. *ACM Transactions on Information Systems, 10*(2), 143-179.

Copyright © 2008, IGI Global. Copying or distributing in print or electronic forms without written permission of IGI Global is prohibited.

Bray, T. (1996, May). *Measuring the Web*. Proceedings of Fifth WWW Conference, Paris. Retrieved from http://www5conf.inria.fr/fich_html/papers/P9/Overview.html

Briand, L. C., & Wieczorek, I. (2002). Software resource estimation. In J. J. Marciniak (Ed.), *Encyclopedia of software engineering: Vol. 2. P-Z* (2nd ed., pp. 1160-1196). New York: John Wiley & Sons.

Calero, C., Ruiz, J., & Piattini, M. (2004). A Web measures survey using WQM. In *Lecture notes in computer science: Vol. 3140. Proceedings of ICWE04* (pp. 147-160).

Christodoulou, S. P., Zafiris, P. A., & Papatheodorou, T. S. (2000). WWW2000: The developer's view and a practitioner's approach to Web engineering. *Proceedings of the 2nd ICSE Workshop on Web Engineering* (pp. 75-92).

Cleary, D. (2000). Web-based development and functional size measurement. *Proceedings of the IFPUG 2000 Conference*.

Conklin, J. (1987). Hypertext: An introduction and survey. *Computer, 20*(9), 17-41.

Cowderoy, A. J. C. (2000). Measures of size and complexity for web-site content. *Proceedings of the 11th ESCOM Conference* (pp. 423-431).

Cowderoy, A. J. C., Donaldson, A. J. M., & Jenkins, J. O. (1998). A measures framework for multimedia creation. *Proceedings of the 5th IEEE International Software Measures Symposium*.

DeMarco, T. (1982). *Controlling software projects: Management, measurement and estimation*. New York: Yourdon Press.

Dhyani, D., Ng, W. K., & Bhowmick, S. S. (2002). A survey of Web measures. *ACM Computing Surveys, 34*(4), 469-503.

Fenton, N. E., & Pfleeger, S. L. (1997). *Software measures: A rigorous & practical approach* (2nd ed.). Boston: PWS Publishing Company & International Thomson Computer Press.

Fletcher, T., MacDonell, S. G., & Wong, W. B. L. (1997). Early experiences in measuring multimedia systems development effort. *Proceedings of Multimedia Technology and Applications* (pp. 211-220).

Hatzimanikatis, A. E., Tsalidis, C. T., & Chistodoulakis, D. (1995). Measuring the readability and maintainability of hyperdocuments. *Journal of Software Maintenance, Research and Practice, 7*, 77-90.

Institute of Electrical and Electronics Engineers (IEEE), Standard Taxonomy for Software Engineering Standards (ANSI). (1986). *The Institute of Electrical and Electronics Engineers Inc.*

Jones, T. C. (1998). *Estimating software costs*. New York: McGraw-Hill.

Copyright © 2008, IGI Global. Copying or distributing in print or electronic forms without written permission of IGI Global is prohibited.

Kitchenham, B. A., Hughes, R. T., & Linkman, S. G. (2001). Modeling software measurement data. *IEEE Transactions on Software Engineering, 27*(9), 788-804.

Mangia, L., & Paiano, R. (2003). MMWA: A software sizing model for Web applications. *Proceedings of WISE'03* (pp. 53-61).

Mendes, E., Counsell, S., & Mosley, N. (2000, June). Measurement and effort prediction of Web applications. *Proceedings of 2nd ICSE Workshop on Web Engineering* (pp. 57-74).

Mendes, E., Hall, W., & Harrison, R. (1999). Applying measurement principles to improve hypermedia authoring. *New Review of Hypermedia and Multimedia, 5*, 105-132.

Mendes, E., Mosley, N., & Counsell, S. (2001). Web measures: Estimating design and authoring effort. *IEEE Multimedia, 8*(1), 50-57.

Mendes, E., Mosley, N., & Counsell, S. (2002a). The application of case-based reasoning to early Web project cost estimation. *Proceedings of IEEE COMPSAC* (pp. 393-398).

Mendes, E., Mosley, N., & Counsell, S. (2002b). Comparison of Web size measures for predicting Web design and authoring effort. *IEE Proceedings Software, 149*(3), 86-92.

Mendes, E., Mosley, N., & Counsell, S. (2003). Investigating early Web size measures for Web costimation. *Proceedings EASE2003 Conference*.

Reifer, D. J. (2000). Web development: Estimating quick-to-market software. *IEEE Software, 17*(6), 57-64.

Rollo, T. (2000). *Sizing e-commerce.* Proceedings of ACOSM 2000, Sydney, Australia.

Umbers, P., & Miles, G. (2004, September). Resource estimation for Web applications. *Proceedings of the 10th International Symposium on Software Measures* (pp. 370-381).

Yamada, S., Hong, J., & Sugita, S. (1995). Development and evaluation of hypermedia for museum education: Validation of measures. *ACM Transactions on Computer-Human Interaction, 2*(4), 284-307.

Copyright © 2008, IGI Global. Copying or distributing in print or electronic forms without written permission of IGI Global is prohibited.

Section II

Techniques for Building Web Cost Models

This section details how to apply three different techniques to estimate costs for Web projects. In addition, it also discusses how to compare different techniques and use this information to improve current estimating practices.

Chapter V

Web Effort Estimation Using Regression Analysis

Abstract

Software effort models and estimates help project managers allocate resources, control costs, and schedule and improve current practices, leading to projects that are finished on time and within budget. In the context of Web development and maintenance, these issues are also crucial, and very challenging, given that Web projects have short schedules and a highly fluidic scope. Therefore, this chapter presents a case study where a real effort prediction model based on data from completed industrial Web projects is constructed step by step using a statistical technique called regression analysis.

Case Study

The case study we present herein describes the construction and further validation of a Web effort estimation model using multivariate regression techniques and data

Copyright © 2008, IGI Global. Copying or distributing in print or electronic forms without written permission of IGI Global is prohibited.

from industrial Web projects, developed by Web companies worldwide from the Tukutuku database (Mendes, Mosley, & Counsell, 2003, 2005). It should be noted that the raw data cannot be presented due to a confidentiality agreement with those companies that volunteered data on their projects. This database is part of the ongoing Tukutuku project (http://www.cs.auckland.ac.nz/tukutuku), which collects data on Web projects for the development of effort estimation models and to benchmark productivity across and within Web companies.

The data set used in this chapter contains data on 87 Web projects: 34 and 13 are from two single Web companies respectively and the remaining 40 projects come from another 23 companies. The Tukutuku database uses 6 variables to store specifics about each company that volunteered projects, 10 variables to store particulars about each project, and 13 variables to store data about each Web application (see Table 1). Company data is obtained once, and both project and application data are gathered for each project a Web company volunteers.

All results presented were obtained using the statistical software package SPSS 12.0 for Windows produced and sold by SPSS Inc. Further details on the statistical methods used throughout this case study are given in Chapter 10. Finally, all the statistical tests set the significance level at 95% ($\alpha = 0.05$). Note that the different types of measurement scales are also detailed in Chapter 10.

The following sections describe our data analysis procedure, adapted from Maxwell (2002), which consists of the following:

1. Data validation
2. Variables and model selection
3. Model inspection
4. Extraction of effort equation
5. Model validation

We also explain step by step how to use SPSS to carry out the analyses described in this chapter. Although you may not have access to SPSS, other commercial statistical tools use a similar methodology of data input and the same statistical algorithms. As such, the detailed instructions provided by this chapter can also be carried out with other statistical software as the options they provide are overall very similar to those offered in SPSS.

Data Validation

Data validation (DV) performs the first screening of the data that have been collected. In general, this involves understanding what the variables are (e.g., their

Copyright © 2008, IGI Global. Copying or distributing in print or electronic forms without written permission of IGI Global is prohibited.

Table 1. Variables for the Tukutuku database

NAME	SCALE	DESCRIPTION
COMPANY DATA		
COUNTRY	Categorical	Country company belongs to
ESTABLISHED	Ordinal	Year when company was established
SERVICES	Categorical	Type of services company provides
NPEOPLEWD	Absolute	Number of people who work on Web design and development
CLIENTIND	Categorical	Industry representative of those clients to whom applications are provided
ESTPRACT	Categorical	Accuracy of a company's own effort estimation practices
PROJECT DATA		
TYPEPROJ	Categorical	Type of project (new or enhancement)
LANGS	Categorical	Implementation languages used
DOCPROC	Categorical	If project followed defined and documented process
PROIMPR	Categorical	If project team was involved in a process improvement programme
METRICS	Categorical	If project team was part of a software metrics programme
DEVTEAM	Absolute	Size of project's development team
TEAMEXP	Absolute	Average team experience with the development language(s) employed
TOTEFF	Absolute	Actual total effort in person hours used to develop the Web application
ESTEFF	Absolute	Estimated total effort in person hours necessary to develop the Web application
ACCURACY	Categorical	Procedure used to record effort data
WEB APPLICATION		
TYPEAPP	Categorical	Type of Web application developed
TOTWP	Absolute	Total number of Web pages (new and reused)
NEWWP	Absolute	Total number of new Web pages
TOTIMG	Absolute	Total number of images (new and reused)
NEWIMG	Absolute	Total number of new images created
HEFFDEV	Absolute	Minimum number of hours to develop a single function/feature by one experienced developer who is considered to possess high-level skills (above average). This number is currently set to 15 hours based on the collected data.
HEFFADPT	Absolute	Minimum number of hours to adapt a single function/feature by one experienced developer who is considered to possess high-level skills (above average). This number is currently set to 4 hours based on the collected data.
HFOTS	Absolute	Number of reused high-effort features/functions without adaptation
HFOTSA	Absolute	Number of reused high-effort features/functions adapted
HNEW	Absolute	Number of new high-effort features/functions
FOTS	Absolute	Number of reused low-effort features without adaptation
FOTSA	Absolute	Number of reused low-effort features adapted
NEW	Absolute	Number of new low-effort features/functions

Copyright © 2008, IGI Global. Copying or distributing in print or electronic forms without written permission of IGI Global is prohibited.

purpose, scale type; see Table 1) and also uses descriptive statistics (e.g., the mean, median, minimum, and maximum are used for numerical variables) to help identify any missing or unusual cases.

Table 2 presents summary statistics for numerical variables. Such statistics are obtained in SPSS by following these steps:

- Select *Analyze* ⇨ *Descriptive Statistics* ⇨ *Frequencies*
- Then click on the button *Statistics* and tick *mean, median, minimum, maximum,* and *Std. deviation*

The output generated by SPSS is similar to that shown in Table 2.

Table 2 suggests that none of the numerical variables seem to exhibit unusual or missing values, although this requires careful examination. For example, one would find it strange to see zero as the minimum value for total images (TOTIMG) or one as the minimum value for total Web pages (TOTWP). However, it is possible to have either a Web application without any images or a Web application that provides all of its content and functionality within a single Web page. Another example relates to the maximum number of Web pages, which has a value of 2,000 Web pages. Although it does not seem possible at first to have such large number of pages, we cannot simply assume this has been a data entry error. When a situation such as this one arises, the first step is to contact the company that provided the data and to

Table 2. Descriptive statistics for numerical variables

Variables	N	Missing	Minimum	Maximum	Mean	Median	Std. Dev.
DEVTEAM	87	0	1	8	2.37	2	1.35
TEAMEXP	87	0	1	10	3.40	2	1.93
TOTWP	87	0	1	2000	92.40	25	273.09
NEWWP	87	0	0	1980	82.92	7	262.98
TOTIMG	87	0	0	1820	122.54	40	284.48
NEWIMG	87	0	0	800	51.90	0	143.25
HEFFDEV	87	0	5	800	62.02	15	141.25
HEFFADPT	87	0	0	200	10.61	4	28.48
HFOTS	87	0	0	3	.08	0	.41
HFOTSA	87	0	0	4	.29	0	.75
HNEW	87	0	0	10	1.24	0	2.35
FOTS	87	0	0	15	1.07	0	2.57
FOTSA	87	0	0	10	1.89	1	2.41
NEW	87	0	0	13	1.87	0	2.84
TOTEFF	87	0	1	5000	261.73	43	670.36
ESTEFF	34	53	1	108	14.45	7.08	20.61

Copyright © 2008, IGI Global. Copying or distributing in print or electronic forms without written permission of IGI Global is prohibited.

confirm the data are correct. Unfortunately, in our case, we were unable to obtain confirmation from the source company. However, further investigation revealed that in relation to the Web project that contains 2,000 Web pages, 1,980 pages were developed from scratch, and numerous new functions and features (five high effort and seven low effort) were also implemented. In addition, the development team consisted of two people who had very little experience with the six programming languages used. The total effort was 947 person hours, which corresponds to a 3-month project assuming both developers worked at the same time. If we only consider number of pages and effort, the ratio of number of minutes per page is 27:1, which seems reasonable given the lack of experience of the development team and the number of different languages they had to use.

Once we have checked the numerical variables, our next step is to check the categorical variables using their frequency tables as a tool (see Tables 3 to 7). To display frequency tables using SPSS, follow the steps below.

- Select *Analyze* ⇨ *Descriptive Statistics* ⇨ *Frequencies*.
- Tick *Display Frequency Tables*.

Tables 4 to 6 show that most projects followed a defined and documented process, and that development teams were involved in a process improvement programme and/or were part of a software metrics programme. These positive trends are mainly due to the two single companies that together volunteered data on 47 projects (54% of our data set). They have answered "yes" to all three categories. No unusual trends are apparent.

Table 3. Frequency table for type of project

Type of Project	Frequency	%	Cumulative %
New	39	44.8	44.8
Enhancement	48	55.2	100.0
Total	87	100.0	

Table 4. Frequency table for documented process

Documented Process	Frequency	%	Cumulative %
No	23	26.4	26.4
Yes	64	73.6	100.0
Total	87	100.0	

Copyright © 2008, IGI Global. Copying or distributing in print or electronic forms without written permission of IGI Global is prohibited.

Table 5. Frequency table for process improvement

Process Improvement	Frequency	%	Cumulative %
No	28	32.2	32.2
Yes	59	67.8	100.0
Total	87	100.0	

Table 6. Frequency table for metrics programme

Metrics Programme	Frequency	%	Cumulative %
No	36	41.4	41.4
Yes	51	58.6	100.0
Total	87	100.0	

Table 7. Frequency table for companies' effort recording procedure

Actual Effort Recording Procedure	Frequency	%	Cumulative %
Poor	12	13.8	13.8
Medium	3	3.4	17.2
Good	24	27.6	44.8
Very good	48	55.2	100
Total	87	100.0	

Table 7 shows that the majority of projects (83%) had the actual effort recorded on a daily basis for each project and/or project task. These numbers are inflated by the two single companies where one chose the category *good* (11 projects) and the other chose the category *very good* (34 projects). The actual effort recording procedure is not an adequate effort estimator per se, being used here simply to show that the effort data gathered seems to be reliable overall.

Once the data validation is complete, we are ready to move on to the next step, namely, variables and model selection.

Variables and Model Selection

The second step in our data analysis methodology is subdivided into two separate and distinct phases: preliminary analysis and model building.

Copyright © 2008, IGI Global. Copying or distributing in print or electronic forms without written permission of IGI Global is prohibited.

Preliminary analysis allows us to choose which variables to use, discard, modify, and, where necessary, create. Model building is used to construct an effort estimation model based on our data set and variables.

Preliminary Analysis

This important phase is used to create new variables based on existing variables, discard unnecessary variables, and modify existing variables (e.g., joining categories). The net result of this phase is to obtain a set of variables that are ready to use in the next phase, model building. Since this phase will construct an effort model using stepwise regression, we need to ensure that the variables comply with the assumptions underlying regression analysis, which are as follows.

1. The input variables (independent variables) are measured without error. If this cannot be guaranteed, then these variables need to be normalised using a transformation.
2. The relationship between dependent and independent variables is linear.
3. No important input variables have been omitted. This ensures that there is no specification error associated with the data set. The use of a prior theory-based model justifying the choice of input variables ensures this assumption is not violated.
4. The variance of the residuals is the same for all combinations of input variables (i.e., the residuals are homoscedastic rather than heteroscedastic). A residual within the context of this book is the difference between actual and estimated effort. Further details are provided in Chapter X.
5. The residuals must be normally distributed.
6. The residuals must be independent, that is, not correlated. Further details are provided in Chapter 10.
7. The independent variables are not linearly dependent; that is, there are no linear dependencies between the independent variables.

The first task within the preliminary analysis phase is to examine the entire set of variables and check if there are any variables containing a significant amount of missing values (> 60%). If there are, they should be automatically discarded as they prohibit the use of imputation methods, which are methods used to replace missing values with estimated values, and will further prevent the identification of useful trends in the data. Table 2 shows that only ESTEFF presented missing values greater than 60%. ESTEFF was gathered to give an idea of each company's own prediction accuracy; however, it will not be included in our analysis since it is not an effort

Copyright © 2008, IGI Global. Copying or distributing in print or electronic forms without written permission of IGI Global is prohibited.

predictor per se. Note that a large number of zero values on certain size variables do not represent missing or rounded values.

Next we present the analysis for numerical variables, followed by the analysis for categorical variables.

Numerical Variables: Looking for Symptoms

Our next step is to look for symptoms (e.g., skewness, heteroscedasticity, and outliers) that may suggest the need for variables to be normalised, that is, having their values transformed such that they more closely resemble a normal distribution. This step uses histograms, boxplots, and scatterplots.

Skewness measures to what extent the distribution of data values is symmetrical about a central value, heteroscedasticity represents unstable variance of values, and outliers are unusual values.

Histograms, or bar charts, provide a graphical display, where each bar summarises the frequency of a single value or range of values for a given variable. They are often used to check if a variable is normally distributed, in which case the bars are displayed in the shape of a bell-shaped curve.

To obtain a histogram for a numerical variable using SPSS, follow these steps:

- Select *Graphs* ⇨ *Histogram*
- Select the variable from the list on the left and click on the arrow button to have it moved to the box labeled *Variable*
- Tick *Display normal curve*

Histograms for the numerical variables (see Figure 1) suggest that all variables present skewed distributions, that is, values not symmetrical about a central value.

Next we use boxplots to check the existence of outliers. Boxplots (see Figure 5) use the median, represented by the horizontal line in the middle of the box, as the central value for the distribution. The box's height is the interquartile range, and contains 50% of the values. The vertical lines up or down from the edges, also known as whiskers, contain observations that are less than 1.5 times the interquartile range. Outliers are taken as values greater than 1.5 times the height of the box. Values greater than 3 times the box's height are called extreme outliers (Kitchenham, MacDonell, Pickard, & Shepperd, 2001).

When upper and lower tails are approximately equal and the median is in the centre of the box, the distribution is symmetric. If the distribution is not symmetric, the relative lengths of the tails and the position of the median in the box indicate the nature of the skewness. The length of the box relative to the length of the tails also

Copyright © 2008, IGI Global. Copying or distributing in print or electronic forms without written permission of IGI Global is prohibited.

Figure 1. Distribution of values for numerical variables

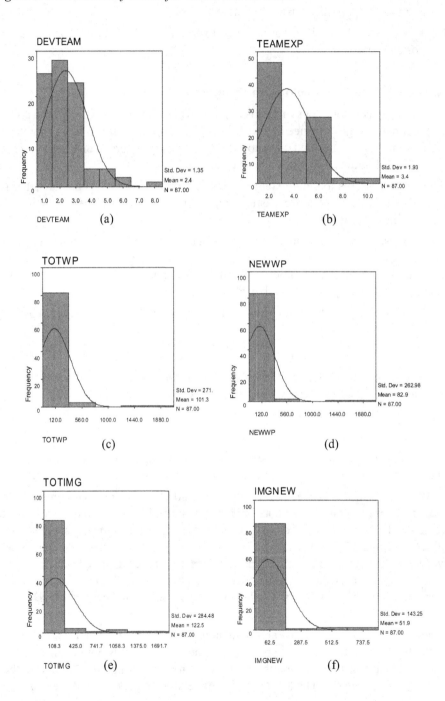

Copyright © 2008, IGI Global. Copying or distributing in print or electronic forms without written permission of IGI Global is prohibited.

Figure 1. continued

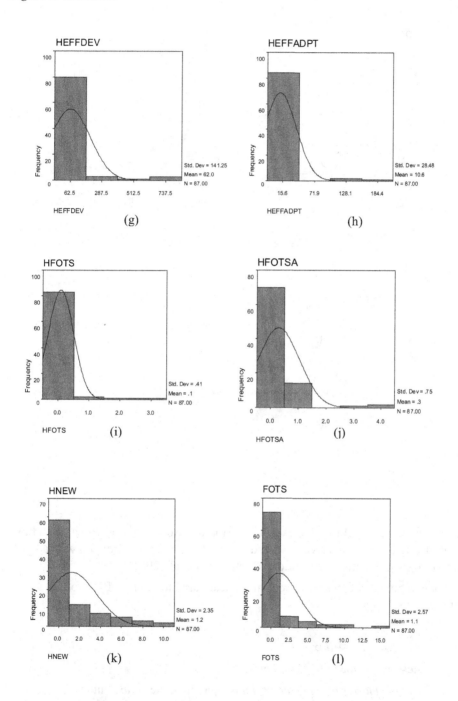

Copyright © 2008, IGI Global. Copying or distributing in print or electronic forms without written permission of IGI Global is prohibited.

Figure 1. continued

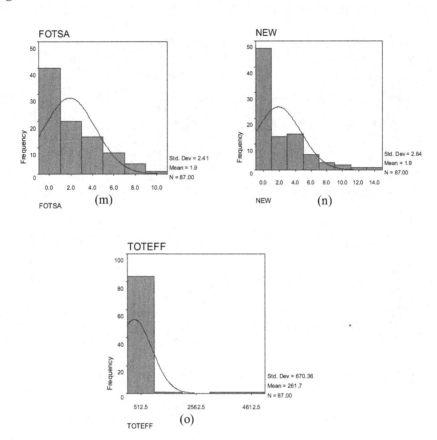

gives an indication of the shape of the distribution. So, a boxplot with a small box and long tails represents a very peaked distribution, whereas a boxplot with a long box represents a flatter distribution (Kitchenham et al., 2001).

To obtain boxplots for one or more numerical variables using SPSS, follow these steps:

*   Select *Graphs* ➪ *Boxplot*
*   Click on the image labeled *Simple*
*   Tick *Summaries of separate variables* and click the *define* button

Copyright © 2008, IGI Global. Copying or distributing in print or electronic forms without written permission of IGI Global is prohibited.

- Select the variables from the list on the left and click on the arrow button to have them moved to the box labeled *Boxes Represent*

- Optionally, select the variable from the list on the left that identifies each project individually (e.g., project ID) and click on the arrow button to have it moved to the box labeled *Label cases by*

The boxplots for numerical variables (see Figure 2) indicate that they present a large number of outliers and peaked distributions that are not symmetric.

Whenever outliers are present they should be investigated further since they may be a result of data entry error. In our analysis we looked at all cases, in particular in relation to projects that exhibited very large effort values, but did not find anything in the data to suggest they should be removed from the data set. Note that when there are doubts about the correctness of the data, the best solution is to contact the data source for confirmation. An assessment should only be based on consistency with other variables if the source is not available.

The histograms and boxplots both indicate symptoms of skewness and outliers. When this situation arises, it is common practice to normalise the data, that is, to transform the data trying to approximate the values to a normal distribution. A common transformation is to take the natural log (ln), which makes larger values smaller and brings the data values closer to each other (Maxwell, 2002). However, before transforming the data, a statistical test can be used to confirm if the data is not normally distributed. This statistical test is called the one-sample Kolmogorov-

Figure 2. Main components of a boxplot

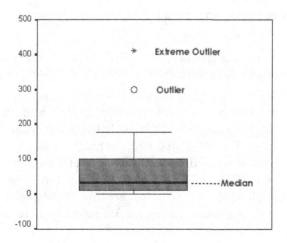

Copyright © 2008, IGI Global. Copying or distributing in print or electronic forms without written permission of IGI Global is prohibited.

Smirnov (K-S) test. It compares an observed distribution to a theoretical distribution. Significance values that are equal to or smaller than 0.05 indicate that the observed distribution differs from the theoretical distribution.

To use the one-sample Kolmogorov-Smirnov test in SPSS, follow these steps:

- Select *Analyze* ⇨ *Nonparametric tests* ⇨ *1-Sample K-S*.
- Then click the test distribution *Normal* and select on the left list all the variables to be checked. Once selected, click the arrow button to show them as part of the test variable list.

We employed the K-S test and found that none of the variables had distributions that matched the normal distribution. Therefore, all variables had to be transformed. The transformation that applied in our case to all numerical variables was the natural log transformation. For consistency, all variables with a value of zero had one added to their values prior to being transformed, as there is no natural log of zero.

To create a variable in SPSS based on transformed values, follow these steps:

- Select *Transform* ⇨ *Compute.*
- Type the name of the new variable to be created (*new_Variable* in Figure 3) to store the values after being transformed.
- Select from the *Functions* list the function to be used (*LN(numexpr)* in Figure 3). Click the arrow button to have the selected function copied to the area identified as *Numeric Expression*.
- Select from the list on the left the variable to be used in the transformation (totimg in Figure 3). Click the right arrow button to have this variable's name added as a parameter to the function LN (*LN(totimg+1)* in Figure 3). One was added to totimg since totimg has a few zero values.

The variable *new_Variable* is automatically added to the data set and contains the values of (totimg+1) after being transformed using a natural log transformation.

The Tukutuku database uses six variables to record the number of features and functions for each application. Their histograms (Figure 4) indicate that each has a large number of zeros, reducing their likelihood of being selected by the stepwise procedure. We therefore decided to group their values by creating two new variables: TOTHIGH (summation of HFOTS, HFOTSA, and HNEW) and TOTNHIGH (summation of FOTS, FOTSA, and NEW). Their histograms are presented in Figure 5. The creation in SPSS of new variables that are a summation of other variables uses steps similar to those presented in Figure 3. The only difference is that here

Copyright © 2008, IGI Global. Copying or distributing in print or electronic forms without written permission of IGI Global is prohibited.

Figure 3. Computing a new variable new_Variable in SPSS

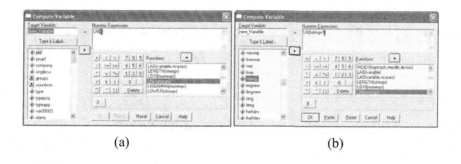

(a)   (b)

Figure 4. Boxplots for numerical variables

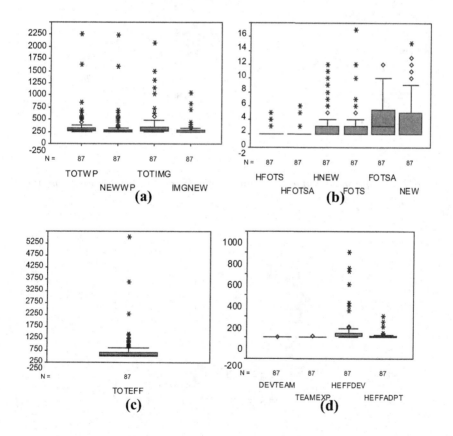

Copyright © 2008, IGI Global. Copying or distributing in print or electronic forms without written permission of IGI Global is prohibited.

we do not select a function and the numeric expression lists all the variables to be summated (e.g., HFOTS + HFOTSA + HNEW).

Finally, we created a new variable called NLANG, representing the number of different implementation languages used per project, replacing the original multi-

Figure 5. Distribution of values for TOTHIGH and TOTNHIGH

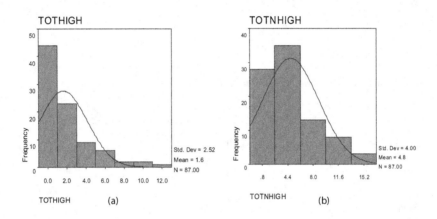

Figure 6. Distribution of values for number of different implementation languages

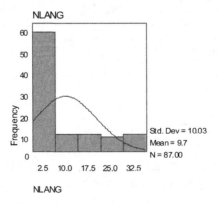

Copyright © 2008, IGI Global. Copying or distributing in print or electronic forms without written permission of IGI Global is prohibited.

valued variable that stored the names of the different implementation languages. The histogram for NLANG is presented in Figure 6.

TOTHIGH, TOTNHIGH, and NLANG were also transformed since they presented skewness and outliers, and their distributions did not resemble a normal distribution. The K-S test also confirmed that these variables were not normally distributed.

In the following sections, any variables that have been transformed have their names identified by an uppercase L, followed by the name of the variables they originated from.

The last part of the preliminary analysis is to check if the relationship between the dependent variable (LTOTEFF) and the independent variables is linear. The tool used to check such relationships is a scatterplot. Further details on scatterplots are provided in Chapter X.

Numerical Variables: Relationship with Total Effort

Scatterplots are used to explore possible relationships between numerical variables. They also help to identify strong and weak relationships between two numerical variables. A strong relationship is represented by observations (data points) falling very close to or on the trend line. Examples of such relationships are shown in Figure 7, Figure 8, and Figure 9. A weak relationship is shown by observations that do not form a clear pattern, which in our case is a straight line. Examples of such relationships are shown in Figure 8 and Figure 9.

To create a scatterplot in SPSS, follow these steps:.

- Select *Graphs* ⇨ *Scatterplot.*
- Then click on the button associated with *Simple* and click the button *Define.*
- Select, using the list on the left, the variable that will be plotted on the Y-axis, and click the right arrow such that this variable's name appears inside the box labeled *Y Axis*. Repeat these steps to select the variable to be plotted on the X-axis.
  - Optionally, select the variable from the list on the left that identifies each project individually (e.g., project ID) and click on the right arrow button to have it moved to the box labeled *Label cases by.*

We can also say that a relationship is positively associated when values on the y-axis tend to increase with those on the x-axis (e.g., Figure 7). When values on the y-axis tend to decrease as those on the x-axis increase, we say that the relationship is negatively associated (e.g., Figure 8 and Figure 9).

Copyright © 2008, IGI Global. Copying or distributing in print or electronic forms without written permission of IGI Global is prohibited.

Figure 7. Scatterplots showing strong relationships between LTOTEFF and several size variables

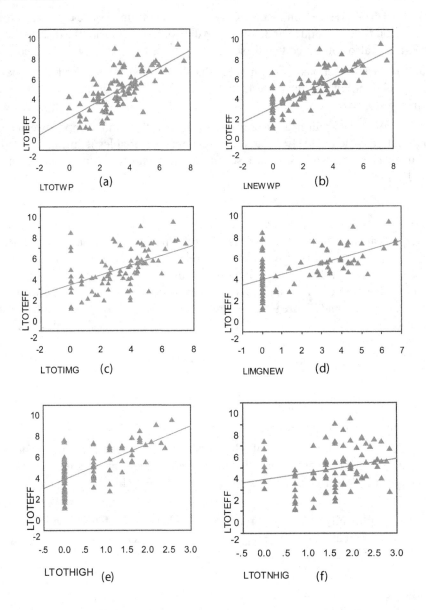

Figures 7 to 9 show that most variables seem to present a positive relationship with LTOTEFF. The scatterplots in Figure 8 clearly show that the large number of zero values for the independent variables causes the dependent variable to exhibit more

Copyright © 2008, IGI Global. Copying or distributing in print or electronic forms without written permission of IGI Global is prohibited.

Figure 8. Scatterplots for strong (d, e, f) and weak (a, b, c) relationships between LTOTEFF and several size variables

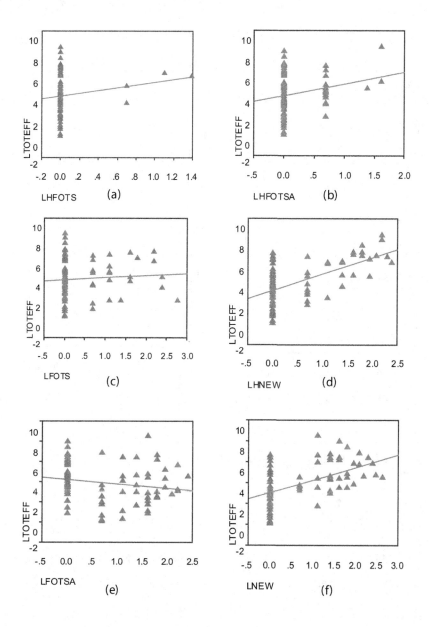

variability at the zero point, that is, when independent variables have zero values compared with nonzero values. This behaviour violates the fourth assumption underlying linear regression. Therefore, within the context of this case study, we will

Copyright © 2008, IGI Global. Copying or distributing in print or electronic forms without written permission of IGI Global is prohibited.

Figure 9. Scatterplots for strong (a-d) and weak (e) relationships between LTOTEFF and independent variables

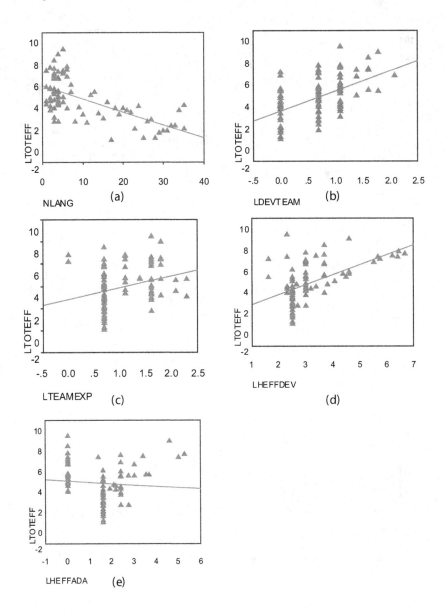

exclude LHFOTS, LHFOSTA, LHNEW, LFOTS, LFOTSA, and LNEW from any subsequent analysis.

Copyright © 2008, IGI Global. Copying or distributing in print or electronic forms without written permission of IGI Global is prohibited.

Our preliminary analysis for numerical variables is finished. Now we can move on and look at our categorical variables.

Categorical Variables: Relationship with Total Effort

This part of the analysis involves the creation of a table for each categorical variable where, for each of this variable's levels, we display the mean and median values of effort and the corresponding number of projects it is based on. The motivation is to check if there is a significant difference in effort by level. If there is, then we need to understand why.

Note that the distinct values of a categorical variable are called levels. For example, the categorical variable DOCPROC has two levels: Yes and No.

To create a table in SPSS for a categorical variable containing statistical summaries for an associated numerical variable, follow these steps:

- Select *Analyze* ⇨ *Reports* ⇨ *Case Summaries*.
- Select, using the list on the left, the numerical variable of interest, and click the right arrow such that this variable's name appears inside the box labeled *Variables*.
- Select using the list on the left the categorical variable of interest, and click the right arrow such that this variable's name appears inside the box labeled *Grouping Variable(s)*.
- Press the button labeled *Statistics* and select using the list on the left the statistic you want to be associated with the numerical variable of interest; click the right arrow such that this statistic is displayed inside the box labeled *Cell statistics*. Repeat the process until all the required statistics have been selected. Finally, click the button labeled *Continue*.

Table 8 shows that on average, new projects require more effort despite being smaller in number than enhancement projects. This should not come as a surprise since we

Table 8. Mean, median effort, and number of projects per type of project category

TYPEPROJ	N	Mean Effort	Median Effort
New	39	329.8	100.0
Enhancement	48	206.4	18.7
Total	87	261.7	43.0

Copyright © 2008, IGI Global. Copying or distributing in print or electronic forms without written permission of IGI Global is prohibited.

generally know that building an application of size *s* from scratch takes longer than if were simply going to enhance an application.

Table 9 shows that on average, despite being smaller in number, projects that did not use any documented process used higher effort than those projects that used a documented process. Further inspection of the data revealed that 70% of the 23 projects that did not use any documented process are new, and that 64% of the 64 projects that used a documented process are enhancement projects. These results are in line with those shown in Table 8.

A similar pattern is observed in Tables 10 and 11, where, on average, projects that are not part of a process improvement or metrics programme required higher effort than projects that are part of a process improvement or metrics programme, despite

Table 9. Mean, median effort, and number of projects per documented process level

DOCPROC	N	Mean Effort	Median Effort
No	23	307.5	50.0
Yes	64	245.3	36.2
Total	87	261.7	43.0

Table 10. Mean, median effort, and number of projects per process improvement level

PROIMPR	N	Mean Effort	Median Effort
No	28	508.1	100.0
Yes	59	144.8	25.2
Total	87	261.7	43.0

Table 11. Mean, median effort, and number of projects per metrics programme level

METRICS	N	Mean Effort	Median Effort
No	36	462.9	112.5
Yes	51	119.7	21.0
Total	87	261.7	43.0

Copyright © 2008, IGI Global. Copying or distributing in print or electronic forms without written permission of IGI Global is prohibited.

being smaller in size (61% of the 28 projects that are not part of a process improvement programme are new projects).

For projects that are not part of a metrics programme, this percentage is also 61% of 36 projects. In both cases, the majority of projects that are part of a process improvement or metrics programme are enhancement projects (63% of 59 and 67% of 51, respectively).

Next we build the effort model using a two-step process. The first step is to use a manual stepwise regression based on residuals to select the categorical and numerical variables that jointly have a statistically significant effect on the dependent variable, LTOTEFF. The second step is to use these selected variables to build the final effort model using multivariate regression, which is a linear regression that uses more than one independent variable.

The size measures used in our case study represent early Web size measures obtained from the results of a survey investigation (Mendes et al., 2005) using data from 133 online Web forms aimed at giving quotes on Web development projects. In addition, the measures were validated by an established Web company and a second survey involving 33 Web companies in New Zealand. Consequently it is our belief that the size measures identified are plausible effort predictors, not an ad hoc set of variables with no underlying rationale.

Building the Model Using a Two-Step Process

This section describes the use of a manual stepwise regression based on residuals to build the effort model. This technique, proposed by Kitchenham (1998), enables the use of information on residuals to handle relationships amongst independent variables. In addition, it only selects the input variables that jointly have a statistically significant effect on the dependent variable, thus avoiding any multicollinearity problems.

The input variables to use are those selected as a result of our preliminary analysis, which are NLANG, LDEVTEAM, LTEAMEXP, LTOTWP, LNEWWP, LTOTIMG, LIMGNEW, LTOTHIGH, LTOTNHIG, TYPEPROJ, DOCPROC, PROIMPR, and METRICS.

The manual stepwise technique applied to categorical variables comprises the following steps (Kitchenham, 1998):

Step 1. Identify the categorical variable that has a statistically significant effect on LTOTEFF and gives the smallest error term (mean square within groups). This is obtained by applying simple analysis of variance (ANOVA) using each categorical variable in turn (CV1). The ANOVA technique enables us to measure the relationship between categorical variables and effort.

Copyright © 2008, IGI Global. Copying or distributing in print or electronic forms without written permission of IGI Global is prohibited.

Step 2. Remove the effect of the most significant categorical variable to obtain residuals (ResC1). This means that for each level of the most significant categorical variable, subtract the mean effort from the project effort values. Note that effort represents the normalised effort: LTOTEFF.

Step 3. Apply ANOVA using each remaining categorical variable in turn, this time measuring their effect on ResC1.

Step 4. Any categorical variables that had a statistically significant effect on LTOTEFF (in Step 1) but have no statistically significant effect on ResC1 are variables related to CV1 and offer no additional information about the dependent variable. They can therefore be eliminated from the stepwise regression.

Step 5. Identify the next most significant categorical variable from Step 4 (CV2). Again, if there are several statistically significant variables, choose the one that minimises the error term.

Step 6. Remove the effect of CV2 to obtain residuals (ResC2).

Step 7. Apply ANOVA using each remaining categorical variable in turn, this time measuring their effect on ResC2.

Step 8. Any categorical variables that had a statistically significant effect on ResC1, but have no statistically significant effect on ResC2, are variables related with CV2 and offer no additional information about the dependent variable. They can therefore be eliminated from the stepwise regression.

Step 9. Repeat the stepwise process until all statistically significant categorical variables are removed or none of the remaining variables have a statistically significant effect on the current residuals.

To measure the relationship between a categorical and a numerical variable in SPSS using ANOVA, follow these steps:

- Select *Analyze* ⇨ *Compare Means* ⇨ *One-Way ANOVA*.
- Select, using the list on the left, the numerical variable of interest, and click the right arrow such that this variable's name appears inside the box labeled *Dependent list*.
- Select using the list on the left the categorical variable of interest, and click the right arrow such that this variable's name appears inside the box labeled *Factor*.

The initial level means for the four categorical variables to be used in our manual stepwise process are presented in Table 12.

Copyright © 2008, IGI Global. Copying or distributing in print or electronic forms without written permission of IGI Global is prohibited.

Table 12. Initial level means for categorical variables

Variable/Level	No. Projects	Total LTOTEFF	Mean LTOTEFF
TYPEPROJ/New	39	186.7	4.8
TYPEPROJ/Enhancement	48	154.1	3.2
DOCPROC/Yes	64	244.3	3.8
DOCPROC/No	23	96.5	4.2
PROIMPR/Yes	59	204.4	3.5
PROIMPR/No	28	136.4	4.9
METRICS/Yes	51	163.2	3.2
METRICS/No	36	177.6	4.9

Numerical variables can also be added to this stepwise procedure. Their impact on the dependent variable can be assessed using linear regression, and for obtaining the mean squares for the regression model and residual. Whenever a numerical variable is the most significant, its effect has to be removed; that is, the obtained residuals are the ones further analysed.

Whenever there are only numerical variables, the manual stepwise technique comprises the following steps:

Step 1. Identify the numerical variable that has a statistically significant effect on LTOTEFF and gives the highest adjusted R^2. This is obtained by applying simple regression analysis using each numerical variable in turn (IV1). Once this variable has been selected, construct the single variable regression equation with effort as the dependent variable using the most highly (and significantly) correlated input variable (IV1).

Step 2. Calculate the residuals (Res1).

Step 3. Correlate the residuals with all the other input variables.

Step 4. Any input variables that were initially significantly correlated with effort but are not significantly correlated with the residual are significantly correlated with IV1 and offer no additional information about the dependent variable. They can therefore be eliminated from the stepwise regression.

Step 5. Construct a single variable regression with the residuals (Res1) as the dependent variable and the variable (IV2) of the remaining input variables that is most highly (and significantly) correlated with Res1.

Step 6. Calculate residuals Res2.

Copyright © 2008, IGI Global. Copying or distributing in print or electronic forms without written permission of IGI Global is prohibited.

Step 7. Correlate the residuals Res2 with the remaining input variables. Any variables that were correlated with Res1 in Step 5 but are not correlated with Res2 are eliminated from the analysis. They are variables that are highly correlated with IV2.

Step 8. Continue in this way until there are no more input variables available for inclusion in the model or none of the remaining variables are significantly correlated with the current residuals.

To use single regression analysis in SPSS, follow these steps:

- Select *Analyze* ⇨ *Regression* ⇨ *Linear*.
- Select, using the list on the left, the numerical variable that is the dependent variable, and click the right arrow such that this variable's name appears inside the box labeled *Dependent*.
- Select, using the list on the left, the numerical variable that is the independent variable, and click the right arrow such that this variable's name appears inside the box labeled *Independent(s)*.

To construct the full regression model, apply a multivariate regression using only the variables that have been selected from the manual stepwise procedure. At each stage of the stepwise process, we also need to verify the stability of the model. This involves identifying large-residual and high-influence data points (i.e., projects), and also checking if residuals are homoscedastic and normally distributed. Several types of plots (e.g., residual, leverage, probability) and statistics are available in most statistics tools to accomplish such a task.

The plots we have employed here are the following:

- A residual plot showing residuals vs. fitted values. This allows us to investigate if the residuals are random and normally distributed. For numerical variables, the plotted data points should be distributed randomly about zero. They should not exhibit patterns such as linear or nonlinear trends, or increasing or decreasing variance. For categorical variables, the pattern of the residuals should appear "as a series of parallel, angled lines of approximately the same length" (Kitchenham, 1998).
- A normal P-P plot (probability plots) for the residuals. Normal P-P plots are generally employed to verify if the distribution of a variable is consistent with the normal distribution. When the distribution is normal, the data points are close to linear.

Copyright © 2008, IGI Global. Copying or distributing in print or electronic forms without written permission of IGI Global is prohibited.

- Cook's D statistic to identify projects that jointly exhibit a large influence and large residual (Maxwell, 2002). Any projects with D greater than $4/n$, where n represents the total number of projects, are considered to have a high influence on the results. With influential projects, the stability of the model is tested by removing these projects and observing the effect their removal has on the model. If the coefficients remain stable and the adjusted R^2 increases, this indicates that the high-influence projects are not destabilising the model and therefore do not need to be removed from further analysis.

To obtain a residual plot in SPSS, follow these steps:

- Select *Analyze* ⇨ *Regression* ⇨ *Linear*.
- Click on the button labeled *Plots*; select, using the list on the left, the label *ZRESID* (standardised residuals) and click the right arrow such that this variable's name appears inside the box labeled *Y*. Select, using the list on the left, the label *ZPRED* (standardised predicted values) and click the right arrow such that this variable's name appears inside the box labeled *X* (see Figure 10); click the button labeled *Continue*.

To obtain a normal P-P Plot in SPSS, follow these steps:

- Select *Analyze* ⇨ *Regression* ⇨ *Linear*.
- Click on the button labeled *Plots*; tick the options *Histogram* and *Normal probability plot*. Click the button labeled *Continue* (see Figure 10).

Figure 10. How to obtain some plots

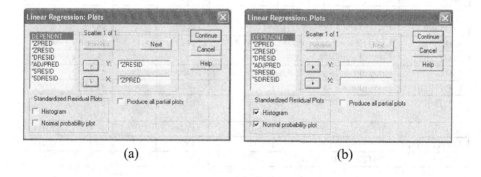

(a)   (b)

Copyright © 2008, IGI Global. Copying or distributing in print or electronic forms without written permission of IGI Global is prohibited.

To obtain Cook's D statistic in SPSS, follow these steps:

- Select *Analyze* ⇨ *Regression* ⇨ *Linear*.
- Click on the button labeled *Save*; tick the option *Cook's* under the group *Distances*. Click the button labeled *Continue*. A new variable will be created named COO_1.

First Cycle

Table 13 shows the results of applying ANOVA to categorical and numerical variables. This is the first cycle in the stepwise procedure. The numerical variable LNEWWP is the most significant since it results in the smallest error term, represented by a within-groups mean square value of 1.47.

The single variable regression equation with LTOTEFF as the dependent or response variable and LNEWWP as the independent or predictor variable gives an adjusted R^2 of 0.597. Two projects are identified with Cook's $D > 0.045$; however,

Table 13. ANOVA for each categorical and numerical variable for first cycle

Variable	Levels	Mean	No. Projects	Between-Groups MS	Within-Groups MS	F Test Level of Significance
TYPEPROJ	New	4.79	39	53.56	3.05	17.56 (p < 0.01)
TYPEPROJ	Enhancement	3.20	48			
DOCPROC	Yes	3.82	64	2.44	3.65	0.42 (n.s.)
DOCPROC	No	4.20	23			
PROIMPR	Yes	3.46	59	37.38	3.24	11.64 (p = 0.001)
PROIMPR	No	4.87	28			
METRICS	Yes	3.20	51	63.54	2.93	21.67 (p < 0.01)
METRICS	No	4.93	36			
LTOTWP	LTOTEFF = 1.183 + 0.841LTOTWP			158.22	1.82	86.97 (p < 0.01)
LNEWWP	**LTOTEFF = 2.165 + 0.731LNEWWP**			**188.21**	**1.47**	**128.36 (p < 0.01)**
LTOTIMG	LTOTEFF = 2.428 + 0.471LTOTIMG			78.55	2.76	28.50 (p < 0.01)
LIMGNEW	LTOTEFF = 2.98 + 0.524LIMGNEW			104.35	2.45	42.54 (p < 0.01)
LTOTHIGH	LTOTEFF = 2.84 + 1.705LTOTHIGH			143.04	2.00	71.61 (p < 0.01)
LTOTNHIG	LTOTEFF = 2.954 + 0.641LTOTNHIG			21.12	3.43	6.15 (p = 0.015)
NLANG	LTOTEFF = -0.585 + 0.372NLANG			14.046	2.857	4.916 (p < 0.01)
LDEVTEAM	LTOTEFF = 0.239 + 0.548LDEVTEAM			15.519	2.747	5.65 (p < 0.01)
LTEAMEXP	LTOTEFF = -0.585 + 0.372NLANG			13.036	2.805	4.647 (p < 0.01)

Copyright © 2008, IGI Global. Copying or distributing in print or electronic forms without written permission of IGI Global is prohibited.

their removal did not seem to destabilise the model; that is, after their removal the coefficients remained stable and the adjusted R^2 increased. Furthermore, there was no indication from the residual and P-P plots that the residuals were non-normal. The residuals resulting from the linear regression are used for the second cycle in the stepwise procedure.

Second Cycle

Table 14 shows the results of applying ANOVA to categorical and numerical variables. This is the second cycle in the stepwise procedure. The numerical variable LTOTHIGH is the most significant since it results in the smallest error term, represented by a within-groups mean square value of 1.118. The linear regression equation with the residual as the dependent or response variable and LTOTHIGH as the independent or predictor variable gives an adjusted R^2 of 0.228. This time five projects are identified with Cook's $D > 0.045$; however, their removal did not destabilise the model. In addition, the residual and P-P plots found no evidence of non-normality.

Table 14 also shows that TYPEPROJ, PROIMPR, METRICS, LTOTWP, NLANG, and LTEAMEXP have no further statistically significant effect on the residuals

Table 14. ANOVA for each categorical and numerical variable for second cycle

Variable	Levels	Mean	No. Projects	Between-Groups MS	Within-Groups MS	F Test Level of Significance
TYPEPROJ	New	-0.0181	39	0.023	1.466	0.016 (n.s.)
TYPEPROJ	Enhancement	0.0147	48			
DOCPROC	Yes	0.0385	64	0.359	1.462	0.246 (n.s.)
DOCPROC	No	-0.1072	23			
PROIMPR	Yes	-0.1654	59	5.017	1.407	3.565 (n.s.)
PROIMPR	No	0.3486	28			
METRICS	Yes	-0.2005	51	4.954	1.408	3.519 (n.s.)
METRICS	No	0.2840	36	0.023	1.466	0.016 (n.s.)
LTOTWP	LTOTEFF = -0.474 + 0.146LTOTWP			4.749	1.410	3.367 (n.s.)
LTOTIMG	LTOTEFF = -0.417 + 0.132LTOTIMG			6.169	1.394	4.427 (p = 0.038)
LIMGNEW	LTOTEFF = -0.33 + 0.184LIMGNEW			12.915	1.314	9.826 (p = 0.002)
LTOTHIGH	**LTOTEFF = -0.49 + 0.775LTOTHIGH**			**29.585**	**1.118**	**26.457 (p < 0.01)**
LTOTNHIG	LTOTEFF = -0.593 + 0.395LTOTNHIG			8.015	1.372	5.842 (p = 0.018)
NLANG	LTOTEFF = -0.896 + 0.274NLANG			1.931	1.413	1.366 (n.s.)
LDEVTEAM	LTOTEFF = -0.768 + 1.073LDEVTEAM			5.517	1.144	4.822 (p < 0.01)
LTEAMEXP	LTOTEFF = -0.157 + 0.144TEAMEXP			1.5	1.445	1.039 (n.s.)

Copyright © 2008, IGI Global. Copying or distributing in print or electronic forms without written permission of IGI Global is prohibited.

obtained in the previous cycle. Therefore, they can all be eliminated from the stepwise procedure. Once this cycle is complete, the remaining input variables are DOCPROC, LTOTIMG, LIMGNEW, LTOTNHIG, and LDEVTEAM.

Third Cycle

Table 15 shows the results of applying ANOVA to the five remaining categorical and numerical variables. This is the third cycle in the stepwise procedure.

The numerical variable LDEVTEAM is the most significant since it results in the smallest error term, represented by a within-groups mean square value of 1.002. The linear regression equation with the residual as the dependent or response variable and LDEVTEAM as the independent or predictor variable gives an adjusted R^2 of 0.101. This time, six projects are identified with Cook's $D > 0.045$; their removal destabilised the model and as such these six projects were removed from further analysis.

Table 15 also shows that LTOTIMG, LIMGNEW, and LTOTNHIGH have no further statistically significant effect on the residuals obtained in the previous cycle. Therefore, they can all be eliminated from the stepwise procedure.

Fourth Cycle

Table 16 shows the results of applying ANOVA to the remaining categorical variable. This is the fourth cycle in the stepwise procedure. DOCPROC has no statistically significant effect on the current residuals, and as such the procedure finishes.

Finally, our last step is to construct the effort model using a multivariate regression analysis with only the input variables selected using the manual stepwise procedure:

Table 15. ANOVA for each categorical and numerical variable for third cycle

Variable	Levels	Mean	No. Projects	Between-Groups MS	Within-Groups MS	F Test Level of Significance
DOCPROC	Yes	0.0097	64	0.023	1.118	0.021 (n.s.)
DOCPROC	No	-0.0272	23			
LTOTIMG	LTOTEFF = -0.109 + 0.034 LTOTIMG			0.419	1.113	0.376 (n.s.)
LIMGNEW	LTOTEFF = -0.162 + 0.091 LIMGNEW			3.126	1.081	2.89 (n.s.)
LTOTNHIG	LTOTEFF = -0.192 + 0.128 LTOTNHIG			0.837	1.108	0.755 (n.s.)
LDEVTEAM	**LTOTEFF = -0.464 + 0.648LDEVTEAM**			**2.477**	**1.002**	**2.472 (p = 0.030)**

Copyright © 2008, IGI Global. Copying or distributing in print or electronic forms without written permission of IGI Global is prohibited.

Table 16. ANOVA for categorical variable for fourth cycle

Variable	Levels	Mean	No. Projects	Between-Groups MS	Within-Groups MS	F Test Level of Significance
DOCPROC	Yes	-0.0745	59	0.109	0.735	0.148 (n.s.)
DOCPROC	No	0.0078	22			

Table 17. Coefficients for the effort model

Variable	Coeff.	Std. Error	t	P>|t|	[95% Conf. Interval]	
(Constant)	1.544	0.185	8.368	0.000	1.177	1.912
LNEWWP	0.523	0.056	9.270	0.000	0.411	0.635
LTOTHIGH	0.797	0.157	5.076	0.000	0.485	1.110
LDEVTEAM	0.860	0.201	4.274	0.000	0.460	1.260

Table 18. Four projects that presented high Cook's distance

ID	NEWWP	TOTHIGH	TOTEFF	Cook's
20	20	0	625	0.073
25	0	4	300	0.138
32	22	8	3150	0.116
45	280	0	800	0.078

LNEWWP, LTOTHIGH, and LDEVTEAM. The coefficients for the effort model are presented in Table 17. Its adjusted R^2 is 0.765, suggesting that LNEWWP, LTOTHIGH, and LDEVTEAM can explain 76.5% of the variation in LTOTEFF.

Four projects had Cook's $D > 0.045$ (see Table 18), and so we followed the procedure adopted previously. We repeated the regression analysis after excluding these four projects from the data set. Their removal did not result in any major changes to the model coefficients and the adjusted R^2 improved (0.820). Therefore, we assume that the regression equation is reasonably stable for this data set and it is not necessary to omit these four projects from the data set.

Figure 11 shows three different plots all related to residuals. The histogram suggests that the residuals are normally distributed, which is further corroborated by the P-P

Copyright © 2008, IGI Global. Copying or distributing in print or electronic forms without written permission of IGI Global is prohibited.

Figure 11. Several residual plots

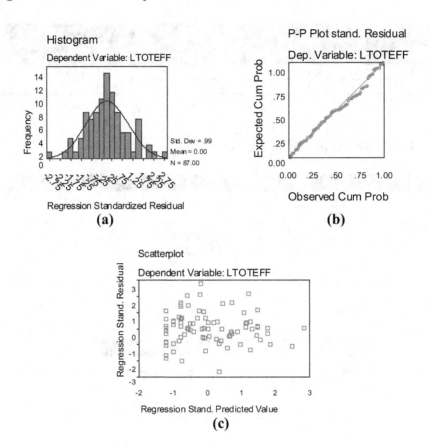

(a)

(b)

(c)

plot. In addition, the scatterplot of standardised residuals vs. standardised predicted values does not show any problematic patterns in the data.

Once the residuals and the stability of the regression model have been checked, we are in a position to extract the equation that represents the model.

Extraction of Effort Equation

The equation obtained from Table 16 is shown to be:

Copyright © 2008, IGI Global. Copying or distributing in print or electronic forms without written permission of IGI Global is prohibited.

$$LTOTEFF = 1.544 + 0.523LNEWWP + 0.797LTOTHIGH + 0.860LDEVTEAM$$

$$\text{(1)}$$

This equation uses three variables that had been previously transformed; therefore, we need to transform it back to its original state, which gives the following equation:

$$TOTEFF = 4.683\,(NEWWP+1)^{0.523}\,(TOTHIGH+1)^{0.797}\,(DEVTEAM)^{0.860}$$

$$\text{(2)}$$

In equation 2, the multiplicative value 4.683 can be interpreted as the effort required to develop a single Web page.

Obtaining a model that has a good fit to the data and alone can explain a large degree of the variation in the dependent variable is not enough to assume this model will provide good effort predictions for new projects. To confirm this, this model also needs to be validated. This is the procedure explained in the next section.

Model Validation

As described previously in Chapter III, to validate a model we need to do the following.

Step 1. Divide data set d into a training set t and a validation set v. Here we may use several training and validation sets; however, within the context of this chapter we will only employ a single training and validation set.

Step 2. Use t to produce an effort estimation model te (if applicable). Note that in this case study we have used a multivariate regression technique, which explicitly builds an effort model. However, there are other effort estimation techniques (e.g., case-based reasoning) that do not build an explicit effort model.

Step 3. Use te to predict effort for each of the projects in v as if these projects were new projects for which effort was unknown.

This process is known as cross-validation. For an n-fold cross-validation, n different training and validation sets are used. In this section, we will show the cross-validation procedure using a one-fold cross-validation, with a 66% split. This split means that 66% of our project data will be used for model building, and the remaining 34% will be used to validate the model; that is, the training set will have 66% of the total number of projects and the validation set will have the remaining 34%.

Copyright © 2008, IGI Global. Copying or distributing in print or electronic forms without written permission of IGI Global is prohibited.

Table 19. Coefficients for effort model using 58 projects

Variable	Coeff.	Std. Error	t	P>|t|	[95% Conf. Interval]	
(Constant)	2.392	0.268	8.908	0.000	1.853	2.930
LNEWWP	0.391	0.069	5.677	0.000	0.253	0.529
LTOTHIGH	0.714	0.157	4.549	0.000	0.399	1.029
LDEVTEAM	0.677	0.225	3.013	0.004	0.227	1.127

Our initial data set had 87 projects. At Step 1 they are split into training and valida-tion sets containing 58 and 29 projects respectively. Generally projects are selected randomly.

As part of Step 2, we need to create an effort model using the 58 projects in the training set. We will create an effort model that only considers the variables that have been previously selected and presented in equation 1. These are LNEWWP, LTOTHIGH, and LDEVTEAM. Here we do not perform the residual analysis or consider Cook's D since it is assumed these have also been done using the generic equation, equation 1. The model's coefficients are presented in Table 19, and the transformed equation is presented as equation 3. The adjusted R^2 is 0.668.

$$TOTEFF = 10.935\,(NEWWP + 1)^{0.391}\,(TOTHIGH + 1)^{0.714}\,(DEVTEAM)^{0.677}$$

$$(3)$$

To measure this model's prediction accuracy, we obtained the mean magnitude of relative error (MMRE), median magnitude of relative error (MdMRE), and predic-tion at 25% (Pred[25]) for the validation set. The model presented as equation 3 is applied to each of the 29 projects in the validation set to obtain estimated effort, and the MRE is computed. Having the calculated estimated effort and the actual effort (provided by the Web companies), we are finally in a position to calculate MRE for each of the 29 projects, and hence MMRE, MdMRE, and Pred(25) for the entire 29 projects. This process is explained in Figure 12.

Table 20 shows the measures of prediction accuracy, calculated from the validation set, assumed to represent the accuracy of the effort estimation model.

How do we know if the prediction obtained for our model is reasonable? Previous studies have suggested that a good prediction model should have an MMRE less than or equal to 25% and Pred(25) greater than or equal to 75% (Conte, Dun-smore, & Shen, 1986). If we consider these suggestions as standard baselines to be

Copyright © 2008, IGI Global. Copying or distributing in print or electronic forms without written permission of IGI Global is prohibited.

Figure 12. Steps used in the cross-validation process

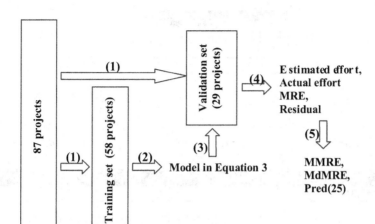

used when assessing effort prediction accuracy, then the values presented in Table 20 suggest that the accuracy of the effort model we built is poor.

However, other factors should also be taken into account. For example, if instead we were to use the average actual effort (average = 261) or the median actual effort for the 87 projects (median = 43) as the estimated effort for each of the projects in the validation set, then prediction accuracy would be considerably worse (see Table 21). This means that, although the accuracy obtained using MMRE, MdMRE, and Pred(25) is worse than the one prescribed in the literature, it would still be advantageous for a Web company to have used our effort model rather than to simply use as estimated effort the mean or median effort for past finished Web projects.

We suggest that a viable approach for a Web company would be to use the effort model described above to obtain an estimated effort, and adapt the obtained values, taking into account factors such as previous experience with similar projects and the skills of the developers. This means that the estimated effort provided by our model could still be calibrated to local circumstances, which would dictate the final estimate to be used for a new Web project.

Another issue that needs to be discussed relates to the cross-validation approach used. In this chapter we measured prediction accuracy based on a single validation set: a one-fold cross-validation (see Table 20). However, research on effort estimation suggests that to have unbiased results for a cross-validation, we should aggregate accuracy from 20 different training and validation sets (Kirsopp & Shepperd, 2001). This would represent for the data set presented here the selection of 20

Copyright © 2008, IGI Global. Copying or distributing in print or electronic forms without written permission of IGI Global is prohibited.

Table 20. Prediction accuracy measures using model-based estimated effort

Measure	%
MMRE	129
MdMRE	73
Pred(25)	17.24

Table 21. Prediction accuracy measures based on average and median effort

	Average Effort as Estimated Effort	Median Effort as Estimated Effort
MMRE	4314%	663%
MdMRE	1413%	149%
Pred(25)	6.89%	3.44%

different training and validation sets and the aggregation of the MMRE, MdMRE, and Pred(25) after the accuracy for all 20 groups has been calculated.

That claim has not yet been corroborated by other studies. In addition, a 20-fold cross-validation that is carried out manually is very time consuming, therefore we will not prescribe its use.

Conclusion

This chapter presented a case study that used data from industrial Web projects held in the Tukutuku database to construct and validate an effort estimation model. The size measures used in the case study represent early Web size measures obtained from the results of a survey investigation (Mendes et al., 2003) using data from 133 online Web forms aimed at giving quotes for Web development projects. In addition, the measures were validated by an established Web company and by a second survey involving 33 Web companies in New Zealand. Consequently, we believe that the size measures identified are plausible effort predictors, not an ad hoc set of variables with no underlying rationale.

Copyright © 2008, IGI Global. Copying or distributing in print or electronic forms without written permission of IGI Global is prohibited.

To build and validate an effort estimation model using multivariate regression we suggested Web companies to apply the following steps.

Data Validation

Data validation performs the first screening of the data that have been collected. It generally involves understanding what the variables are (e.g., their purpose, scale type) and also uses descriptive statistics (e.g., the mean, median, minimum, and maximum are used for numerical variables) to help identify any missing or unusual cases.

Variables and Model Selection

The second step in our data analysis methodology is subdivided into two separate and distinct phases: preliminary analysis and model building.

Preliminary analysis is used to create variables based on existing variables, discard unnecessary variables, and modify existing variables (e.g., joining categories). The net result of this phase is to obtain a set of variables that are ready to use in the next phase, model building. Model building is used to construct an effort estimation model based on our data set and variables. To build an effort model, we first apply a manual stepwise procedure (Kitchenham, 1998) to select only the variables that are strongly associated with effort. These variables are then used to build the effort model using multivariate regression.

Within the context of our case study, the three variables that were selected by the effort estimation model were the total number of new Web pages, the total number of high-effort features and functions in the application, and the size of a project's development team. Together they explained 76.5% of the variation in total effort. Note that the effort model constructed and the selected variables are applicable only to projects belonging to the data set from which they were built, or projects that are similar to those in the data set.

Model Inspection

This step is used to verify, at each stage of the stepwise process, the stability of the effort model. This involves identifying large-residual and high-influence data points (i.e., projects), and also checking if residuals are homoscedastic and normally distributed. Several types of plots (e.g., residual, leverage, probability) and statistics are available in most statistics tools to accomplish such a task.

Copyright © 2008, IGI Global. Copying or distributing in print or electronic forms without written permission of IGI Global is prohibited.

Extraction of Effort Equation

This step is used to extract an effort equation once the model has been built using multivariate regression.

Model Validation

This step uses a cross-validation mechanism to assess the prediction accuracy of an effort model. Cross-validation represents splitting the original data set into training and validation sets; the training set is then used to build an effort model, and the projects in the validation set are used to obtain effort estimates for each of the projects in this validation set, which once measured, are compared to their corresponding actual effort. The closer the estimated effort is to the actual effort, the better the prediction accuracy.

The case study presented in this chapter details the mechanism that can be used by any Web company to construct and validate its own effort estimation model. Alternatively, Web companies that do not have a data set of past projects may be able to benefit from the cross-company effort estimation models provided within the context of the Tukutuku project, provided they are willing to volunteer data on three of their past finished projects. Further details are provided in Chapter 9.

References

Conte, S. D., Dunsmore, H. E., & Shen, V. Y. (1986). *Software engineering metrics and models.* Benjamin-Cummins.

Kirsopp, C., & Shepperd, M. (2001). *Making inferences with small numbers of training sets* (Tech. Rep. No. TR02-01). Bournemouth, UK: Bournemouth University.

Kitchenham, B. A. (1998). A procedure for analyzing unbalanced datasets. *IEEE Transactions on Software Engineering, 24*(4), 278-301.

Kitchenham, B. A., MacDonell, S. G., Pickard, L. M., & Shepperd, M. J. (2001). What accuracy statistics really measure. *IEE Proceedings Software, 148*(3), 81-85.

Maxwell, K. (2002). *Applied statistics for software managers.* Englewood Cliffs, NJ: Prentice Hall PTR.

Copyright © 2008, IGI Global. Copying or distributing in print or electronic forms without written permission of IGI Global is prohibited.

Mendes, E., Mosley, N., & Counsell, S. (2003). Early Web size measures and effort prediction for Web costimation. *Proceedings of the IEEE Metrics Symposium* (pp. 18-29).

Mendes, E., Mosley, N., & Counsell, S. (2005). Investigating Web size metrics for early Web cost estimation. *Journal of Systems and Software, 77*(2), 157-172.

Copyright © 2008, IGI Global. Copying or distributing in print or electronic forms without written permission of IGI Global is prohibited.

Chapter VI

Web Effort Estimation Using Case-Based Reasoning

Abstract

Software practitioners recognise the importance of realistic effort estimates to the successful management of software projects, the Web being no exception. Having realistic estimates at an early stage in a project's life cycle allow project managers and development organisations to manage resources effectively. Several techniques have been proposed to date to help organisations estimate effort for new projects. One of these is a machine-learning technique called case-based reasoning. This chapter presents a case study that details step by step, using real data from completed industrial Web projects, how to obtain effort estimates using case-based reasoning, and how to assess the prediction accuracy of this technique. The reason to describe the use of case-based reasoning for effort estimation is motivated by its previous use with promising results in Web effort estimation studies.

Copyright © 2008, IGI Global. Copying or distributing in print or electronic forms without written permission of IGI Global is prohibited.

Introduction

The effort estimation technique described in this chapter is called case-based reasoning (CBR). This technique, proposed by the machine-learning community, uses the following claim as its basis: Similar problems provide similar solutions.

CBR provides effort estimates for new projects by comparing the characteristics of the current project to be estimated against a library of historical data from completed projects with known effort (case base). It involves the following (Angelis & Stamelos, 2000).

1. Characterising a new project p for which an effort estimate is required, with variables (features) common to those completed projects stored in the case base. In terms of Web and software effort estimation, features represent size measures and cost drivers, which have a bearing on effort. This means that if a Web company has stored data on past projects where, for example, the data represents the features effort, size, development team size, and tools used, the data used as input to obtaining an effort estimate will also need to include these same features.

2. Use of this characterisation as a basis for finding similar (analogous) completed projects for which effort is known. This process can be achieved by measuring the distance between two projects at a time (project p and one finished project) based on the features' values for all features (k) characterising these projects. Each finished project is compared to a project p, and the finished project presenting the shortest distance overall is the most similar project to project p. Although numerous techniques can be used to measure similarity, nearest-neighbour algorithms using the unweighted Euclidean distance measure have been the most widely used to date in Web and software engineering.

3. Generation of an effort estimate for project p based on the effort for those completed projects that are similar to p. The number of similar projects to take into account to obtain an effort estimate will depend on the size of the case base. For small case bases (e.g., up to 90 cases), typical values are to use the most similar finished project, the two most similar finished projects, or the three most similar finished projects (one, two, and three closest neighbours or analogues). For larger case bases, no conclusions have been reached to date regarding the best number of similar projects to use. There are several choices to calculate estimated effort, such as the following:

    a.   To use the same effort value as the closest neighbour.

    b.   To use the mean effort for the two or more closest neighbours.

    c.   To use the median effort for the two or more closest neighbours.

Copyright © 2008, IGI Global. Copying or distributing in print or electronic forms without written permission of IGI Global is prohibited.

d.   To use the inverse rank weighted mean, which allows higher ranked neighbours to have more influence than lower ones. For example, if we use three neighbours, the closest neighbour (*CN*) would have weight 3, the second closest (*SN*) weight 2, and the last one (*LN*) weight 1. The estimation would then be calculated as $(3CN + 2SN + LN)/6$. These are the common choices in Web and software engineering.

It is important to note that when using CBR for effort estimation, there are several parameters that need to be decided upon. However, existing literature on the use of CBR for Web and software effort estimation has not yet provided a consensus on what should be the best combination of parameters to provide the best effort predictions. Therefore, the choice of parameters will depend on what combination works best based on the available data being used. In addition, some parameters may not be available in the CBR tool being used by a Web company.

The six parameters that can have a bearing on the estimations obtained using CBR are as follows (Stensrud, Foss, Kitchenham, & Myrtveit, 2002):

- Feature subset selection
- Similarity measure
- Scaling
- Number of analogies
- Analogy adaptation
- Adaptation rules

Although these parameters have been previously presented in Chapter II, they will also be briefly described here since we do not assume that readers are already familiar with Chapter II.

Feature Subset Selection

Feature subset selection involves determining the optimum subset of features that yields the most accurate estimation. Some of the existing CBR tools optionally offer this functionality using a brute-force algorithm, which searches the solution domain for all possible feature subset combinations looking for the one that provides the best results. Other CBR tools offer no such functionality, and as such, to obtain estimated effort, we must use all of the known features of a new project to retrieve the most similar finished projects. For the purpose of this chapter, CBR-Works v4.2.1 was

Copyright © 2008, IGI Global. Copying or distributing in print or electronic forms without written permission of IGI Global is prohibited.

used, which does not offer the option to use a subset of features when looking for the most similar projects in the case base.

Similarity Measure

The similarity measure measures the level of likeness between different cases. Although several similarity measures have been proposed in the literature, the most popular similarity measures used in the most recent Web and software engineering literature (Angelis & Stamelos, 2000; Mendes, Mosley, & Counsell, 2003a; Stensrud et al., 2002) is the Euclidean distance. In terms of the use of the Euclidean distance, two different versions of this similarity measure have been used.

Unweighted Euclidean distance: The unweighted Euclidean distance measures the Euclidean (straight-line) distance d between two cases, where each case has n features. The equation used to calculate the distance between two cases x and y is the following:

$$d(x, y) = \sqrt{\left|x_0 - y_0\right|^2 + \left|x_1 - y_1\right|^2 + \ldots + \left|x_{n-1} - y_{n-1}\right|^2 + \left|x_n - y_n\right|^2}, \tag{1}$$

where

x_0 to x_n represent features 0 to n of case x and

y_0 to y_n represent features 0 to n of case y.

This measure has a geometrical meaning as the shortest distance between two points in an n-dimensional Euclidean space (Angelis & Stamelos, 2000). The number of features employed determines the number of dimensions, En.

If using the weighted Euclidean distance, then the closeness between projects is also taken into account. For example, if the distance between Projects 1 and 3 is smaller than the distance between Projects 1 and 2, Project 3 is considered more similar to Project 1 than Project 2.

Weighted Euclidean Distance: The weighted Euclidean distance is used when features are given weights that reflect their relative importance. The weighted Euclidean distance measures the Euclidean distance d between two cases x and y. Each case is assumed to have n features, and each feature has a weight

Copyright © 2008, IGI Global. Copying or distributing in print or electronic forms without written permission of IGI Global is prohibited.

w_n. The equation used to calculate the distance between two cases x and y is the following:

$$d(x, y) = \sqrt{w_0|x_0 - y_0|^2 + w_1|x_1 - y_1|^2 + \ldots + w_{n-1}|x_{n-1} - y_{n-1}|^2 + w_n|x_n - y_n|^2} \quad , (2)$$

where

x_0 to x_n represent features 0 to n of case x,

y_0 to y_n represent features 0 to n of case y, and

w_0 to w_n are the weights for features 0 to n.

Scaling

Scaling, which is also known as standardisation, represents the transformation of feature values according to a defined rule. This is done such that all features present values within the same range and as a consequence have the same degree of influence on the results (Angelis & Stamelos, 2000). A common method of scaling is to assign zero to the minimum observed value and one to the maximum observed value (Kitchenham, 1998). Original feature values are normally standardised (between 0 and 1) by case-based reasoning tools to guarantee that they all influence the results similarly. This approach is automatically done by the CBR tool we use in the case study described in this chapter.

Number of Analogies

The number of analogies represents the number of most similar cases that will be used to generate an effort estimate. With small sets of data, it is reasonable to consider only a small number of most similar analogues (Angelis & Stamelos, 2000). This is the approach employed in several studies in Web and software engineering. For example, Conte, Dunsmore, and Shen (1986) and Schroeder et al. (1998) used only the closest case or analogue ($k = 1$) to obtain an estimated effort for a new project. Other studies have also used the two or three closest analogues (Angelis & Stamelos, 2000; Kemerer, 1987; Kirsopp & Shepperd, 2001; Mendes et al., 2003a; Mendes, Mosley, & Counsell, 2003c; Myrtveit & Stensrud, 1999; Shepperd & Schofield, 1997); however no more than three closest analogues have been used in most studies.

Copyright © 2008, IGI Global. Copying or distributing in print or electronic forms without written permission of IGI Global is prohibited.

Analogy Adaptation

Once a similarity measure has been used to find the most similar cases, and these have been selected, the next step is to decide how to generate (adapt) an effort estimate for project P_{new}. Choices of analogy adaptation techniques presented in the literature vary from the nearest neighbour (Conte et al., 1986; Kirsopp & Shepperd, 2001), the mean of the closest analogues (Mendes, Watson, Triggs, Mosley, & Counsell, 2002b), the median of the closest analogues (Angelis & Stamelos, 2000), the inverse distance weighted mean, and inverse rank weighted mean (Mendes, Watson, et al., 2002), to illustrate just a few. The adaptations used to date for Web engineering are the nearest neighbour, mean of the closest analogues (Mendes, Counsell, & Mosley, 2000; Mendes, Mosley, & Counsell, 2001), and the inverse rank weighted mean (Mendes et al., 2003a; Mendes, Watson, et al., 2002). The nearest neighbour uses as the estimated effort for P_{new} the same effort of its closest analogue. The mean of the closest analogues uses as the estimated effort for P_{new} the average of its closest k analogues, when $k > 1$. This is a typical measure of central tendency, often used in the Web and software engineering literature. It treats all analogues as being equally important toward the outcome: the estimated effort. Finally, the inverse rank weighted mean allows higher ranked analogues to have more influence over the outcome than lower ones. For example, if we use three analogues, then the closest analogue (CA) would have weight 3, the second closest analogue (SC) would have weight 2, and the third closest analogue (LA) would have weight 1. The estimated effort would then be calculated as:

$$InverseRankWeighedMean = \frac{3CA + 2SC + LA}{6}.$$
(3)

Adaptation Rules

Adaptation rules are used to adapt the estimated effort according to a given criterion such that it reflects the characteristics of the target project, which is the new project for which an estimate is required, more closely. For example, within the context of effort prediction, it seems plausible that the estimated effort to develop an application be adapted such that it also takes into consideration the estimated size value of the application for which effort is to be estimated. The adaptation rule that has been employed to date in Web engineering is based on the linear size adjustment to the estimated effort (Mendes et al., 2003c). The linear size adjustment to the estimated effort is obtained as follows:

Copyright © 2008, IGI Global. Copying or distributing in print or electronic forms without written permission of IGI Global is prohibited.

- Once the most similar analogue in the case base has been retrieved, its effort value is adjusted and used as the effort estimate for the target project (new project).
- A linear extrapolation is performed along the dimension of a single measure, which is a size measure strongly correlated with effort. The linear size adjustment is calculated using the equation presented below.

$$Effort_{new\,Project} = \frac{Effort_{finished\,Project}}{Size_{finished\,Project}}\,Size_{new\,Project}$$

(4)

This type of adaptation assumes that all projects present similar productivity; however, this may not necessarily be representative of the Web development context of numerous Web companies worldwide.

In the case study that will be presented later in this chapter, we will use and compare different combinations of parameters in order to assess which combination provides the most accurate predictions given the data set being used.

Previous Studies that Used CBR for Web Cost Estimation

This section presents a survey of previous studies in Web engineering that have applied case-based reasoning for Web effort estimation. Each work is described and finally summarised in Table 1. Note that this is a subset of the complete survey that was presented in Chapter II. The reason for also including the CBR-related studies in this chapter is to make all chapters self-contained, and to avoid having any required reading.

First Study: Measurement and Effort Prediction for Web Applications

Mendes et al. (2000) investigated the use of case-based reasoning, linear regression, and stepwise regression techniques to estimate development effort for Web applications. The two data sets (HEL and LEL) employed had data on Web applications developed by second-year computer science students from the University of Southampton, United Kingdom, and had 29 and 41 data points respectively. HEL represented data from students with high experience in Web development, whereas

Copyright © 2008, IGI Global. Copying or distributing in print or electronic forms without written permission of IGI Global is prohibited.

LEL had data from inexperienced students. The size measures collected were as follows: page count, the total number of HTML (hypertext markup language) pages created from scratch; reused page count, the total number of reused HTML pages; connectivity, the total number of links in the application; compactness (Botafogo et al., 1992), the interconnectedness in an application on a scale from 1 (*no connections*) to 5 (*totally connected application*); stratum (Botafogo et al.), the level of linearity of an application on a scale from 1 (*no sequential navigation*) to 5 (*totally sequential navigation*); and structure, which represents the topology of the application's backbone, and can be either sequential, hierarchical, or network. The effort estimations were obtained using an existing freeware case-based reasoning tool, ANGEL, developed at the University of Bournemouth, United Kingdom. The most similar Web projects were retrieved using the unweighted Euclidean distance using the "leave one out" cross-validation. Estimated effort was generated using both the closest analogue and the mean of two and three analogues. Finally, prediction accuracy was measured using the mean magnitude of relative error (MMRE; Conte et al., 1986) and the median magnitude of relative error (MdMRE; Conte et al.). The effort estimates obtained using data on Web applications developed by the group with previous experience in Web development (HEL group) were statistically significantly superior to the estimates obtained using data on Web applications developed by the inexperienced group (LEL group). In addition, case-based reasoning showed the best results overall.

Second Study: The Application of Case-Based Reasoning to Early Web Project Cost Estimation

Mendes, Mosley, and Counsell (2002) harvested Web project data at different points in the Web development life cycle, and using a different set of size measures, compared their suitability as effort predictors and to find whether different size measures would lead to significantly different prediction accuracy. Their aim was to investigate if using early and late measures would make a difference in relation to the effort estimates obtained. Their rationale for this work was as follows.

Most work on Web effort estimation proposes models based on late product size measures, such as the number of HTML pages, number of images, and so forth. However, for the successful management of Web projects, estimates are necessary throughout the whole development life cycle. Preliminary (early) effort estimates in particular are essential when bidding for a contract or when determining a project's feasibility in terms of cost-benefit analysis.

Their effort estimates were obtained using case-based reasoning, where several different parameters were used: similarity measure, scaling, the number of closest analogues, analogy adaptation, and feature subset selection. Their study was based on data from 25 Web applications developed by pairs of postgraduate computer

Copyright © 2008, IGI Global. Copying or distributing in print or electronic forms without written permission of IGI Global is prohibited.

science students from the University of Auckland, New Zealand. The prediction accuracy measures employed were MMRE, MdMRE, prediction at the 25% level (Pred[25]), and boxplots of residuals. Contrary to the expected, late size measures did not show statistically significant better predictions than early size measures.

Third Study: A Comparison of Development Effort Estimation Techniques for Web Hypermedia Applications

Mendes, Watson, et al. (2002) present an in-depth comparison of Web cost estimation models. The steps they followed were as follows.

1. Compare the prediction accuracy of three CBR techniques to estimate the effort to develop Web applications

2. Compare the prediction accuracy of the best CBR technique, according to their findings in the previous step, against three commonly used effort prediction models, namely, multiple linear regression, stepwise regression, and regression trees.

The data set used in this investigation contained data on 37 Web applications developed by honours and postgraduate computer science students from the University of Auckland, New Zealand. The measures that were used in this investigation were the following.

- Page count: The number of HTML or SHTML files used in the Web application

- Media count: The number of media files used in the Web application

- Program count: The number of JavaScript files and Java applets used in the Web application

- Reused media count: The number of reused or modified media files used in the Web application

- Reused program count: The number of reused or modified programs used in the Web application

- Connectivity density: Computed as the total number of internal links divided by the page count

- Total page complexity: The average number of different types of media per Web page

Copyright © 2008, IGI Global. Copying or distributing in print or electronic forms without written permission of IGI Global is prohibited.

- Total effort: The effort in person hours to design and author a Web application

Note that only size measures were used as effort predictors. In addition, the authors did not use external links to other Web hypermedia applications; that is, all the links pointed to pages within the original application only. Regarding the use of case-based reasoning, they employed several parameters, detailed as follows:

- Three similarity measures (unweighted Euclidean, weighted Euclidean, and maximum)
- Three choices for the number of analogies (one, two, and three)
- Three choices for the analogy adaptation (mean, inverse rank weighted mean, and median)
- Two alternatives regarding the standardisation of the attributes (*Yes* for standardised and *No* for not standardised)

Prediction accuracy was measured using MMRE, MdMRE, Pred(25), and boxplots of residuals. Their results showed that different measures of prediction accuracy gave different results. MMRE and MdMRE showed better prediction accuracy for effort estimates obtained using multivariate regression models, whereas boxplots showed better effort estimation accuracy for CBR.

Fourth Study: Do Adaptation Rules Improve Web Cost Estimation?

Mendes et al. (2003a) compared several methods of CBR-based effort estimation in order to investigate the following.

1. Whether the use of adaptation rules was a contributing factor for better effort estimation accuracy
2. If the level of "messiness" of a data set would have an impact upon the accuracy of the effort estimates obtained

They used two data sets, where both contained data on Web applications developed by students at the University of Auckland, New Zealand. The difference between these data sets was the level of messiness each had. Messiness was evaluated by the

Copyright © 2008, IGI Global. Copying or distributing in print or electronic forms without written permission of IGI Global is prohibited.

number of outliers and the amount of collinearity (Shepperd & Kadoda, 2001). The data set that presented a smaller level of messiness than the other data set presented a continuous cost function, translated as a strong linear relationship between size and effort. The messiest data set, on the other hand, presented a discontinuous effort function, where there was no linear or log-linear relationship between size and effort. Two types of effort adaptation were used and compared: one with weights, the other without weights. Results showed that none of the adaptation rules provided superior predictions for the messier data set; however, for the less messy data set, one type of adaptation rule, the one using weights, presented good effort prediction accuracy. Prediction accuracy was measured using MMRE, Pred(25), and boxplots of absolute residuals.

Discussion

Table 1 summarises the studies presented above and indicates that in general the data sets used in these studies were relatively small, no greater than 41 data points.

The first study used only one distance measure to find the most similar projects and three analogy adaptations, which were the following:

1.   Estimated effort equal to the actual effort for the most similar project
2.   Estimated effort equal to the average actual effort for the two most similar projects
3.   Estimated effort equal to the average actual effort for the three most similar projects

The other three studies used much wider combinations of CBR parameters, containing different similarity measures, more than three analogy adaptations, and in one instance (Mendes et al., 2003a) adaptation rules based on the linear size adjustment to the estimated effort procedure. CBR does not always provide the best results when used in combination with other effort estimation techniques. In addition, another issue that must be considered is that data sets employed in all the studies were based on data from students' projects; thus, these results may not scale up to industrial practices.

Copyright © 2008, IGI Global. Copying or distributing in print or electronic forms without written permission of IGI Global is prohibited.

Table 1. Summary of literature in CBR for Web effort estimation

Study	Type (case study, experiment, survey)	# Data Sets (# data points)	Participants (students, professionals)	Size Measures	Prediction Techniques	Best Technique(s)	Measure Prediction Accuracy
1st	Case study	2 (29 and 41)	Second-year computer science students	Page count, reused page count, connectivity, compactness, stratum, structure	Case-based reasoning, linear regression, stepwise regression	Case-based reasoning for high-experience group	MMRE
2nd	Case study	1 (25)	Honours and postgraduate computer science students	Requirements and design measures, application measures	Case-based reasoning	-	MMRE, MdMRE, Pred(25), boxplots of residuals
3rd	Case study	1 (37)	Honours and postgraduate computer science students	Page count, media count, program count, reused media count, reused program count, connectivity density, total page complexity	Case-based reasoning, linear regression, stepwise regression, classification and regression trees	Linear/ stepwise regression or case-based reasoning (depends on the measure of accuracy employed)	MMRE, MdMRE, Pred(25), boxplots of residuals
4th	Case study	2 (37 and 25)	Honours and postgraduate computer science students	Page count, media count, program count, reused media count (only one data set), reused programcount (only one data set), connectivity density, total page complexity	Case-based reasoning	-	MMRE, Pred(25), boxplots of absolute residuals

Copyright © 2008, IGI Global. Copying or distributing in print or electronic forms without written permission of IGI Global is prohibited.

Case Study

The case study described in this chapter details the use of case-based reasoning to estimate effort and the validation of the prediction accuracy of this technique. It employs data on industrial Web projects, developed by Web companies worldwide, from the Tukutuku database (Mendes, Mosley, & Counsell, 2003b). Note that the raw data cannot be displayed here due to a confidentiality agreement with those companies that have volunteered data on their projects. This database is part of the ongoing Tukutuku project (http://www.cs.auckland.ac.nz/tukutuku), which collects data on Web projects to be used with effort estimation models and techniques, and to benchmark productivity across and within Web companies.

The data set used in this chapter contains data on 87 Web projects: 34 and 13 come from two single Web companies respectively and the remaining 40 projects come from another 23 companies. The Tukutuku database uses 6 variables to store specifics about each of the companies that volunteer data on their projects, 10 variables to store particulars about each project, and 13 variables to store data about each Web application (see Table 2). Company data are obtained only once and both project and application data are gathered for each volunteered project.

The results using CBR were obtained using a commercial case-based reasoning tool called CBR-Works version 4.2.1 from tec:inno. The statistical results presented here were obtained using the statistical software SPSS 12.0.1 for Windows from SPSS Inc. Further details on the statistical methods used throughout this case study are given in Chapter X. Finally, all the statistical tests set the significance level at 95% ($\alpha = 0.05$). Note that the different types of measurement scale are also detailed in Chapter X.

Before we use CBR-Works to obtain effort estimates, we still need to validate the data we are going to use, and also select the variables that should be used with CBR. Therefore validation and selection phases need to be conducted prior to using the CBR tool.

Data Validation

Data validation (DV) performs the first screening of the collected data. It generally involves understanding what the variables are (e.g., purpose, scale type; see Table 1) and also uses descriptive statistics (e.g., mean, median, minimum, maximum) to help identify any missing or unusual cases.

Table 3 presents summary statistics for numerical variables. Such statistics are obtained in SPSS by following these steps:

Copyright © 2008, IGI Global. Copying or distributing in print or electronic forms without written permission of IGI Global is prohibited.

Table 2. Variables for the Tukutuku database

NAME	SCALE	DESCRIPTION
COMPANY DATA		
COUNTRY	Categorical	Country company belongs to
ESTABLISHED	Ordinal	Year when company was established
SERVICES	Categorical	Type of services company provides
NPEOPLEWD	Absolute	Number of people who work on Web design and development
CLIENTIND	Categorical	Industry representative of those clients to whom applications are provided
ESTPRACT	Categorical	Accuracy of a company's own effort estimation practices
PROJECT DATA		
TYPEPROJ	Categorical	Type of project (new or enhancement)
LANGS	Categorical	Implementation languages used
DOCPROC	Categorical	If project followed defined and documented process
PROIMPR	Categorical	If project team was involved in a process improvement programme
METRICS	Categorical	If project team was part of a software metrics programme
DEVTEAM	Absolute	Size of project's development team
TEAMEXP	Absolute	Average team experience with the development language(s) employed
TOTEFF	Absolute	Actual total effort in person hours used to develop a Web application
ESTEFF	Absolute	Estimated total effort in person hours necessary to develop a Web application
ACCURACY	Categorical	Procedure used to record effort data
WEB APPLICATION		
TYPEAPP	Categorical	Type of Web application developed
TOTWP	Absolute	Total number of Web pages (new and reused)
NEWWP	Absolute	Total number of new Web pages
TOTIMG	Absolute	Total number of images (new and reused)
NEWIMG	Absolute	Total number of new images created
HEFFDEV	Absolute	Minimum number of hours to develop a single function/feature by one experienced developer that is considered to have high-level skill (above average). This number is currently set to 15 hours based on the collected data.
HEFFADPT	Absolute	Minimum number of hours to adapt a single function/feature by one experienced developer that is considered to have high-level skill (above average). This number is currently set to 4 hours based on the collected data.
HFOTS	Absolute	Number of reused high-effort features/functions without adaptation
HFOTSA	Absolute	Number of reused high-effort features/functions adapted
HNEW	Absolute	Number of new high-effort features/functions
FOTS	Absolute	Number of reused low-effort features without adaptation
FOTSA	Absolute	Number of reused low-effort features adapted
NEW	Absolute	Number of new low-effort features/functions

Copyright © 2008, IGI Global. Copying or distributing in print or electronic forms without written permission of IGI Global is prohibited.

- Select *Analyze* ⇨ *Descriptive Statistics* ⇨ *Frequencies*.
- Then click on the button *Statistics* and tick *mean, median, minimum, maximum,* and *Std. deviation*

The output generated by SPSS is similar to the one shown in Table 3.

Table 3 suggests that none of the numerical variables seem to exhibit unusual or missing values, although this requires careful examination. For example, one would find it strange to see zero as minimum value for total images (TOTIMG) or one as the minimum value for the total Web pages (TOTWP). However, it is possible to have either a Web application without any images or a Web application that provides all its content and functionality within a single Web page. Another example relates to the maximum number of Web pages, which is 2,000 Web pages. Although it does not seem possible at first to have such a large number of pages, we cannot simply assume this has been a data entry error. We were unable to obtain confirmation from the source company. However, further investigation revealed that 1,980 pages were developed from scratch, and numerous new functions and features (five high effort and seven low effort) were also implemented. In addition, the development team consisted of two people who had very little experience with the six programming languages used. The total effort was 947 person hours, which can correspond to a 3-month project assuming both developers worked at the same time. If we only

Table 3. Descriptive statistics for numerical variables

Variables	N	Missing	Minimum	Maximum	Mean	Median	Std. Dev.
DEVTEAM	87	0	1	8	2.37	2	1.35
TEAMEXP	87	0	1	10	3.40	2	1.93
TOTWP	87	0	1	2000	92.40	25	273.09
NEWWP	87	0	0	1980	82.92	7	262.98
TOTIMG	87	0	0	1820	122.54	40	284.48
NEWIMG	87	0	0	800	51.90	0	143.25
HEFFDEV	87	0	5	800	62.02	15	141.25
HEFFADPT	87	0	0	200	10.61	4	28.48
HFOTS	87	0	0	3	.08	0	.41
HFOTSA	87	0	0	4	.29	0	.75
HNEW	87	0	0	10	1.24	0	2.35
FOTS	87	0	0	15	1.07	0	2.57
FOTSA	87	0	0	10	1.89	1	2.41
NEW	87	0	0	13	1.87	0	2.84
TOTEFF	87	0	1	5000	261.73	43	670.36
ESTEFF	34	53	1	108	14.45	7.08	20.61

Copyright © 2008, IGI Global. Copying or distributing in print or electronic forms without written permission of IGI Global is prohibited.

consider the number of pages and effort, the ratio of number of minutes per page is 27:1, which seems reasonable given the lack of experience of the development team and the number of different languages they had to use.

Once we have checked the numerical variables, our next step is to check the categorical variables using their frequency tables as a tool (see Tables 4 to 8). To display frequency tables using SPSS, follow these steps:

- Select *Analyze* ⇨ *Descriptive Statistics* ⇨ *Frequencies*.
- Tick *Display Frequency Tables*.

Tables 4 to 7 show that most projects followed a defined and documented process, and that development teams were involved in a process improvement program and/or were part of a software metrics programme. These positive trends are mainly due to the two single companies that together volunteered data on 47 projects (54% of our data set). They have answered "yes" to all three categories. No unusual trends seem to exist.

Table 8 shows that the majority of projects (83%) had the actual effort recorded on a daily basis for each project and/or project task. These numbers are inflated by the two single companies where one chose the category *Good* (11 projects) and the other chose the category *Very Good* (34 projects). The actual effort recording procedure

Table 4. Frequency table for type of project

Type of Project	Frequency	%	Cumulative %
New	39	44.8	44.8
Enhancement	48	55.2	100.0
Total	87	100.0	

Table 5. Frequency table for documented process

Documented Process	Frequency	%	Cumulative %
No	23	26.4	26.4
Yes	64	73.6	100.0
Total	87	100.0	

Copyright © 2008, IGI Global. Copying or distributing in print or electronic forms without written permission of IGI Global is prohibited.

Table 6. Frequency table for process improvement

Process Improvement	Frequency	%	Cumulative %
No	28	32.2	32.2
Yes	59	67.8	100.0
Total	87	100.0	

Table 7. Frequency table for metrics programme

Metrics Programme	Frequency	%	Cumulative %
No	36	41.4	41.4
Yes	51	58.6	100.0
Total	87	100.0	

Table 8. Frequency table for companies' effort recording procedure

Actual Effort Recording Procedure	Frequency	%	Cumulative %
Poor	12	13.8	13.8
Medium	3	3.4	17.2
Good	24	27.6	44.8
Very good	48	55.2	100
Total	87	100.0	

is not an adequate effort estimator per se, being used here simply to show that the effort data gathered seem to be reliable overall.

Once the data validation is complete, we are ready to move on to the next step, namely, variables selection.

Variables Selection

This phase is used to create new variables based on existing variables, discard unnecessary variables, and modify existing variables (e.g., joining categories). The

Copyright © 2008, IGI Global. Copying or distributing in print or electronic forms without written permission of IGI Global is prohibited.

net result of this phase is to obtain a set of variables that are ready to use in the next phase, obtaining effort estimates.

This phase is extremely important given that the CBR tool we use does not provide the feature subset selection parameter option.

The first task within this phase is to examine the entire set of variables and check if there are any variables that have a significant amount of missing values (> 60%). If there are, they should be automatically discarded as they prohibit the use of imputation methods and will further prevent the identification of useful trends in the data. (Imputation methods are methods used to replace missing values with estimated values.) Table 2 shows that only ESTEFF presented missing values greater than 60%. ESTEFF was gathered to give an idea of each company's own prediction accuracy; however, it will not be included in our analysis since it is not an effort predictor per se. Note that a large number of zero values on certain size variables do not represent missing or rounded values.

The Tukutuku database uses six variables to record the number of features or functions for each application. They all had a large number of zeros, reducing their contribution to finding the most similar projects. We therefore decided to group them into two new variables: TOTHIGH (summation of HFOTS, HFOTSA, and HNEW) and TOTNHIGH (summation of FOTS, FOTSA, and NEW). We also created a variable called NLANG, representing the number of different implementation languages used per project, replacing the original multivalued variable that stored the names of the different implementation languages.

The last part of the variables selection phase is to identify which variables are significantly associated with effort. This step is carried out in order to simulate the features subset selection parameter.

In order to measure the level of association between numerical variables and effort, we used a statistical test to confirm if the numerical variables were normally distributed. This statistical test is called the one-sample Kolmogorov-Smirnov test (K-S test). It compares an observed distribution to a theoretical distribution. Significance values equal to, or smaller than, 0.05 indicate that the observed distribution differs from the theoretical distribution.

To use the one-sample Kolmogorov-Smirnov test in SPSS, we suggest you follow these steps:

- Select *Analyze* ⇨ *Nonparametric tests* ⇨ *1-Sample K-S*
- Then click the test distribution *Normal* and select on the left list all the variables to be checked. Once selected, click the arrow button to show them as part of the test variable list.

Copyright © 2008, IGI Global. Copying or distributing in print or electronic forms without written permission of IGI Global is prohibited.

We employed the K-S test and found that none of the numerical variables had distributions that matched the normal distribution. This suggests that a nonparametric test needs to be used to measure the level of association between numerical variables and effort. The test used was the Spearman's correlation test. It calculates Spearman's rho, r_s, which measures the strength and the direction of the relationship between two variables that were measured on an ordinal scale. It is also the technique of choice whenever interval, ratio, and absolute variables are not normally distributed and are part of a small data sample.

To obtain Spearman's correlation coefficient in SPSS, follow the steps outlined here:

- Select *Analyze* ⇨ *Correlate* ⇨ *Bivariate*.
- Select the two variables from the list on the left whose association you want to measure and click on the arrow button to have them moved to the box labeled *Variables*.
- Tick the option *Spearman* in the group labeled *Correlation Coefficients*.
- Tick the option *Two-tailed* in the group labeled *Test of Significance*.
- Optionally, tick the option *Flag significant correlations*.

Here again, the choice of a two-tailed test of significance depends on whether or not you know in advance the direction of the association. If you do not know the direction, you should use a two-tailed test of significance; otherwise, you should use a one-tailed test of significance.

The results obtained using SPSS for the Tukutuku data are shown in Table 9. Spearman's correlation test shows the correlation coefficients taking into account all the possible combinations of variables. Since we used 14 variables, results show 14x14 correlation coefficients. A correlation coefficient between a variable and itself is always equal to 1 since this represents a perfect linear association.

Table 9 shows that 12 attributes are significantly associated (correlated) with effort. Significant correlations are highlighted via the use of one or two asterisks, which flag a statistically significant correlation. These 12 attributes are the following: typeproj, nlang, proimprn, metricsn, devteam, teamexp, totwp, newwp, totimg, imgnew, tothigh, and totnhigh. These will be the attributes that we will use with the CBR tool to obtain effort estimates.

Copyright © 2008, IGI Global. Copying or distributing in print or electronic forms without written permission of IGI Global is prohibited.

Table 9. Spearman's correlation test results in SPSS

		toteff	typeproj	nlang	docpron	proimprn	metricsn	devteam	teamexp	totwp	newwp	toting	imgnew	tothigh	totnhigh
toteff	Correlation Coefficient	1.000	.438(**)	.282(**)	.083	.332(**)	.463(**)	.507(**)	.333(**)	.705(**)	.781(**)	.551(**)	.566(**)	.628(**)	.311(**)
	Sig. (two-tailed)	.	.000	.008	.447	.002	.000	.000	.002	.000	.000	.000	.000	.000	.003
typeproj	Correlation Coefficient	.438(**)	1.000	-.001	.298(**)	.220(*)	.275(**)	.145	.497(**)	.183	.598(**)	.251(*)	.294(**)	-.030	-.081
	Sig. (two-tailed)	.000	.	.996	.005	.041	.010	.180	.000	.089	.000	.019	.006	.781	.456
nlang	Correlation Coefficient	.282(**)	-.001	1.000	.177	.387(**)	.306(**)	.131	.308(**)	.119	.164	.252(*)	.340(**)	.415(**)	.229(*)
	Sig. (two-tailed)	.008	.996	.	.102	.000	.004	.226	.004	.273	.130	.019	.001	.000	.033
docpron	Correlation Coefficient	.083	.298(**)	.177	1.000	.647(**)	.502(**)	-.209	.422(**)	-.025	.130	.077	.252(*)	-.120	.115
	Sig. (two-tailed)	.447	.005	.102	.	.000	.000	.052	.000	.819	.190	.476	.019	.268	.288
proimprn	Correlation Coefficient	.332(**)	.220(*)	.387(**)	.647(**)	1.000	.770(**)	-.168	.369(**)	.130	.286(**)	.209	.388(**)	.149	.206
	Sig. (two-tailed)	.002	.041	.000	.000	.	.000	.120	.000	.231	.078	.052	.000	.169	.056
metricsn	Correlation Coefficient	.463(**)	.275(**)	.306(**)	.502(**)	.770(**)	1.000	-.081	.419(**)	.221(*)	.416(**)	.340(**)	.476(**)	.207	.287(**)
	Sig. (two-tailed)	.000	.010	.004	.000	.000	.	.457	.000	.039	.000	.001	.000	.207	.007
devteam	Correlation Coefficient	.507(**)	.145	.131	-.209	-.168	-.081	1.000	.115	.361(**)	.280(**)	.232(*)	.355(**)	.360(**)	.062
	Sig. (two-tailed)	.000	.180	.226	.052	.120	.457	.	.288	.001	.009	.031	.001	.001	.571
teamexp	Correlation Coefficient	.333(**)	.497(**)	.308(**)	.422(**)	.369(**)	.419(**)	.115	1.000	.141	.392(**)	.452(**)	.461(**)	.132	.213(*)
	Sig. (two-tailed)	.002	.000	.004	.000	.000	.000	.288	.	.191	.000	.000	.000	.221	.132
totwp	Correlation Coefficient	.705(**)	.183	.119	-.025	.130	.221(*)	.361(**)	.141	1.000	.692(**)	.498(**)	.339(**)	.478(**)	.489(**)
	Sig. (two-tailed)	.000	.089	.273	.819	.231	.039	.001	.191	.	.000	.000	.001	.000	.000

**Correlation is significant at the 0.01 level (two-tailed)
*Correlation is significant at the 0.05 level (two-tailed)

Copyright © 2008, IGI Global. Copying or distributing in print or electronic forms without written permission of IGI Global is prohibited.

Table 9. continued

		toteff	typeproj	nlang	docpron	proimprm	metricsn	devteam	teamexp	totwp	newwp	totimg	imgnew	tothigh	totnhigh
newwp	Correlation Coefficient	.781(**)	.598(**)	.164	.190	.286(**)	.416(**)	.280(**)	.392(**)	.692(**)	1.000	.484(**)	.435(**)	.423(**)	.172
	Sig. (two-tailed)	.000	.000	.130	.078	.007	.000	.009	.000	.000	.	.000	.000	.000	.111
totimg	Correlation Coefficient	.551(**)	.251(*)	.252(*)	.077	.209	.340(**)	.232(*)	.452(**)	.498(**)	.484(**)	1.000	.680(**)	.332(**)	.319(**)
	Sig. (two-tailed)	.000	.019	.019	.476	.052	.001	.031	.000	.000	.000	.	.000	.002	.003
imgnew	Correlation Coefficient	.566(**)	.294(**)	.340(**)	.252(*)	.388(**)	.476(**)	.355(**)	.461(**)	.339(**)	.435(**)	.680(**)	1.000	.272(*)	.123
	Sig. (two-tailed)	.000	.006	.001	.019	.000	.000	.001	.000	.001	.000	.000	.	.011	.258
tothigh	Correlation Coefficient	.628(**)	-.030	.415(**)	-.120	.149	.207	.360(**)	.132	.478(**)	.423(**)	.332(**)	.272(*)	1.000	.353(**)
	Sig. (two-tailed)	.000	.781	.000	.268	.169	.055	.001	.221	.000	.000	.002	.011	.	.001
totnhigh	Correlation Coefficient	.311(**)	-.081	.229(*)	.115	.206	.287(**)	.062	.213(*)	.489(**)	.172	.319(**)	.123	.353(**)	1.000
	Sig. (two-tailed)	.003	.456	.033	.288	.056	.007	.571	.048	.000	.111	.003	.258	.001	.

**Correlation is significant at the 0.01 level (two-tailed)
*Correlation is significant at the 0.05 level (two-tailed)

Copyright © 2008, IGI Global. Copying or distributing in print or electronic forms without written permission of IGI Global is prohibited.

Obtaining Effort Estimates

This section describes the use of CBR-Works to obtain effort estimates for the Web projects from the Tukutuku database. The first step of this process is to store the project data on the CBR-Works case base. This can be accomplished by manually entering data on each project, or by importing data from an existing database. The Tukutuku database was already stored in an MS Access database, so the steps we will use assume the data are already stored on a database file. Please note that if your data are stored on an MS Excel file, it can readily be converted into an MS Access database. Just make sure that all the fields in your Excel file are of the same type before importing your data into MS Access.

Please note that we are providing as much detail as possible on how to use a CBR tool because it is our belief that the functionality offered by CBR tools will be similar to the functionality offered by CBR-Works and therefore the knowledge of how to use one CBR tool may be useful and readily applicable when using a CBR tool other than CBR-Works.

Connecting CBR-Works to a Database

The first step is to enable CBR-Works to connect to the MS Access database that contains the data using an ODBC driver. To do this, you need to create a new data source by following these steps:

1. Using the *Start* button on your computer, open the Control Panel and click on the icon *Administrative Tools*, then on the icon *Data Sources (ODBC)*. A dialog screen will open (see Figure 1). Select the tab labeled *User DSN*.

2. Click the *Add* button in order to add a new data source. This will immediately open another dialog screen (see Figure 2) where you need to select the type of driver to be associated with the new data source. In the context of this case study, the driver we selected was a Microsoft Access driver (*.mdb). When you click the button labeled *Finish*, this dialog screen will be replaced by another (see Figure 3), which is to be used to type the name of the data source (to be used in CBR-Works) in the *Data Source Name* text field, and to provide the location of the MS Access database file by pressing the button *Select*. The name of the data source used in our example is *tukutuku new* (see Figure 3).

Once a new data source has been created and associated to the database file to be used within CBR-Works, our next step is to configure CBR-Works to connect to that database file and to use its data and field descriptions as a case base. The explanations

Copyright © 2008, IGI Global. Copying or distributing in print or electronic forms without written permission of IGI Global is prohibited.

Figure 1. ODBC data source administrator screen

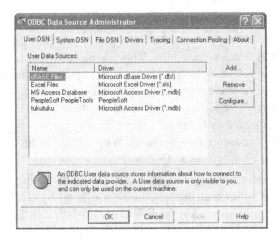

Figure 2. Creating a new data source

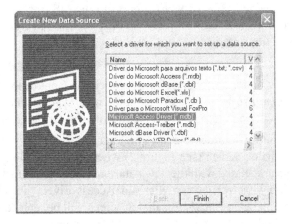

on how to create a new data source and connect from CBR-Works to a database are also available from the CBR-Works as well as additional documentation on using CBR-Works with databases. Here we present a compact version only.

Copyright © 2008, IGI Global. Copying or distributing in print or electronic forms without written permission of IGI Global is prohibited.

Figure 3. ODBC MS Access setup dialog

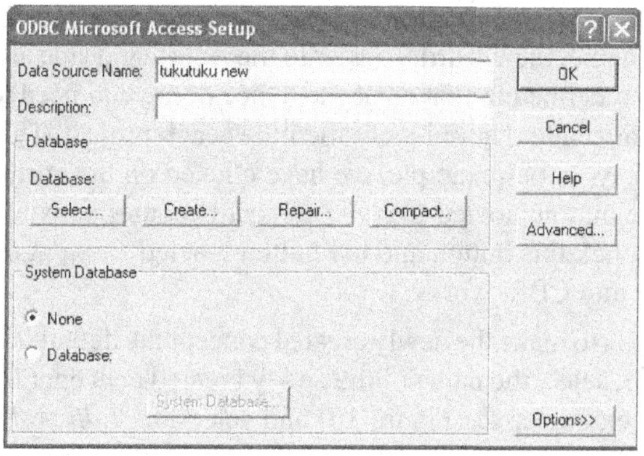

Connecting CBR-Works to a Database to Import Data and Metadata

In order to connect CBR-Works to the database, we followed the steps below.

1. Create a new domain in CBR-Works using the *File* ⇨ *New* option.

2. Select the *File* ⇨ *Preferences* ⇨ *Database* option. A database options dialog will open, and you need to type the name of the data source that has been previously created in the *Data Source* text field. In our example, the data source name is *tukutuku new*. When you click *OK*, if you do not get an error message, this means that CBR-Works is connected to the database you have specified.

3. The next step is to import the data types from the database into CBR-Works' domain model. To do so you need to first click the *Type* icon (see Figure 5).

4. Select the *Edit* ⇨ *Create Type from Database* option. A wizard dialog screen will open (see Figure 6) allowing you to select the name of the table from where you obtain your attributes, the column name associated to the attribute of interest, and its data type. You will need to repeat Steps 3 and 4 until you have selected all the table columns of interest, and have associated them to CBR-Works' attributes.

5. Once finished, you move onto the next step, which is to import the database metadata into CBR-Works. You need to click first the icon *Concepts* (see Figure 7).

Copyright © 2008, IGI Global. Copying or distributing in print or electronic forms without written permission of IGI Global is prohibited.

6. Select the *Edit* ⇨ *Create Concepts from Database* option. A concept wizard dialog screen will open (see Figure 8), showing on the left-hand side the name of the database (*tukutuku eighty seven* in our example). When you click on the database name, the wizard loads onto the right-hand side all the attributes that have been defined in that database. Once done, you need to click on the name of the attribute that uniquely identifies each project. This is known as the primary key. In our example, we have clicked on the attribute *ID*. When complete, the button labeled *Create Concept* becomes active (see Figure 9). You need to click this button and the button labeled *Done* in order to import the metadata into CBR-Works.

7. The next step is to make the newly created concept the default case concept. In order to do so, select the name of the newly created concept (*Tukutuku eighty seven* in our example; see Figure 10) and select the *Edit* ⇨ *Define as Case* option. The folder associated with the new case *Tukutuku eighty seven* is now open and also has an arrow on it (see Figure 11). This means that *Tukutuku eighty seven* is now the case concept. Once this step has been completed, the next part of the process is to associate the data types you have imported from the database to the attributes that have also been imported from the same database. Figure 12 shows the list of attributes that have been imported and the default data types that have been associated with each. So, for example, for the attribute labeled *devteam*, its default data type is *Real*. When you click on the pull-down menu associated with this data type, a list of data types is displayed in alphabetical order. You then select the data type that corresponds to the attribute's correct data type. In our example, we selected the data type *Devteam* to be associated with the attribute *devteam* (see Figure 13). This step needs to be repeated for each of the attributes that have been imported.

8. The next step is to import the data from the database into the CBR-Works case base. You need to first click the case base icon (see Figure 14) and select the name of the case base, which in this example would be *Tukutuku eighty seven*, and then select the *Edit* ⇨ *Add Cases from DB* option. A wizard automatically opens (see Figure 15) and you need to select the attribute that represents the primary key for your data. In our example, this attribute is *ID*. Click the *OK* button. All data are automatically loaded and uniquely identified using the original primary key values (see Figure 16). So, in our example, the *ID* attribute has values ranging from 1 to 87; therefore, these are the values that are associated with each individual case.

9. Finally, save the case base by clicking on the icon *Save*, or by selecting the *File* ⇨ *Save* option. This will open a dialog screen for you to select the location of where the case based is to be saved to.

Copyright © 2008, IGI Global. Copying or distributing in print or electronic forms without written permission of IGI Global is prohibited.

Figure 4. Database options dialog

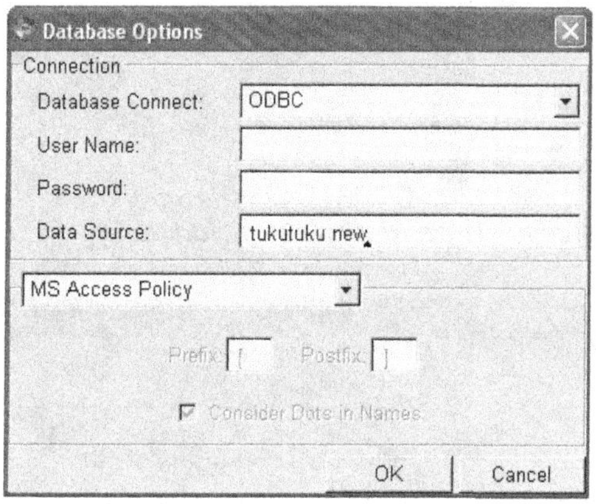

Figure 5. Type icon

Figure 6. Type wizard dialog screen

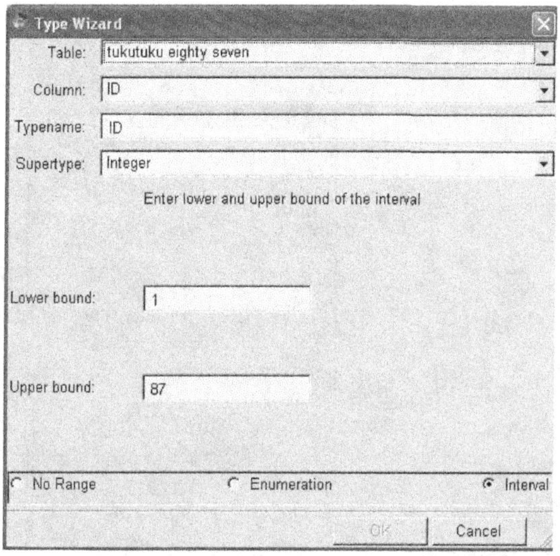

Copyright © 2008, IGI Global. Copying or distributing in print or electronic forms without written permission of IGI Global is prohibited.

Figure 7. Concepts icon

Figure 8. Using the concept wizard to load the metadata

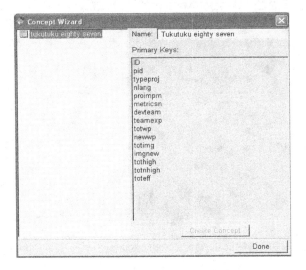

Figure 9. Using the concept wizard to select the primary key and create a new concept

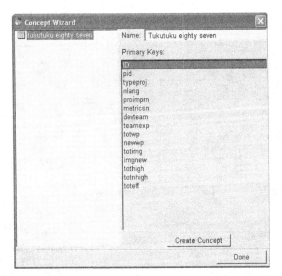

Copyright © 2008, IGI Global. Copying or distributing in print or electronic forms without written permission of IGI Global is prohibited.

Figure 10. Selecting the new concept to be the default case concept

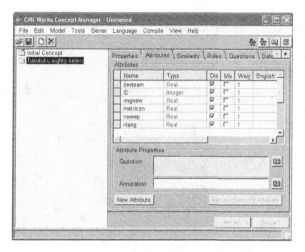

Figure 11. The default case concept

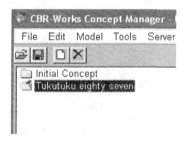

Figure 12. Associating types to attributes

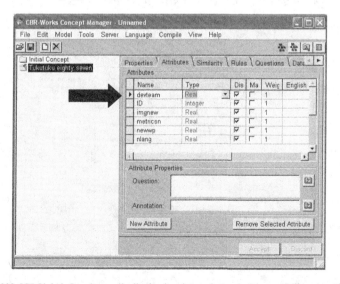

Copyright © 2008, IGI Global. Copying or distributing in print or electronic forms without written permission of IGI Global is prohibited.

Figure 13. Associating data type Devteam to attribute devteam

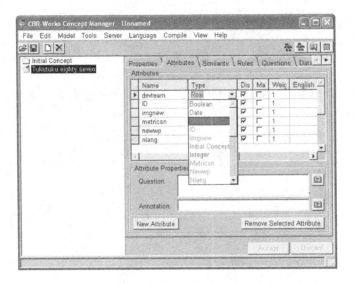

Figure 14. Case base icon

Figure 15. Importing cases from a database into the case base

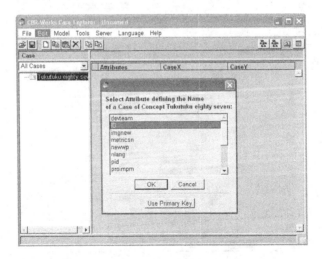

Copyright © 2008, IGI Global. Copying or distributing in print or electronic forms without written permission of IGI Global is prohibited.

Figure 16. Imported cases identified using values from the ID attribute

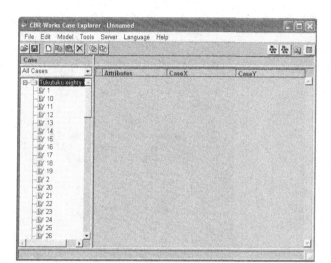

Once the data have been loaded, we need to choose some of the parameters using CBR-Works, and then obtain estimated effort for each of the projects in the case base.

Using CBR-Works to Obtain Effort Estimates

To choose the similarity measure to be used to retrieve the most similar cases to the case being estimated, you need to click the *Concepts* icon (see Figure 7) and the tab labeled *Similarity* (see Figure 17). There are several similarity measures already implemented in CBR-Works, and they can also be defined by the user. The similarity measure that we will use in our example is the Euclidean distance (*Euclidean* in Figure 17). You will then need to click the button labeled *Accept*. You can also assign different weights to attributes using the tab labeled *Attributes*; however, in this example we will assume that all attributes have the same influence over effort, thus their weights are all the same (e.g., 1).

CBR-Works does not automatically provide an estimated effort for a project that has been defined as new. What it does do is provide us with a list of the most similar projects to that new project, and then we have to decide how to obtain the estimated effort. Remember that when using CBR we are not building a model such as the equations that are obtained using multivariate regression analysis (see Chapter 5). As already stated, in this chapter our objective is to obtain estimated effort for each

Copyright © 2008, IGI Global. Copying or distributing in print or electronic forms without written permission of IGI Global is prohibited.

Figure 17. Choosing a similarity measure

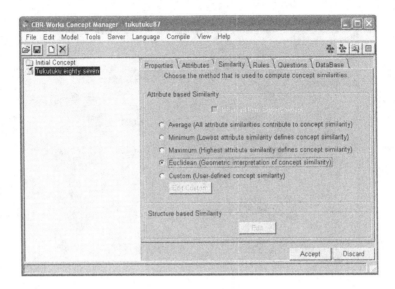

one of the 87 Web projects in the case base. This means that for each project p_i, one at a time, we will use the remaining 86 projects to find the most similar projects to p_i (where i is 1 to 87). Estimated effort will be calculated using the same effort as the most similar project to p_i, and the average effort for the two and three most similar projects to p_i. Other parameters can be used as well (e.g., the inverse rank weighted mean). In addition, we will not employ adaptation rules in our example. Therefore, in terms of the six parameters that need to be configured when using CBR, our example will employ the following configurations.

- Feature subset selection: This parameter is not available in the CBR tool we use, therefore we decided to only use the attributes that have shown significant association with effort.

- Similarity measure: This is the similarity measure to be used is the Euclidean distance.

- Scaling: CBR-Works automatically scales all attributes to have values between 0 and 1.

- Number of analogies: We use one, two, and three analogies in our example.

Copyright © 2008, IGI Global. Copying or distributing in print or electronic forms without written permission of IGI Global is prohibited.

- Analogy adaptation: The analogy adaptations used in our example are the use of the estimated effort equal to the one of the closest analogy, and estimated effort corresponding to the average of the closest two and three analogies.

- Adaptation rules: Adaptation rules will not be used in this example.

To obtain the most similar projects to project p_i (where i is from 1 to 87), we need to follow these steps:

1. Click the case base icon (see Figure 14), and select the project on the list displayed on the left-hand side in which the most similar projects in the case base are to be found. We will show this step for project ID = 1, however this step has to be repeated 87 times, once for each different project in the case base.

2. Click on the project identified as 1.

3. Select the *Edit ⇨ Case Mode ⇨ Unconfirmed* option. By doing so, you are telling the CBR tool's engine that project ID = 1 is not to be used when looking for the most similar projects. Once done, the icon for project ID = 1 will change to a question mark (see Figure 18).

4. Select the *Edit ⇨ Case as Query* option. In so doing, so you are telling the CBR tool's engine that project ID = 1 is the new project for which the most similar projects need to be found.

5. Click the *Case navigator* icon (see Figure 19), which will take you to the case navigator screen. Then click the *search* facility, used to find the most similar cases, represented by a pair of binoculars (see Figure 20).

6. Once the binoculars icon is clicked, CBR-Works automatically displays in a column from left to right, in descending order or similarity (high to low), the cases that are most similar to the target case. Figure 21 shows that the most similar case to Case 1 (ID = 1) is Case 5, followed by Case 11. As we click the forward icon more cases are shown, one by one. For the project ID = 1, the three most similar cases are Cases 5, 11, and 3.

Once this information is recorded elsewhere, for example, on a spreadsheet, it is time to change the project that was labeled as *Unconfirmed* to *Confirmed,* and to move on to the next project, which will be changed from *Confirmed* to *Unconfirmed.* The table resulting from our 87 Web projects from the Tukutuku database is shown as Table 10.

Copyright © 2008, IGI Global. Copying or distributing in print or electronic forms without written permission of IGI Global is prohibited.

Figure 18. Labeling a project as unconfirmed

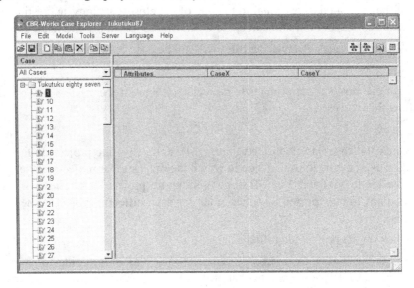

Figure 19. Case navigator icon

Figure 20. Find the most similar cases

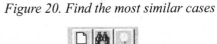

Figure 21. Most similar cases to Case 1

Attributes	1	5	11
devteam	4	3	5
ID	1	6	11
imgnew	0	0	76
metricsn	1		1
newwp	125	130	120
nlang	3	3	3
pid	1.0	50	11.0
proimpm	1	1	1
teamexp	5	5	5
toteff	340	410	100
tothigh	2	3	0
totimg	168	0	76
totnhigh	7	2	5
totwp	125	130	120
typepro		1	1

Number of Cases found (max, 10): 10 | **Similarity:** 0.95 | **Similarity:** 0.944

Starts the retrieval process.

Copyright © 2008, IGI Global. Copying or distributing in print or electronic forms without written permission of IGI Global is prohibited.

Table 10. Results from using CBR on 87 Web projects

Case ID	Actual Effort	Case A1	Effort A1	Case A2	Effort A2	Case A3	Effort A3	Est. Effort A1	MRE	Pred.	Est. Effort A1-A2	MRE	Pred.	Est. Effort A1-A3	MRE	Pred.
1	340	5	410	11	100	3	75	410	0.21	TRUE	255	0.25	TRUE	195.00	0.43	FALSE
2	300	5	410	3	75	66	8.15	410	0.37	FALSE	242.5	0.19	TRUE	164.38	0.45	FALSE
3	75	12	50	4	24	62	5.3	50	0.33	FALSE	37	0.51	FALSE	26.43	0.65	FALSE
4	24	8	21	3	75	12	50	21	0.13	TRUE	48	1.00	FALSE	48.67	1.03	FALSE
5	410	1	340	3	75	2	300	340	0.17	TRUE	207.5	0.49	FALSE	238.33	0.42	FALSE
6	40	7	130	12	50	3	75	130	2.25	FALSE	90	1.25	FALSE	85.00	1.13	FALSE
7	130	12	50	6	40	3	75	50	0.62	FALSE	45	0.65	FALSE	55.00	0.58	FALSE
8	21	4	24	3	75	12	50	24	0.14	TRUE	49.5	1.36	FALSE	49.67	1.37	FALSE
9	1786	11	100	7	130	5	410	100	0.94	FALSE	115	0.94	FALSE	213.33	0.88	FALSE
10	900	5	410	2	300	7	130	410	0.54	FALSE	355	0.61	FALSE	280.00	0.69	FALSE
11	100	1	340	5	410	3	75	340	2.40	FALSE	375	2.75	FALSE	275.00	1.75	FALSE
12	50	7	130	3	75	6	40	130	1.60	FALSE	102.5	1.05	FALSE	81.67	0.63	FALSE
13	429	17	6	7	130	12	50	6	0.99	FALSE	68	0.84	FALSE	62.00	0.86	FALSE
14	90	11	100	20	625	49	35	100	0.11	TRUE	362.5	3.03	FALSE	253.33	1.81	FALSE
15	34	21	105	31	105	8	21	105	0.82	FALSE	55.5	0.63	FALSE	44.00	0.29	FALSE
16	363	14	90	20	625	11	100	90	0.75	FALSE	357.5	0.02	TRUE	271.67	0.25	FALSE
17	6	13	429	42	35	47	90	429	70.50	FALSE	232	37.67	FALSE	184.67	29.78	FALSE
18	38	19	30	37	120	22	16	30	0.21	TRUE	75	0.97	FALSE	55.33	0.46	FALSE
19	30	18	38	30	43	22	16	38	0.27	FALSE	40.5	0.35	FALSE	32.33	0.08	TRUE
20	625	11	100	4	24	5	410	100	0.84	FALSE	62	0.90	FALSE	178.00	0.72	FALSE
21	6	31	105	29	100	34	90	105	16.50	FALSE	102.5	16.08	FALSE	98.33	15.39	FALSE
22	16	41	20	21	6	23	26	20	0.25	TRUE	13	0.19	TRUE	17.33	0.08	TRUE
23	26	40	30	21	6	31	105	30	0.15	TRUE	18	0.31	TRUE	47.00	0.81	FALSE
24	102	17	6	47	90	28	100	6	0.94	FALSE	48	0.53	FALSE	65.33	0.36	FALSE
25	300	28	100	23	26	31	105	100	0.67	FALSE	63	0.79	FALSE	77.00	0.74	FALSE
26	600	46	60	29	100	31	105	60	0.90	FALSE	80	0.87	FALSE	88.33	0.85	FALSE
27	655	47	90	39	120	17	6	90	0.86	FALSE	105	0.84	FALSE	72.00	0.89	FALSE
28	100	25	300	48	45	23	26	300	2.00	FALSE	172.5	0.73	FALSE	123.67	0.24	TRUE
29	100	31	105	21	6	34	90	105	0.05	TRUE	55.5	0.45	FALSE	67.00	0.33	FALSE
30	43	31	105	21	6	29	100	105	1.44	FALSE	55.5	0.29	FALSE	70.33	0.64	FALSE

Copyright © 2008, IGI Global. Copying or distributing in print or electronic forms without written permission of IGI Global is prohibited.

Table 10. continued

Case ID	Actual Effort	Case A1	Effort A1	Case A2	Effort A2	Case A3	Effort A3	Est. Effort A1	MRE	Pred.	Est. Effort A1-A2	MRE	Pred.	Est. Effort A1-A3	MRE	Pred.
31	105	21	6	29	100	30	43	6	0.94	FALSE	53	0.50	FALSE	49.67	0.53	FALSE
32	3150	38	600	52	640	48	45	600	0.81	FALSE	620	0.80	FALSE	428.33	0.86	FALSE
33	750	38	600	40	30	23	26	600	0.20	TRUE	315	0.58	FALSE	218.67	0.71	FALSE
34	90	21	6	36	500	42	35	6	0.93	FALSE	253	1.81	FALSE	180.33	1.00	FALSE
35	5000	32	3150	40	30	33	750	3150	0.37	FALSE	1590	0.68	FALSE	1310.00	0.74	FALSE
36	500	41	20	34	90	42	35	20	0.96	FALSE	55	0.89	FALSE	48.33	0.90	FALSE
37	120	18	38	30	43	31	105	38	0.68	FALSE	40.5	0.66	FALSE	62.00	0.48	FALSE
38	600	33	750	52	640	25	300	750	0.25	TRUE	695	0.16	TRUE	563.33	0.06	TRUE
39	120	44	120	47	90	45	800	120	0.00	TRUE	105	0.13	TRUE	336.67	1.81	FALSE
40	30	42	35	23	26	41	20	35	0.17	TRUE	30.5	0.02	TRUE	27.00	0.10	TRUE
41	20	42	35	22	16	36	500	35	0.75	FALSE	25.5	0.28	FALSE	183.67	8.18	FALSE
42	35	41	20	46	60	48	45	20	0.43	FALSE	40	0.14	TRUE	41.67	0.19	TRUE
43	150	44	120	30	43	66	8.15	120	0.20	TRUE	81.5	0.46	FALSE	57.05	0.62	FALSE
44	120	43	-150	39	120	29	100	150	0.25	TRUE	135	0.13	TRUE	123.33	0.03	TRUE
45	800	39	120	44	120	47	90	120	0.85	FALSE	120	0.85	FALSE	110.00	0.86	FALSE
46	60	42	35	48	45	34	90	35	0.42	FALSE	40	0.33	FALSE	56.67	0.06	TRUE
47	90	17	6	40	30	44	120	6	0.93	FALSE	18	0.80	FALSE	52.00	0.42	FALSE
48	45	42	35	46	60	34	90	35	0.22	TRUE	47.5	0.06	TRUE	61.67	0.37	FALSE
49	35	5	410	69	21	71	20.2	410	10.71	FALSE	215.5	5.16	FALSE	150.40	3.30	FALSE
50	947	53	490	52	640	33	750	490	0.48	FALSE	565	0.40	FALSE	626.67	0.34	FALSE
51	351	48	45	52	640	42	35	45	0.87	FALSE	342.5	0.02	FALSE	240.00	0.32	FALSE
52	640	53	490	51	351	38	600	490	0.23	TRUE	420.5	0.34	FALSE	480.33	0.25	TRUE
53	490	52	640	51	351	48	45	640	0.31	FALSE	495.5	0.01	TRUE	345.33	0.30	FALSE
54	8	61	12	62	5.3	65	13.1	12	0.44	FALSE	8.65	0.04	TRUE	10.13	0.22	TRUE
55	63	57	20.31	64	91	59	6	20.31	0.68	FALSE	55.655	0.11	TRUE	39.10	0.37	TRUE
56	58	63	72.3	65	13.1	60	22	72.3	0.24	TRUE	42.7	0.27	FALSE	35.80	0.38	FALSE
57	20	55	62.5	64	91	59	6	62.5	2.08	FALSE	76.75	2.78	FALSE	53.17	1.62	FALSE
58	178	60	22	63	72.3	56	58.16	22	0.88	FALSE	47.15	0.74	FALSE	50.82	0.71	FALSE
59	6	57	20.31	55	62.5	64	91	20.31	2.39	FALSE	41.405	5.90	FALSE	57.94	8.66	FALSE
60	22	65	13.1	63	72.3	61	12	13.1	0.40	FALSE	42.7	0.94	FALSE	32.47	0.48	FALSE

Copyright © 2008, IGI Global. Copying or distributing in print or electronic forms without written permission of IGI Global is prohibited.

Table 10. continued

Case ID	Actual Effort	Case A1	Effort A1	Case A2	Effort A2	Case A3	Effort A3	Est. Effort A1	MRE	Pred.	Est. Effort A1-A2	MRE	Pred.	Est. Effort A1-A3	MRE	Pred.
61	12	62	5.3	54	8.33	65	13.1	5.3	0.56	FALSE	6.815	0.43	FALSE	8.91	0.26	FALSE
62	5	61	12	54	8.33	67	37.3	12	1.26	FALSE	10.165	0.92	FALSE	19.21	2.62	FALSE
63	72	65	13.1	56	58.16	60	22	13.1	0.82	FALSE	35.63	0.51	FALSE	31.09	0.57	FALSE
64	91	55	62.5	57	20.31	63	72.3	62.5	0.31	FALSE	41.405	0.55	FALSE	51.70	0.43	FALSE
65	13	61	12	63	72.3	60	22	12	0.08	TRUE	42.15	2.22	FALSE	35.43	1.70	FALSE
66	8	72	16.15	71	20.2	69	21	16.15	0.98	FALSE	18.175	1.23	FALSE	19.12	1.35	FALSE
67	37	71	20.2	69	21	62	5.3	20.2	0.46	FALSE	20.6	0.45	FALSE	15.50	0.58	FALSE
68	1	76	1.3	78	7.15	80	2	1.3	0.18	TRUE	4.225	2.84	FALSE	3.48	2.17	FALSE
69	21	71	20.2	66	8.15	72	16.15	20.2	0.04	TRUE	14.175	0.33	FALSE	14.83	0.29	FALSE
70	11	74	3.15	77	6.15	81	2.45	3.15	0.72	FALSE	4.65	0.59	FALSE	3.92	0.66	FALSE
71	20	69	21	72	16.15	67	37.3	21	0.04	TRUE	18.575	0.08	TRUE	24.82	0.23	TRUE
72	16	66	8.15	71	20.2	69	21	8.15	0.50	FALSE	14.175	0.12	TRUE	16.45	0.02	TRUE
73	13	82	2.42	83	4.07	84	4.12	2.42	0.82	FALSE	3.245	0.76	FALSE	3.54	0.73	FALSE
74	3	77	6.15	81	2.45	70	11.45	6.15	0.95	FALSE	4.3	0.37	FALSE	6.68	1.12	FALSE
75	25	76	1.3	78	7.15	80	2	1.3	0.95	FALSE	4.225	0.83	FALSE	3.48	0.86	FALSE
76	1	78	7.15	80	2	68	1.1	7.15	4.50	FALSE	4.575	2.52	FALSE	3.42	1.63	FALSE
77	6	74	3.15	81	2.45	79	1.33	3.15	0.49	FALSE	2.8	0.54	FALSE	2.31	0.62	FALSE
78	7	76	1.3	80	2	79	1.33	1.3	0.82	FALSE	1.65	0.77	FALSE	1.54	0.78	FALSE
79	1	80	2	86	3	78	7.15	2	0.50	FALSE	2.5	0.88	FALSE	4.05	2.05	FALSE
80	2	78	7.15	76	1.3	79	1.33	7.15	2.58	FALSE	4.225	1.11	FALSE	3.26	0.63	FALSE
81	2	77	6.15	74	3.15	79	1.33	6.15	1.51	FALSE	4.65	0.90	FALSE	3.54	0.45	FALSE
82	2	83	4.07	84	4.12	73	13.28	4.07	0.68	FALSE	4.095	0.69	FALSE	7.16	1.96	FALSE
83	4	84	4.12	82	2.42	73	13.28	4.12	0.01	TRUE	3.27	0.20	TRUE	6.61	0.62	FALSE
84	4	83	4.07	82	2.42	73	13.28	4.07	0.01	TRUE	3.245	0.21	TRUE	6.59	0.60	FALSE
85	17	65	13.1	87	26.14	81	2.45	13.1	0.24	TRUE	19.62	0.14	TRUE	13.90	0.19	TRUE
86	3	79	1.33	80	2	78	7.15	1.33	0.56	FALSE	1.665	0.45	FALSE	3.49	0.16	TRUE
87	26	72	16.15	71	20.2	84	4.12	16.15	0.38	FALSE	18.175	0.30	FALSE	13.49	0.48	FALSE
								MMRE	181.60		MMRE	141.85		MMRE	141.62	
								MdMRE	55.83		MdMRE	59.39		MdMRE	62.44	
								Pred(25)	28.74		Pred(25)	21.84		Pred(25)	16.09	

Copyright © 2008, IGI Global. Copying or distributing in print or electronic forms without written permission of IGI Global is prohibited.

Measuring Effort Prediction Accuracy

Table 10 shows the MMRE, MdMRE, and Pred(25) for the three different types of analogy adaptation.

We can see that the MMRE, MdMRE, and Pred(25) for the three different types of analogy adaptation used to obtain estimated effort provide very similar values. However, in order to test and verify if there is a best analogy adaptation, we need to first check if the absolute residuals (actual effort - estimated effort) for these three types of analogy adaptation are statistically different from one another. The two techniques of choice to check for statistical significance are the one-way analysis of variance (ANOVA) test (parametric test) and Friedman's test (nonparametric test). Both are paired samples and are described in Chapter 10. For the example shown, we will employ Friedman's test as the data sample is not large enough and the residuals are not normally distributed, confirmed using the one-sample Kolmogorov-Smirnov test (see Table 11).

The results for Friedman's test (see Table 12) show that there are no statistically significant differences between the three groups of absolute residuals (Asymp. Sig. > 0.05), which suggests that, at least for the data set we used in this example, predictions could have been obtained using an analogy adaptation, where estimated effort is based on the effort of the most similar project, or where estimated effort is based on the average effort for the two or three most similar projects.

As we have seen in Chapter III, an effort estimation model or technique is considered good if the MMRE and MdMRE are less than or equal to 25%, and Pred(25)

Table 11. One-sample Kolmogorov-Smirnov test results

		resA1	resA12	resA123
N		87	87	87
Normal Parameters (a, b)	Mean	169.00	179.33	185.58
	Std. Deviation	393.854	492.338	520.809
Most Extreme Differences	Absolute	.334	.358	.361
	Positive	.306	.325	.344
	Negative	-.334	-.358	-.361
Kolmogorov-Smirnov Z		3.115	3.340	3.367
Asymp. Sig. (two-tailed)		.000	.000	.000

a Test distribution is normal
b Calculated from data

Copyright © 2008, IGI Global. Copying or distributing in print or electronic forms without written permission of IGI Global is prohibited.

Table 12. Friedman's test results comparing the three samples of absolute residuals

Test Statistics (a)	
N	87
Chi-Square	1.885
df	2
Asymp. Sig.	.390

a Friedman's test

is greater than or equal to 75%. If we look at the values for each of the three different analogy adaptations employed, it is clear that their MMRE and MdMRE are all greater than 25%, and their Pred(25) are all smaller than 75%, thus in principle indicating that CBR provided poor predictions. However, although the MMRE, MdMRE, and Pred(25) values may not look good, we need to compare these values to a benchmark. The benchmark to be used can either be based on the estimated effort suggested for each project by means of expert opinion or on the use of the

Table 13. Comparing CBR effort estimations to a benchmark

	Mean Effort	CBR1	CBR2	CBR3
MMRE	2220.07	181.60	141.85	141.62
MdMRE	508.67	55.83	59.39	62.44
Pred(25)	3.45	28.74	21.84	16.09

Table 14. Friedman's test comparing CBR effort estimations to a benchmark

Test Statistics (a)	
N	87
Chi-Square	67.115
df	3
Asymp. Sig.	.000

a Friedman's test

Copyright © 2008, IGI Global. Copying or distributing in print or electronic forms without written permission of IGI Global is prohibited.

mean or median actual effort for the projects in the data set. We chose to use the mean actual effort (261.73) as a benchmark (see Table 13), which gives MMRE, MdMRE, and Pred(25) values much worse than any of those presented in Table 11. When we apply Friedman's test on all four absolute residuals, the rank differences among these residuals become statistically significant (see Table 14). This means that if a Web company had decided to use the mean effort for past projects as the estimated effort for a new project, it would have obtained much worse predictions than using any of the CBR approaches presented herein.

The effort estimates we have shown in Table 10 are assumed to be optimistic as each time the entire data set -1 was used to look for the most similar projects. We have used here a cross-validation approach (see Chapter III) called the leave-one-out cross-validation, or 87-fold cross-validation. Ideally, we should use a validation set that is greater than 1. This is the procedure presented in the next section.

Model Validation

As described in Chapter III, to validate a model we need to do the following.

Step 1. Divide data set d into a training set t and a validation set v.

Step 2. Use t to produce an effort estimation model te (if applicable).

Step 3. Use te to predict effort for each of the projects in v as if these projects were new projects for which effort was unknown.

This process is known as cross-validation. For an n-fold cross-validation, n different training or validation sets are used. In this section, we will detail the cross-validation procedure using a one-fold cross-validation, with a 66% split. This split means that 66% of our project data will be used as a training set, and the remaining 34% will be used as a validation set to assess the accuracy of the effort estimation technique; that is, the training set will have 66% of the total number of projects and the validation set will have the remaining 34%.

Our initial data set had 87 projects. At Step 1 they are split into training and validation sets containing 58 and 29 projects respectively. Generally projects are selected randomly. As part of Step 2 we sometimes need to create an effort model using the 58 projects in the training set. However, this step is not available when using CBR. Instead, change the case mode for each of the projects in the validation set from confirmed to unconfirmed (see Figure 22). By doing so, they will not be used by the CBR engine when it is looking for the most similar projects in the case base. To measure the CBR technique's prediction accuracy, we obtained the MMRE,

Copyright © 2008, IGI Global. Copying or distributing in print or electronic forms without written permission of IGI Global is prohibited.

MdMRE, and Pred(25) for the validation set. Using CBR-Works, the training set of 58 projects is used to obtain estimated effort for each of the 29 projects in the validation set, and MRE is computed. Since we have the calculated estimated effort and the actual effort (provided by the Web companies), we are finally in a position

Figure 22. Projects in the validation set are all changed to unconfirmed

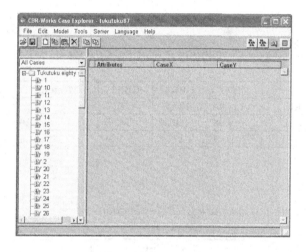

Figure 23. Steps used in the cross-validation process

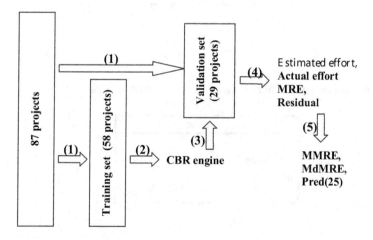

Copyright © 2008, IGI Global. Copying or distributing in print or electronic forms without written permission of IGI Global is prohibited.

to calculate MRE for each of the 29 projects, and hence MMRE, MdMRE, and Pred(25) for the entire 29 projects. This process is explained in Figure 23.

Table 18 shows the estimated effort and MRE for the 29 projects used as a validation set, and summary prediction accuracy measures based on the validation set are presented in Table 15. Here again Friedman's test shows any statistically significant differences between the CBR predictions (see Table 16); however, as previously found when using a leave-one-out cross-validation, Friedman's test also shows that the mean effort provides significantly worse predictions than CBR (see Table 17).

Table 15. Summary accuracy measures from using CBR on 29 Web projects

	CBR1	CBR2	CBR3	Mean Effort
MMRE	135.93	127.57	138.96	555.76
MdMRE	59.05	50.67	64.76	118.11
Pred(25)	20.69	17.24	17.24	6.90

Table 16. Friedman's test comparing CBR estimations

Test Statistics (a)	
N	29
Chi-Square	1.103
df	2
Asymp. Sig.	.576

a Friedman's test

Table 17. Friedman's test comparing CBR estimations to mean effort

Test Statistics (a)	
N	29
Chi-Square	12.434
df	3
Asymp. Sig.	.006

a Friedman's test

Copyright © 2008, IGI Global. Copying or distributing in print or electronic forms without written permission of IGI Global is prohibited.

Table 18. Results from using CBR on 29 Web projects

Case ID	Actual Effort	Case A1	Effort A1	Case A2	Effort A2	Case A3	Effort A3	Est. Effort A1	MRE	Pred	Est. Effort A1-A2	MRE	Pred	Est. Effort A1-A3	MRE	Pred
1	340	56	58.16	2	300	63	72.3	58.16	0.83	FALSE	179.08	0.47	FALSE	143.49	0.58	FALSE
3	75	12	50	4	24	62	5.3	50.00	0.33	FALSE	37.00	0.51	FALSE	26.43	0.65	FALSE
5	410	2	300	4	24	71	20.2	300.00	0.27	FALSE	162.00	0.60	FALSE	114.73	0.72	FALSE
7	130	12	50	6	40	61	12	50.00	0.62	FALSE	45.00	0.65	FALSE	34.00	0.74	FALSE
9	1786	56	58.16	12	50	2	300	58.16	0.97	FALSE	54.08	0.97	FALSE	136.05	0.92	FALSE
11	100	20	625	12	50	4	24	625.00	5.25	FALSE	337.50	2.38	FALSE	233.00	1.33	FALSE
13	429	12	50	61	12	30	43	50.00	0.88	FALSE	31.00	0.93	FALSE	35.00	0.92	FALSE
15	34	8	21	20	625	34	90	21.00	0.38	FALSE	323.00	8.50	FALSE	245.33	6.22	FALSE
17	6	42	35	48	45	22	16	35.00	4.83	FALSE	40.00	5.67	FALSE	32.00	4.33	FALSE
19	30	18	38	30	43	22	16	38.00	0.27	FALSE	40.50	0.35	FALSE	32.33	0.08	TRUE
21	6	34	90	22	16	30	43	90.00	14.00	FALSE	53.00	7.83	FALSE	49.67	7.28	FALSE
23	26	40	30	22	16	42	35	30.00	0.15	TRUE	23.00	0.12	TRUE	27.00	0.04	TRUE
25	300	28	100	38	600	18	38	100.00	0.67	FALSE	350.00	0.17	FALSE	246.00	0.18	TRUE
27	655	20	625	44	120	18	38	625.00	0.05	TRUE	372.50	0.43	FALSE	261.00	0.60	FALSE
29	100	34	90	30	43	40	30	90.00	0.10	TRUE	66.50	0.34	FALSE	54.33	0.46	FALSE
31	105	30	43	42	35	40	30	43.00	0.59	FALSE	39.00	0.63	FALSE	36.00	0.66	FALSE
33	750	38	600	40	30	36	500	600.00	0.20	TRUE	315.00	0.58	FALSE	376.67	0.50	FALSE
35	5000	32	3150	40	30	38	600	3150.00	0.37	FALSE	1590.00	0.68	FALSE	1260.00	0.75	FALSE
37	120	18	38	30	43	22	16	38.00	0.68	FALSE	40.50	0.66	FALSE	32.33	0.73	FALSE
39	120	44	120	40	30	36	500	120.00	0.00	TRUE	75.00	0.38	FALSE	216.67	0.81	FALSE
41	20	42	35	22	16	36	500	35.00	0.75	FALSE	25.50	0.28	FALSE	183.67	8.18	FALSE
43	150	44	120	30	43	66	8.15	120.00	0.20	TRUE	81.50	0.46	FALSE	57.05	0.62	FALSE
45	800	44	120	60	22	10	900	120.00	0.85	FALSE	71.00	0.91	FALSE	347.33	0.57	FALSE
47	90	40	30	44	120	58	178	30.00	0.67	FALSE	75.00	0.17	TRUE	109.33	0.21	TRUE
49	35	69	21	71	20.2	66	8.15	21.00	0.40	FALSE	20.60	0.41	FALSE	16.45	0.53	FALSE
51	351	48	45	52	640	42	35	45.00	0.87	FALSE	342.50	0.02	TRUE	240.00	0.32	FALSE
53	490	52	640	48	45	30	43	640.00	0.31	FALSE	342.50	0.30	FALSE	242.67	0.50	FALSE
55	62.5	64	91	59	6	63	72.3	91.00	0.46	FALSE	48.50	0.22	TRUE	56.43	0.10	TRUE
57	20.31	64	91	59	6	61	12	91.00	3.48	FALSE	48.50	1.39	FALSE	36.33	0.79	FALSE

Copyright © 2008, IGI Global. Copying or distributing in print or electronic forms without written permission of IGI Global is prohibited.

If we consider that a good prediction model has an MMRE less than or equal to 25% and Pred(25) greater than or equal to 75%, then the values presented in Table 15 suggest that the prediction accuracy obtained using CBR to estimate effort is rated overall to be poor. However, if instead we were to use the mean actual effort (432.44) as the estimated effort, then accuracy would be considerably worse (see Table 15). One viable approach for a Web company would be to use CBR to obtain an estimated effort, and to adapt the obtained values, taking into account factors such as previous experience with similar projects and the skills of the developers.

Table 15 presents the results for a one-fold cross-validation. However, research on effort estimation suggests that to have unbiased results for a cross-validation, we should actually use at least a 20-fold cross-validation analysis (Kirsopp & Shepperd, 2001). This would represent, at least for the data set presented herein, the selection of 20 different training and validation sets and the aggregation of the MMRE, MdMRE, and Pred(25) after accuracy for all 20 groups has been calculated. Note that we are not aware of any other studies that have investigated this claim, therefore further investigation is necessary before we can suggest Web companies use at least a 20-fold cross-validation when assessing the prediction accuracy of model and effort estimation techniques.

Conclusion

This chapter presented a case study that used data from industrial Web projects held in the Tukutuku database to obtain effort estimates using an effort estimation technique named case-based reasoning. The size measures used in the case study represent early Web size measures, obtained from the results of a survey investigation (Mendes et al., 2003b), using data from 133 online Web forms aimed at giving quotes for Web development projects. These measures were also validated by an established Web company, and by a second survey involving 33 Web companies in New Zealand. Consequently, we believe that the size measures identified are plausible effort predictors, not an ad hoc set of variables with no underlying rationale.

The case study details the use of CBR for effort estimation, using three different types of analogy adaptation. Results have shown that there were no significant differences in prediction accuracy between the absolute residuals obtained using each of the analogy adaptations. However, when using as a benchmark the mean effort as an effort estimate, the predictions obtained were much worse than those obtained using CBR. Our case study shows that it is important to use a benchmark that reflects the context in which the effort estimation technique is being used, and

Copyright © 2008, IGI Global. Copying or distributing in print or electronic forms without written permission of IGI Global is prohibited.

that MMRE, MdMRE, and Pred(25) values suggested in the literature may not be applicable to a company's circumstances.

We have detailed the use of a CBR tool in such a way that any Web company that wishes to investigate this technique to obtain effort estimates similar to those described above has at hand a basic knowledge base regarding the overall functionality offered by generic CBR tools.

Alternatively, Web companies that do not have a data set of past projects may be able to benefit from the cross-company effort estimation models, later detailed in Chapter 9.

References

Angelis, L., & Stamelos, I. (2000). A simulation tool for efficient analogy based cost estimation. *Empirical Software Engineering, 5*, 35-68.

Conte, S., Dunsmore, H., & Shen, V. (1986). *Software engineering metrics and models.* Menlo Park, CA: Benjamin/Cummings.

Kemerer, C. F. (1987). An empirical validation of software cost estimation models. *Communications of the ACM, 30*(5), 416-429.

Kirsopp, C., & Shepperd, M. (2001). *Making inferences with small numbers of training sets* (Tech. Rep. No. TR02-01). Bournemouth University.

Kitchenham, B. A. (1998). A procedure for analyzing unbalanced datasets. *IEEE Transactions on Software Engineering, 24*(4), 278-301.

Mendes, E., Counsell, S., & Mosley, N. (2000, June). Measurement and effort prediction of Web applications. *Proceedings of the 2nd ICSE Workshop on Web Engineering* (pp. 57-74).

Mendes, E., Mosley, N., & Counsell, S. (2001). Web metrics: Estimating design and authoring effort. *IEEE Multimedia, 8*(1), 50-57.

Mendes, E., Mosley, N., & Counsell, S. (2002). The application of case-based reasoning to early Web project cost estimation. *Proceedings of COMPSAC* (pp. 393-398).

Mendes, E., Mosley, N., & Counsell, S. (2003a). Do adaptation rules improve Web cost estimation? *Proceedings of the ACM Hypertext Conference 2003* (pp. 173-183).

Mendes, E., Mosley, N., & Counsell, S. (2003b, September). Early Web size measures and effort prediction for Web costimation. *Proceedings of the IEEE Metrics Symposium* (pp. 18-29).

Copyright © 2008, IGI Global. Copying or distributing in print or electronic forms without written permission of IGI Global is prohibited.

Mendes, E., Mosley, N., & Counsell, S. (2003c). A replicated assessment of the use of adaptation rules to improve Web cost estimation. *Proceedings of the ACM and IEEE International Symposium on Empirical Software Engineering* (pp. 100-109).

Mendes, E., Watson, I., Triggs, C., Mosley, N., & Counsell, S. (2002, June). A comparison of development effort estimation techniques for Web hypermedia applications. *Proceedings of the IEEE Metrics Symposium* (pp. 141-151).

Myrtveit, I., & Stensrud, E. (1999). A controlled experiment to assess the benefits of estimating with analogy and regression models. *IEEE Transactions on Software Engineering, 25*(4), 510-525.

Shepperd, M. J., & Kadoda, G. (2001). Using simulation to evaluate prediction techniques. *Proceedings of the IEEE 7th International Software Metrics Symposium* (pp. 349-358).

Shepperd, M. J., & Schofield, C. (1997). Estimating software project effort using analogies. *IEEE Transactions on Software Engineering, 23*(11), 736-743.

Stensrud, E., Foss, T., Kitchenham, B. A., & Myrtveit, I. (2002). An empirical validation of the relationship between the magnitude of relative error and project size. *Proceedings of the IEEE 8th Metrics Symposium* (pp. 3-12).

Copyright © 2008, IGI Global. Copying or distributing in print or electronic forms without written permission of IGI Global is prohibited.

Chapter VII

Web Effort Estimation Using Classification and Regression Trees

Abstract

The use of realistic effort estimates is fundamental to both software and Web project management as they help project managers allocate resources, control costs and schedule, and improve current practices, leading to projects that are finished on time and within budget. Different effort techniques have been used to obtain effort estimates for Web projects. Two—stepwise regression and case-based reasoning—have already been presented in Chapters V and VI respectively. In this chapter we detail a third technique used to obtain effort estimates for Web projects, known as classification and regression trees (CART), that is considered a machine-learning technique. We detail its use by means of a case study where a real effort prediction model based on data from completed industrial Web projects is constructed step by step.

Copyright © 2008, IGI Global. Copying or distributing in print or electronic forms without written permission of IGI Global is prohibited.

Introduction

The effort estimation technique that will be used in this chapter is called classification and regression trees (CART; Brieman, Friedman, Olshen, & Stone, 1984). This is, in addition to case-based reasoning (CBR), one of the techniques proposed by the machine-learning community, and has also been one of the techniques used in a previous study to estimate effort for Web applications.

CART uses independent variables (predictors) to build binary trees where each leaf node either represents a category to which an estimate belongs, or a value for an estimate. The former situation occurs with classification trees and the latter occurs with regression trees; that is, whenever predictors are categorical (e.g., *Yes* or *No*), the tree is called a classification tree, and whenever predictors are numerical, the tree is called a regression tree.

In order to obtain an estimate, one has to traverse the tree nodes from root to leaf by selecting the nodes that represent the category or value for the independent variables associated with the case to be estimated.

For example, assume we wish to obtain an effort estimate for a new Web project using as its basis the simple regression tree structure presented in Figure 4 (deemed a regression tree because effort is a numerical variable measured on a ratio scale). In this example, we assume the tree was generated from data obtained from past finished Web applications, taking into account their existing values of effort and independent variables (e.g., new Web pages [WP], new images [IM], and new features/functions [FN]). The data used to build a CART model are called a learning sample.

Figure 1. Example of a regression tree for Web effort estimation

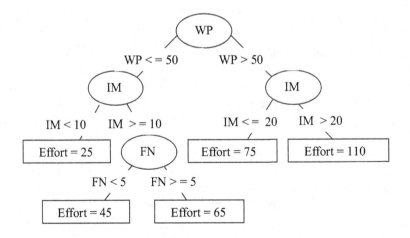

Copyright © 2008, IGI Global. Copying or distributing in print or electronic forms without written permission of IGI Global is prohibited.

Once the tree has been built, it can be used to estimate effort for new projects. For example and with reference to Figure 1, assuming that the estimated values for WP, IM, and FN for a new Web project are 25, 15, and 3, respectively, we would obtain an estimated effort of 45 person hours after navigating the tree from its root down to leaf: Effort = 45.

Again, using the same figure, if now we assume that the estimated values for WP, IM, and FN for a new Web project are 56, 34, and 22, respectively, we would obtain an estimated effort of 110 person hours after navigating the tree from its root down to leaf: Effort = 110.

A simple example of a classification tree for Web cost estimation is depicted in Figure 2. It uses the same variable names as shown in Figure 1; however, these variables are now all categorical, where possible categories (classes) are *Yes* and *No*. The effort estimate obtained using this classification tree is also categorical, where possible categories are *High effort* and *Low effort*. Therefore, the tree presented in Figure 2 is a classification tree rather than a regression tree.

A CART model constructs a binary tree by recursively partitioning the predictor space (set of all values or categories for the independent variables judged relevant) into subsets where the distribution of values or categories for the dependent variable (e.g., effort) is successively more uniform. The partition (split) of a subset *S1*

Figure 2. Example of a classification tree for Web effort estimation

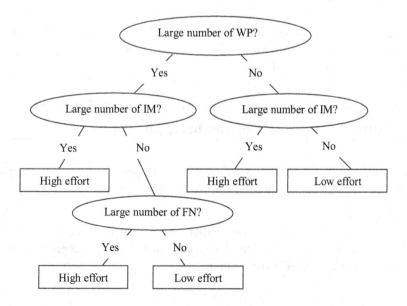

Copyright © 2008, IGI Global. Copying or distributing in print or electronic forms without written permission of IGI Global is prohibited.

is decided on the basis that the data in each of the descendant subsets should be "purer" than the data in *S1*. Thus, node "impurity" is directly related to the amount of different values or classes in a node; that is, the greater the mix of classes or values, the higher the node impurity. A pure node means that all the cases (e.g., Web projects) belong to the same class, or have the same value.

As such, the partition of subsets continues until a node contains only one class or value. Note that not all the initial independent variables are necessarily used to build a CART model; that is, only those variables that are related to the dependent variable are selected by the model. This suggests that a CART model can be used not only to produce a model that can be applicable for effort prediction, but also to obtain insight and understanding into the factors that are relevant to estimate a given dependent variable.

The tree is the model, built and then used to obtain predictions for new cases. Although the model here is not an equation as, say, using multivariate regression, it too is built from previous available data on finished projects and is used later to obtain effort estimations for new projects.

In the case study presented later in this chapter, we will build and compare different configurations of trees in order to assess which combination provides the most accurate predictions given the data set being used.

Previous Study that Used CART for Web Cost Estimation

This section describes the single study to date in Web engineering that has applied classification and regression trees for Web effort estimation. This work is described below and is summarised in Table 1.

Study: A Comparison of Development Effort Estimation Techniques for Web Hypermedia Applications

Mendes, Watson, Triggs, Mosley, and Counsell (2002) present an in-depth comparison of Web effort estimation models comprising the following steps:

Step 1: The first step is to compare the prediction accuracy of three CBR techniques to estimate the effort to develop Web applications. The Web applications used are all Web hypermedia applications.

Copyright © 2008, IGI Global. Copying or distributing in print or electronic forms without written permission of IGI Global is prohibited.

Regarding the use of CBR, Mendes et al. (2002) employed several parameters, as follows: three similarity measures (unweighted Euclidean, weighted Euclidean, and maximum), three choices for the number of analogies (one, two, and three), three choices for the analogy adaptation (mean, inverse rank weighted mean, and median), and two alternatives regarding the standardisation of the attributes (*Yes* for standardised and *No* for not standardised). The CBR technique that presents the best prediction accuracy is used in Step 2.

Step 2: The second step compares the prediction accuracy of the best CBR technique, obtained in Step 1, against three commonly used prediction models, namely, multiple linear regression, stepwise regression, and regression trees.

Mendes et al. (2002) employed one data set containing data from 37 Web applications developed by honours and postgraduate computer science students from the University of Auckland, New Zealand.

The measures used in the study are as follows:

- Page count: Number of HTML or SHTML files used in a Web application
- Media count: Number of media files used in a Web application
- Program count: Number of JavaScript files and Java applets used in a Web application
- Reused media count: Number of reused or modified media files used in a Web application
- Reused program count: Number of reused or modified programs used in a Web application
- Connectivity density: Total number of internal links divided by page count
- Total page complexity: Average number of different types of media per Web page
- Total effort: The effort in person hours to design and author a Web application

Note that participants did not use external links to other Web hypermedia applications; that is, all the links pointed to pages within the original Web application only.

Prediction accuracy was measured using the mean magnitude of relative error (MMRE; Conte, Dunsmore, & Shen, 1986), the median magnitude of relative error (MdMRE; Conte et al.), prediction at 25% level (Pred[25]; Conte et al.), and boxplots of absolute residuals. Their results showed that different measures of prediction accuracy gave different results. MMRE and MdMRE showed better prediction ac-

Copyright © 2008, IGI Global. Copying or distributing in print or electronic forms without written permission of IGI Global is prohibited.

Table 1. Summary of literature on CART for Web cost estimation

Study	Type (case study, experiment, survey)	# Data Sets (# data points)	Participants (students, professionals)	Size Measures	Prediction Techniques	Best Technique(s)	Measure Prediction Accuracy
1st	Case study	1 (37)	Honours and postgraduate computer science students	Page count, media count, program count, reusedmedia count, reused program count, connectivity density, total page complexity	Case-based reasoning, linear regression, stepwise regression, classification and regression trees	Linear/ stepwise regression or case-based reasoning (depends on the measure of accuracy employed)	MMRE, MdMRE, Pred(25), Boxplots of residuals

curacy for estimates obtained using multiple regression, whereas boxplots showed better accuracy for CBR. Regression trees provided the worse accuracy.

The two main issues related to this study are the size of the data set employed and the use of data from students' projects. The data set was relatively small and this pattern may have influenced the results obtained for CART. In addition, using data from students' projects may not scale up to industrial practices as it is often the case that the students participating in a case study do not have large industrial experience in Web development.

Case Study

The case study we present here describes the construction and further validation of a Web effort estimation model using a CART model, and data on industrial Web projects developed by Web companies worldwide from the Tukutuku database (Mendes, Mosley, & Counsell, 2003). Note that the raw data cannot be displayed here due to a confidentiality agreement with those companies that have volunteered data on their projects. This database is part of the ongoing Tukutuku project (http://www.cs.auckland.ac.nz/tukutuku), which collects data on Web projects for the development of effort estimation models and to benchmark productivity across and within Web companies.

Copyright © 2008, IGI Global. Copying or distributing in print or electronic forms without written permission of IGI Global is prohibited.

Table 2. Variables for the Tukutuku database

NAME	SCALE	DESCRIPTION
COMPANY DATA		
COUNTRY	*Categorical*	*Country company belongs to*
ESTABLISHED	*Ordinal*	*Year when company was established*
SERVICES	*Categorical*	*Type of services company provides*
NPEOPLEWD	*Absolute*	*Number of people who work on Web design and development*
CLIENTIND	*Categorical*	*Industry representative of those clients to whom applications are provided*
ESTPRACT	*Categorical*	*Accuracy of a company's own effort estimation practices*
PROJECT DATA		
TYPEPROJ	*Categorical*	*Type of project (new or enhancement)*
LANGS	*Categorical*	*Implementation languages used*
DOCPROC	*Categorical*	*If project followed defined and documented process*
PROIMPR	*Categorical*	*If project team was involved in a process improvement programme*
METRICS	*Categorical*	*If project team was part of a software metrics programme*
DEVTEAM	*Absolute*	*Size of project's development team*
TEAMEXP	*Absolute*	*Average team experience with the development language(s) employed*
TOTEFF	*Absolute*	*Actual total effort in person hours used to develop the Web application*
ESTEFF	*Absolute*	*Estimated total effort in person hours necessary to develop the Web application*
ACCURACY	*Categorical*	*Procedure used to record effort data*
WEB APPLICATION		
TYPEAPP	*Categorical*	*Type of Web application developed*
TOTWP	*Absolute*	*Total number of Web pages (new and reused)*
NEWWP	*Absolute*	*Total number of new Web pages*
TOTIMG	*Absolute*	*Total number of images (new and reused)*
NEWIMG	*Absolute*	*Total number of new images created*
HEFFDEV	*Absolute*	*Minimum number of hours to develop a single function/feature by one experienced developer whose skill is considered high (above average). This number is currently set to 15 hours based on the collected data*
HEFFADPT	*Absolute*	*Minimum number of hours to adapt a single function/feature by one experienced developer whose skill is considered high (above average). This number is currently set to 4 hours based on the collected data*
HFOTS	*Absolute*	*Number of reused high-effort features/functions without adaptation*
HFOTSA	*Absolute*	*Number of reused high-effort features/functions adapted*
HNEW	*Absolute*	*Number of new high-effort features/functions*
FOTS	*Absolute*	*Number of reused low-effort features without adaptation*
FOTSA	*Absolute*	*Number of reused low-effort features adapted*
NEW	*Absolute*	*Number of new low-effort features/functions*

Copyright © 2008, IGI Global. Copying or distributing in print or electronic forms without written permission of IGI Global is prohibited.

The data set used in this chapter contains data on 87 Web projects: 34 and 13 come from two single Web companies respectively and the remaining 40 projects come from another 23 companies. The Tukutuku database uses 6 variables to store specifics about each company that volunteered projects, 10 variables to store particulars about each project, and 13 variables to store data about each Web application (see Table 1). Company data are obtained once and both project and application data are gathered for each volunteered project.

The results for CART were obtained using a commercial classification and regression tree tool called AnswerTree 3.1, from SPSS Inc. The statistical results presented were obtained using the statistical software SPSS 12.0.1 for Windows, from SPSS Inc. Further details on the statistical methods used throughout this case study are given in Chapter 10. Finally, all the statistical tests set the significance level at 95% ($\alpha = 0.05$). Note that the different types of measurement scales are also detailed in Chapter 10.

Before using the CART tool AnswerTree to build an effort model, which is later used to obtain effort estimates, we need first to validate the data we intend to use with the CART tool, and in addition we need to select the variables that should be used. As such validation and selection phases need to be conducted prior to using the CART tool.

Data Validation

Data validation (DV) performs the first screening of the collected data. It generally involves understanding what the variables are (e.g., purpose, scale type; see Table 2) and also uses descriptive statistics (e.g., mean, median, minimum, maximum) to help identify any missing or unusual cases.

Table 3 presents summary statistics for numerical variables. Such statistics are obtained in SPSS by following these steps:

- Select *Analyze* ⇨ *Descriptive Statistics* ⇨ *Frequencies.*
- Then click on the button *Statistics* and tick *mean, median, minimum, maximum,* and *Std. deviation.*

The output generated by SPSS is similar to the one shown in Table 3.

Table 3 suggests that none of the numerical variables seem to exhibit unusual or missing values, although this requires careful examination. For example, one would find it strange to see zero as the minimum value for the total images (TOTIMG) or one as the minimum value for total Web pages (TOTWP). However, it is possible to have either a Web application without any images or a Web application that pro-

Copyright © 2008, IGI Global. Copying or distributing in print or electronic forms without written permission of IGI Global is prohibited.

Table 3. Descriptive statistics for numerical variables

Variables	N	Missing	Minimum	Maximum	Mean	Median	Std. Dev.
DEVTEAM	87	0	1	8	2.37	2	1.35
TEAMEXP	87	0	1	10	3.40	2	1.93
TOTWP	87	0	1	2000	92.40	25	273.09
NEWWP	87	0	0	1980	82.92	7	262.98
TOTIMG	87	0	0	1820	122.54	40	284.48
NEWIMG	87	0	0	800	51.90	0	143.25
HEFFDEV	87	0	5	800	62.02	15	141.25
HEFFADPT	87	0	0	200	10.61	4	28.48
HFOTS	87	0	0	3	.08	0	.41
HFOTSA	87	0	0	4	.29	0	.75
HNEW	87	0	0	10	1.24	0	2.35
FOTS	87	0	0	15	1.07	0	2.57
FOTSA	87	0	0	10	1.89	1	2.41
NEW	87	0	0	13	1.87	0	2.84
TOTEFF	87	0	1	5000	261.73	43	670.36
ESTEFF	34	53	1	108	14.45	7.08	20.61

vides all its content and functionality within a single Web page. Another example relates to the maximum number of Web pages, which is 2,000 Web pages. Although it does not seem possible at first to have such large number of pages, we cannot simply assume this has been a data entry error. When a situation such as this arises, it is common practice to contact the company that provided the data to ensure the values given are correct. In our case, we contacted the source Web company but were unable to obtain confirmation as the company did not respond to our inquiry. However, further investigation revealed that 1,980 pages were developed from scratch, and numerous new functions and features (five high effort and seven low effort) were also implemented.

In addition, the development team consisted of two people who had very little experience with the six programming languages used. The total effort was 947 person hours, which can correspond to a 3-month project assuming both developers worked at the same time. If we only consider the number of pages and effort, the ratio of minutes per page is 27:1, which seems reasonable given the lack of experience of the development team and the number of different languages they had to use.

Once we have checked the numerical variables, our next step is to check the categorical variables using their frequency tables as a tool (see Tables 4 to 8).

Copyright © 2008, IGI Global. Copying or distributing in print or electronic forms without written permission of IGI Global is prohibited.

To display frequency tables using SPSS, follow these steps:

* Select *Analyze ⇨ Descriptive Statistics ⇨ Frequencies*.
* Tick *Display Frequency Tables*.

Tables 4 to 7 show that most projects followed a defined and documented process, and that development teams were involved in a process improvement programme and/or were part of a software metrics programme. These positive trends are mainly

Table 4. Frequency table for type of project

Type of Project	Frequency	%	Cumulative %
New	39	44.8	44.8
Enhancement	48	55.2	100.0
Total	87	100.0	

Table 5. Frequency table for documented process

Documented Process	Frequency	%	Cumulative %
No	23	26.4	26.4
Yes	64	73.6	100.0
Total	87	100.0	

Table 6. Frequency table for process improvement

Process Improvement	Frequency	%	Cumulative %
No	28	32.2	32.2
Yes	59	67.8	100.0
Total	87	100.0	

Table 7. Frequency table for metrics programme

Metrics Programme	Frequency	%	Cumulative %
No	36	41.4	41.4
Yes	51	58.6	100.0
Total	87	100.0	

Copyright © 2008, IGI Global. Copying or distributing in print or electronic forms without written permission of IGI Global is prohibited.

Table 8. Frequency table for companies' effort recording procedure

Actual Effort Recording Procedure	Frequency	%	Cumulative %
Poor	12	13.8	13.8
Medium	3	3.4	17.2
Good	24	27.6	44.8
Very good	48	55.2	100
Total	87	100.0	

due to the two single companies that together volunteered data on 47 projects (54% of our data set). They have answered "yes" to all three categories. No unusual trends seem to exist.

Table 8 shows that the majority of projects (83%) had the actual effort recorded on a daily basis for each project and/or project task. These numbers are inflated by the two single companies where one chose the category *good* (11 projects) and the other chose the category *very good* (34 projects). The actual effort recording procedure is not an adequate effort estimator per se, being used here simply to show that the effort data gathered seems to be reliable overall.

Once the data validation is complete, we are ready to move on to the next step, namely, variables selection.

Variables Selection

This important phase is used to create variables based on existing variables, discard unnecessary variables, and modify existing variables (e.g., joining categories). The net result of this phase is to obtain a set of variables that are ready to use in the next phase, model building. This phase is extremely important given that the use of variables that should have been discarded can make the generation of CART trees considerably slow and inefficient, and can also bias the results.

The first task within this phase is to examine the entire set of variables and check if there is a significant amount of missing values (> 60%). If there are, they should be automatically discarded as they prohibit the use of imputation methods and will further prevent the identification of useful trends in the data (imputation methods are methods used to replace missing values with estimated values). Table 3 shows that only ESTEFF presented missing values greater than 60%. ESTEFF was gathered to give an idea of each company's own prediction accuracy; however, it will not be included in our analysis since it is not an effort predictor per se. Note that a

Copyright © 2008, IGI Global. Copying or distributing in print or electronic forms without written permission of IGI Global is prohibited.

large number of zero values on certain size variables do not represent missing or rounded values.

The Tukutuku database uses six variables to record the number of features and functions for each application. They all exhibited a large number of zeros, reducing their contribution toward finding the most similar projects. We therefore decided to group their values by creating two new variables: TOTHIGH (summation of HFOTS, HFOTSA, and HNEW) and TOTNHIGH (summation of FOTS, FOTSA, and NEW).

We also created a new variable called NLANG, representing the number of different implementation languages used per project, replacing the original multivalued variable that stored the names of the different implementation languages.

The last part of the variables selection phase is to identify which variables are significantly associated with effort. This step is carried out in order to reduce the set of variables to be used to build the CART model to only those that are significantly related with effort.

In order to measure the level of association between numerical variables and effort, we used a statistical test to confirm if the numerical variables were normally distributed. This statistical test is called the one-sample Kolmogorov-Smirnov test (K-S test). It compares an observed distribution to a theoretical distribution. Significance values equal to, or smaller than, 0.05 indicate that the observed distribution differs from the theoretical distribution.

To use the one-sample K-S test in SPSS, follow these steps:

- Select *Analyze* ⇨ *Nonparametric tests* ⇨ *1-Sample K-S.*
- Then click the test distribution *Normal* and select on the left list all the variables to be checked. Once selected, click the arrow button to show them as part of the test variable list.

We employed the K-S test and its results showed that none of the numerical variables had distributions that matched the normal distribution. This means that a nonparametric test needs to be used to measure the level of association between numerical variables and effort. The test used was Spearman's correlation test. It calculates Spearman's rho, r_s, to measure the strength and the direction of the relationship between two variables that were measured on an ordinal scale. It is also the technique of choice whenever interval, ratio, and absolute variables are not normally distributed and are part of a small data sample.

To obtain Spearman's correlation coefficient in SPSS, follow these steps:

Copyright © 2008, IGI Global. Copying or distributing in print or electronic forms without written permission of IGI Global is prohibited.

- Select *Analyze* ⇨ *Correlate* ⇨ *Bivariate*.
- Select the two variables from the list on the left whose association you want to measure and click on the arrow button to have them moved to the box labeled *Variables*.
- Tick the option *Spearman* in the group labeled *Correlation Coefficients*.
- Tick the option *Two-tailed* in the group labeled *Test of Significance*.
- Optionally, tick the option *Flag significant correlations*.

Here again, the choice of a two-tailed test of significance depends on whether or not you know in advance the direction of the association (positive or negative). If the direction the association takes is unknown, use a two-tailed test of significance; otherwise, use a one-tailed test of significance.

The results obtained using SPSS for the Tukutuku data are shown in Table 9. Spearman's correlation test shows the correlation coefficients taking into account all the possible combinations of variables. Since we used 14 variables, results show 14x14 correlation coefficients. A correlation coefficient between a variable and itself is always equal to 1 since this represents a perfect linear association.

Table 9 shows that 12 attributes are significantly associated (correlated) with effort. This is signalled via the use of one or two asterisks, which flag a statistically significant correlation. These 12 attributes are the following: typeproj, nlang, proimprn, metricsn, devteam, teamexp, totwp, newwp, totimg, imgnew, tothigh, and totnhigh. These will be the attributes that we will use with the CART tool to obtain effort estimates.

Obtaining Effort Estimates

This section describes the use of AnswerTree, from SPSS Inc., to build an effort model and obtain effort estimates for Web projects from the Tukutuku database. The first step of this process is to import the Tukutuku data onto AnswerTree. This can be accomplished by importing data from an existing database or file. The Tukutuku database was already stored on an SPSS data file, therefore the steps will take that into account. Please note that if your data are stored on a database, on an MS Excel file, or in a text file (ASCII), it can readily be imported into AnswerTree. In this chapter we provide as much detail as possible on how to use a CART tool as it is our belief that the functionality offered by CART tools will be similar to the functionality offered in AnswerTree, therefore the knowledge of how to use one CART tool may be useful and readily applicable when using a CART tool other than AnswerTree. In so doing, we are not advocating the use of AnswerTree.

Copyright © 2008, IGI Global. Copying or distributing in print or electronic forms without written permission of IGI Global is prohibited.

Table 9. Spearman's correlation test results in SPSS

		toteff	typeproj	nlang	docpron	proimpm	metricsn	devteam	teamexp	totwp	newwp	totimg	imgnew	totbigh	totnhigh
toteff	Correlation Coefficient	1.000	.438(**)	.282(**)	.083	.332(**)	.463(**)	.507(**)	.333(**)	.705(**)	.781(**)	.551(**)	.566(**)	.628(**)	.311(**)
	Sig. (2-tailed)	.	.000	.008	.447	.002	.000	.000	.002	.000	.000	.000	.000	.000	.003
typeproj	Correlation Coefficient	.438(**)	1.000	-.001	.298(**)	.220(*)	.275(**)	.145	.497(**)	.183	.598(**)	.251(*)	.294(**)	-.030	-.081
	Sig. (2-tailed)	.000	.	.996	.005	.041	.010	.180	.000	.089	.000	.019	.006	.781	.456
nlang	Correlation Coefficient	.282(**)	-.001	1.000	.177	.387(**)	.306(**)	.131	.308(**)	.119	.164	.252(*)	.340(**)	.415(**)	.229(*)
	Sig. (2-tailed)	.008	.996	.	.102	.000	.004	.226	.004	.130	.190	.019	.001	.000	.033
docpron	Correlation Coefficient	.083	.298(**)	.177	1.000	.647(**)	.502(**)	-.209	.422(**)	-.025	.190	.077	.252(*)	-.120	.115
	Sig. (2-tailed)	.447	.005	.102	.	.000	.000	.052	.000	.819	.078	.476	.019	.268	.288
proimpm	Correlation Coefficient	.332(**)	.220(*)	.387(**)	.647(**)	1.000	.770(**)	-.168	.369(**)	.130	.286(**)	.209	.388(**)	.149	.206
	Sig. (2-tailed)	.002	.041	.000	.000	.	.000	.120	.000	.231	.007	.052	.000	.169	.056
metricsn	Correlation Coefficient	.463(**)	.275(**)	.306(**)	.502(**)	.770(**)	1.000	-.081	.419(**)	.221(*)	.416(**)	.340(**)	.476(**)	.207	.287(**)
	Sig. (2-tailed)	.000	.010	.004	.000	.000	.	.457	.000	.039	.000	.001	.000	.055	.007
devteam	Correlation Coefficient	.507(**)	.145	.131	-.209	-.168	-.081	1.000	.115	.361(**)	.280(**)	.232(*)	.355(**)	.360(**)	.062
	Sig. (2-tailed)	.000	.145	.226	.052	.120	.457	.	.288	.001	.009	.031	.001	.001	.571
teamexp	Correlation Coefficient	.333(**)	.497(**)	.308(**)	.422(**)	.369(**)	.419(**)	.115	1.000	.141	.392(**)	.452(**)	.461(**)	.132	.213(*)
	Sig. (2-tailed)	.002	.000	.004	.000	.000	.000	.115	.	.191	.000	.000	.000	.221	.048
totwp	Correlation Coefficient	.705(**)	.183	.119	-.025	.130	.221(*)	.361(**)	.141	1.000	.692(**)	.498(**)	.339(**)	.478(**)	.489(**)
	Sig. (2-tailed)	.000	.089	.273	.819	.231	.039	.001	.191	.	.000	.000	.001	.000	.000
newwp	Correlation Coefficient	.781(**)	.598(**)	.164	.190	.286(**)	.416(**)	.280(**)	.392(**)	.692(**)	1.000	.484(**)	.435(**)	.423(**)	.172
	Sig. (2-tailed)	.000	.000	.130	.078	.007	.000	.009	.000	.000	.	.000	.000	.000	.111

**Correlation is significant at the 0.01 level (two-tailed)
*Correlation is significant at the 0.05 level (two-tailed)

Copyright © 2008, IGI Global. Copying or distributing in print or electronic forms without written permission of IGI Global is prohibited.

Table 9. continued

		toteff	typeproj	nlang	docpron	proimprn	metricsn	devteam	teamexp	totwp	newwp	totimg	imgnew	tothigh	totnhigh
totimg	Correlation Coefficient	.551(**)	.251(*)	.252(*)	.077	.209	.340(**)	.232(*)	.452(**)	.498(**)	.484(**)	1.000	.680(**)	.332(**)	.319(**)
	Sig. (2-tailed)	.000	.019	.019	.476	.052	.001	.031	.000	.000	.000	.	.000	.002	.003
imgnew	Correlation Coefficient	.566(**)	.294(**)	.340(**)	.252(*)	.388(**)	.476(**)	.355(**)	.461(**)	.339(**)	.435(**)	.680(**)	1.000	.272(*)	.123
	Sig. (2-tailed)	.000	.006	.001	.019	.000	.000	.001	.000	.001	.000	.000		.011	.123
tothigh	Correlation Coefficient	.628(**)	-.030	.415(**)	-.120	.149	.207	.360(**)	.132	.478(**)	.423(**)	.332(**)	.272(*)	1.000	.353(**)
	Sig. (2-tailed)	.000	.781	.000	.268	.169	.055	.001	.221	.000	.000	.002	.011	.	.001
totnhigh	Correlation Coefficient	.311(**)	-.081	.229(*)	.115	.206	.287(**)	.062	.213(*)	.489(**)	.172	.319(**)	.123	.353(**)	1.000
	Sig. (2-tailed)	.003	.456	.033	.288	.056	.007	.571	.048	.000	.111	.003	.258	.001	.

**Correlation is significant at the 0.01 level (two-tailed)*
Correlation is significant at the 0.05 level (two-tailed)

Copyright © 2008, IGI Global. Copying or distributing in print or electronic forms without written permission of IGI Global is prohibited.

To enable AnswerTree to import an SPSS data file, follow these steps:

1.   Create a new project by selecting *File* ⇨ *New Project.*
2.   A data source screen will open (see Figure 3) so that you can select the data source. Once you click the *OK* button, an *Open file* dialog will allow you to select the data source file.
3.   Once you select the file (see Figure 4) and click *Open,* a wizard screen will automatically open (see Figure 5) to take you through a four-step process where parameters are chosen and used to build the CART model. The first screen on this wizard asks you to choose the method to be used to build the tree model (grow the tree). Since in this chapter we are applying CART for Web effort estimation, the option to choose is *C&RT*; click the *Next* button.
4.   The second screen in the four-step process is used to select the variables that will be used to build the CART tree (see Figure 6). Within the context of this case study, our target or response variable is TOTEFF (this is the variable that we wish to estimate), and all remaining variables are to be used as predictor variables. Therefore, we drag TOTEFF from the list displayed on the left-hand side of the screen and drop it beside the *Target* list. As we are using all the remaining variables as predictors, we tick the option *All others* under category *Predictors.* Click *Next.*
5.   The third screen in the four-step process is used to choose the method, if any, to be used to validate the tree (see Figure 7). Tree validation or model validation is a way to assess how good the model is at explaining the variation in the target variable. In terms of validation, the three possible choices are as follows.

   a.   *Do not validate the tree:* This option does not split the data into training and validation sets. It simply uses the entire data set to build the tree and also to validate the tree.

   b.   *Partition my data into subsamples:* This option splits the original data set into training and validation sets. The user defines, by means of a slider control, the percentages of data to be used as training and validation sets. The training set is used to generate and build the tree; the validation set is used to test and validate the model. If the model generated provides good predictions for the projects in the validation set, this suggests that the model is a good fit to the data, and perhaps may also be useful to obtain predictions for other projects that are not currently part of the validation set. To generate a model only based on the training set, you need to select from the main menu *View* ⇨ *Sample* ⇨ *Training.* Once the model has been created, you select *View* ⇨ *Sample* ⇨ *Testing* in order to have the model tested using the validation set.

Copyright © 2008, IGI Global. Copying or distributing in print or electronic forms without written permission of IGI Global is prohibited.

    c.   *Cross-validation:* This option carries out a cross-validation where the original data set is split into training and validation sets. However, this time the split is automatically chosen by AnswerTree. The only parameter you can set relates to the number of cross-validations that you wish AnswerTree to carry out. The measures of goodness of fit that we will detail later in this chapter are based on the average goodness of fit obtained for each model that was created and validated in this cross-validation. So, if we use a 20-fold cross-validation, this means that 20 alternative trees will be built and validated, and the average of their goodness of fit will be the overall measure of goodness of fit presented. AnswerTree uses as default a 10-fold cross-validation; however, for our example we have set it to 20-fold cross-validation.

    d.   Figure 7 also shows another parameter that sets the starting value for the random-number generator (random seed). When this value is set, all the validation sets that were defined with the same random number seed will always allocate the same data points to the same sets, therefore if you wish to compare validation techniques, you can do so. AnswerTree's default setting is 2000000.

6.   Click the *Next* button.

7.   The fourth and last screen in the four-step process is used to select and configure advanced parameters, or to simply opt to use the defaults provided by AnswerTree itself (see Figure 8). As the data set we are using in our case study is small, we need to change some of the advanced parameters in order to reflect this by clicking the button *Advanced Options* (see Figure 9[a]). You will be presented with three separate tabs: *Stopping Rules*, *C&RT*, and *Pruning*. Figure 9(a) shows the defaults that are provided by AnswerTree. In our example, we need to change the values for the minimum number of cases for the parent node and child node, so we set the minimum number of cases for the parent node to 5 and the minimum number of cases for the child node to 1 (see Figure 9[b]). Nodes with fewer cases than the minimum number of cases will not be split. As we will see later, these values may not provide the best CART model for the data we have, and as such we may need to change these settings further down the line and assess their effectiveness in providing a model that has large explanatory power in regard to TOTEFF. We also kept the number of levels that the CART tree can grow to (levels below root under the category *Maximum Tree Depth*) and the minimum change in impurity (under the category *C&RT*) unchanged. AnswerTree will try to split a node if the results for an impurity value are greater than the minimum change in impurity.

8.   Next, we move to the tab labeled *C&RT* (see Figure 10). This screen allows you to choose the impurity measure to be used when the target variable is

Copyright © 2008, IGI Global. Copying or distributing in print or electronic forms without written permission of IGI Global is prohibited.

categorical. The most well-known measure to be used in these circumstances is the Gini impurity measure (Brieman et al., 1984), which is the default. As our target variable TOTEFF is numerical, the measure of impurity to be used is the least squares deviation (Brieman et al.). We also kept the maximum number of surrogates unchanged.

Figure 3. Creating a new project and choosing the data source

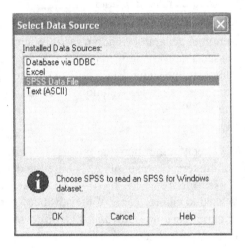

Figure 4. Selecting the data source file

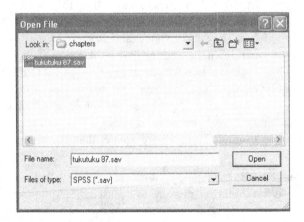

Copyright © 2008, IGI Global. Copying or distributing in print or electronic forms without written permission of IGI Global is prohibited.

9.   Finally, we move to the next tab labelled *Pruning* (see Figure 11). It provides
     two choices for selecting subtrees: standard error rule and minimum risk. If
     the former is selected, AnswerTree selects the smallest subtree that has a risk

Figure 5. Tree wizard: Growing method

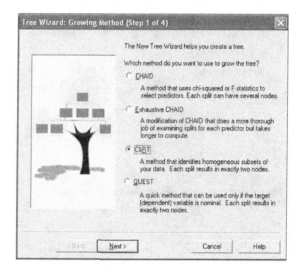

Figure 6. Tree wizard: Model definition

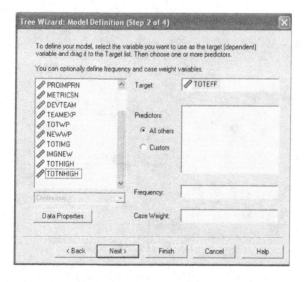

Copyright © 2008, IGI Global. Copying or distributing in print or electronic forms without written permission
of IGI Global is prohibited.

value similar to that of the subtree with the smallest risk. This is the default option. If the latter is selected, AnswerTree selects the subtree that has the smallest risk. We also kept the default setting unchanged. Once this is finished,

Figure 7. Tree wizard: Validation

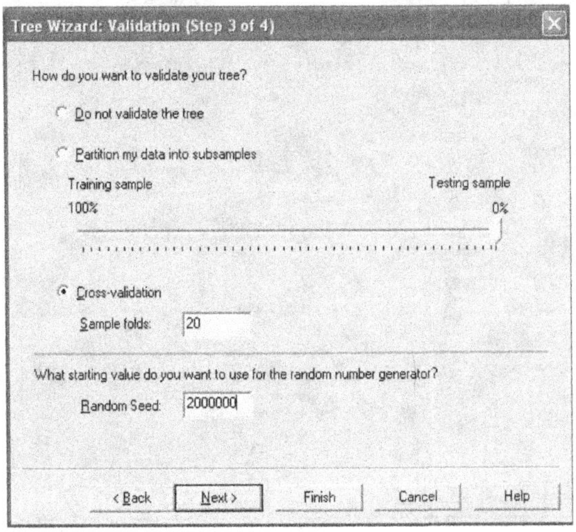

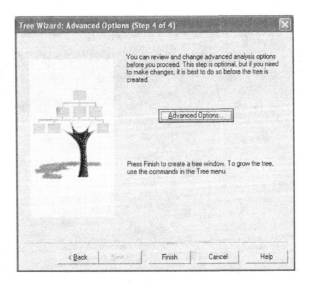

Figure 8. Tree wizard: Advanced options

Copyright © 2008, IGI Global. Copying or distributing in print or electronic forms without written permission of IGI Global is prohibited.

we click the button *OK*, which takes us back to Screen 4 of the wizard (see Figure 8). We then click the button *Finish*. AnswerTree automatically shows the root tree node in another window (see Figure 12). We can now save this project by selecting *File* ⇨ *Save Project*.

Figure 9. Advanced options: Stopping rules

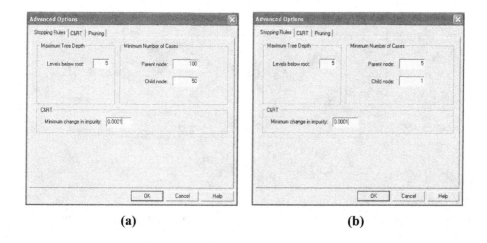

(a)   (b)

Figure 10. Advanced options: C&RT

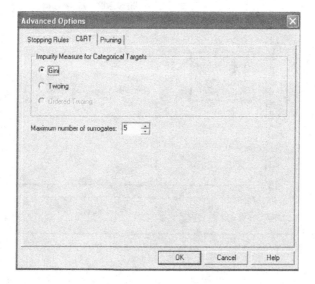

Copyright © 2008, IGI Global. Copying or distributing in print or electronic forms without written permission of IGI Global is prohibited.

Figure 11. Advanced options: Pruning

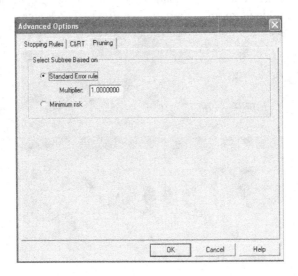

Figure 12. AnswerTree main window with tree window showing root tree node

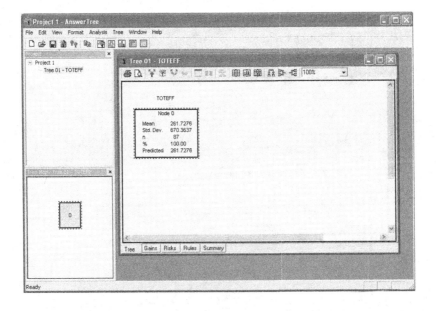

Copyright © 2008, IGI Global. Copying or distributing in print or electronic forms without written permission of IGI Global is prohibited.

The root node of the tree about to be constructed or grown (see Figure 12) shows a few statistics for TOTEFF, for example, average effort, standard deviation for effort values, percentage of cases that are in this node, and predicted effort. To grow this tree step by step, we need to select *Tree ⇨ Grow Tree One Level*. We can see that two new nodes were added to the tree, one containing 1 case (1.15% of cases) and the other containing 86 cases (98.85% of cases). The predictor variable used for this split was TOTHIGH; if we were to traverse the tree as is to obtain estimated effort for new projects, we would go from the root node to Node 2 if TOTHIGH was greater than 11, and from the root node to Node 1 if TOTHIGH was smaller or equal to 11. On the left-hand side of the main screen we can also see the tree structure using a tree map (see Figure 13).

When we select *Tree ⇨ Grow Tree One Level*, we can see that the tree has not grown uniformly (see Figure 14). Only Node 1 was split further. One of the reasons why AnswerTree did not split Node 2 further was this node had only a single case, which is the value that had been previously set as the minimum number of cases for the child node. The other reason is that it is not possible to split a node that has less than two cases, for obvious reasons. The variable used to split Node 1 further was also TOTHIGH. Node 3 contains 76 cases and Node 4 contains 10 cases. Growing another level of this tree splits Nodes 3 and 4 further (see Figure 15).

Figure 13. AnswerTree main window with tree window showing root tree plus one level

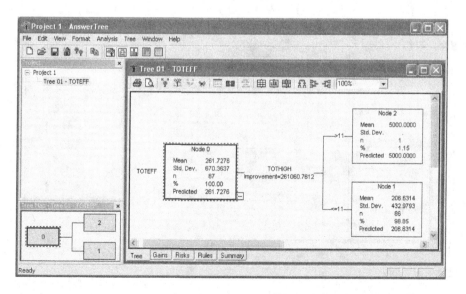

Copyright © 2008, IGI Global. Copying or distributing in print or electronic forms without written permission of IGI Global is prohibited.

Figure 14. AnswerTree main window with tree window showing root tree plus two levels

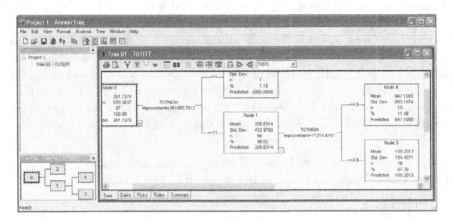

Figure 15. AnswerTree main window with tree window showing further split of Nodes 3 and 4

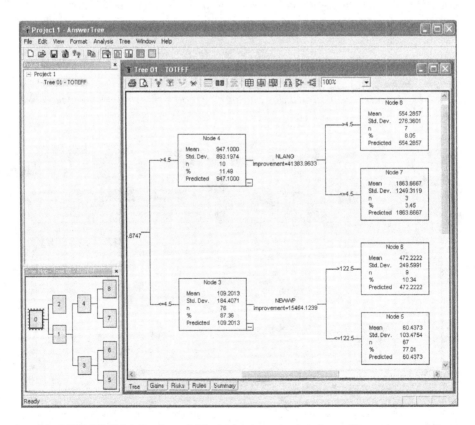

Copyright © 2008, IGI Global. Copying or distributing in print or electronic forms without written permission of IGI Global is prohibited.

We can see that the variable used to split Nodes 3 and 4 further is no longer TO-THIGH. For Node 4, NLANG was used, whereas for Node 3, NEWWP was used. We still remain with a single node containing 67 cases (Node 5). In addition, of the original 12 predictor variables used, the only variables that have been selected are TOTHIGH, NLANG, and NEWWP. This suggests that these three variables are amongst the best predictors of effort, given our data set. When we split the tree one level further (see Figures 16 and 17), we can see that the variable TOTIMG was used to split Nodes 5 and 6 further, whereas the variable PROIMPRN was used to split Node 8 further. Thus, two more variables are added to the list of best predictors: TOTIMG and PROIMPRN.

Growing the tree another level splits Nodes 9, 10, 11, and 14 further (see Figures 18 and 19), adding two new variables as selected predictors: DEVTEAM and IMGNEW.

When we select *Tree ⇨ Grow Tree One Level*, AnswerTree shows the message, "The tree cannot be grown further because one or more stopping rules are met." Now we need to remove unnecessary splits by applying a pruning algorithm to the final tree.

Figure 16. AnswerTree main window with Nodes 5 and 6 split further

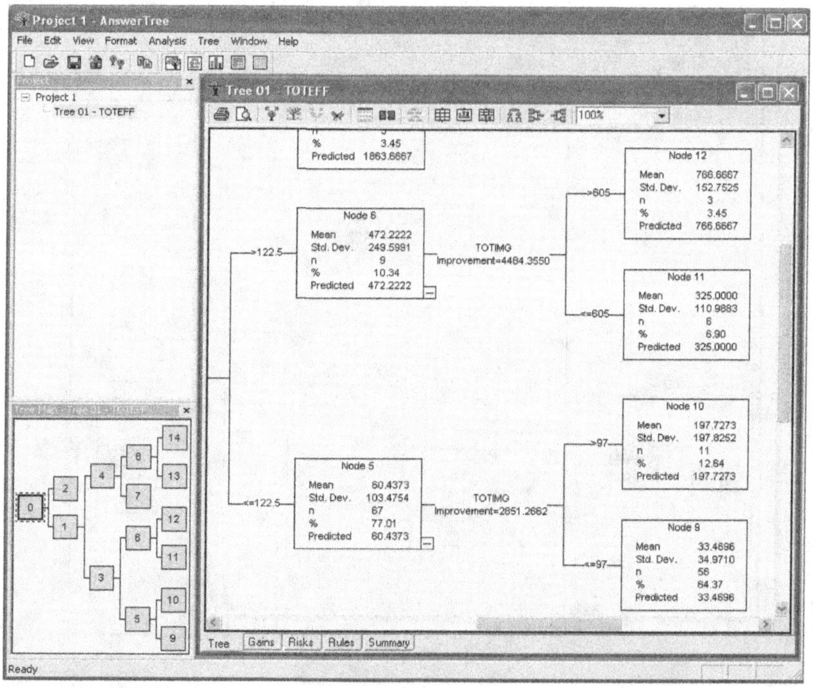

Copyright © 2008, IGI Global. Copying or distributing in print or electronic forms without written permission of IGI Global is prohibited.

Figure 17. AnswerTree main window with Node 8 split further

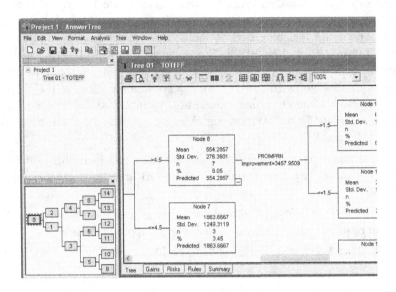

Figure 18. AnswerTree main window with Nodes 9 and 10 split further

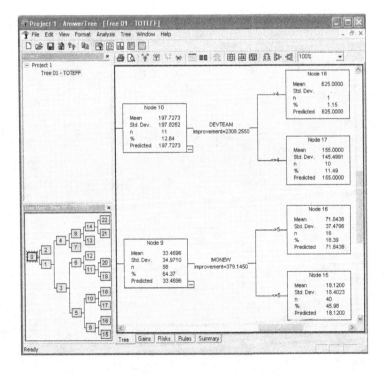

Copyright © 2008, IGI Global. Copying or distributing in print or electronic forms without written permission of IGI Global is prohibited.

Figure 19. AnswerTree main window with Nodes 11 and 14 split further

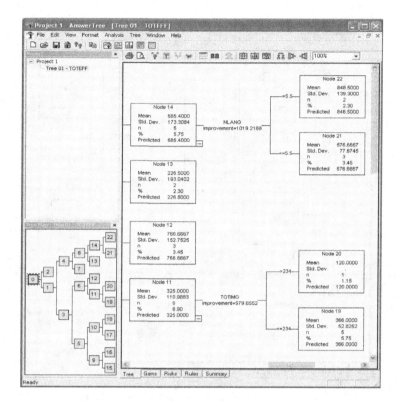

This is accomplished by selecting *Tree ⇨ Grow Tree and Prune*. When this function is finished, we have a tree that is two levels smaller (see Figure 20[b]) than the one initially created (see Figure 20[a]). This means that only variables TOTHIGH, NLANG, and NEWWP are really necessary to build a CART model.

In order to assess the goodness of fit of the CART model in predicting effort, we need to examine the risk summary for the tree by selecting the *Risks* tab on the right-hand side (see Figure 21).

The risk estimate corresponds to the within-node (error) variance. The total variance, which represents the risk estimate for the CART model with only a single node, is equal to the within-node variance plus the between-node (explained) variance (Brieman et al., 1984). Within the context of our example, the within-node variance is 25409.6, and the total variance is 54998.6. The variance ratio due to

Copyright © 2008, IGI Global. Copying or distributing in print or electronic forms without written permission of IGI Global is prohibited.

Figure 20. Tree before and after pruning

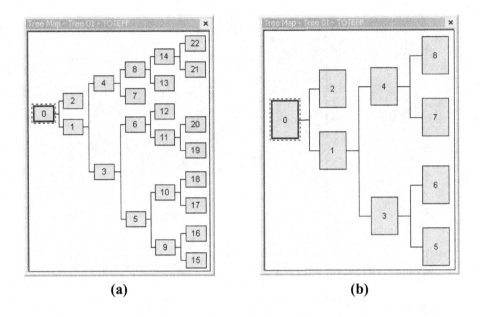

(a)   **(b)**

Figure 21. Risk estimate for tree

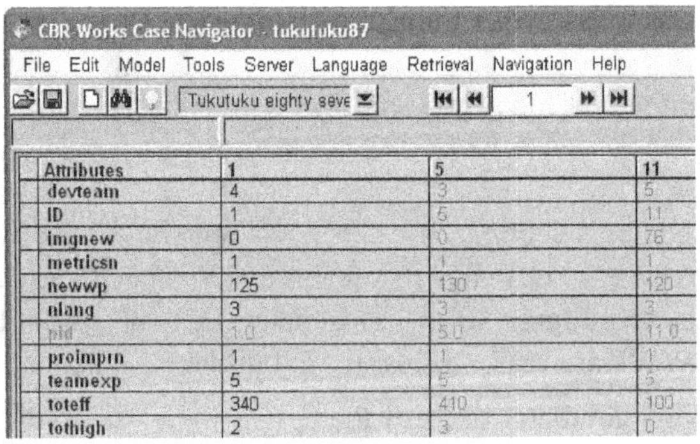

error corresponds to the within-node variance divided by the total variance, thus 25409.6 divided by 54998.6, which corresponds to 0.46 (46%). This suggests that the amount of variance explained by the CART model corresponds to 100% - 46%, that is, 54%. As a result, this indicates this CART model can only explain 54% of

Copyright © 2008, IGI Global. Copying or distributing in print or electronic forms without written permission of IGI Global is prohibited.

the variation in TOTEFF. This small percentage also suggests that the model may not have captured the most important variables. In this instance, we now revisit the advanced parameters that were used to build this model to assess if any new settings may affect the goodness of the fit of the model, given our particular data. We accomplish this by creating new trees and changing some of the settings. As you might guess, this step requires a certain amount of trial and error.

The settings for the group of models that provide the best fit for the data are shown in Figure 22. They are all under the same project: Project 1. For each tree, we present its goodness of fit, maximum number of levels, and minimum number of cases for the parent and child nodes. Tree 13 provided the best fit overall, showing that the model can explain 77% of the variation in TOTEFF. It used nine levels, a minimum of two cases in the parent node, and a minimum of one case in the child node. All original predictor variables have been selected by this model: TOTHIGH, NLANG, PROIMPRN, TYPEPROJ, TEAMEXP, NEWWP, TOTIMG, IMGNEW, TOTWP, DEVTEAM, TOTNHIGH, and METRICSN. This is an excellent result, in particular when compared to the adjusted R^2 of 76.5% obtained for the same data set using regression analysis (see Chapter V).

Figure 22. Different tree models, each with different goodness of fit

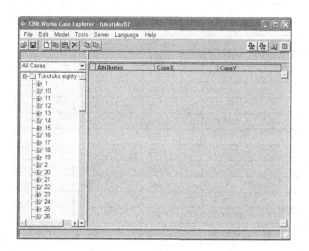

Copyright © 2008, IGI Global. Copying or distributing in print or electronic forms without written permission of IGI Global is prohibited.

Table 10. Results from applying CART to 87 Web projects

Case ID	Actual Effort	Estimated Effort	MRE	Residual	Pred
1.00	340.00	340.00	0.00	0.00	TRUE
2.00	300.00	300.00	0.00	0.00	TRUE
3.00	75.00	68.50	0.09	6.50	TRUE
4.00	24.00	25.03	0.04	1.03	TRUE
5.00	410.00	410.00	0.00	0.00	TRUE
6.00	40.00	45.75	0.14	5.75	TRUE
7.00	130.00	130.00	0.00	0.00	TRUE
8.00	21.00	25.03	0.19	4.03	TRUE
9.00	1786.00	1786.00	0.00	0.00	TRUE
10.00	900.00	900.00	0.00	0.00	TRUE
11.00	100.00	100.00	0.00	0.00	TRUE
12.00	50.00	50.00	0.00	0.00	TRUE
13.00	429.00	429.00	0.00	0.00	TRUE
14.00	90.00	90.00	0.00	0.00	TRUE
15.00	34.00	34.00	0.00	0.00	TRUE
16.00	363.00	363.00	0.00	0.00	TRUE
17.00	6.00	6.00	0.00	0.00	TRUE
18.00	38.00	45.75	0.20	7.75	TRUE
19.00	30.00	34.50	0.15	4.50	TRUE
20.00	625.00	625.00	0.00	0.00	TRUE
21.00	6.00	5.26	0.12	0.74	TRUE
22.00	16.00	21.00	0.31	5.00	FALSE
23.00	26.00	21.00	0.19	5.00	TRUE
24.00	102.00	96.00	0.06	6.00	TRUE
25.00	300.00	300.00	0.00	0.00	TRUE
26.00	600.00	600.00	0.00	0.00	TRUE
27.00	655.00	655.00	0.00	0.00	TRUE
28.00	100.00	100.00	0.00	0.00	TRUE
29.00	100.00	100.00	0.00	0.00	TRUE
30.00	43.00	34.50	0.20	8.50	TRUE
31.00	105.00	105.00	0.00	0.00	TRUE
32.00	3150.00	3150.00	0.00	0.00	TRUE
33.00	750.00	750.00	0.00	0.00	TRUE
34.00	90.00	96.00	0.07	6.00	TRUE
35.00	5000.00	5000.00	0.00	0.00	TRUE
36.00	500.00	500.00	0.00	0.00	TRUE
37.00	120.00	120.00	0.00	0.00	TRUE
38.00	600.00	600.00	0.00	0.00	TRUE
39.00	120.00	120.00	0.00	0.00	TRUE
40.00	30.00	34.50	0.15	4.50	TRUE
41.00	20.00	25.03	0.25	5.03	FALSE
42.00	35.00	25.03	0.28	9.97	FALSE

Copyright © 2008, IGI Global. Copying or distributing in print or electronic forms without written permission of IGI Global is prohibited.

Table 10. continued

Case ID	Actual Effort	Estimated Effort	MRE	Residual	Pred
43.00	150.00	150.00	0.00	0.00	TRUE
44.00	120.00	120.00	0.00	0.00	TRUE
45.00	800.00	800.00	0.00	0.00	TRUE
46.00	60.00	45.75	0.24	14.25	TRUE
47.00	90.00	90.00	0.00	0.00	TRUE
48.00	45.00	45.75	0.02	0.75	TRUE
49.00	35.00	34.50	0.01	0.50	TRUE
50.00	947.00	947.00	0.00	0.00	TRUE
51.00	351.00	351.00	0.00	0.00	TRUE
52.00	640.00	640.00	0.00	0.00	TRUE
53.00	490.00	490.00	0.00	0.00	TRUE
54.00	8.33	5.26	0.37	3.07	FALSE
55.00	62.50	62.50	0.00	0.00	TRUE
56.00	58.16	68.50	0.18	10.34	TRUE
57.00	20.31	20.31	0.00	0.00	TRUE
58.00	178.00	178.00	0.00	0.00	TRUE
59.00	6.00	6.00	0.00	0.00	TRUE
60.00	22.00	21.32	0.03	0.68	TRUE
61.00	12.00	5.26	0.56	6.74	FALSE
62.00	5.30	5.26	0.01	0.04	TRUE
63.00	72.30	68.50	0.05	3.80	TRUE
64.00	91.00	91.00	0.00	0.00	TRUE
65.00	13.10	13.10	0.00	0.00	TRUE
66.00	8.15	12.15	0.49	4.00	FALSE
67.00	37.30	37.30	0.00	0.00	TRUE
68.00	1.10	5.26	3.78	4.16	FALSE
69.00	21.00	21.32	0.02	0.32	TRUE
70.00	11.45	5.26	0.54	6.19	FALSE
71.00	20.20	21.32	0.06	1.12	TRUE
72.00	16.15	12.15	0.25	4.00	TRUE
73.00	13.28	5.26	0.60	8.02	FALSE
74.00	3.15	5.26	0.67	2.11	FALSE
75.00	25.15	25.03	0.00	0.12	TRUE
76.00	1.30	5.26	3.05	3.96	FALSE
77.00	6.15	5.26	0.14	0.89	TRUE
78.00	7.15	5.26	0.26	1.89	FALSE
79.00	1.33	5.26	2.95	3.93	FALSE
80.00	2.00	5.26	1.63	3.26	FALSE
81.00	2.45	5.26	1.15	2.81	FALSE
82.00	2.42	5.26	1.17	2.84	FALSE
83.00	4.07	5.26	0.29	1.19	FALSE
84.00	4.12	5.26	0.28	1.14	FALSE

Copyright © 2008, IGI Global. Copying or distributing in print or electronic forms without written permission of IGI Global is prohibited.

Table 10. continued

Case ID	Actual Effort	Estimated Effort	MRE	Residual	Pred
85.00	17.24	21.32	0.24	4.08	TRUE
86.00	3.00	5.26	0.75	2.26	FALSE
87.00	26.14	21.32	0.18	4.82	TRUE
		MMRE	25.79		
		MdMRE	0.75		
		Pred(25)	78.16		

Tree 13 has 99 nodes of which 46 are leaf nodes. Using this tree model, we obtained the estimated effort for each of the 87 projects in our data set and also measures of prediction accuracy (see Table 10). Unfortunately, it is impossible to reproduce this tree here.

As we have seen in Chapter 3, an effort estimation model or technique is considered good if results present an MMRE and MdMRE less than or equal to 25% and Pred(25) greater than or equal to 75%. If we look at the values of MMRE, MdMRE, and Pred(25) obtained using the model represented by Tree 13 (see Table 10), it is clear that MMRE is very close to 25%, MdMRE is much lower than 25%, and Pred(25) is greater than 75%, thus in principle indicating that CART provided very good predictions. However, the CART model was generated based on the entire data set and as such, predictions are very likely to be optimistic. What we need to do is to use part of the data set to build a new CART tree (training set) and to use the remaining data to validate that model. This cross-validation process will be detailed in the next section.

Model Validation

As described in Chapter III, to validate a model, we need to do the following:

Step 1. Divide data set d into a training set t and a validation set v.

Step 2. Use t to produce an effort estimation model te (if applicable).

Step 3. Use te to predict effort for each of the projects in v as if these projects were new projects for which effort was unknown.

Copyright © 2008, IGI Global. Copying or distributing in print or electronic forms without written permission of IGI Global is prohibited.

This process is known as cross-validation. For an *n*-fold cross-validation, *n* different training and validation sets are used. In this section, we will show the cross-validation procedure using a one-fold cross-validation with a 66% split. This split means that 66% of our project data will be used for model building and the remaining 34% will be used to validate the model; that is, the training set will have 66% of the total number of projects and the validation set will have the remaining 34%.

Our initial data set had 87 projects. At Step 1 they are split into training and validation sets containing 58 and 29 projects respectively. Generally, projects are selected randomly. As part of Step 2, sometimes we need to create an effort model using the 58 projects in the training set as is the approach used with CART.

To measure the CART's prediction accuracy, we obtained the MMRE, MdMRE, and Pred(25) for the validation set. Using AnswerTree, the training set of 58 projects is used to build a tree model that is then used to manually obtain estimated effort for each of the 29 projects in the validation set; then MRE is computed. Having the calculated estimated effort and the actual effort (provided by the Web companies), we are finally in a position to calculate MRE for each of the 29 projects, and hence MMRE, MdMRE, and Pred(25) for the entire 29 projects. This process is explained in Figure 23.

We reduced the original data set of 87 projects to 58 randomly selected projects. This subset was then used to build a CART tree with a maximum of nine levels, a minimum of two cases for the parent node, and a minimum of one case for the child node. This was the same configuration used to build Tree 13, described in the previous section. The tree we obtained used 69 nodes (see Figure 24) and 11

Figure 23. Steps used in the cross-validation process

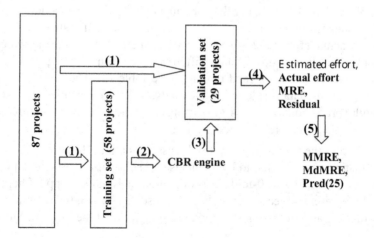

Copyright © 2008, IGI Global. Copying or distributing in print or electronic forms without written permission of IGI Global is prohibited.

Figure 24. Tree generated using data on 58 projects

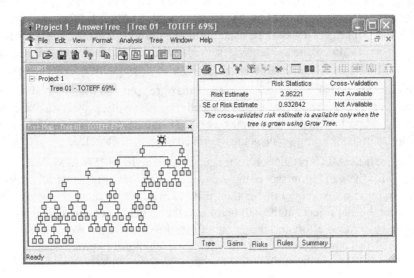

predictor variables: TOTHIGH, NLANG, TYPEPROJ, TOTIMG, IMGNEW, TOTNHIGH, TEAMEXP, PROIMPR, DEVTEAM, TOTWP, and NEWWP. This model explained 68.5% of the variation in TOTEFF. It is not possible to reproduce this tree here as it is too large.

Table 11 shows the estimated effort and MRE for the 29 projects used as the validation set, and the summary prediction accuracy measures.

Here again, if we consider that a good prediction model has an MMRE less than or equal to 25% and Pred(25) greater than or equal to 75%, then the values presented in Table 11 suggest the accuracy of CART is overall poor. If instead we were to use the mean actual effort (432.44) as the estimated effort, both sets of predictions would not be statistically significantly different, as confirmed using the nonparametric paired test Wilcoxon signed-rank test (see Table 13). These results suggest that, at least for the data employed in the analysis, Web companies are likely to obtain similar predictions using CART or using estimations based on a simple effort average calculated from past finished projects.

Table 12 presents the results for a one-fold cross-validation. However, research on effort estimation suggests that to have unbiased results for a cross-validation, we should actually use at least a 20-fold cross-validation analysis (Kirsopp & Shepperd). This would represent, at least for the data set presented herein, the selection of 20 different training and validation sets and the aggregation of the MMRE, MdMRE,

Copyright © 2008, IGI Global. Copying or distributing in print or electronic forms without written permission of IGI Global is prohibited.

Table 11. Results from applying CART to 29 Web projects

Case ID	Actual Effort	Estimated Effort	MRE	Residual	Pred
1	340.00	6.00	0.98	334.00	FALSE
3	75.00	40.15	0.46	34.85	FALSE
5	410.00	6.00	0.99	404.00	FALSE
7	130.00	91.00	0.30	39.00	FALSE
9	1786.00	58.16	0.97	1727.84	FALSE
11	100.00	640.00	5.40	540.00	FALSE
13	429.00	6.00	0.99	423.00	FALSE
15	34.00	625.00	17.38	591.00	FALSE
17	6.00	35.00	4.83	29.00	FALSE
19	30.00	23.38	0.22	6.62	TRUE
21	6.00	6.25	0.04	0.25	TRUE
23	26.00	14.00	0.46	12.00	FALSE
25	300.00	14.00	0.95	286.00	FALSE
27	655.00	947.00	0.45	292.00	FALSE
29	100.00	91.00	0.09	9.00	TRUE
31	105.00	10.15	0.90	94.85	FALSE
33	750.00	40.15	0.95	709.85	FALSE
35	5000.00	363.00	0.93	4637.00	FALSE
37	120.00	50.00	0.58	70.00	FALSE
39	120.00	300.00	1.50	180.00	FALSE
41	20.00	23.38	0.17	3.38	TRUE
43	150.00	40.00	0.73	110.00	FALSE
45	800.00	300.00	0.63	500.00	FALSE
47	90.00	90.00	0.00	0.00	TRUE
49	35.00	40.15	0.15	5.15	TRUE
51	351.00	6.00	0.98	345.00	FALSE
53	490.00	40.15	0.92	449.85	FALSE
55	62.50	72.30	0.16	9.80	TRUE
57	20.31	72.30	2.56	51.99	FALSE
		MMRE	157.47		
		MdMRE	90.33		
		Pred(25)	24.14		

Table 12. Summary prediction accuracy for CART and mean effort

	CART	Mean Effort
MMRE	157.47	555.76
MdMRE	90.33	118.11
Pred(25)	24.14	13.79

Copyright © 2008, IGI Global. Copying or distributing in print or electronic forms without written permission of IGI Global is prohibited.

Table 13. Wilcoxon test comparing CART estimations to mean effort

Test Statistics[b]	
	resMean - resCART
Z	-1.233[a]
Asymp. Sig. (two-tailed)	.218

[a] *Based on negative ranks*
[b] *Wilcoxon signed-ranks test*

and Pred(25) after the accuracy for all 20 groups has been calculated. Note that we are not aware of any other studies that have investigated this claim and suggest that further investigation is necessary before it can be asserted that Web companies use a minimum 20-fold cross-validation when assessing the prediction accuracy of model and effort estimation techniques.

Conclusion

This chapter presented a case study that used a machine-learning effort estimation technique named classification and regression trees to obtain effort estimates for Web applications. CART is a technique where independent variables (predictors) are used to build binary trees where each leaf node either represents a category to which an estimate belongs or a value for an estimate. The former situation occurs with classification trees and the latter occurs with regression trees; that is, whenever predictors are categorical (e.g., *Yes* or *No*), the tree is called a classification tree, and whenever predictors are numerical, the tree is called a regression tree. To obtain an estimate, one must traverse the tree nodes from root to leaf by selecting the nodes that represent the category or value for the independent variables associated with the case to be estimated.

The data set employed in the case study described in this chapter represents data on industrial projects from the Tukutuku database. The size measures used in the case study represent early Web size measures obtained from the results of a survey investigation (Mendes et al., 2003) using data from 133 online Web forms aimed at giving quotes for Web development projects. In addition, the measures were validated by an established Web company and by a second survey involving 33 Web companies in New Zealand. Consequently, we believe that the size measures

Copyright © 2008, IGI Global. Copying or distributing in print or electronic forms without written permission of IGI Global is prohibited.

identified are plausible effort predictors, not an ad hoc set of variables with no underlying rationale.

The case study details the use of CART for effort estimation. Results have shown that there were no significant differences in prediction accuracy between predictions obtained using CART and those obtained using average effort.

We have detailed the use of CART such that it can be used by any Web company to estimate effort for its projects. Alternatively, Web companies that do not have a data set of past projects may be able to benefit from the cross-company effort estimation models, as detailed in Chapter 9.

References

Brieman, L., Friedman, J., Olshen, R., & Stone, C. (1984). *Classification and regression trees.* Belmont: Wadsworth.

Conte, S., Dunsmore, H., & Shen, V. (1986). *Software engineering metrics and models.* Menlo Park, CA: Benjamin/Cummings.

Mendes, E., Mosley, N., & Counsell, S. (2003, September). Early Web size measures and effort prediction for Web costimation. *Proceedings of the IEEE Metrics Symposium* (pp. 18-29).

Mendes, E., Watson, I., Triggs, C., Mosley, N., & Counsell, S. (2002, June). A comparison of development effort estimation techniques for Web hypermedia applications. *Proceedings of IEEE Metrics Symposium* (pp. 141-151).

Copyright © 2008, IGI Global. Copying or distributing in print or electronic forms without written permission of IGI Global is prohibited.

Chapter VIII

What is the Best Technique?

Abstract

Although numerous studies on Web effort estimation have been carried out to date, there is no consensus on what constitutes the best effort estimation technique to be used by Web companies. It seems that not only the effort estimation technique itself can influence the accuracy of predictions, but also the characteristics of the data set used (e.g., skewness, collinearity; Shepperd & Kadoda, 2001). Therefore, it is often necessary to compare different effort estimation techniques, looking for those that provide the best estimation accuracy for the data set being employed. With this in mind, the use of graphical aids such as boxplots is not always enough to assess the existence of significant differences between effort prediction models. The same applies to measures of prediction accuracy such as the mean magnitude of relative error (MMRE), median magnitude of relative error (MdMRE), and prediction at level 1 (Pred[25]). Other techniques, which correspond to the group of statistical significance tests, need to be employed to check if the different residuals obtained for each of the effort estimation techniques compared come from the same population. This chapter details how to use such techniques and how their results should be interpreted.

Copyright © 2008, IGI Global. Copying or distributing in print or electronic forms without written permission of IGI Global is prohibited.

Introduction

Previous studies in Web effort estimation have used different techniques to estimate effort for new projects, each with a varying degree of success. We have seen in Chapter II that to date there is no single effort estimation technique that always provides the most accurate prediction, and that the identification of such a technique may perhaps never occur. It seems that there is a relationship between the success of a particular technique and factors such as the size of the training set, the nature of the effort estimation function (e.g., continuous or discontinuous), and also characteristics of the data set (e.g., outliers, collinearity; Shepperd & Kadoda, 2001). This suggests that in many cases we are faced with having to use different techniques to estimate effort and consequently to compare their prediction accuracy in order to find out which one presents the best accuracy for the data set employed in the evaluation.

The aim of this chapter, therefore, is to help answer the following question:

How do we compare effort estimation techniques in order to find out which one provides the best estimation accuracy, given the data set employed?

Before explaining how such a comparison can be carried out, we will present a survey of previous studies in Web effort estimation that have compared different techniques. This is done so that the reader is aware of the techniques that have been used and the one, whenever applicable, that provided the best results for that particular data set. This survey is a subset of the survey presented in Chapter II and the motivation for including this subset here is so that readers who have not previously read Chapter II will also be informed about the results from previous studies.

Survey of Web Effort Estimation Studies that Compared Different Techniques

This section presents the results from previous studies in Web effort estimation that compared different effort estimation techniques. Each work is described and summarised in Table 1. Studies will be presented in chronological order.

Copyright © 2008, IGI Global. Copying or distributing in print or electronic forms without written permission of IGI Global is prohibited.

Studies Published in 2000 (Mendes, Counsell, & Mosley, 2000)

Mendes et al. (2000) investigated the use of case-based reasoning (CBR), linear regression, and stepwise regression techniques to estimate development effort for Web applications. These applications were developed by both experienced and inexperienced students. The case-based reasoning estimations were generated using a freeware tool, ANGEL, developed at the University of Bournemouth, United Kingdom. For the CBR technique, the following were used:

- The measure of similarity employed in the study was the unweighted Euclidean distance using a jackknife approach.

- For each Web project for which effort was to be estimated, three effort estimates were obtained: one using the same effort value as the one from the most similar project in the case base, another using as effort the mean effort of the two most similar projects in the case base, and finally the third as effort the mean effort of the three most similar projects in the case base.

In terms of the linear and stepwise regression techniques, both were carried out using SPSS.

The study used two separate data sets (HEL and LEL) containing data respectively on 29 and 41 Web applications developed by second-year computer science students from the University of Southampton, United Kingdom. HEL contains data on projects developed by students who had high experience in Web development previous to participating in the study, whereas LEL contains data on projects developed by students who had very low experience in Web development previous to participating in the study.

The size measures collected for each of the Web projects were the following.

- Page count: Total number of HTML (hypertext markup language) pages created from scratch in a Web application

- Reused page count: Total number of reused HTML pages in a Web application

- Connectivity: Total number of links in a Web application

- Compactness (Botafogo, Rivlin, & Shneiderman, 1992): Level of interconnectedness of the Web pages. Compactness was measured using an ordinal scale from 1 to 5, where 1 represented no connectedness and 5 represented a totally connected application.

Copyright © 2008, IGI Global. Copying or distributing in print or electronic forms without written permission of IGI Global is prohibited.

- Stratum (Botafogo et al., 1992): A measure of how linear an application is. Stratum was also measured using an ordinal scale from 1 to 5, where 1 represented no sequential navigation and 5 represented sequential navigation without any branching.

- Structure: Topology of the application's backbone. Structure was measured using a nominal scale with values sequential, hierarchical, or network.

Prediction accuracy was measured using mean magnitude of relative error (MMRE; Conte, Dunsmore, & Shen, 1986) and the median magnitude of relative error (MdMRE; Conte et al.). The accuracy of the prediction obtained using data on Web projects developed by the HEL group was significantly superior to the accuracy of the predictions obtained using data on Web projects developed by the LEL group. In addition, case-based reasoning showed the best results overall.

Studies Published in 2001 (Mendes, Mosley, & Counsell, 2001)

Mendes et al. (2001) compared the prediction accuracy between several Web effort estimation models using two multivariate regression techniques: linear regression and stepwise regression.

These effort estimation models were classified into two different categories: top-down and bottom-up. Top-down effort estimation models used Web application size measures as independent variables and the effort employed to develop an entire Web application as the dependent variable. Conversely, bottom-up effort estimation models used Web page, media, and program size measures as independent variables, and the effort employed to author Web pages, media, and programs as dependent variables.

The data set used in the study contained data on 37 Web applications developed by honours and postgraduate computer science students from the University of Auckland, New Zealand.

The measures that were gathered were organised into five categories: length size, reusability, complexity size, effort, and confounding factors (factors that, if not controlled, could influence the validity of the evaluation). Each measure was also associated to one of the following entities: application, page, media, and program.

Effort estimation models were generated for each entity and prediction accuracy was measured using the MMRE measure. Results showed that the best predictions were obtained for the entity program based on nonreused program measures (code length and code comment length).

Copyright © 2008, IGI Global. Copying or distributing in print or electronic forms without written permission of IGI Global is prohibited.

Studies Published in 2002 (Mendes, Watson, Triggs, Mosley, & Counsell, 2002)

Mendes et al. (2002) present an in-depth comparison of Web effort estimation models using four different techniques: CBR, linear regression, stepwise regression, and classification and regression trees (CARTS). This was the first study to compare more than three different effort estimation techniques. In addition, the way in which these techniques were compared differed from what had been done in previous studies in Web and software engineering.

Their study employed a two-step approach. As part of Step 1, they compared the prediction accuracy among three CBR configurations to estimate the effort to develop Web applications.

The different CBR configurations were as follows:

- Three similarity measures (unweighted Euclidean, weighted Euclidean, and maximum)
- Three choices for the number of closest projects to use when obtaining effort estimates (one, two, and three)
- Three choices for the type of effort adaptation to employ (mean effort of closest projects in the case base, inverse rank weighted mean of closest projects in the case base, and median effort of closest cases in the case base)
- Two alternatives regarding the standardisation of the attributes (*Yes* for standardised and *No* for not standardised)

Once the first step was complete, Mendes et al. (2002) compared the prediction accuracy between the best CBR configuration (obtained from Step 1) and three commonly used prediction models, namely, multiple linear regression, stepwise regression, and classification and regression trees.

The data set used contained data on 37 Web hypermedia applications developed by honours and postgraduate computer science students from the University of Auckland, New Zealand.

The measures obtained were as follows.

- Page count: The number of HTML or SHTML files used in a Web application
- Media count: The number of media files used in a Web application
- Program count: The number of JavaScript files and Java applets used in a Web application

Copyright © 2008, IGI Global. Copying or distributing in print or electronic forms without written permission of IGI Global is prohibited.

- Reused Media count: The number of reused or modified media files in a Web application

- Reused Program count: The number of reused or modified programs in a Web application

- Connectivity density: The total number of internal links divided by page count

- Total page complexity: The average number of different types of media per Web page

- Total effort: The total effort in person hours used to design and author a Web application

Note that participants did not use external links from their Web applications to other Web hypermedia applications. All the links pointed to Web pages within the original application only.

Prediction accuracy was measured using MMRE, MdMRE, prediction at 25% (Pred[25]), and boxplots of residuals. Their results showed that different measures of prediction accuracy gave different results. MMRE and MdMRE showed better prediction accuracy for multiple regression models whereas boxplots showed better accuracy for CBR.

Studies Published in 2003 (Ruhe, Jeffery, & Wieczorek, 2003)

Ruhe et al. (2003) investigated whether the COBRA™ (Cost Estimation Benchmarking and Risk Analysis) method, previously employed in software engineering, was adequate to obtain accurate effort estimates for Web applications (COBRA is a registered trademark of the Fraunhofer Institute for Experimental Software Engineering [IESE], Germany). It is a hybrid effort estimation technique that mixes expert judgment and multiple regression, building a productivity estimation model. The objective of using the COBRA method is to develop an understandable effort estimation model based on a company-specific data set. Data sets do not need to be large in order to be used by this technique. Ruhe et al. adapted COBRA to Web projects using a small data set of 12 industrial projects developed by an Australian Web company. The size measure employed was Web objects (Reifer, 2000), measured for each one of the 12 finished Web applications used in this study. The effort estimates obtained using COBRA were compared to those using expert opinion and linear regression. Prediction accuracy was measured using MMRE and Pred(25). As expected, COBRA provided the most accurate results.

Copyright © 2008, IGI Global. Copying or distributing in print or electronic forms without written permission of IGI Global is prohibited.

Table 1. Summary of literature on Web cost estimation where several estimation techniques are compared

Study	Prediction Techniques	Best Technique(s)	Measure Prediction Accuracy
Mendes et al. (2000)	Case-based reasoning, linear regression, stepwise regression	Case-based reasoning for high-experience group	MMRE
Mendes et al. (2001)	Linear regression, stepwise regression	Linear regression	MMRE
Mendes et al. (2002)	Case-based reasoning, linear regression, stepwise regression, classification and regression trees	Linear and stepwise regression or case-based reasoning (depends on the measure of accuracy employed)	MMRE, MdMRE, Pred(25), boxplots of residuals
Ruhe et al. (2003)	COBRA, expert opinion, linear regression	COBRA	MMRE, Pred(25), boxplots of residuals

Discussion

Table 1 summarises the studies previously presented and shows that a minimum of two and a maximum of four different effort estimation techniques have been used. Linear regression has been used by all these previous studies, followed by stepwise regression, which was used in three studies. MMRE was the measure of accuracy used in all studies, followed by Pred(25) and boxplots of residuals.

Comparing Effort Estimation Techniques

Chapter III presented several measures of prediction accuracy: magnitude of relative error (MRE), MMRE, MdMRE, Pred(25), and absolute residuals, which are obtained as part of a cross-validation process. Chapter III also detailed the process used to obtain these measures, using as example real data on Web projects.

This section will detail the use of statistical significance techniques that are used to assess if differences among different predictions are legitimate or due to chance.

Copyright © 2008, IGI Global. Copying or distributing in print or electronic forms without written permission of IGI Global is prohibited.

Table 2. Prediction accuracy for two imaginary techniques

	Technique 1	Technique 2
MMRE (%)	56	36
MdMRE (%)	47	33
Pred(25) (%)	52	60

To start, let us suppose that you are presented with the data shown in Table 2.

We have seen that MMRE and MdMRE with values up to 25%, and Pred(25) at 75% or above, are often used to indicate good prediction accuracy. Given the MMRE, MdMRE, and Pred(25) values in Table 2, one would suggest that Technique 2 provides more accurate predictions than Technique 1. However, despite their difference in values, they may still provide similar effort prediction accuracy. In other words, MMRE, MdMRE, and Pred(25) alone provide an indication of the prediction accuracy obtained using a given technique; however, when you are comparing techniques, in addition to measuring its prediction accuracy using, for example, MMRE, MdMRE, and Pred(25), you also need to verify if the absolute residuals obtained using each of the techniques being compared have come from the same distribution of absolute residual values. In such cases where they have, this suggests that the differences in absolute residual values obtained using different techniques have occurred by chance.

However, if the absolute residuals obtained using each of the techniques being compared have not come from the same distribution of absolute residual values, this suggests there is a legitimate difference between absolute residuals obtained using these different techniques, implying that the differences in prediction accuracy that have been observed did not occur by chance; that is, they are legitimate, and the differences are statistically significant.

The choice to use absolute residuals is motivated by the fact that we are not interested in the direction of the differences between actual and estimated efforts, but rather in the absolute differences themselves. To compare the estimation accuracy between different techniques, we need to know if the differences between actual effort and estimated effort for different techniques could have come from the same population.

Effort estimation techniques that provide over- or underestimation prompts a different question to investigate and will be discussed later on in this chapter.

Assuming that residuals are calculated as actual effort minus estimated effort, a negative residual indicates overestimation; that is, the estimated effort is greater than the

Copyright © 2008, IGI Global. Copying or distributing in print or electronic forms without written permission of IGI Global is prohibited.

actual effort. Conversely, a positive residual indicates underestimation, where the actual effort is greater than the estimated effort. Figure 1, previously presented in Chapter III, shows the steps to be followed when you are measuring the prediction accuracy of a single effort estimation technique (technique *t*).

Figure 1. Overall process to measure prediction accuracy

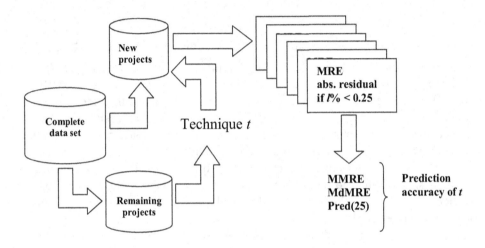

Figure 2. Comparing prediction accuracy between different effort estimation techniques

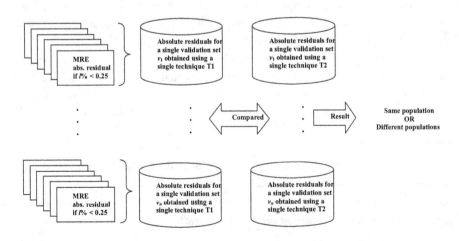

Copyright © 2008, IGI Global. Copying or distributing in print or electronic forms without written permission of IGI Global is prohibited.

Figure 2 expands the process used to measure prediction accuracy by adding further steps to be used when comparing prediction accuracy between two or more effort estimation techniques. Here, once absolute residuals have been obtained for a validation set v_1 for a given technique $T1$, they are compared to the absolute residuals obtained for the same validation set v_1 using another effort estimation technique $T2$. It is important to compare absolute residuals for the same validation set across all the techniques so that we can precisely assess the impact these different techniques had on a single project for each of the projects in a validation set. Before the comparison takes place, we aggregate as a single set of absolute residuals, for each effort estimation technique used, each set of absolute residuals for each validation set. Therefore, if we are comparing two different effort estimation techniques, we will have two sets of absolute residual values to compare.

Checking the Residuals for Symptoms of Non-Normality

Before carrying out a comparison between absolute residuals, it is important to look at their characteristics and whether they are normally distributed or not. This step is necessary in order to decide what statistical technique to use to compare these absolute residuals. The tools that are generally used here are histograms and boxplots. Histograms, or bar charts, provide a graphical display, where each bar summarises the frequency of a single value or range of values for a given variable. They are often used to check if a variable is normally distributed, in which case the bars are displayed in the shape of a bell-shaped curve.

To obtain a histogram for a numerical variable in SPSS, from SPSS Inc., follow these steps:

- Select *Graphs* ⇨ *Histogram*.
- Select the variable from the list on the left and click on the arrow button to have it moved to the box labeled *Variable*.
- Tick *Display normal curve*.

Next, we can also use boxplots to check the existence of outliers. Boxplots (see Figure 3) use the median, represented by the horizontal line in the middle of the box, as the central value for the distribution. The box's height is the interquartile range, and contains 50% of the values. The vertical lines up or down from the edges (whiskers) contain observations that are less than 1.5 times the interquartile range. Outliers are taken as values greater than 1.5 times the height of the box. Values greater than 3 times the box's height are called extreme outliers (Kitchenham, MacDonell, Pickard, & Shepperd, 2001).

Copyright © 2008, IGI Global. Copying or distributing in print or electronic forms without written permission of IGI Global is prohibited.

Figure 3. Main components of a boxplot

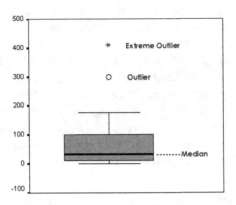

When upper and lower tails are approximately equal and the median is in the centre of the box, the distribution is symmetric. If the distribution is not symmetric, the relative lengths of the tails and the position of the median in the box indicate the nature of the skewness. The length of the box relative to the length of the tails gives an indication of the shape of the distribution. So, a boxplot with a small box and long tails represents a very peaked distribution, whereas a boxplot with a long box represents a flatter distribution (Kitchenham et al., 2001).

To obtain boxplots for one or more numerical variables in SPSS, follow these steps:

- Select *Graphs* ⇨ *Boxplot*.
- Click on the image labeled *Simple*.
- Tick *Summaries of separate variables* and click the *define* button.
- Select the variables from the list on the left and click on the arrow button to have them moved to the box labeled *Boxes Represent*.
- Optionally, select the variable from the list on the left that identifies each project individually (e.g., project ID) and click on the arrow button to have it moved to the box labeled *Label cases by*.

The last step is to use a statistical test called the one-sample Kolmogorov-Smirnov test (K-S test) to check if the observed distribution, represented by the residual

Copyright © 2008, IGI Global. Copying or distributing in print or electronic forms without written permission of IGI Global is prohibited.

values, corresponds to a theoretical distribution, which in our case is the normal distribution. This test can be applied to one or more numerical variables.

To use the K-S test for one or more numerical variables in SPSS, follow these steps:

- Select *Analyze* ⇨ *Nonparametric tests* ⇨ *1-Sample K-S*.
- Tick *Normal* under *Test Distribution*.
- Select the variables from the list on the left and click on the arrow button to have them moved to the box labeled *Test Variable List*.

If any of the residual sets are not normally distributed, their comparison will have to be carried out using nonparametric tests. These tests do not make any assumptions regarding the distribution of data and as such can be employed when the data are not normally distributed. Otherwise, in the case that all residual sets are normally distributed, we can employ parametric statistical tests as their assumption of normally distributed data would apply to these residual sets.

Comparing Two Groups at a Time

If you are comparing the prediction accuracy between two effort estimation techniques, Technique 1 and Technique 2, you will have two sets of absolute residuals: Set 1 and Set 2, where Set 1 contains the absolute residuals obtained by applying Technique 1, and Set 2 contains the residuals obtained by applying Technique 2 (see Figure 4).

In Figure 4, projects are identified as *Project + p*, absolute residual values are identified as *Residual + p/t*, and effort estimation techniques are identified as *Technique + t*.

Their interpretation is as follows: *p* represents a project, identified by a number, and *t* represents an effort estimation technique, also identified by a number.

Absolute residual sets are identified in Figure 4 using shades of grey, thus we have two sets. The number of projects in each absolute residual set is the same, and the projects to which those absolute residuals relate to are also the same, even when more than one validation set has been used. So, when we compare these two absolute residual sets using a statistical test, we have to use a paired test rather than an independent-samples test.

Examples of pairs are as follows.

- First pair: *Residual 1/1* and *Residual 1/2*
- Second pair: *Residual 10/1* and *Residual 10/2*

Copyright © 2008, IGI Global. Copying or distributing in print or electronic forms without written permission of IGI Global is prohibited.

Figure 4. Comparing two different residual sets

		Technique 1	Technique 2
Validation Set 1	Project 1	Residual 1/1	Residual 1/2
	Project 10	Residual 10/1	Residual 10/2
	Project 90	Residual 90/1	Residual 90/2
	Project 34	Residual 34/1	Residual 34/2
Validation Set 2	Project 67	Residual 67/1	Residual 67/2
	Project 4	Residual 4/1	Residual 4/2
	Project 66	Residual 66/1	Residual 66/2
	Project 87	Residual 87/1	Residual 87/2

....

Validation Set n	Project 23	Residual 23/1	Residual 23/2
	Project 45	Residual 45/1	Residual 45/2
	Project 3	Residual 3/1	Residual 3/2
	Project 9	Residual 9/1	Residual 9/2

- Third pair: *Residual 90/1* and *Residual 90/2*
- Fourth pair: *Residual 34/1* and *Residual 34/2*

The two statistical tests that need to be considered are the paired-samples T-test, which is a parametric test, and the Wilcoxon test, which is a nonparametric test and equivalent to the paired-samples T-test. Both tests will be detailed further in Chapter X.

Comparing More than Two Groups

If you are comparing the prediction accuracy between three effort estimation techniques, Technique 1, Technique 2, and Technique 3, you will have three sets of absolute residuals: Set 1, Set 2, and Set 3, where Set 1 contains the absolute residuals obtained by applying Technique 1, Set 2 contains the absolute residuals obtained by applying Technique 2, and Set 3 contains the absolute residuals obtained by applying Technique 3 (see Figure 5). In Figure 5, projects are identified as *Project* + *p*, absolute residual values are identified as *Residual* + *p/t*, and effort estimation techniques are identified as *Technique* + *t*. Their interpretation is as follows: *p*

Copyright © 2008, IGI Global. Copying or distributing in print or electronic forms without written permission of IGI Global is prohibited.

represents a project, identified by a number, and t represents an effort estimation technique, also identified by a number.

Absolute residual sets are identified in Figure 5 using shades of grey, thus we have three sets. The number of projects in each absolute residual set is the same, and the projects to which those absolute residuals relate to are also the same, even when more than one validation set has been used. This means that when we compare these three absolute residual sets using a statistical test, we have to use a test similar to the paired test, which allows three or more values of absolute residuals to be compared, all relative to the same original Web project.

Examples of three-valued groups are as follows:

- First group: *Residual 1/1, Residual 1/2, Residual 1/3*
- Second group: *Residual 10/1, Residual 10/2, Residual 10/3*
- Third group: *Residual 90/1, Residual 90/2, Residual 90/3*
- Fourth group: *Residual 34/1, Residual 34/2, Residual 34/3*

The two statistical tests that need to be considered are the one-way ANOVA (analysis of variance), which is a parametric test, and Kendall's W H test, which is a non-parametric test equivalent to the one-way ANOVA test.

Figure 5. Comparing three different absolute residual sets

		Technique 1	Technique 2	Technique 3
	Project 1	Residual 1/1	Residual 1/2	Residual 1/3
Validation Set 1	Project 10	Residual 10/1	Residual 10/2	Residual 10/3
	Project 90	Residual 90/1	Residual 90/2	Residual 90/3
	Project 34	Residual 34/1	Residual 34/2	Residual 34/3
	Project 67	Residual 67/1	Residual 67/2	Residual 67/3
Validation Set 2	Project 4	Residual 4/1	Residual 4/2	Residual 4/3
	Project 66	Residual 66/1	Residual 66/2	Residual 66/3
	Project 87	Residual 87/1	Residual 87/2	Residual 87/3
		...		
	Project 23	Residual 23/1	Residual 23/2	Residual 23/3
Validation Set n	Project 45	Residual 45/1	Residual 45/2	Residual 45/3
	Project 3	Residual 3/1	Residual 3/2	Residual 3/3
	Project 9	Residual 9/1	Residual 9/2	Residual 9/3

Copyright © 2008, IGI Global. Copying or distributing in print or electronic forms without written permission of IGI Global is prohibited.

Detailed Example

This section will present an example where two and then three effort estimation techniques are compared using absolute residuals to identify which techniques, if any, provide significantly better prediction accuracy than the others. The effort data used in this section represents real effort data on industrial Web projects, developed by Web companies worldwide, from the Tukutuku database (Mendes, Mosley, & Counsell, 2003). Note that the raw data for all the variables that characterise Web projects cannot be displayed here due to a confidentiality agreement with those companies that have volunteered data on their projects. However, we will present the effort data for those projects since this cannot in itself be used to identify any Web company specifically. The Tukutuku database is part of the ongoing Tukutuku project (http://www.cs.auckland.ac.nz/tukutuku), which collects data on Web projects to be used to estimate effort for Web projects, and to benchmark productivity across and within Web companies.

The Tukutuku database uses 6 variables to store specifics about each of the Web companies that volunteered projects, 10 variables to store particulars about each Web project, and 13 variables to store data about each Web application (see Table 3). Company data are obtained once and both Web project and application data are gathered for each volunteered project. This database currently has data on 150 Web projects; however, for simplicity, we will use in this section three small validation sets containing data on seven Web projects each.

All results presented in this section were obtained using the statistical software SPSS 12.0.1 for Windows from SPSS Inc. Further details on the statistical methods used throughout this section are given in Chapter 10. Finally, all the statistical tests set the significance level at 95% ($\alpha = 0.05$). Note that the different types of measurement scales are detailed in Chapter XIII.

We are assuming here that the following steps have already been carried out.

Step 1: Splitting of the project data set into training and validation sets, keeping seven projects in the validation set and the remaining projects in the training set

Step 2: Selection of an effort estimation technique (e.g., stepwise regression, case-based reasoning, regression trees) to be used to obtain estimated effort for the projects in the validation set

Step 3: If applicable, construction of an effort estimation model that will later be used to obtain estimated effort for all the projects in the validation set. This model can be an equation in case the effort estimation technique is stepwise regression or linear regression; it can also be a binary tree, in case the effort estimation technique is a regression tree. If the technique used is CBR, there

Copyright © 2008, IGI Global. Copying or distributing in print or electronic forms without written permission of IGI Global is prohibited.

Table 3. Variables for the Tukutuku database

NAME	SCALE	DESCRIPTION
COMPANY DATA		
COUNTRY	Categorical	Country company belongs to
ESTABLISHED	Ordinal	Year when company was established
SERVICES	Categorical	Type of services company provides
NPEOPLEWD	Absolute	Number of people who work on Web design and development
CLIENTIND	Categorical	Industry representative of those clients to whom applications are provided
ESTPRACT	Categorical	Accuracy of a company's own effort estimation practices
PROJECT DATA		
TYPEPROJ	Categorical	Type of project (new or enhancement)
LANGS	Categorical	Implementation languages used
DOCPROC	Categorical	If project followed defined and documented process
PROIMPR	Categorical	If project team was involved in a process improvement programme
METRICS	Categorical	If project team was part of a software metrics programme
DEVTEAM	Absolute	Size of project's development team
TEAMEXP	Absolute	Average team experience with the development language(s) employed
TOTEFF	Absolute	Actual total effort in person hours used to develop the Web application
ESTEFF	Absolute	Estimated total effort in person hours necessary to develop the Web application
ACCURACY	Categorical	Procedure used to record effort data
WEB APPLICATION		
TYPEAPP	Categorical	Type of Web application developed
TOTWP	Absolute	Total number of Web pages (new and reused)
NEWWP	Absolute	Total number of new Web pages
TOTIMG	Absolute	Total number of images (new and reused)
NEWIMG	Absolute	Total number of new images created
HEFFDEV	Absolute	Minimum number of hours to develop a single function/feature by one experienced developer whose skill is considered high (above average) This number is currently set to 15 hours based on the collected data.
HEFFADPT	Absolute	Minimum number of hours to adapt a single function/feature by one experienced developer whose skill is considered high (above average). This number is currently set to 4 hours based on the collected data.
HFOTS	Absolute	Number of reused high-effort features/functions without adaptation
HFOTSA	Absolute	Number of reused high-effort features/functions adapted
HNEW	Absolute	Number of new high-effort features/functions
FOTS	Absolute	Number of reused low-effort features without adaptation
FOTSA	Absolute	Number of reused low-effort features adapted
NEW	Absolute	Number of new low-effort features/functions

Copyright © 2008, IGI Global. Copying or distributing in print or electronic forms without written permission of IGI Global is prohibited.

is no explicit model per se. These are the three techniques mentioned here as they are the ones described in this book.

Step 4: Application of the model generated in Step 3, or, if using CBR, application of a CBR software to each of the projects in the validation set in order to obtain their estimated effort

Our example uses a three-fold cross-validation, allowing for three different training and validation sets to be selected at random; the four steps mentioned above will be applied to each of these training and validation sets. Note that the same training and validation sets will be used with each of the effort estimation techniques to be compared. Therefore, if we are comparing two effort estimation techniques, we would have the same three training and validation sets used with each of the effort estimation techniques. This is the same reasoning to be used if we were to compare three or more effort estimation techniques.

The use of a three-fold cross-validation does not mean that this is the best choice when measuring the prediction accuracy of effort estimation techniques. In fact, a previous study suggests that we should use at least 20 different training and validation sets (Kirsopp & Shepperd, 2001); however, this solution may not be feasible when using small data sets since we would end up having a repetition of projects in different validation sets, which behaves similarly to double counting. In addition, no other studies have investigated the issue regarding the minimum number of validation sets to be used when measuring prediction accuracy, therefore we do not recommend the use of 20 different training and validation sets.

First Case: Comparing Two Different Effort Estimation Techniques

Table 4 shows the actual effort for 21 Web projects and their corresponding estimated effort and absolute residuals for two different effort estimation techniques: *Tech1* and *Tech2*. The MMRE, MdMRE, and Pred(25) for each of these effort estimation techniques are shown in Table 5.

Table 5 shows that technique *Tech1* seems to have provided much worse prediction accuracy than technique *Tech2*. Both MMRE and MdMRE for *Tech1* are well above 25%, and Pred(25) is well below the minimum 75% used to indicate good prediction accuracy. On the other hand, both MMRE and MdMRE for *Tech2* are exceptionally good and below 25%, and Pred(25) is excellent too, well above 75%. By carrying out a statistical significance test comparing the absolute residuals of both effort estimation techniques, we will be able to determine if there is a legitimate difference in the prediction accuracy obtained with each of these techniques, or whether the differences have occurred in this instance by chance.

Copyright © 2008, IGI Global. Copying or distributing in print or electronic forms without written permission of IGI Global is prohibited.

Table 4. Actual effort, estimated effort, and residuals for T1 and T2

	Project ID	Actual Effort	Estimated Effort Using *Tech1*	Abs. Residual	Estimated Effort Using *Tech2*	Abs. Residual
First Validation Set	1	340	450	110	350	10
	3	300	600	300	230	70
	5	75	167	92	67	8
	7	24	67	43	21	3
	9	410	400	10	340	70
	11	40	78	38	34	6
	13	130	100	30	123	7
Second Validation Set	15	21	15	6	34	13
	17	1786	2500	714	1589	197
	19	900	700	200	789	111
	21	100	76	24	78	22
	23	50	23	27	39	11
	25	429	89	340	401	28
	27	90	147	57	79	11
Third Validation Set	29	34	21	13	30	4
	31	363	500	137	345	18
	33	6	2	4	5	1
	35	38	12	26	29	9
	37	30	56	26	28	2
	39	625	467	158	634	9
	41	6	1	5	5	1

Table 5. MMRE, MdMRE, and Pred(25) for Tech1 and Tech2

Accuracy Measure	Technique *Tech1*	Technique *Tech2*
MMRE (%)	61	15
MdMRE (%)	54	12
Pred(25) (%)	19	95

Before using a statistical test to compare the absolute residuals between effort estimation technique *Tech1* and effort estimation technique *Tech2*, we need to find out if the absolute residuals are normally distributed or not. As previously mentioned, the two visual tools used to investigate if data appear normally distributed

Copyright © 2008, IGI Global. Copying or distributing in print or electronic forms without written permission of IGI Global is prohibited.

are histograms and boxplots. When employing histograms and boxplots, we will use two sets of absolute residuals, one for each of the effort estimation techniques being compared. Each of these sets contains 21 absolute residual values, and aggregates the absolute residual values that result from obtaining effort estimates for the projects in the three validation sets. In other words, we do not analyse validation sets independently.

Figure 6 shows the histograms for absolute residuals for each of the two effort estimation techniques being compared as part of our example.

Figure 6 suggests that absolute residuals obtained using technique *Tech 1* resemble a bell shape, which is characteristic of a normal distribution, much more closely than the absolute residuals using technique *Tech 2*. The latter presents a large number of residuals between 0 and 25, and then shows sporadic values in the ranges 25 to 50, 50 to 75, 100 to 125, and 175 to 200.

Figure 7 shows that the values for the absolute residuals for technique *Tech 1* spread much further than those using technique *Tech 2*, which shows a very compact distribution with most values scattered around the median. Both boxplots present unusual values (outliers), although there are two extreme outliers for absolute residuals using technique *Tech 2*. Both boxplots show a common project as an extreme outlier: Project 17. This project presented a very large actual effort: 1,786 person hours. The other extreme outlier, for Project 19, also presents a large actual effort: 900 person hours. This may suggest that the projects used as part of the training set had smaller actual effort values and therefore both techniques were unable to calibrate their models for projects containing large effort values.

Figure 6. Histograms of absolute residuals using Tech 1 and Tech 2

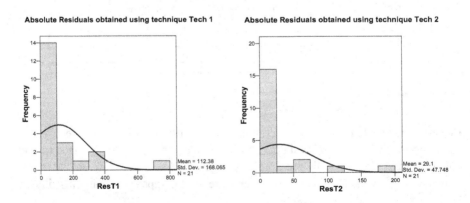

Copyright © 2008, IGI Global. Copying or distributing in print or electronic forms without written permission of IGI Global is prohibited.

Figure 7. Boxplots of absolute resic' als using Tech 1 and Tech 2

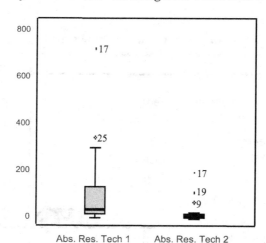

Our next step is to use the statistical test one-sample K-S test to check if the observed distribution, represented by the absolute residual values, corresponds to a theoretical distribution, which in our case is the normal distribution.

This test can be applied to one or more numerical variables. The output for the K-S test for each of the absolute residual sets is shown in Figures 8 and 9. The most important piece of information in Figures 8 and 9 is the significance value (indicated by a dark arrow in Figures 8 and 9, and by the label Asymp. Sig. [two-tailed]). Whenever this value is greater than 0.05, this means that the hypothesis that there are no differences between the observed distribution and a theoretical distribution (in other words, that the observed distribution corresponds to a theoretical distribution), which represents the null hypothesis, cannot be rejected using a statistical significance α of 0.05. Therefore the K-S test indicates that absolute residuals obtained using technique *Tech 1* are normally distributed, and those obtained using technique *Tech 2* are not.

Given that one of the absolute residual sets is not normally distributed, we will need to use a nonparametric test to compare both absolute residual sets and verify if values for both sets come from the same distribution. The statistical test to use is the Wilcoxon test.

Copyright © 2008, IGI Global. Copying or distributing in print or electronic forms without written permission of IGI Global is prohibited.

Figure 8. Kolmogorov-Smirnov test for absolute residuals for Tech 1

One-Sample Kolmogorov-Smirnov Test

		ResT1
N		21
Normal Parameters [a,b]	Mean	112.38
	Std. Deviation	168.065
Most Extreme Differences	Absolute	.260
	Positive	.248
	Negative	-.260
Kolmogorov-Smirnov Z		1.189
Asymp. Sig. (2-tailed)		.118

a. Test distribution is Normal.

b. Calculated from data.

Figure 9. Kolmogorov-Smirnov test for absolute residuals for Tech 2

One-Sample Kolmogorov-Smirnov Test

		ResT2
N		21
Normal Parameters [a,b]	Mean	29.10
	Std. Deviation	47.748
Most Extreme Differences	Absolute	.321
	Positive	.321
	Negative	-.278
Kolmogorov-Smirnov Z		1.471
Asymp. Sig. (2-tailed)		.026

a. Test distribution is Normal.

b. Calculated from data.

Copyright © 2008, IGI Global. Copying or distributing in print or electronic forms without written permission of IGI Global is prohibited.

To use the Wilcoxon test in SPSS, follow the steps below.

- Select *Analyze* ⇨ *Nonparametric tests* ⇨ *2-Related Samples*.
- Tick *Wilcoxon* under *Test Type*.
- Select the variables from the list on the left that are to be paired and compared, and click on the arrow button to have them moved to the box labeled *Test Pair(s) List*.

The output for the Wilcoxon test, comparing residual sets between techniques *Tech 1* and *Tech 2*, is shown in Figure 10. The important piece of information in Figure 10 is the significance value (indicated by a dark arrow by the label Asymp. Sig. [two-tailed]). Whenever this value is greater than 0.05, this means that the hypothesis that there are no differences between the distributions of the observed variables, which represents the null hypothesis, cannot be rejected using a statistical significance α of 0.05. Conversely, significance values smaller or equal to 0.05 indicate that there are differences between the distributions of the observed variables, and that the null hypothesis should therefore be rejected. The Wilcoxon test indicates that absolute residual values for technique *Tech1* definitely come from a different distribution than absolute residual values for technique *Tech 2*.

The results for the Wilcoxon test indicate that the prediction accuracy between the two effort estimation techniques being compared is significantly different. The boxplots shown in Figure 7 suggest that absolute residuals for technique *Tech 1* are overall larger than the absolute residuals obtained for technique *Tech 2* since they

Figure 10. Wilcoxon test comparing absolute residuals between Tech 1 and Tech 2

Test Statistics[b]

	ResT2 - ResT1
Z	-3.424[a]
Asymp. Sig. (2-tailed)	.001

a. Based on positive ranks.

b. Wilcoxon Signed Ranks Test

Copyright © 2008, IGI Global. Copying or distributing in print or electronic forms without written permission of IGI Global is prohibited.

Table 6. Sum of absolute residuals for Tech 1 and Tech 2

	Technique *Tech 1*	Technique *Tech 2*
Sum of absolute residuals	2360	611

spread further up the *Y*-axis. However, another way to find out what technique gives the most accurate predictions is to sum up all the absolute residuals and see which one provides the smallest sum. Table 6 shows the sum of absolute residuals for both techniques, and clearly shows that technique *Tech 2* presented the best accuracy since it showed the smallest sum of absolute residuals.

Second Case: Comparing Three Different Effort Estimation Techniques

Table 7 shows the actual effort for 21 Web projects and their corresponding estimated effort and absolute residuals for the effort estimation techniques used in the previous example, *Tech 1* and *Tech 2*, and a third technique: *Tech 3*. The MMRE, MdMRE, and Pred(25) for each of these three techniques are shown in Table 8.

Table 8 shows that MMRE, MdMRE, and Pred(25) for technique *Tech 1* are much worse than those for either technique *Tech 2* or *Tech 3*. Technique *Tech 2* presented exceptionally good predictions, with MMRE and MdMRE well below 25% and Pred(25) well above 75%. Prediction accuracy using technique *Tech 3* was not bad either, with MMRE and MdMRE below 25% and Pred(25) close to 75%. We know by now that a statistical significance test comparing the absolute residuals of techniques *Tech 1* and *Tech 2* showed a significant difference in prediction accuracy between these two techniques, therefore adding a third technique to the comparison will also lead to similar results. However, for the sake of showing how to compare three or more effort estimation techniques, we will carry on and use a statistical significance test to compare absolute residuals of techniques *Tech 1*, *Tech 2*, and *Tech 3*.

Before using a statistical test to compare the absolute residuals between effort estimation techniques *Tech 1*, *Tech 2*, and *Tech 3*, we need to find out if the absolute residuals are normally distributed or not. We have seen histograms and boxplots of absolute residuals for techniques *Tech 1* and *Tech 2* and by now we also know that residuals for technique *Tech 2* are not normally distributed, which means that we will have to use a nonparametric statistical test. Although we already know these facts, we will still show the histogram (see Figure 11) of absolute residuals for technique *Tech 3*, and boxplots comparing all three techniques (see Figure 12).

Copyright © 2008, IGI Global. Copying or distributing in print or electronic forms without written permission of IGI Global is prohibited.

Table 7. Actual effort, estimated effort, and residuals for Tech 1, Tech 2, and Tech 3

	Project ID	Actual Effort	Estimated Effort Using Tech 1	Abs. Res.	Estimated Effort Using Tech 2	Abs. Res.	Estimated Effort Using Tech 3	Abs. Res.
First Validation Set	1	340	450	110	350	10	300	40
	3	300	600	300	230	70	250	50
	5	75	167	92	67	8	67	8
	7	24	67	43	21	3	20	4
	9	410	400	10	340	70	390	20
	11	40	78	38	34	6	25	15
	13	130	100	30	123	7	120	10
Second Validation Set	15	21	15	6	34	13	15	6
	17	1786	2500	714	1589	197	1699	87
	19	900	700	200	789	111	800	100
	21	100	76	24	78	22	79	21
	23	50	23	27	39	11	42	8
	25	429	89	340	401	28	390	39
	27	90	147	57	79	11	67	23
Third Validation Set	29	34	21	13	30	4	28	6
	31	363	500	137	345	18	350	13
	33	6	2	4	5	1	3	3
	35	38	12	26	29	9	28	10
	37	30	56	26	28	2	21	9
	39	625	467	158	634	9	600	25
	41	6	1	5	5	1	4	2

Table 8. MMRE, MdMRE, and Pred(25) for Tech 1, Tech 2, and Tech 3

Accuracy Measure	Technique *Tech 1*	Technique *Tech 2*	Technique *Tech 3*
MMRE (%)	61	15	18
MdMRE (%)	54	12	17
Pred(25) (%)	19	95	67

Figure 11 suggests that, similar to *Tech 1*, absolute residuals obtained using technique *Tech 3* resemble a bell shape much more closely than the absolute residuals using technique *Tech 2*.

Copyright © 2008, IGI Global. Copying or distributing in print or electronic forms without written permission of IGI Global is prohibited.

Figure 11. Histogram of absolute residuals using Tech 3

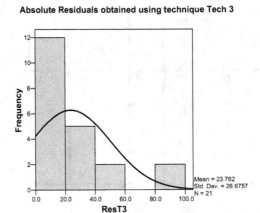

Figure 12. Boxplots of absolute residuals using Tech 1, Tech 2, and Tech 3

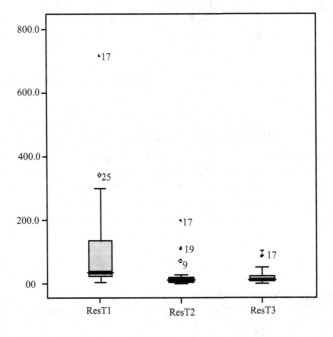

Copyright © 2008, IGI Global. Copying or distributing in print or electronic forms without written permission of IGI Global is prohibited.

Figure 12 shows that the distribution of values for the absolute residuals for technique *Tech 3* is compact, and similar to the distribution of values for the absolute residuals for technique *Tech 2*; both differ from *Tech 1*, where absolute residual values spread much further. In addition, medians for techniques *Tech 2* and *Tech 3* are lower than the median for technique *Tech 1*. All three boxplots present unusual values (outliers), and Project 17 also remains an extreme outlier when using technique *Tech 3*.

Our next step is to use the K-S test to check if the observed distribution, represented by the absolute residual values, corresponds to a theoretical distribution, which in our case is the normal distribution. The output for the K-S test for the absolute residual set for technique *Tech 3* is shown in Figure 13. As previously mentioned, the most important piece of information in Figure 13 is the significance value (indicated by a dark arrow and by the label Asymp. Sig. [two-tailed]). Whenever this value is greater than 0.05, this means that the hypothesis that there are no differences between the observed distribution and a theoretical distribution (in other words, that the observed distribution corresponds to a theoretical distribution), which represents the null hypothesis, cannot be rejected using a statistical significance α of 0.05. Therefore, the K-S test indicates that absolute residuals obtained using technique *Tech 3* are normally distributed.

As we already know, given that one of the residual sets is not normally distributed, we will need to use a nonparametric test to compare the three residual sets and to

Figure 13. Kolmogorov-Smirnov test for absolute residuals for Tech 3

One-Sample Kolmogorov-Smirnov Test

		ResT3
N		21
Normal Parameters [a,b]	Mean	23.762
	Std. Deviation	26.6757
Most Extreme Differences	Absolute	.243
	Positive	.243
	Negative	-.207
Kolmogorov-Smirnov Z		1.115
Asymp. Sig. (2-tailed)		.166

a. Test distribution is Normal.

b. Calculated from data.

Copyright © 2008, IGI Global. Copying or distributing in print or electronic forms without written permission of IGI Global is prohibited.

verify if their values come from the same distribution. The statistical test to use is Kendall's W test.

To use SPSS to execute the Kendall's W test, follow these steps:

- Select *Analyze* ⇨ *Nonparametric tests* ⇨ *K Related Samples*.
- Tick *Kendall's W* under *Test Type*
- Select from the list on the left the variables that contain the residuals to be compared and click on the arrow button to have it moved to the box labeled *Test Variables*.

The output for Kendall's W test comparing residual sets among techniques *Tech 1*, *Tech 2*, and *Tech 3* is shown in Figure 14. The important piece of information in Figure 14 is the significance value (indicated by a dark arrow by the label Asymp. Sig. [two-tailed]). Whenever this value is greater than 0.05, this means that the hypothesis that there are no differences between the distributions of the observed variables, which represents the null hypothesis, cannot be rejected using a statistical significance α of 0.05. Conversely, significance values smaller or equal to 0.05 indicate that there are differences between the distributions of the observed variables, and the null hypothesis should therefore be rejected. Kendall's W test indicates that residual values for at least one of the techniques come from a different distribution than residual values for the remaining techniques.

The results for Kendall's W test indicate that the prediction accuracies of the three effort estimation techniques being compared are significantly different. The boxplots shown in Figure 12 suggest that absolute residuals for technique *Tech 1* are overall larger than absolute residuals obtained for techniques *Tech 2* and *Tech 3* since they

Figure 14. Kendall's W test comparing absolute residuals among Tech 1, Tech 2, and Tech 3

Test Statistics

N	21
Kendall's W [a]	.541
Chi-Square	22.707
df	2
Asymp. Sig.	.000

a. Kendall's Coefficient of Concordance

Copyright © 2008, IGI Global. Copying or distributing in print or electronic forms without written permission of IGI Global is prohibited.

Table 9. Sum of absolute residuals for Tech 1, Tech 2, and Tech 3

	Technique *Tech 1*	Technique *Tech 2*	Technique *Tech 3*
Sum of absolute residuals	2360	611	499

Figure 15. Wilcoxon test comparing absolute residuals between Tech 2 and Tech 3

Test Statistics^b

	ResT3 - ResT2
Z	-.224^a
Asymp. Sig. (2-tailed)	.823

a. Based on negative ranks.

b. Wilcoxon Signed Ranks Test

spread further up the *Y*-axis, and the median is higher too. However, as previously mentioned, another way to find out what technique gives the most accurate predictions is to sum up all the absolute residuals and see which one provides the smallest sum. Table 9 shows the sum of absolute residuals for all three techniques, and clearly shows that technique *Tech 1* presented the worst accuracy since it showed the greatest sum of absolute residuals. Table 9 also shows that techniques *Tech 2* and *Tech 3* presented similar sums of absolute residuals, thus similar prediction accuracy. To definitely know if the small difference in prediction accuracy between techniques *Tech 2* and *Tech 3* was not statistically significant, we need to compare their residuals using this time the previously used Wilcoxon test. The results for the Wilcoxon test indicate that the prediction accuracy between the two effort estimation techniques *Tech 2* and *Tech 3* is not significantly different. This means that either technique could have been chosen to obtain effort estimates with good prediction accuracy.

Copyright © 2008, IGI Global. Copying or distributing in print or electronic forms without written permission of IGI Global is prohibited.

Management Implications

This chapter has detailed the steps a company can follow in order to compare two or more effort estimation techniques. These techniques can be some of those that are presented in this book, or may also include other techniques that are outside the scope of the book (e.g., fuzzy systems, neural networks, Bayesian networks). We suggest, however, that one of the techniques to be used be representative of the company's own expert-based effort estimation procedures, and that it is used to establish a benchmark against which to compare the accuracy of any other techniques.

This will provide the means to realistically assess if any new techniques really add value to the effort estimates currently obtained by the company. Why do we think that it is important to include the company's own effort estimation procedures as a benchmark? Let us suppose that you work for a Web company that has employed three new effort estimation techniques to estimate effort for its Web projects. All these techniques provided similar estimation accuracy: Their MMREs were 60%, 62%, and 65%, respectively, and their Pred(25) were 7%, 9%, and 10%, respectively. Given this scenario, one would think that suggesting your company use any of these three techniques would be a waste of time. However, let us assume that your company also measured prediction accuracy using its own expert-based effort estimation procedure and obtained MMRE of 85%, and Pred(25) of 0%. Here the company's own estimates are much worse than those obtained using any of the three new effort estimation techniques. Therefore, using any of the three techniques would be advantageous for the company, despite the overall poor effort estimation accuracy based on MMRE and Pred(25). The point here is that unless the company's own effort estimates are also used for comparison, it is impossible to determine if a new effort estimation technique would be an improvement over the current procedures used by that company to estimate effort.

However, if a company does not record expert-based effort estimates for its projects, an alternative is to use the mean or median effort for past finished Web projects as the estimated effort for a new project, and to compare its accuracy with that obtained from using the new effort estimation techniques. If we use as the estimated effort the mean effort (261) and median effort (35) obtained using the projects from the Tukutuku data set, after removing the 21 projects used as part of our three validation sets (see Table 7), Table 7 would be as follows (see Table 10).

And the accuracy measures would then be (see Table 11) as follows:

The output for Kendall's W test, comparing residual sets among techniques *Tech 1*, *Tech 2*, and *Tech 3*, and the median and mean effort, is shown in Figure 16.

As previously stated, the important piece of information is the significance value (indicated by a dark arrow by the label Asymp. Sig. [two-tailed]). Whenever this value is greater than 0.05, this means that the hypothesis that there are no differ-

Copyright © 2008, IGI Global. Copying or distributing in print or electronic forms without written permission of IGI Global is prohibited.

Table 10. Actual effort, estimated effort, and residuals for Tech 1, Tech 2, and Tech 3, and median and mean effort

	Proj. ID	Actual Effort	Est. Effort *Tech 1*	Abs. Res.	Est. Effort *Tech 2*	Abs. Res.	Est. Effort *Tech 3*	Abs. Res.	Median	Abs. Res.	Mean	Abs. Res.
First Validation Set	1	340	450	110	350	10	300	40	35	305	261	79
	3	300	600	300	230	70	250	50	35	265	261	39
	5	75	167	92	67	8	67	8	35	40	261	186
	7	24	67	43	21	3	20	4	35	11	261	237
	9	410	400	10	340	70	390	20	35	375	261	149
	11	40	78	38	34	6	25	15	35	5	261	221
	13	130	100	30	123	7	120	10	35	95	261	131
Second Validation Set	15	21	15	6	34	13	15	6	35	14	261	240
	17	1786	2500	714	1589	197	1699	87	35	1751	261	1525
	19	900	700	200	789	111	800	100	35	865	261	639
	21	100	76	24	78	22	79	21	35	65	261	161
	23	50	23	27	39	11	42	8	35	15	261	211
	25	429	89	340	401	28	390	39	35	394	261	168
	27	90	147	57	79	11	67	23	35	55	261	171
Third Validation Set	29	34	21	13	30	4	28	6	35	1	261	227
	31	363	500	137	345	18	350	13	35	328	261	102
	33	6	2	4	5	1	3	3	35	29	261	255
	35	38	12	26	29	9	28	10	35	3	261	223
	37	30	56	26	28	2	21	9	35	5	261	231
	39	625	467	158	634	9	600	25	35	590	261	364
	41	6	1	5	5	1	4	2	35	29	261	255

Table 11. MMRE, MdMRE, and Pred(25) for Tech 1, Tech 2, Tech 3, and median and mean effort models

Accuracy Measure	Technique *Tech 1*	Technique *Tech 2*	Technique *Tech 3*	Median Model	Mean Model
MMRE (%)	61	15	18	699.22	102.00
MdMRE (%)	54	12	17	190.00	73.08
Pred(25) (%)	19	95	67	9.52	19.05

Copyright © 2008, IGI Global. Copying or distributing in print or electronic forms without written permission of IGI Global is prohibited.

Figure 16. Kendall's W Test comparing absolute residuals among Tech 1, Tech 2, Tech 3, and median and mean effort models

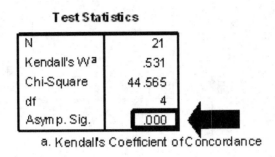

Figure 17. Wilcoxon signed-ranks test comparing different pairs of absolute residuals

Test Statistics[b]

	Median - ResT1	Mean - ResT1	Median - ResT2	Mean - ResT2	Median - ResT3	Mean - ResT3
Z	-2.972[a]	-1.860[a]	-3.980[a]	-3.633[a]	-3.980[a]	-3.530[a]
Asymp. Sig. (2-tailed)	.003	.063	.000	.000	.000	.000

a. Based on negative ranks.

b. Wilcoxon Signed Ranks Test

ences between the distributions of the observed variables, which represents the null hypothesis, cannot be rejected using a statistical significance α of 0.05. Kendall's W test indicates that at least one set of absolute residual values come from a different distribution than absolute residual values for the remaining sets.

We know that the prediction accuracy using technique *Tech 1* was significantly worse than the prediction accuracy using techniques *Tech 2* and *Tech 3*; however, using solely Kendall's W test, we cannot determine if any other predictions were also very poor. Therefore, we can compare pairs of absolute residual sets, using the Wilcoxon signed-ranks test, in order to find out this information.

Except for the pair Mean and ResT1, all remaining pairs show significant differences.

Copyright © 2008, IGI Global. Copying or distributing in print or electronic forms without written permission of IGI Global is prohibited.

Table 12. Sum of absolute residuals for Tech 1, Tech 2, Tech 3, and median and mean effort

	Technique Tech 1	Technique Tech 2	Technique Tech 3	Median	Mean
Sum of absolute residuals	2360	611	499	5814	5240

To find out what residual sets give the worst predictions, we sum up all the absolute residuals and see which ones provide the largest sums. Table 12 shows the sum of absolute residuals for all three techniques, median, and mean, and clearly shows that the mean and median effort models provide the largest sums of absolute residuals. Therefore, according to our results, the mean effort model provides significantly worse accuracy than techniques *Tech 2* and *Tech 3*, and the median effort model provides significantly worse accuracy than any of the three effort estimation techniques.

Another point that we see to be relevant to the discussion in this chapter is that, regardless of the number of different effort estimation techniques a given company c wishes to compare, they should all in theory be applied to data on past finished Web projects developed by company c. However, this may bring problems whenever a Web company does not have a priori data to use in the comparison. Such problems are as follows (Briand, Langley, & Wieczorek, 2000):

- The time required to accumulate enough data on past projects from a single company may be prohibitive.
- By the time the data set is large, technologies used by the company may have changed, and older projects may no longer be representative of current practices.
- Care is necessary as data need to be collected in a consistent manner.

These three problems have motivated the use of cross-company data sets (data sets containing data from several companies) for effort estimation and productivity benchmarking. Such data sets can be used by a given Web company c in numerous ways, such as the following:

- To obtain a productivity baseline to be used by company c to compare its projects against. A baseline is an average that represents what is typical. Thus, once this

Copyright © 2008, IGI Global. Copying or distributing in print or electronic forms without written permission of IGI Global is prohibited.

baseline is obtained, a project that has its productivity above the baseline can indicate a project that presents above-average productivity and, conversely, a project that has its productivity below the productivity baseline can indicate a project that presents below-average productivity. Projects with productivity values very close to the baseline are considered of average productivity. The cross-company data to be used to obtain the productivity baseline need to correspond to projects that are very similar to those developed by company c; otherwise, the productivity baseline will not be applicable to company c's projects.

- To select a subject of projects similar to those developed by company c to be used with effort estimation techniques to obtain estimated effort for the new Web projects developed by company c. The similarity of projects is very important because you may end up using the wrong data and obtaining estimates that are highly inadequate. If a company is willing to compare several techniques, then the approach that has been described in this chapter can be readily applied. As for using company c's own expert-based estimations, this will be more difficult when you are using data from a cross-company data set since it is unlikely that such data sets will have requirements information available, and your company's expert-based effort estimates may turn out to be guesswork. Often the data available in such data sets represent effort, size, and cost drivers only (e.g., developers' experience with using the technology, number of different programming languages used in the project).

We suggest that a cross-company effort estimation model can be useful for companies that do not have past projects from which to develop its own models. For example, small or immature software companies will not initially have past projects from which to develop its own models (Moses, 1999). Therefore, the ability to estimate effort using, as a reference, similar projects developed by diverse Web companies is more realistic than to estimate effort without historical data or previous experience.

A cross-company data set should only be used for effort estimation until it is possible for a Web company to use its own data to build an effort estimation model. This is even more appropriate for Web companies that develop Web projects of the same type, using standard technologies and the same staff. Unfortunately, it is not possible to know in advance how many projects of a single Web company are necessary and sufficient to construct a useful company data set since it depends on several factors and specific circumstances (e.g., the stability of the development process and the number of variables included in the model). However, the Web effort estimation literature has examples where effort estimation models of good prediction accuracy were obtained using 12 or 13 Web projects; therefore, in some circumstances, a data set of 12 or 13 is sufficient.

Copyright © 2008, IGI Global. Copying or distributing in print or electronic forms without written permission of IGI Global is prohibited.

To date, the only cross-company data set specifically designed to record data on Web projects developed by Web companies worldwide is the Tukutuku data set, which is part of the Tukutuku project that has been briefly introduced at the start of this chapter and shown in Table 3. Any company can use this data when it volunteers three of its own projects to the Tukutuku project to be included in the data set.

Conclusion

This chapter begins by presenting a survey of Web effort estimation studies where two or more effort estimation techniques were compared, looking for the one that presented the best estimation accuracy. The survey shows that a minimum of two and a maximum of four different effort estimation techniques have been used in previous studies. In addition, linear regression has been used by all these previous studies, followed by stepwise regression, which was used in three studies. Finally, MMRE was the measure of accuracy used in all studies, followed by Pred(25) and boxplots of residuals.

This chapter also goes on to explain the steps necessary to compare using statistical significance tests sets of residuals obtained for the same validation set(s), using two or more effort estimation techniques. If two sets of absolute residuals are to be compared, and at least one of them is not normally distributed, then a nonparametric test, the Wilcoxon test, is to be used. Otherwise, if two sets of absolute residuals are to be compared and they are both normally distributed, then the parametric test to use is the paired-samples T-test.

When more than two sets of absolute residuals are to be compared, and at least one of them is not normally distributed, then a nonparametric test, Kendall's W H test, is to be used. Otherwise, if all sets of absolute residuals are to be compared and they are all normally distributed, then the statistical test to use is the one-way ANOVA parametric test.

Finally, the chapter provides an example, using data from the Tukutuku data set, where two and later three effort estimation techniques are compared.

References

Botafogo, R., Rivlin, A. E., & Shneiderman, B. (1992). Structural analysis of hypertexts: Identifying hierarchies and useful measures. *ACM Transactions on Information Systems, 10*(2), 143-179.

Copyright © 2008, IGI Global. Copying or distributing in print or electronic forms without written permission of IGI Global is prohibited.

Briand, L. C., Langley, T., & Wieczorek, I. (2000). A replicated assessment of common software cost estimation techniques. *Proceedings of the 22ⁿᵈ International Conference on Software Engineering* (pp. 377-386).

Conte, S., Dunsmore, H., & Shen, V. (1986). *Software engineering metrics and models.* Menlo Park, CA: Benjamin/Cummings.

Kirsopp, C., & Shepperd, M. (2001). *Making inferences with small numbers of training sets* (Tech. Rep. No. TR02-01). Bournemouth, United Kingdom: Bournemouth University.

Kitchenham, B. A., MacDonell, S. G., Pickard, L. M., & Shepperd, M. J. (2001). What accuracy statistics really measure. *IEE Proceedings Software, 148*(3), 81-85.

Mendes, E., Counsell, S., & Mosley, N. (2000, June). Measurement and effort prediction of Web applications. *Proceedings of the 2ⁿᵈ ICSE Workshop on Web Engineering* (pp. 57-74).

Mendes, E., Mosley, N., & Counsell, S. (2001). Web metrics: Estimating design and authoring effort. *IEEE Multimedia, 8*(1), 50-57.

Mendes, E., Mosley, N., & Counsell, S. (2003, April). Investigating early Web size measures for Web cost estimation. *Proceedings of EASE2003 Conference* (pp. 1-22).

Mendes, E., Watson, I., Triggs, C., Mosley, N., & Counsell, S. (2002, June). A comparison of development effort estimation techniques for Web hypermedia applications. *Proceedings IEEE Metrics Symposium* (pp. 141-151).

Moses, J. (1999). Learning how to improve effort estimation in small software development companies. *Proceedings of the 24ᵗʰ International Computer Software and Applications Conference* (pp. 522-527).

Reifer, D. J. (2000). Web development: Estimating quick-to-market software. *IEEE Software, 17*(6), 57-64.

Ruhe, M., Jeffery, R., & Wieczorek, I. (2003). Cost estimation for Web applications. *Proceedings of ICSE 2003* (pp. 285-294).

Shepperd, M. J., & Kadoda, G. (2001). Using simulation to evaluate prediction techniques. *Proceedings of the IEEE 7ᵗʰ International Software Metrics Symposium* (pp. 349-358).

Copyright © 2008, IGI Global. Copying or distributing in print or electronic forms without written permission of IGI Global is prohibited.

Chapter IX

How to Improve Your Company's Effort Estimation Practices

Abstract

Numerous Web development companies worldwide do not employ formal techniques to estimate effort for new projects, thus relying on expert-based opinion (McDonald & Welland, 2001; Mendes, Mosley, & Counsell, 2005). In addition, many Web companies do not gather any data on past projects, which can later be used to estimate effort for new projects, and as a consequence they are not aware of how effort is used throughout their projects and if it could be used more effectively. This chapter provides a set of guidelines we believe can be of benefit to Web companies to help them improve their effort estimation practices. Our guidelines are particularly targeted at small Web development companies.

Copyright © 2008, IGI Global. Copying or distributing in print or electronic forms without written permission of IGI Global is prohibited.

Introduction

Expert-based effort estimation represents the process by which effort for a new project to be developed is estimated by subjective means, and is often based on previous experience from developing or managing similar projects. This is by far the most used technique for Web effort estimation (Mendes et al., 2005; McDonald & Welland, 2001). Estimates can be suggested by a project manager or by a group of people mixing project managers and developers, usually by means of a brainstorming session.

Within the context of Web development, our experience suggests that expert-based effort estimates are obtained using one of the following mechanisms.

- An estimate that is based on a detailed effort breakdown taking into account all the lowest level parts of an application or tasks. These lowest level parts and tasks are each attributed effort estimates, which are then combined into higher level estimates until we finally obtain an estimate that is the sum of all lower level estimates. Each part or task can represent a functional (the application must provide a shopping cart) or nonfunctional (the application must offer a high level of security) requirement. Such type of estimation is called bottom-up. Each estimate can be an educated guess, based on previous experience, or a mix of both.

- An estimate representing an overall process or product. A total estimate is suggested and used to calculate estimates for the component parts as relative portions of the whole. Each component part, as with the bottom-up estimation, will be related to a functional or nonfunctional requirement. This type of estimation is called top-down. As with bottom-up effort estimates, each estimate can also be an educated guess, based on previous experience, or a combination of both.

- An estimate that corresponds to a client's budget, which has been pre-agreed upon. From this point on, a top-down approach is used to identify the components that are to be delivered. This estimate will be based on the company's average or fixed rate for Web development projects.

All the three different ways to derive an effort estimate above mentioned will also be influenced by the type of process model used by a Web company. In general a software development process (and Web development is no exception) produces what is named a software life cycle (or process model), which in general comprises the following phases (Abernethy et al., 2007; Bennett, McRobb, & Farmer, 2002).

Copyright © 2008, IGI Global. Copying or distributing in print or electronic forms without written permission of IGI Global is prohibited.

- Requirements analysis
- Design
- Implementation (or coding)
- Testing
- Installation
- Maintenance

The Waterfall Model

The way in which these phases interact with each other determines a specific process model. For example, if the phases are organised as shown in Figure 1, then this life cycle model represents the commonly known waterfall model (Royce, 1970/1987).

The use of a waterfall model means that the analysis of the requirements associated with a given application must be well-understood and finished before the design phase begins, and this same principle applies to all consecutive phases. In other words, a phase must be complete before moving to the next phase, and there is no iteration among phases. The waterfall model aims to deliver a final working Web application

Figure 1. Waterfall life cycle model

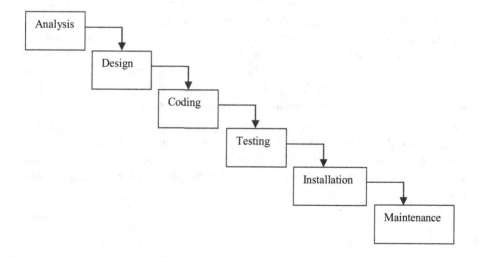

Copyright © 2008, IGI Global. Copying or distributing in print or electronic forms without written permission of IGI Global is prohibited.

as the finished product, which means that the customer and end users only become familiar with how the application works when this application is delivered.

When a Web company uses a waterfall model, this means that effort estimates relating to the entire development of a Web application will be derived during or as soon as the requirements analysis phase is complete, and it is very unlikely that these estimates will be changed later on in the development life cycle unless the requirements change significantly (Jørgensen & Sjøberg, 2001). Either top-down, bottom-up, or budget-based approaches are applicable here. If later on in the development life cycle there are significant changes to the initial requirements, then it is common practice to revisit the initial contract such that these changes are taken into account in the final costs. If this is the case, the original effort estimate will also be revisited.

In addition, some Web companies budget separately the requirements analysis phase from the rest of the project. This means that customers are charged for an initial and complete requirements document, and only then an effort estimate for the project is proposed, and costs for the remainder of the project budgeted.

The lack of flexibility inherent to this process model led to the proposal of other models that present iteration at different levels, and models that were created specifically to be used to develop Web applications, or to be used as extensions of traditional software development life cycles that took into account Web development needs. Some of these models will be presented next.

Extension to the Waterfall Model

An extension to the waterfall model that allows for iteration is presented in Figure 2. When a Web company uses an iterative waterfall model, this also means that, similar to the traditional waterfall model, effort estimates relating to the entire development of a Web application will be derived early on, during or as soon as the requirements analysis phase is complete; again, it is very unlikely that these estimates will be changed later on in the development life cycle, unless there are significant changes to the initial requirements (Jørgensen & Sjøberg, 2001). Either top-down, bottom-up, or budget-based approaches are applicable here.

Since 1999, several process models specifically targeted at Web development have been proposed (Burdman, 1999; McDonald, 2004), and evolutions to traditional software engineering processes have been extended to accommodate for Web development (Ward & Kroll, 1999). They are briefly presented in this chapter, and detailed in McDonald and Welland (2001).

Copyright © 2008, IGI Global. Copying or distributing in print or electronic forms without written permission of IGI Global is prohibited.

Figure 2. Waterfall life cycle model with iteration

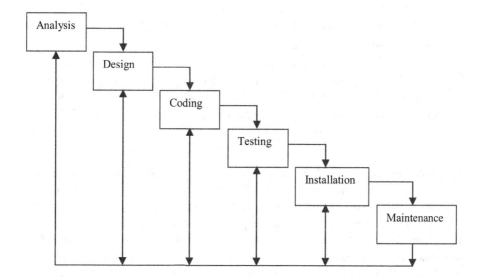

Collaborative Web Development

The collaborative Web development (CWD) process model (Burdman, 1999) is detailed in Figure 3, and its four phases are described below, quoted from Burdman.

- Phase I: *Strategy.* During this phase, either a strategic planner, account executive, or project manager and/or the client is determining the objective for the site based on a dedicated research effort. The culmination or deliverable of this phase is the creative brief, which clearly outlines the objectives, requirements, and key insights of the target audience. The creative brief provides a foundation for every team member's work.

- Phase II: *Design.* During this phase, the creative and technical teams are doing a parallel design of the site. The creative team is designing the user interface and interactions, and the technical team is designing the back-end applications that will be used on the site. The culmination of this phase is the functional and/or technical specification, site architecture, schematics, and designs of the site. Sign-off by the client is critical to proceed.

Copyright © 2008, IGI Global. Copying or distributing in print or electronic forms without written permission of IGI Global is prohibited.

- Phase III: *Production.* During this phase, we are building the site. Any major changes in functionality and features have to be monitored closely. If the client requests a change at this point, a change order is issued. The culmination of this phase is, of course, the site, which will go into Phase IV. A production guide is also created during this phase.

- Phase IV: *Testing.* During this phase we are testing the site and getting ready to publish it on the live, or production, Web server. Our QA (quality assurance) manager develops a test plan based on the scope document and functional specification, and tests against this plan. Bugs are reported and fixed. The site is ready to go live at the end of this phase.

Within the context of the CWD process model, effort estimates are obtained after Phase II is complete, which means that both the requirements analysis and the design of the application must be finished in order to obtain an effort estimate. This seems to be a common practice among Web companies worldwide (McDonald & Welland, 2001); however, ideally an estimate should be prepared before the design of an application commences. Both bottom-up and top-down estimations are applicable here. Finally, this process model is not iterative, and is not incremental either.

Figure 3. The CWD Web project development life cycle (Adapted from Burdman, 1999)

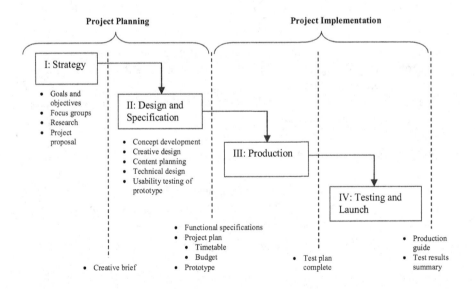

Copyright © 2008, IGI Global. Copying or distributing in print or electronic forms without written permission of IGI Global is prohibited.

Extended Rational Unified Process

The extended rational unified process (extended RUP) to Web applications (Ward & Kroll, 1999) is a process model that focuses predominantly on the initial phases of a development life cycle, and how the creative design process inherent to Web development can be integrated to the traditional RUP, which is a software engineering process.

The life cycle described in Figure 4 shows that the extended RUP relates to using the deliverables that are normally developed as part of RUP (e.g., use-case diagrams) as input to processes that are Web specific (e.g., initial Web UI prototype).

Figure 4. The extended RUP life cycle (Ward & Kroll, 1999)

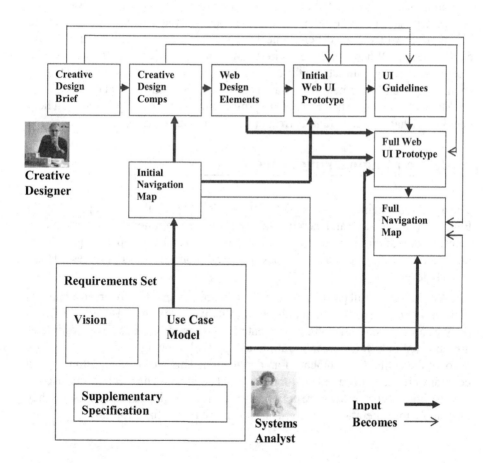

Copyright © 2008, IGI Global. Copying or distributing in print or electronic forms without written permission of IGI Global is prohibited.

The traditional RUP life cycle incorporates the following four phases (McDonald, 2004).

1. *Inception:* This phase's goal is to obtain agreement among all stakeholders regarding the project's life cycle objectives.
2. *Elaboration:* This phase's goal is to analyse the problem domain, prepare a basis for the application's architecture that is robust, and work on a project plan that reduces the project's most challenging risks.
3. *Construction:* This phase's goal is to develop and integrate into the product all remaining components and application features and functions. In addition, features, components, and functions are all tested systematically.
4. *Transition:* This phase's goal is to deliver the product to the customer and users.

The process model presented in Figure 4 is iterative and incremental. However, it is expected that an effort estimate be obtained once the requirements analysis phase is complete. All the three different mechanisms used to obtain effort estimates are applicable here. Whenever there are iterations to a Web project in practice, it will be likely that an initial estimate for the entire development is proposed and used to plan each iteration and increment. This way, a customer can be informed at the start about the likely effort and costs for the entire project and, whenever applicable, can help decide on what iterations (and corresponding increments) will be carried out.

Agile Web Engineering Process

The agile Web engineering process (AWE) model (McDonald, 2004), presented in Figure 5, is an iterative and incremental process where iterations are centred on the identification of problems that are seen by customers and developers as presenting the highest risk. In addition, it focuses specifically on architectural issues relating to Web development.

The AWE assumes full participation of all stakeholders and developers in all phases of the development life cycle. Finally, the only deliverable required to be produced is the Web application itself. Within the context of this process model, effort estimates are obtained only for a given iteration, as opposed to being obtained taking into account the entire development of an application. This means that customers and company are likely to negotiate iteration-based contracts. The mechanisms used to obtain effort estimates that were previously presented need to be scaled down as they only apply to an iteration or increment. It is more likely that a top-down approach

Copyright © 2008, IGI Global. Copying or distributing in print or electronic forms without written permission of IGI Global is prohibited.

Figure 5. The AWE process life cycle

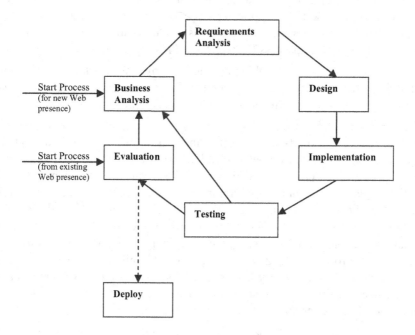

will be used on each iteration or increment to obtain effort estimates; however, a bottom-up mechanism may also occur.

Accuracy of Estimates

A survey of 32 Web companies in New Zealand conducted in 2004 (Mendes et al., 2005) showed that 32% of the companies prepared an effort estimate during the requirements gathering phase, 62% prepared an estimate during the design phase, and 6% did not have to provide any effort estimates at all to their customers. Of these 32 companies, 38% did not refine their effort estimate, and 62% did refine estimates but not often. This indicated that at least for the surveyed companies, the initial effort estimate was used as their final estimate, and work was adjusted to fit the initial estimate. These results corroborated those in Jørgensen and Sjøberg (2001). These results also suggest that many Web companies only provide an effort estimate for a new project once the requirements are understood. This is an option that can

Copyright © 2008, IGI Global. Copying or distributing in print or electronic forms without written permission of IGI Global is prohibited.

be pursued by Web companies that do not have to bid for projects and thus do not need to provide early effort estimates; however, for those companies that have to bid, it is imperative that they are able to provide early estimates despite the fact that in many instances requirements are notoriously fluidic and difficult to gather until later in the development process (Lowe, 2003; Pressman, 2000; Reifer, 2000).

Regardless of the process model being employed by a Web company to develop their Web applications, deriving an accurate effort estimate is more likely to occur when there is previous knowledge and data about completed projects very similar to the one having its effort estimated.

Within the scope of expert-based effort estimation, the attainment of accurate effort estimates relies on the competence and experience of individuals (e.g., project manager, developer). Given a new project p, the greater the experience with application domains and technologies similar to what is required in p, the greater the chances that the suggested estimated effort will be closer to the actual effort that will be required to develop p. However, in particular for small Web development companies, the reality is that in order to remain competitive, these companies often have to bid for projects in domain areas they are not familiar with, and that require the use of technologies that they have not previously used (Moses, 1999). In such circumstances the probability that the estimated effort for a new project becomes simply guesswork is very high.

It is in our view very important that those companies that wish to improve their effort estimates record on a database (experience base) the main problems and solutions encountered for each project, and that this experience base contain data on successful as well as unsuccessful projects. Such data can later be used to understand better and learn from past projects, which will be very likely useful when estimating effort for new projects and negotiating contracts. It is also important to use simple project management practices, where each project should have the following.

- An associated process model identifying phases, activities, tasks, and deliverables.

- A work breakdown structure, which is a hierarchy detailing tasks and activities within each task. This can also be associated with a Gantt chart (see Figure 6). A Gantt chart is a time-charting technique where horizontal bars are used to represent project activities, and the horizontal axis represents time using dates, weeks, and so forth. The length of a bar determines the duration of an activity, and activities are listed vertically so it is easy to identify activities that run in parallel and activities that are interdependent. Both work breakdown structures and Gantt charts are useful tools to help project managers allocate resources effectively.

- A critical path analysis that is used to identify a project's critical path. This means that the project manager(s) and developer(s) know what the sequence

Copyright © 2008, IGI Global. Copying or distributing in print or electronic forms without written permission of IGI Global is prohibited.

of activities is where if one is delayed, the entire project is also delayed. An example is given in Figure 7, showing that the path A to D is critical.

- Company baselines that are used as often as possible to check against actual results.

- Existing standards applied whenever available.

- Continuous feedback and continuous improvement. Early feedback is crucial to help remedy any problems that have been identified with an ongoing project. This means that the project manager and developers must develop a communication channel that is constant. Weekly or even daily meetings may be very helpful to keep a project on target.

- A time logging mechanism where developers and project managers enter, preferably on a daily basis, the amount of time spent on each of the activities relating to an ongoing project. This is in our view one of the most difficult problems currently faced by Web companies worldwide. They simply do not gather effort data, and the only data available is what is written on the invoice used to charge a client for the work done. In our view, without reliable effort data, it is very difficult, and likely impossible, to use any of the techniques introduced in this book to help improve effort estimates for new Web projects.

Figure 6. Example of a Gantt chart

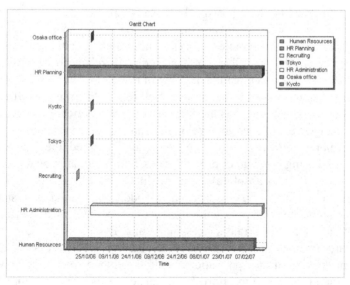

Copyright © 2008, IGI Global. Copying or distributing in print or electronic forms without written permission of IGI Global is prohibited.

Figure 7. Critical path analysis example

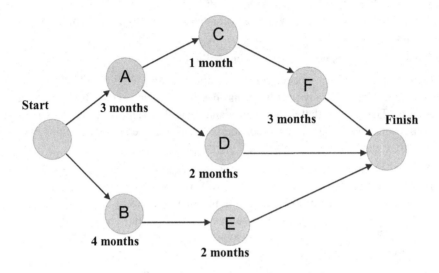

There are Web companies that document the effort spent developing past projects; however, they do not use these data to help improve their effort estimation practices and to obtain accurate estimates for new projects. One of the reasons that we have observed for effort data not being used is because companies do not make it their priority and consequently do not put any time aside to understand the set of factors that have a bearing on the estimation process within their specific contexts. This should involve not only the identification of factors directly related to the applications developed (e.g., size of the application, amount of reuse of content and structure), but also factors that are related to the project itself (e.g., type of project [new, enhancement], how well requirements are understood, the experience of developers with the technologies being used to develop the application, number of people as part of the development team). Once such factors are identified, they can even be initially measured using nominal or ordinal scales, which can later be replaced by other scale types (e.g., ratio, absolute). Using qualitative data to understand current practices is better than not using any data at all. In addition, without understanding the factors that influence effort within the context of a specific company, effort data alone are not sufficient to warrant successful results. Even if a company wishes to first compare productivity amongst team members, it is still necessary to also gather data on the size of the applications being developed since productivity is calculated as the ratio of size to effort. Unfortunately, it is our experience that a

Copyright © 2008, IGI Global. Copying or distributing in print or electronic forms without written permission of IGI Global is prohibited.

large number of Web companies worldwide do not actually gather any data at all. We believe the main factors that prevent companies from gathering data on past projects are as follows:

- Unwillingness of the development team to record the time spent on activities since it can be used later for accountability and to help measure their productivity.

- Timing software tools that use the metaphor of a stopwatch, thus still requiring Web developers to control when and how timing takes place. This author has surveyed several commercial timing software tools and found only one that does not require the users' interference (MetriQ, http://www.metriq.biz). This is the timing software we currently use; it is easy to use and straightforward to set up.

- No widespread awareness in the Web industry of useful Web application size measures, despite the existence of several proposals in the Web engineering literature (details on these measures are provided in Chapter IV). This means that Web companies willing to gather data on their projects have to many times blindly decide upon the size measures to use, and since this task can take some time, companies simply postpone their decision and data collection.

- Many companies employ ad hoc processes to develop applications and as a consequence there is never time for gathering data since all the available time has to be devoted to finishing often delayed projects and starting other projects. The main concern under such circumstances is for a company to survive, and clearly data gathering and the formalisation of effort estimation are not considered to be their main priorities.

There are drawbacks in the use of expert-based estimation that have motivated the software and Web engineering communities to look for the use of systematic techniques to obtain effort estimates. Some of the drawbacks are as follows.

1. It is very difficult for an expert to quantify and to determine those factors that have been used to derive an estimate, making it difficult to repeat success.

2. When a company finally builds up its expertise with developing Web applications using a given set of technologies, other technologies appear and are rapidly adopted (mostly due to hype), thus leaving behind the knowledge that had been accumulated.

3. Obtaining an effort estimate based on experience with past similar projects can be misleading when projects vary in their characteristics. For example, knowing that a Web application containing 10 new static pages using HTML (hypertext

Copyright © 2008, IGI Global. Copying or distributing in print or electronic forms without written permission of IGI Global is prohibited.

markup language) and 10 new images was developed by one person who took 40 person hours does not mean that a similar application developed by two people will also use 40 person hours. Two people may need additional time to communicate, and may also have different experience with using HTML. In addition, another application eight times its size is unlikely to take exactly eight times longer.

4.   Developers and project managers are known for providing optimistic effort estimates (DeMarco, 1982; Moløkken & Jørgensen, 2005). Optimistic estimates lead to underestimated effort, and the consequences are projects over budget and past due.

To deal with underestimation, it is suggested that experts provide three different estimates (Vliet, 2000): an optimistic estimate o, a realistic estimate r, and a pessimistic estimate p. Based on a beta distribution, the estimated effort E is then calculated as:

$$E = (o + 4r + p)/6..$$ (1)

This measure is likely to be better than a simple average of o and p; however, caution is still necessary.

Within the context of conventional software development, Jørgensen (2004) has reported the results of 14 studies that compared expert-based and model-based effort estimation accuracy for software development and maintenance work. Of these, 5 have found that expert-based effort estimates provided better accuracy (Kitchenham, Pfleeger, McColl, & Eagan, 2002; Kusters, Genuchten, & Heemstra, 1990; Mukhopadhyay, Vicinanza, & Prietula, 1992; Pengelly, 1995; Vicinanza, Mukhopadhyay, & Prietula, 1991), 4 have found that model-based effort estimates provided better accuracy than expert-based effort estimates (Atkinson & Shepperd, 1994; Jørgensen, 1997; Jørgensen & Sjøberg, 2002; Myrtveit & Stensrud, 1999), and the remaining 5 studies have found no differences between expert-based and model-based effort estimates (Bowden, Hargreaves, & Langensiepen, 2000; Heemstra & Kusters, 1991; Lederer & Prasad, 2000; Ohlsson, Wohlin, & Regnell, 1998; Walkerden & Jeffery, 1999). Although no clear evidence is presented in favour of expert-based effort estimations or in favour of model-based effort estimations, there are a few studies that have reported that when used in combination with other less subjective techniques (e.g., algorithmic models), expert-based effort estimation can be an effective estimating tool (Gray et al., 1999; Mendes et al., 2002; Reifer, 2000).

This is actually the approach we would like to suggest Web companies employ in order to improve their current estimation practices. We believe that within contexts where many of the new Web applications to be developed are similar (e.g., scope,

Copyright © 2008, IGI Global. Copying or distributing in print or electronic forms without written permission of IGI Global is prohibited.

application domain, technologies) to previously developed applications, the use of expert-based estimations and more formal techniques (e.g., multivariate regression) in combination can help adjust the estimate up to an optimal level. For example, as we have seen in previous chapters, techniques such as multivariate regression and classification and regression trees help identify the variables that are really contributing toward the effort estimate. This information can be used by experts to help them calibrate their own estimates. In addition, the estimated effort provided using more formal techniques can also be used in conjunction with the estimated effort obtained by means of expert opinion in order to obtain an aggregated effort estimate. To know the set of variables that have a bearing on effort is also important for other related reasons. For example, if multivariate regression shows that larger development teams are actually not providing economies of scale, this information can be used by project managers in the future when allocating resources for new Web projects.

In addition, this book has provided chapters detailing the steps a company can follow in order to compare two or more effort estimation techniques. These techniques can be some of those that are presented in this book, or may also include other techniques that are outside the scope of this book (e.g., fuzzy systems, neural networks, Bayesian networks). We suggest, however, that one of the techniques to be used be representative of the company's own expert-based effort estimation procedures, and that it is used to establish a benchmark against which to compare the accuracy of any other techniques. This will provide the means to realistically assess whether any new techniques really add value to the effort estimates currently obtained by the company. Why do we think that it is important to include the company's own effort estimation procedures as a benchmark? Let us suppose that your company has applied three new techniques to estimate effort for your Web projects. All these techniques provided similar estimation accuracy: Their mean magnitudes of relative error (MMREs) were 60%, 62%, and 65%, and their prediction at 25% (Pred[25]) were 7%, 9%, and 10%. Given this scenario, one would think that suggesting your company to use any of these three techniques would be a waste of time. However, let us assume that your company also measured prediction accuracy using its own expert-based effort estimation procedure, and obtained an MMRE of 85% and Pred(25) of 0%. Here the company's own estimates are much worse than those obtained using any of the three new effort estimation techniques. Therefore, using any of the three techniques would be advantageous for the company, despite the overall poor effort estimation accuracy based on MMRE and Pred(25). The point here is that unless the company's own effort estimates are also used for comparison, it is impossible to determine if a new effort estimation technique would be an improvement over the current procedures used by that company to estimate effort.

Another option, as we will see in the next section, is to use existing cross-company data sets to help provide effort estimates for new Web projects until a company is able to gather its own data.

Copyright © 2008, IGI Global. Copying or distributing in print or electronic forms without written permission of IGI Global is prohibited.

The Value of Cross-Company Data Sets

When a Web company decides to gather data on its past projects because it wishes to use these data to improve its effort estimation practices, it is important to keep into perspective the three following problems that might occur (Briand, Langley, & Wieczorek, 2000).

- The time required to accumulate enough data on past projects from a single company may be prohibitive
- By the time the data set is large enough, technologies used by the company may have changed, and older projects may no longer be representative of current practices
- Care is necessary as data need to be collected in a consistent manner, otherwise results may end up being biased and the entire effort in gathering data becomes worthless

These three problems have motivated the use of cross-company data sets (data sets containing data from several companies) for effort estimation and productivity benchmarking. Such data sets can be used by a given Web company c in numerous ways, such as the following:

- To obtain a productivity baseline to be used by company c to compare its projects against. A baseline is an average that represents what is typical. Thus, once this baseline is obtained, a project that has its productivity above the baseline can indicate a project that presents above-average productivity and, conversely, a project that has its productivity below the productivity baseline can indicate a project that presents below-average productivity. Projects with productivity values very close to the baseline are considered of average productivity. The cross-company data to be used to obtain the productivity baseline needs to correspond to projects that are very similar to those developed by company c; otherwise, the productivity baseline will not be applicable to company c's projects.
- To select a subject of projects similar to those developed by company c to be used with effort estimation techniques to obtain estimated effort for the new Web projects developed by company c. Similarity of projects is very important as otherwise you will end up using the wrong data and obtaining estimates that are highly inadequate. As for using company c's own expert-based estimations, this will be more difficult when you are using data from a cross-company data set since it is unlikely that such data sets will have requirements information

Copyright © 2008, IGI Global. Copying or distributing in print or electronic forms without written permission of IGI Global is prohibited.

available, and your company's expert-based effort estimates may turn out to be guesswork. Often, the data available in such data sets represent effort, size, and cost drivers (e.g., developers' experience with using the technology, number of different programming languages used in the project) only.

Note that for the remainder of this section we will assume that the effort estimation technique(s) being used explicitly build effort prediction models.

We suggest that using a cross-company data set to build an effort prediction model to be used to estimate effort can be useful to companies that do not have past projects from which to build a model, or by companies that currently have a very small number of projects. For example, small or immature software companies will not initially have past projects from which to develop their own models (Moses, 1999). Therefore, the ability to estimate effort using, as a reference, similar projects developed by diverse Web companies is more realistic than to estimate effort without historical data or from previous experience.

A cross-company data set should only be used for effort estimation until it is possible for a Web company to use its own data to build an effort estimation model. This is even more appropriate for Web companies that develop Web projects of the same type, using standard technologies and the same staff. Another alternative is for a Web company to continue using the cross-company data set but to also volunteer to that data set data on its recently finished projects. This means that the cross-company data set will incorporate a Web company's own recent projects and also similar projects that have been developed by other Web companies, and will progressively contain more projects similar to those developed by the company.

To date, it is not possible to know in advance the exact number of projects from a single Web company that are necessary and sufficient to construct a useful single-company effort estimation model since it depends on several factors and specific circumstances (e.g., the stability of the development process and the number of variables included in the model). However, the Web cost estimation literature has examples where effort estimation models of good prediction accuracy were obtained using 12 or 13 Web projects; therefore, in some circumstances, a data set of 12 or 13 may be sufficient.

Assessing the Effectiveness of Cross-Company Models

How can a Web company assess if using its own data to build an effort model will provide better predictions for its new projects than to use an effort model built from cross-company data? This requires that two questions be answered:

Copyright © 2008, IGI Global. Copying or distributing in print or electronic forms without written permission of IGI Global is prohibited.

1. How successful is a Web cross-company model at estimating effort for projects from a single Web company?

2. How successful is a Web cross-company model compared to a Web single-company model?

A Web cross-company model is a model that is built using data volunteered by several different Web companies; conversely, a Web single-company model is a model built using data volunteered by a single Web company. Both questions need to be assessed in combination because even if a Web cross-company effort model provides accurate effort estimates for the projects that belong to the single company, this does not mean that using the cross-company model is the best choice for this company. Perhaps using the company's own data to build an effort model would provide even more accurate effort estimates than using the cross-company model. This means that we need to compare the prediction accuracy obtained from applying a cross-company model to estimate effort for the single-company projects to the prediction accuracy obtained from applying a single-company model to estimate effort for the same single-company projects that have been used to validate the cross-company model.

The steps to follow in order to answer Question 1 are as follows.

CC1. Apply an effort estimation technique (e.g., multivariate regression, or classification and regression trees) to build a cross-company cost model using the cross-company data set. This data set does not contain the data that belong to the single company. It is not applicable to case-based reasoning since no explicit model is built.

CC2. Use the model in Step CC1 to estimate effort for each of the single-company projects. The single-company projects are the validation set used to obtain effort estimates. The estimated effort obtained for each project is also used to calculate accuracy statistics (e.g., MMRE, absolute residuals). The equivalent for case-based reasoning is to use the cross-company data set as a case base to estimate effort for each of the single-company projects.

CC3. The overall model accuracy is aggregated from the validation set (e.g., MMRE, MdMRE [median magnitude of relative error]). The same goes for case-based reasoning.

These steps are used to simulate a situation where a single company uses a cross-company model to estimate effort for its new projects.

Copyright © 2008, IGI Global. Copying or distributing in print or electronic forms without written permission of IGI Global is prohibited.

The steps to follow in order to answer Question 2 are as follows.

SC1. Apply an effort estimation technique (multivariate regression, or classification and regression trees) to build a single-company cost model using the single-company data set. This is not applicable to case-based reasoning.

SC2. Obtain the prediction accuracy of estimates for the model obtained in SC1 using a leave-one-out cross-validation. Cross-validation is the splitting of a data set into training and validation sets. Training sets are used to build models and validation sets are used to validate models. A leave-one-out cross-validation means that the original data set is divided into n different subsets (n is the size of the original data set) of training and validation sets, where each validation set has one project. The equivalent for case-based reasoning is to use the single-company data set as a case base after removing one project, and then to estimate effort for the project that has been removed. This step is iterated n times, each time removing a different project. The estimated effort obtained for each project is also used to calculate accuracy statistics (e.g., MMRE, absolute residuals).

SC3. The overall model accuracy is aggregated across the n validation sets. The same goes for case-based reasoning.

SC4. Compare the accuracy obtained in Step SC2 to that obtained for the cross-company model in CC2. Do the same for case-based reasoning. To carry out this step, it is important to use the absolute residuals obtained in steps CC2 and SC2. If any of the residual sets are not normally distributed, then it will be necessary to use a nonparametric paired statistical test (Wilcoxon signed-ranks test) to compare the statistical significance of the results, that is, to assess whether the two sets of residuals come from the same or from different distributions. If the residual sets are large, or normally distributed, then the paired-samples T-test is the choice to compare the samples.

Steps 1 to 3 simulate a situation where a single company builds a model using its own data set, and then uses this model to estimate effort for its new projects.

To date, the only cross-company data set specifically designed to record data on Web projects developed by Web companies worldwide is the Tukutuku data set (http://www.cs.auckland.ac.nz/tukutuku), which has been used throughout this book. Any Web companies can use this data set as long as they contribute at least three of their own projects to the Tukutuku project to be included in the Tukutuku data set.

Copyright © 2008, IGI Global. Copying or distributing in print or electronic forms without written permission of IGI Global is prohibited.

How to Start?

If a Web company wishes to start gathering data on past projects to be used to understand its current practices and to build effort estimation models, there is probably one question that comes to mind: What do I need to gather?

The answer to this question does not need to be complicated. The first measure has to be effort, which is one of the most difficult measures to gather since developers do not wish to be distracted from their work by having to fill out timing sheets, and also do not wish to use tools that require the constant use of a stopwatch. As previously mentioned, there is one tool we are aware of that we strongly believe is not disruptive since we have used it for a while now to time all the work we do.

Once effort is dealt with, we still have the challenge to decide on what the measures are that should be used to predict effort. Ideally these measures should be gathered early so that they can be used at the bidding stage. The only set of early measures for Web cost estimation that has been proposed to date in the literature is the set of measures used in the Tukutuku project. These measures were identified by means of a survey. The purpose of this survey (S1) was to identify Web size metrics and factors used by Web companies to estimate effort for Web projects early on in the development cycle (Mendes et al., 2005). The target population was that of Web companies that offer online Web project price quotes to customers. There was no need to contact Web companies directly, only to download their online Web project price quote forms from the Web.

The four research questions that were answered using this survey were as follows.

Question 1. What are the size measures and factors used as early effort estimators by Web companies?

Question 2. Which size measures are used the most?

Question 3. Which size measures are characteristic of Web hypermedia applications?

Question 4. Which size metrics are characteristic of Web software applications?

Example of How to Define your Own Size Measures and Cost Drivers

To obtain a sample of the population of interest, Mendes et al. (2005) used a Web search engine (http://www.google.com) to carry out a search on the 7th of August, 2002, using the sentence "quote Web development project." Google.com was chosen

Copyright © 2008, IGI Global. Copying or distributing in print or electronic forms without written permission of IGI Global is prohibited.

because at the time it was the fourth most popular search engine in the world, and those ranked 1 and 3 both licensed Google technology for their own Web searches. About half of all Web searches in the world are performed with Google, and it is translated into 86 languages. The authors' objective was to obtain Web addresses (URLs, uniform resource locators) for Web companies that had online price quotes for Web development projects so that these quotes could be used to identify size metrics and cost factors. Two hundred and fifty nine (259) Web addresses were retrieved. Of those, 38 did not contain any forms or useful descriptions. Of the remaining 221 URLs, 88 presented online quotes that were too general to obtain any useful information.

The data collected from the 133 online quotes were organised into six categories.

- Web application static measures
- Web application dynamic measures
- Cost drivers
- Web project measures
- Web company measures
- Web interface style measures

Web application static measures corresponded to attributes that have been commonly used to size Web hypermedia applications (e.g., number of Web pages, number of graphics, etc.). Web application dynamic measures referred to any features or functionality mentioned (e.g., database integration, online secure order form, etc.), which is taken as an abstract measure of functionality and therefore size (Fenton & Pfleeger, 1997). Cost drivers corresponded to attributes that might influence effort but did not characterise application size. Web project measures incorporated measures believed to have a bearing on the contingency and/or profit costs that are provided in a price quote (Kitchenham, Pickard, Linkman, & Jones, 2003; e.g., project budget). Web company measures are attributes that characterised a Web company (e.g., target audience), and Web interface style measures are attributes that characterised the final appearance (style) of the Web application (e.g., background colour, style, etc.). The full list of measures per category is given in Table 1. This table also shows the percentage and corresponding number of Web companies that have included that measure in their quote forms. Two measures stood out: total number of Web pages, and features and functionality. Both can be taken as size measures as the first is a typical length size metric and the second an abstract measure of functionality (Fenton & Pfleeger, 1997).

Seventy four (74) Web companies also asked for the available Web project budget. Mendes et al. (2005) believed this measure could have a bearing on the contingency

Copyright © 2008, IGI Global. Copying or distributing in print or electronic forms without written permission of IGI Global is prohibited.

and/or profit costs that are provided in a price quote (Kitchenham et al., 2003). Project estimated end date, project estimated start date, and application type also were important to help set priorities and perhaps decide on what skills are necessary and available for the project.

Examples of features and functionality are as follows: auction or bid utility, bulletin boards, discussion forums and newsgroups, chat rooms, e-postcards, e-mail a friend, mailing lists for sites, subscriptions, vote systems, Web-based e-mail, database creation, database integration, other persistent storage integration (e.g., flat files), credit card authorization, member log-in, online secure order forms, password-protected pages, online content updating, online feedback forms, shopping cart services, invoices and billing, calendars and event calendars, displays of current date, CSS (style sheets) charts, file upload and download, human resource handbooks, job accounting, job scheduling, specialized reports, live data (stock quotes, etc.), performance reviews, time tracking, traffic statistics, knowledge bases, language translation, page counters, personalisation, search engines, user guest books, visitor statistics, cell phone optimisations, and palm PDA (personal digital assistant) Web clipping.

The types of Web applications that were elicited were academic, corporate, e-commerce, e-trading, educational, entertainment, extranet, family, functional, intranet, media, multimedia presentations, news and information, nonprofit, online communities and forums, one-page presence, personal, political, portals (vertical or horizontal), professional, promotional, search engines, short-term promotion, small businesses, support sites and video chat, and virtual marketplaces (B2B, business to business).

Companies' target audiences were the following: business people and professionals, mainly women, mainly men, teenagers and young adults, children, students, college or trade schools, and anyone and everyone.

The preferred style of the site was the following: whimsical, bright and vivid, techno-futuristic, gritty, aggressive, mass-consumer oriented, really "clean" looking, sports oriented, fun and wacky, for women only, and others.

The answers obtained for the survey questions were as follows:

- The size measures and factors used as early effort estimators by Web companies were identified in Table 1 under Web application static measures and Web application dynamic measures. Those that have been ranked highest are possibly the most important given that they were suggested by the greatest number of Web companies.

- The size measures used the most were the total number of Web pages and features and functionality. Together they represented 70% and 66% of the Web companies included in the survey, respectively.

Copyright © 2008, IGI Global. Copying or distributing in print or electronic forms without written permission of IGI Global is prohibited.

Table 1. Measures organised by category and ranking (Mendes et al., 2005)

Category	Measures	%	# Companies
Web Application Static Measures	1. Total number of Web pages	**70**	**92**
	2. Total number images provided by customer	31	41
	3. Total number of text pages provided by customer	30	39
	4. Total number of photos provided by customer	30	40
	5. Total number of products to sell	28	37
	6. Total number of flash animations	27	35
	7. Total number of photos from a library	23	30
	8. Total number of images from a library	22	29
	9. Total number of audio clips	20	27
	10. Total number of video clips	20	26
	11. Total number of photos to scan	15	20
	12. Total number of images to scan	14	19
	13. Total number of gif animations	14	18
	14. Total number of photos to process/create	11	15
	15. Total number of text pages to type	11	13
	16. Total number of images to process/create	9	12
	17. Total number of icons/buttons	8	10
	18. Total number of text pages to scan (OCR, optical character reader)	8	10
	19. Total number of existing components to add	4	5
	20. Total number of PDF (Portable Document Format)/ Word documents to download	2	3
	21. Total amount of graphics per product	2	3
	22. Average length of audio clips	2	2
	23. Average length of video clips	2	2
	24. How much text necessary for each product	1	1
Web Application Dynamic Measures	**Which Features/Functionality**	**66**	**87**
Cost Drivers	1. New application or enhancement	31	41
Web Project Measures	1. Budget for the project	56	74
	2. Project estimated end date	35	46
	3. Web application type	34	44
	4. Project estimated start date	32	42
	5. Will customer provide page mock-ups?	4	4
	6. Will the application be translated into different idioms?	3	4
	7. Will customer provide Web site map?	3	4
	8. What kind of Internet access most likely for customers?	1	1

Copyright © 2008, IGI Global. Copying or distributing in print or electronic forms without written permission of IGI Global is prohibited.

Table 1. continued

Category	Measures		%	# Companies
Web Company Measures	1.	Contact information (e-mail)	100	133
	2.	Description of company's business	19	25
	3.	Company's target audience	18	24
Web Interface Style Measures	1.	What is the preferred style for the site?	17	23
	2.	Give three URLs for sites you like	17	23
	3.	What type of colours for the site?	13	17
	4.	What type of colours for the background?	5	7
	5.	What type of colours for pages?	5	7

- The size measures identified in the survey that were characteristic of Web hypermedia applications comprised the category of Web application static measures (see Table 1).

- The size measures identified in the survey that were characteristic of Web software applications comprised the category of Web application dynamic measures (see Table 1).

The survey just described was used to identify measures related to a project's price quote. However, price is the result of three components (Kitchenham et al., 2003): estimated effort, contingency, and profit. Therefore, a case study and a second survey were conducted in order to identify only those measures specifically targeted at effort estimation. The case study involved the participation of a well-established and mature Web company, who validated the effort-estimation-related measures that had been obtained using the first survey. The second survey involved the participation of 33 Web companies in Auckland, New Zealand, who answered a questionnaire that was also used to validate the effort-estimation-related measures that were obtained using the first survey and confirmed using the case study. After both were conducted, the set of measures that was identified is the set that is used in all the chapters that employ the Tukutuku data set.

In summary, the size measures used in Tukutuku represent early Web size measures obtained from the results of a survey investigation, using data from 133 online Web forms aimed at giving quotes on Web development projects. In addition, the measures were validated by an established Web company, and a second survey involving 33 Web companies in New Zealand. Consequently it is our belief that the size measures identified are plausible effort predictors, not an ad hoc set of variables with no underlying rationale.

Copyright © 2008, IGI Global. Copying or distributing in print or electronic forms without written permission of IGI Global is prohibited.

We suggest that Web companies employ the Tukutuku early measures at least as a starting point until they can assess whether additional measures are also necessary.

Conclusion

This chapter discusses the role of expert-based effort estimations and has also presented examples of existing life cycle models (process models) that are used to develop Web applications.

We discussed the need for proper project management to help improve effort estimates, and also introduced the need for the use of complementary techniques that can help improve a company's current effort estimation practices. Many of these techniques, however, require that data on past projects be gathered and used to build effort models, and currently there are many Web companies that do not gather any data at all or only gather effort data. We also discuss the use of cross-company data sets in helping companies obtain effort estimates that can be compared to that company's own expert-based estimations, and alternatively used to adjust the original effort estimate suggested via expert opinion. A company can also gather data on their past projects and use some of the techniques presented in this book to build different effort models, which can then be compared and/or aggregated to expert-based estimations. Finally, the chapter also provides steps to follow in order to compare cross-company-based effort predictions to single-company-based predictions.

References

Atkinson, K., & Shepperd, M. (1994). *Using function points to find cost analogies.* Paper presented at the European Software Cost Modeling Meeting, Ivrea, Italy.

Bennett, S., McRobb, S., & Farmer, R. (2002). *Object-oriented systems analysis and design using UML.* McGraw Hill.

Bowden, P., Hargreaves, M., & Langensiepen, C. S. (2000). Estimation support by lexical analysis of requirement documents. *Journal of Systems and Software, 51*(2), 87-98.

Briand, L. C., Langley, T., & Wieczorek, I. (2000). A replicated assessment of common software cost estimation techniques. *Proceedings of the 22nd International Conference on Software Engineering* (pp. 377-386).

Copyright © 2008, IGI Global. Copying or distributing in print or electronic forms without written permission of IGI Global is prohibited.

Burdman, J. (1999). *Collaborative Web development: Strategies and best practices for Web teams.* Addison-Wesley.

Fenton, N. E., & Pfleeger, S. L. (1997). *Software metrics: A rigorous & practical approach* (2nd ed.). Boston: PWS Publishing Company & International Thomson Computer Press.

Haire, B., Henderson-Sellers, B., & Lowe, D. (2001). Supporting Web development in the OPEN process: Additional tasks. *Proceedings COMPSAC2001: International Computer Software and Applications Conference* (pp. 383-392).

Heemstra, F. J., & Kusters, R. J. (1991). Function point analysis: Evaluation of a software cost estimation model. *European Journal of Information Systems, 1*(4), 223-237.

Jørgensen, M. (1997). *An empirical evaluation of the MkII FPA estimation model.* Paper presented at the Norwegian Informatics Conference, Voss, Norway.

Jørgensen, M. (2004). A review of studies on expert estimation of software development effort. *Journal of Systems and Software, 7*(1-2), 37-60.

Jørgensen, M., & Sjøberg, D. (2001). Impact of effort estimates on software project work. *Information and Software Technology, 43*, 939-948.

Jørgensen, M., & Sjøberg, D. I. K. (2002). Impact of experience on maintenance skills. *Journal of Software Maintenance Evolution, 14*, 1-24.

Kitchenham, B., Pfleeger, S. L., McColl, B., & Eagan, S. (2002). An empirical study of maintenance and development estimation accuracy. *Journal of Systems and Software, 64*, 57-77.

Kitchenham, B. A., Pickard, L., Linkman, S., & Jones, P. (2003). Modelling software bidding risks. *Transactions on Software Engineering, 29*(6), 542-554.

Kusters, R. J., Genuchten, M. J. I. M., & Heemstra, F. J. (1990). Are software cost-estimation models accurate? *Information and Software Technology, 32*(3), 187-190.

Lederer, A. L., & Prasad, J. (2000). Software management and cost estimation error. *Journal of Systems and Software, 50*, 33-42.

Lowe, D. (2003). Emergent knowledge in Web development. In A. Aurum, R. Jeffery, C. Wohlin, & M. Handzic (Eds.), *Managing software engineering knowledge* (pp. 157-176). Berlin, Germany: Springer Verlag.

Mcdonald, A. (2004). *The agile Web engineering (AWE) process.* Unpublished doctoral dissertation, Department of Computing Science, University of Glasgow, Glasgow, Scotland.

McDonald, A., & Welland, R. (2001). Web engineering in practice. *Proceedings of the Fourth WWW10 Workshop on Web Engineering* (pp. 21-30).

Copyright © 2008, IGI Global. Copying or distributing in print or electronic forms without written permission of IGI Global is prohibited.

Mendes, E., Mosley, N., & Counsell, S. (2005). Investigating Web size metrics for early Web cost estimation. *Journal of Systems and Software, 77*(2), 157-172.

Moløkken, K., & Jørgensen, M. (2005). Expert estimation of Web-development projects: Are software professionals in technical roles more optimistic than those in non-technical roles? *Empirical Software Engineering, 10*(1), 7-30.

Moses, J. (1999). Learning how to improve effort estimation in small software development companies. *Proceedings of the 24th International Computer Software and Applications Conference* (pp. 522-527).

Mukhopadhyay, T., Vicinanza, S. S., & Prietula, M. J. (1992). Examining the feasibility of a case-based reasoning model for software effort estimation. *MIS Quarterly*, 155-171.

Myrtveit, I., & Stensrud, E. (1999). A controlled experiment to assess the benefits of estimating with analogy and regression models. *Transactions on Software Engineering, 25*, 510-525.

Ohlsson, N., Wohlin, C., & Regnell, B. (1998). A project effort estimation study. *Information and Software Technology, 40*, 831-839.

Pengelly, A. (1995). Performance of effort estimating techniques in current development environments. *Software Engineering Journal*, 162-170.

Pressman, R. S. (2000). What a tangled web we weave. *IEEE Software, 17*(1), 18-21.

Reifer, D. J. (2000). Web development: Estimating quick-to-market software. *IEEE Software, 17*(6), 57-64.

Royce, W. W. (1987). Managing the development of large software systems: Concepts and techniques. *Proceedings of the Ninth International Conference on Software Engineering*, 328-338. (Reprinted from *WESCON technical papers*, Vol. 14, pp. A/1-1–A/1-9, 1970, Los Angeles: WESCON)

Vicinanza, S. S., Mukhopadhyay, T., & Prietula, M. J. (1991). Software effort estimation: An exploratory study of expert performance. *Information Systems Research, 2*(4), 243-262.

Walkerden, F., & Jeffery, R. (1999). An empirical study of analogy-based software effort estimation. *Journal of Empirical Software Engineering, 4*, 135-158.

Ward, S., & Kroll, P. (1999). *Building Web solutions with the rational unified process: Unifying the creative design process and the software engineering process*. Rational Software Corporation. Retrieved from http://www.rational.com/

Copyright © 2008, IGI Global. Copying or distributing in print or electronic forms without written permission of IGI Global is prohibited.

Section III

An Introduction to Statistics

This section provides an introduction to statistics and empirical studies.

Chapter X

Understanding
Project Data

Abstract

The objective of this chapter is to provide an introduction to statistical techniques and concepts that are frequently used when dealing with data for effort estimation. The concepts presented here are in no way exhaustive since statistics comprises a very large body of knowledge where entire books are devoted to specific topics. The parts that are the focus of this chapter are those that are necessary to use when building effort estimation models, and also when comparing different effort estimation techniques.

Introduction

This book focuses on the use of data on past finished Web projects to help estimate effort for future Web projects. As part of this process, it is fundamental to under-

Copyright © 2008, IGI Global. Copying or distributing in print or electronic forms without written permission of IGI Global is prohibited.

stand the project data we have as this will determine the techniques to be used to analyse such data. Without such understanding, it is very likely that we may obtain biased results that are misleading and present a distorted view of the reality. The field of statistics provides a wide range of techniques devised with specific aims. For example, if your objective is to obtain a baseline based on previous productivity figures for past projects, then the technique to use will be to obtain the mean and median for these past projects (median and mean are introduced later in this chapter); if you wish to use data on past projects to predict effort for new projects by means of an equation (model), then the technique to use to obtain such an equation is linear regression or to general linear models (GLMs are outside the scope of this chapter). The field of statistics comprises a large body of knowledge used to describe, and often also to analyse, quantitative as well as qualitative data. Within the context of this book, the use of statistics will help investigative and answer questions such as the ones below:

- Are effort values for past Web projects normally distributed?
- What is the average effort used by projects that applied process improvement principles?
- What is the range of values for the total number of Web pages?
- Is there a strong relationship between the total number of Web pages and effort?
- What is the strength of the relationship between the total number of Web pages and effort?
- Are the effort values for the past finished Web projects too far apart from the average effort for these projects?
- What is the percentage of Web projects that used three different programming languages?

Note that this chapter has been provided in this book for those who wish to understand in more depth the techniques that have been used in the previous chapters.

Measurement Scales

The data from past finished Web projects used to help us estimate effort for new projects represent attributes (variables) of entities that we wish to measure. For example, within the Tukutuku context, examples of attributes are the total number of new Web pages, the project team's average number of years of experience developing

Copyright © 2008, IGI Global. Copying or distributing in print or electronic forms without written permission of IGI Global is prohibited.

Web applications, and the type of project. Each attribute is associated with an entity, which it characterises. So, the attribute *new Web pages* is a characteristic of a Web application (entity), and the project's team average number of years of experience developing Web applications and the type of the project are characteristics of a Web project. The data associated with the attributes of entities we wish to measure can be collected using different scales of measurement. The characteristics of each scale type determine the choice of methods and statistics that can be used to analyse the data and to interpret their corresponding measures. In this section we describe the five main scale types (Fenton & Pfleeger, 1997):

- Nominal
- Ordinal
- Interval
- Ratio
- Absolute

Nominal Scale Type

The nominal scale type represents the most primitive form of measurement. It identifies classes or categories where each category groups a set of entities based on their attribute's value. Here, entities can only be organised into classes or categories and there is no notion of ranking between classes. Classes can be represented as symbols or numbers; however, if we use numbers, they do not have any numerical meaning.

Examples of using a nominal scale are given in Table 1.

Table 1. Examples of nominal scale measures

Entity	Attribute	Categories
Web Application	Type	E-Commerce, Academic, Corporate, Entertainment
Programming Language	Type	ASP (VBScript, .Net), Coldfusion, J2EE (JSP, Servlet, EJB), PHP
Web Project	Type	New, Enhancement, Redevelopment
Web Company	Type of Service	1, 4, 5, 7, 9, 34, 502, 8

Copyright © 2008, IGI Global. Copying or distributing in print or electronic forms without written permission of IGI Global is prohibited.

Table 2. Examples of ordinal scale measures

Entity	Attribute	Categories
Web Application	Complexity	Very Low, Low, Average, High, Very High
Web Page	Design Quality	Very Poor, Poor, Average, Good, Very Good
Web Project	Priority	1, 2, 3, 4, 5, 6, 7

Ordinal Scale Type

The ordinal scale supplements the nominal scale with information about the ranking of classes or categories. As with the nominal scale, it also identifies classes or categories where each category groups a set of entities based on their attribute's value. The difference between an ordinal scale and a nominal scale is that here there is the notion of ranking between classes. Classes can be represented as symbols or numbers; however, if we use numbers, they do not have any numerical meaning and represent ranking only. Therefore, addition, subtraction, and other arithmetic operations cannot be applied to classes.

Examples of using an ordinal scale are given in Table 2.

Interval Scale Type

The interval scale supplements the ordinal scale with information about the size of the intervals that separate the classes or categories. As with the nominal and ordinal scales, it also identifies classes or categories, where each category groups a set of entities based on their attribute's value. As with the ordinal scale, there are ranks between classes or categories. The difference between an interval scale and an ordinal scale is that here there is the notion that the size of intervals between classes or categories remains constant. Although the interval scale is a numerical scale and numbers have a numerical meaning, the class zero does not mean the complete absence of the attribute we measured. To illustrate that, let us look at temperatures measured using the Celsius scale. The difference between 1°C and 2°C is the same as the difference between 6°C and 7°C: exactly 1°. There is a ranking between two classes; thus, 1°C has a lower rank than 2°C, and so on. Finally, the temperature 0°C does not represent the complete absence of temperature, where molecular motion stops. In this example, 0°C was arbitrarily chosen to represent the freezing point of water. This means that operations such as addition and subtraction between two categories are permitted (e.g., 50°C - 20°C = 70°C - 40°C; 5°C + 25°C = 20°C +

Copyright © 2008, IGI Global. Copying or distributing in print or electronic forms without written permission of IGI Global is prohibited.

Table 3. Examples of interval scale measures

Entity	Attribute	Categories
Web Project	Number of Days Relative to Start of Project	0, 1, 2, 3, 4, 5...
Human Body	Temperature (Celsius or Fahrenheit)	Decimal Numbers

10°C). However, calculating the ratio of two categories (e.g., 40°C/20°C) is not meaningful (40°C is not twice as hot as 20°C since the amount of temperature from the real zero temperature point to 40°C is not twice the amount of temperature from the real zero temperature point to 20°C), so multiplication and division cannot be calculated directly from categories. If ratios are to be calculated, they need to be based on the differences between categories.

Examples of using an interval scale are given in Table 3.

Ratio Scale Type

The ratio scale supplements the interval scale with the existence of a zero element, representing total absence of the attribute measured. As with the interval scale, it also provides information about the size of the intervals that separate the classes or categories. As with the interval and ordinal scales, there are ranks between classes or categories, and like the interval, ordinal, and nominal scales, it also identifies classes or categories, where each category groups a set of entities based on their attribute's value. The difference between a ratio scale and an interval scale is the existence of an absolute zero. The ratio scale is also a numerical scale and numbers have a numerical meaning. This means that any arithmetic operations between two categories are permitted.

Examples of using a ratio scale are given in Table 4.

Table 4. Examples of ratio scale measures

Entity	Attribute	Categories
Web Project	Effort	Decimal Numbers
Web Application	Size	Integer Numbers
Human Body	Temperature in Kelvin	Decimal Numbers

Copyright © 2008, IGI Global. Copying or distributing in print or electronic forms without written permission of IGI Global is prohibited.

Absolute Scale Type

The absolute scale supplements the ratio scale by restricting the classes or categories to a specific unit of measurement. As with the ratio scale, it also has a zero element, representing the total absence of the attribute measured. Like the ratio and interval scales, it provides information about the size of the intervals that separate the classes or categories, and like the interval and ordinal scale, there are ranks between classes or categories. Also, as with the ratio, interval, ordinal, and nominal scales, it also identifies classes or categories, where each category groups a set of entities based on their attribute's value.

The difference between an absolute scale and the ratio scale is the existence of a fixed unit of measurement associated with the attribute being measured. For example, using a ratio scale, if we were to measure the attribute *effort* of a Web project, we could obtain an effort value that could represent effort in the number of hours, or effort in the number of days, and so on. In case we want all effort measures to be kept using the number of hours, we can convert effort in number of days to effort in number of hours, or effort in number of weeks to effort in number of hours. Thus, an attribute measured using a given unit of measurement (e.g., number of weeks) can have its class converted into another using a different unit of measurement, but keeping the meaning of the obtained data unchanged. Therefore, assuming a single developer, a Web project's effort of 40 hours is equivalent to a Web project effort of a week. Thus, the unit of measurement changes, however the data that have been gathered remain unaffected. If we were to measure the attribute *effort* of a Web project using an absolute scale, we would need to determine in advance the unit of measurement to be used. Therefore, once the unit of measurement is determined, it is the one used when effort data are being gathered. Using our example on Web project effort, if the unit of measurement associated with the attribute *effort* was chosen to be the number of hours, then all the effort data gathered would represent effort in number of hours only.

Table 5. Examples of absolute scale measures

Entity	Attribute	Categories
Web Project	Effort (in number of hours)	Decimal Numbers
Web Application	Size (in number of HTML [hypertext markup language] files)	Integer Numbers
Web Developer	Experience in Developing Web Applications (in number of years)	Integer Numbers

Copyright © 2008, IGI Global. Copying or distributing in print or electronic forms without written permission of IGI Global is prohibited.

Finally, as with the ratio scale, operations between two categories, such as addition, subtraction, multiplication, and division, are also permitted.

Examples of using an absolute scale are given in Table 5.

Summary of Scale Types

Table 6 presents one of the summaries we are providing regarding scale types. It has been adapted from Maxwell (2005). It is also important to note that the nominal and ordinal scales do not provide classes or categories that have numerical meaning,

Table 6. Summary of scale type definitions

Scale Type	Is Ranking Meaningful?	Are Distances Between Classes the Same?	Does the Class Include an Absolute Zero?
Nominal	No	No	No
Ordinal	Yes	No	No
Interval	Yes	Yes	No
Ratio	Yes	Yes	Yes
Absolute	Yes	Yes	Yes

Table 7. Summary of suitable statistics

Scale Type	Examples of Suitable Statistics	Suitable Statistical Tests
Nominal	Mode Frequency	Nonparametric
Ordinal	Median Percentile	Nonparametric
Interval	Mean Standard Deviation	Nonparametric and Parametric
Ratio	Mean Geometric Mean Standard Deviation	Nonparametric and Parametric
Absolute	Mean Geometric Mean Standard Deviation	Nonparametric and Parametric

Copyright © 2008, IGI Global. Copying or distributing in print or electronic forms without written permission of IGI Global is prohibited.

and for this reason their attributes are called categorical or qualitative. Conversely, given that the interval, ratio, and absolute scales provide classes or categories that have numerical meaning, their attributes are called numerical or quantitative (Maxwell).

In relation to the statistics relevant to each measurement scale type, Table 7 presents a summary adapted from Fenton and Pfleeger (1997).

The statistics presented in Table 7 will be detailed in the next section.

It is important to understand that the type of data you are investigating will have a substantial influence on the type of analyses that you can carry out; that is, they affect the set of operations and statistics that can be applied to the data. It is fundamental, therefore, to be able to identify the scale types associated with the data that is to be manipulated.

Finally, data can also be categorised into two types: continuous and discrete. Continuous data can take values between whole numbers. For example, one can say that the temperature today is of 12.5°C, or that someone is 40.5 years old. Conversely, discrete data are only meaningful when associated with whole numbers. For example, it would not make sense to say a bookcase contains 30.5 books or that a crate of beer bottles contains 24.5 bottles (Sapsford & Jupp, 2006).

How Good are Your Data?

Every new or updated data set that is going to be used for statistical analysis needs to undergo a detailed examination such that the person carrying out the analysis understands as much as possible what sort of data and corresponding trends are present in the data set.

There are two types of statistics that we will look at, each with a specific aim and in a way taken as complementary to each other. These two types are descriptive statistics and inferential statistics (Sapsford & Jupp, 2006). In a nutshell, descriptive statistics are used to describe the data in a way that provides the means to show their main trends, and inferential statistics are used to observe similarities and differences between variables, to observe relationships between variables, and to use sample data in order to obtain conclusions about a wider population. Descriptive statistics will be presented in this section, and some of the existing inferential statistics will be described in the remainder of this chapter.

Copyright © 2008, IGI Global. Copying or distributing in print or electronic forms without written permission of IGI Global is prohibited.

Descriptive Statistics

Descriptive statistics represent the use of measures that summarise and describe the distribution of values associated with each of the variables being investigated. To do so, it is important to provide information that shows, given a variable v, where its central values or typical values lie; in addition, it is also important to indicate the variability (spread) among the values of v. Typical values are obtained using measures of central tendency, and variability among values is obtained using measures of spread.

Commonly used measures of central tendency are the mean, the median, and the mode. Figure 1 shows the values for these measures, in addition to *sum*, all calculated using the data values for the 16 observations of variable *Webpages*, which are also displayed in Figure 1.

The mean, or arithmetic mean, represents the average. Thus, to obtain the mean for the variable *Webpages*, we sum all values for its 16 observations, which equal to 958, and divide the sum by the number of observations, which is 16.

Figure 1. Sample data with three measures of central tendency

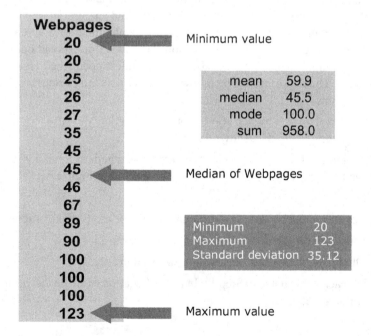

Copyright © 2008, IGI Global. Copying or distributing in print or electronic forms without written permission of IGI Global is prohibited.

The median represents the value of the observation that is in the middle of a set of observations whose values have been sorted in ascending order. When a distribution comprises an odd number of observations, the median will be the observation represented by the number of observations divided by 2, plus 1. Thus, if there are nine observations that have been sorted, the median will be obtained by 9/2+1, thus the fifth element. When the distribution comprises an even number of observations, then the median will be the average of the values for the two observations obtained by dividing the total number of observations by 2, and by dividing the total number of observations by 2, plus 1, respectively. Thus, if there are eight observations that have been sorted, the median will be the average of the values between the observation obtained by 8/2 = 4 and the observation obtained by 8/2+1 = 5.

To obtain the median for *Webpages*, we need to sort in ascending order the values of its 16 observations (see Figure 1), and the median will sit at exactly the middle of the ranking. In the example presented in Figure 1, since there is an even number of observations, the median sits between the eighth and ninth observations, corresponding to values 45 and 46 respectively; therefore, the median will be the average between 45 and 46, which is 45.5.

The mode is the value of the most commonly occurring observation. In the example presented in Figure 1, the value corresponds to 100. If there are two or more observations that contain the most frequent value, they will all be selected. Conversely, sometimes there is no mode whenever there is no single value that is the most commonly occurring.

Commonly used measures of spread are the minimum and maximum values and the standard deviation (see Figure 1). Minimum and maximum values provide an idea of the range of values for the observations obtained for a given variable, and the standard deviation gives an indication of how values spread out about the mean. The minimum value of a variable is the smallest occurring value that variable contains. The maximum value of a variable is the largest occurring value that variable contains.

Here we will explain step by step how to obtain the standard deviation for *Webpages*, using as an example the data shown in Table 8.

The following are the steps to follow to obtain the standard deviation for the 16 original values for *Webpages*, presented in Table 8 and in Figure 1.

Step 1: For variable *Webpages*, list original values for all its observations.

Step 2: Calculate the mean for the values listed in Step 1.

Step 3: Obtain the number of observations n listed in Step 1.

Step 4: For each value listed in Step 1, obtain its deviation from the mean, calculated as value - mean.

Copyright © 2008, IGI Global. Copying or distributing in print or electronic forms without written permission of IGI Global is prohibited.

Table 8. How to obtain the standard deviation

Original Values	Mean	Deviation from Mean = Value - Mean	Squared Deviation
20	59.9	-40	1592.01
20	59.9	-40	1592.01
25	59.9	-35	1218.01
26	59.9	-34	1149.21
27	59.9	-33	1082.41
35	59.9	-25	620.01
45	59.9	-15	222.01
45	59.9	-15	222.01
46	59.9	-14	193.21
67	59.9	7	50.41
89	59.9	29	846.81
90	59.9	30	906.01
100	59.9	40	1608.01
100	59.9	40	1608.01
100	59.9	40	1608.01
123	59.9	63	3981.61
Sum of Squared Deviation			18499.76
Sum of Squared Deviation Divided by (Number of Values - 1)			18499.76 / 15 = 1233.317

Step 5: For each deviation value obtained in Step 4, calculate its squared value.

Step 6: Sum all the squared values obtained in Step 5.

Step 7: Divide the sum obtained in Step 6 by n -1.

Step 8: Calculate the square root for the total obtained in Step 7. This is the standard deviation for *Webpages*.

Thus, the standard deviation is calculated as the square root of 1233.317, which is 35.12.

The Normal Distribution

The values for the 16 observations in *Webpages* that have been presented both in Figure 1 and in Table 8 represent measures that have been taken for this variable. For example, it is very likely that they represent the total number of pages for 16 differ-

Copyright © 2008, IGI Global. Copying or distributing in print or electronic forms without written permission of IGI Global is prohibited.

ent Web projects. When observing the values for all the observations in *Webpages*, arranged from lowest to highest value (see Figure 1), we can consider how much these values spread out and also how much they cluster together. What we are doing is looking at their distribution. One simple way to show a distribution of values is to use a graphical representation such as the one in Figure 2(a). This graphical representation, to be explained later, shows on the *Y*-axis the frequency of values in the range determined using the *X*-axis. Therefore, there are six projects with Web pages in the range of 20 to 40, and one project with Web pages in the range of 60 to 80. When this graphical representation has a bell shape and shows that 68.2% of the data points fall within one standard deviation from the mean, 95.4% of the data points fall within two standard deviations from the mean, 99.6% of the data points fall within three standard deviations from the mean, and the mean and median are the same, we have a special type of distribution called a normal distribution (see Figure 3). It presents a bell shape such as the one in Figure 2(b). What is important about this distribution is that many statistical techniques (parametric tests) assume that either the data values are normally distributed, or that the mean of the data (data sample) we are going to investigate is normally distributed. The latter assumption is only possible due to the central limit theorem (CLT; Sapsford & Jupp, 2006).

The CLT states that if we were to obtain numerous large samples that may or may not have data that are normally distributed, and for each one we were to calculate the mean, we would observe that after a large number of samples the distribution

Figure 2. Distribution of data

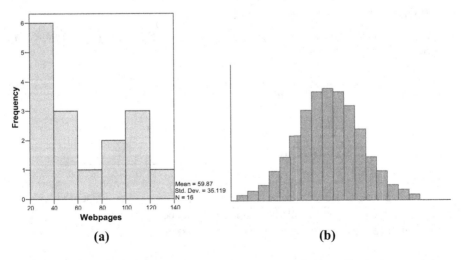

(a)   (b)

Copyright © 2008, IGI Global. Copying or distributing in print or electronic forms without written permission of IGI Global is prohibited.

of the means would move closer and closer to a bell shape, representing a normal distribution. The consequence of this is that statistical methods that use the mean to make statistical inferences can therefore be applied to any data samples as long as they are large samples (Sapsford & Jupp, 2006). The CLT is a very important theorem in statistics given that it proves that large samples can have their data analysed as if they were all normally distributed.

Inferential Statistics

As previously mentioned, inferential statistics are used to observe similarities and differences between variables, to observe relationships between variables, and to use sample data in order to obtain conclusions about a wider population. Inferential statistics comprise the remainder of this chapter.

Parametric vs. Nonparametric Tests

First, it is important to understand the difference between parametric and nonparametric tests. Parametric tests assume that the data sample is normally distributed, or that the sample's mean is normally distributed. It employs the mean to make any statistical inferences. Conversely, nonparametric tests do not make any assumptions regarding the distribution of the data, and in this sense are called distribution free. They do not take into account how far apart the observations are but rather the order (rank) in which observations fall. In addition, they also tend not to be sensitive to the existence of outliers in the data (Wild & Seber, 2000). An outlier is a value that is far from the others. The drawback of nonparametric tests and the reason for their use only when necessary is the fact that they are not as powerful as parametric tests when it comes to their ability to detect if the data being investigated show a departure from the null hypothesis (false null hypothesis).

Visualising Variables and Relationships

There are different graphic representation tools that can be used to provide further information about numerical variables in a data sample. Such information refers to the variables' distributions, the existence of unusual values (outliers), and also the relationship between two or more variables. The visual tools to be described in this section are histograms, boxplots, and scatterplots.

Copyright © 2008, IGI Global. Copying or distributing in print or electronic forms without written permission of IGI Global is prohibited.

Histograms

Histograms are represented by boxes that may differ in their number, height, and width. Figure 2(a) shows an example of a histogram, which is the histogram for *Webpages*. The width of a box represents a range of values in the *X*-axis. All boxes in the same histogram have the same width, which is obtained by taking into account the smallest and highest values, and arranging these values into equal intervals. The height of a box represents the number of observations with values falling within that box's width. Heights are represented in the *Y*-axis. Using as an example the histogram in Figure 2(a), we have six boxes, where each box uses as width a range of 20 Web pages. The first box indicates Web pages ranging from 20 to 40; the second box indicates Web pages ranging from 40 to 60, and so on. The first box's height is equal to 6, since there are six projects that have Web pages in the range from 20 to 40 (exclusive). Histograms are a very good way to identify if the distribution of values for the variable being investigated resembles a bell shape. Whenever a variable is normally distributed, the boxes are displayed in the shape of a bell-shaped curve.

To obtain a histogram in SPSS, from SPSS Inc., follow these steps:

* Select *Graphs* ⇨ *Histogram*.
* Select the variable from the list on the left for which a histogram is to be generated, and click on the arrow button to have it moved to the box labeled Variable.
* Optionally, in case you also wish to display the normal curve associated with the distribution of values for the selected variable, you can also tick the option *Display normal curve*.

Boxplots

Boxplots (see Figure 3) use the median, represented by the horizontal line in the middle of the box, as the central value for the distribution. The box's height is the interquartile range (IQR) and contains 50% of the values. The vertical (whiskers) lines up or down from the edges contain observations that are less than 1.5 times the IQR. Outliers are taken as values greater than 1.5 times the height of the box. Values greater than 3 times the box's height are called extreme outliers (Kitchenham, MacDonell, Pickard, & Shepperd, 2001). The first quartile is the median of the lower half of the distribution, also taking into account the median of the entire distribution (45.5 is the median for the example used in Figure 3). The same rationale is used to obtain the third quartile. The IQR, using the example given in Figure 3, is 90 - 27 = 63.

Copyright © 2008, IGI Global. Copying or distributing in print or electronic forms without written permission of IGI Global is prohibited.

Figure 3. Main components of a boxplot

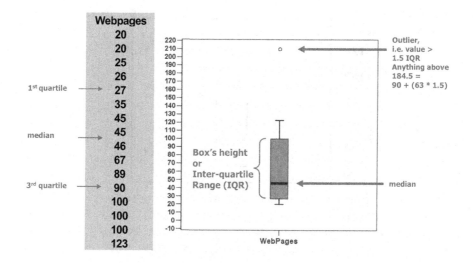

When upper and lower tails are approximately equal and the median is in the centre of the box, the distribution is symmetric. If the distribution is not symmetric, the relative lengths of the tails and the position of the median in the box indicate the nature of the skewness. The length of the box relative to the length of the tails gives an indication of the shape of the distribution. So, a boxplot with a small box and long tails represents a very peaked distribution, whereas a boxplot with a long box represents a flatter distribution (Kitchenham et al., 2001).

The boxplot for variable *Webpages* is displayed in Figure 4, where it shows that the distribution of data is not symmetrical and is right skewed. It also shows that there are no outliers and that the median falls above 40 and below 50.

The box in Figure 4 is a long box, suggesting that the distribution of data is not peaked around the median, but is rather flat. Finally, since 50% of the data points are always within the boundaries of the box's length, we know that 50% of the projects represented in *Webpages* have Web pages ranging from about 25 to about 95.

To obtain a boxplot in SPSS, follow these steps:

- Select *Graphs* ⇨ *Boxplot*.
- Select the icon *simple*, tick the option *Summaries of separate_variables*, and press the *Define* button.

Copyright © 2008, IGI Global. Copying or distributing in print or electronic forms without written permission of IGI Global is prohibited.

Figure 4. Boxplot for Webpages

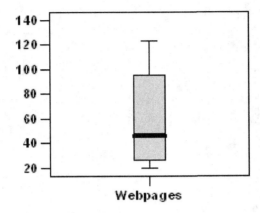

Webpages

- Select the variable(s) from the list on the left for which the boxplot is to be generated, and click on the arrow button to have it moved to the box labeled *Variable.*
- Optionally, in case you also wish to identify individually each of the projects in the scatterplot, select the variable from the list on the left that is used as a project identifier, and click on the arrow button to have it moved to the box labeled *Label Cases by.*

Scatterplots

Scatterplots provide the means to visually explore possible relationships between numerical variables. They also help to identify strong and weak relationships between two numerical variables. A strong relationship is represented by observations (data points) falling very close to or on the trend line. One example of such relationships is shown in Figure 5. A weak relationship is shown by observations that do not form a clear pattern, which in our case is a straight line. An example of such relationships is shown in Figure 6.

We can also say that a relationship is positively associated when values on the Y-axis tend to increase with those on the X-axis. This is the case with the boxplot in Figure 5. When values on the Y-axis tend to decrease as those on the X-axis increase, we say

Copyright © 2008, IGI Global. Copying or distributing in print or electronic forms without written permission of IGI Global is prohibited.

that the relationship is negatively associated, which is illustrated in Figure 7. When all points fall on the line, we say that the relationship between the two variables is perfectly positive, as in Figure 8, or perfectly negative, as in Figure 9.

Figure 5. Strong relationship in a scatterplot

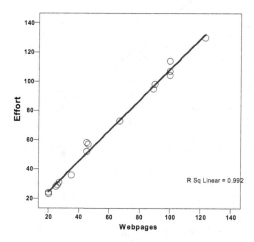

Figure 6. Weak relationship in a scatterplot

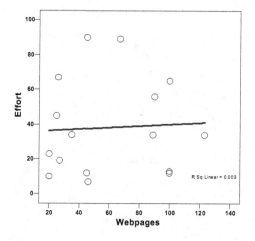

Copyright © 2008, IGI Global. Copying or distributing in print or electronic forms without written permission of IGI Global is prohibited.

Figure 7. Negative relationship in a scatterplot

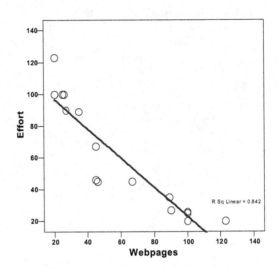

Figure 8. Perfect positive relationship in a scatterplot

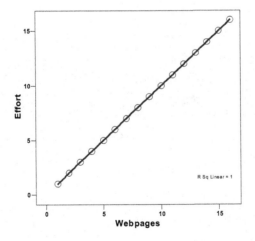

Copyright © 2008, IGI Global. Copying or distributing in print or electronic forms without written permission of IGI Global is prohibited.

Figure 9. Perfect negative relationship in a scatterplot

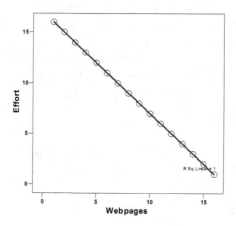

To obtain a scatterplot in SPSS, follow these steps:

- Select *Graphs* ⇨ *Scatter*.
- Select the icon *simple* and press the *Define* button.
- Select the variable from the list on the left that is to be plotted in the *Y*-axis, and click on the arrow button to have it moved to the box labeled *Y Axis*.
- Select the variable from the list on the left that is to be plotted in the *X*-axis, and click on the arrow button to have it moved to the box labeled *X Axis*.
- Optionally, in case you also wish to identify individually each of the projects in the scatterplot, select the variable from the list on the left that is used as a project identifier, and click on the arrow button to have it moved to the box labeled *Label Cases by:*.

How to Identify Relationships between Variables

Often, as part of a data analysis, it is necessary to use statistical methods to confirm whether there is a true relationship between two variables. In other words, given two variables *a* and *b*, one wishes to investigate in what ways the distribution of

Copyright © 2008, IGI Global. Copying or distributing in print or electronic forms without written permission of IGI Global is prohibited.

b can affect the distribution of *a*. This type of analysis is called bivariate analysis. For example, we may have used a scatterplot to investigate if there is a relationship between *Webpages* and *Effort*, and the scatterplot may have indicated that there is. However, it does not provide a single measure that can express the strength of this relationship or association. Also, we may wish to predict or explain the behaviour of *Effort* in terms of the behaviour of *Webpages* and to generate an equation that describes that behaviour. A scatterplot cannot help us with that either.

The statistical methods presented in this section allow a researcher or practitioner to answer questions such as the following:

- Given that the scatterplot suggests there is a relationship between the numerical variables *a* and *b*, what is the strength of this relationship? Is this relationship statistically significant?
- Is there an equation that can be used to represent the relationship between the numerical variables *a* and *b*?
- Is there a relationship between two categorical variables *c* and *d*?

It is important to know that the choice of statistical methods to use will change depending on the objective of the investigation. In addition, once the objective of the investigation is clear, the statistical method to use may also change depending on the nature of the data being compared and also, in some cases, depending on whether the data are normally distributed or not.

Finally, it is also important to explain what the dependent and independent variables are given that these two types of variables are used when we describe regression analysis and analysis of variance. Let us assume that we wish to predict or explain the behaviour of *Effort* in terms of the behaviour of *Webpages*. The variable whose behaviour we wish to predict or explain is called the dependent variable; the variable that we believe can help predict or explain the dependent variable is called the independent variable (Wild & Seber, 2000).

Measures of Association

Measures of association are used as a way for representing the strength of a relationship using a single measure. Depending on the type of the variables whose relationship we wish to measure, and sometimes also on the type of distribution of these variables, we will need to use different types of statistical techniques. This is detailed in Table 9. If we are investigating whether or not there is a relationship between two nominal variables, or between a nominal variable and an ordinal variable, then the statistical technique to use is the Chi-square test. If both variables are

Copyright © 2008, IGI Global. Copying or distributing in print or electronic forms without written permission of IGI Global is prohibited.

ordinal, then we can either use the Chi-square test or the Spearman's correlation test. If the variables to compare are either interval, ratio, or absolute, then the techniques to use can either be the Spearman's correlation test or the Pearson's correlation test. In this case, the choice of technique will very much depend on the distribution of the data and also on the number of observations. Normally distributed data, or large samples, can use the Pearson's correlation test; otherwise, the Spearman's correlation test is the correct choice.

It is also important to distinguish between the Chi-square test and Pearson's and Spearman's correlation tests. The Chi-square test only identifies the existence of an association between variables; however, it does not provide the type or the strength of the association. Conversely, both Pearson's and Spearman's correlation tests measure the correlation between two variables. Correlation is a form of association where it is possible to identify if high values of one variable are associated with high values of another variable, or if high values of one variable are associated with low values of another variable. The former case indicates that both variables are positively correlated and the latter indicates that both are negatively correlated (Sapsford & Jupp, 2006). Both Pearson's and Spearman's correlation tests also measure the strength of the association between two variables, where strength varies from -1 to 1. A correlation of -1 represents a perfect linear negative association,

Table 9. Techniques used to measure association

Variable Type	Nominal	Ordinal	Interval	Ratio	Absolute
Nominal	Chi-square test	Chi-square test			
Ordinal	Chi-square test	Spearman's correlation, chi-square test	Spearman's correlation	Spearman's correlation	Spearman's correlation
Interval		Spearman's correlation	Spearman's correlation, Pearson's correlation	Spearman's correlation, Pearson's correlation	Spearman's correlation, Pearson's correlation
Ratio		Spearman's correlation	Spearman's correlation, Pearson's correlation	Spearman's correlation, Pearson's correlation	Spearman's correlation, Pearson's correlation
Absolute		Spearman's correlation	Spearman's correlation, Pearson's correlation	Spearman's correlation, Pearson's correlation	Spearman's correlation, Pearson's correlation

Copyright © 2008, IGI Global. Copying or distributing in print or electronic forms without written permission of IGI Global is prohibited.

a correlation of 1 represents a perfect linear positive association, and a correlation of zero represents no association.

Each of these techniques will be detailed next.

Chi-Square Test

The Chi-square test measures if two nominal or ordinal variables are independent of each other, that is, have no association (Sapsford & Jupp, 2006). This measurement uses a contingency table, also known as cross-tabulation (see Table 10 for an example). This type of table shows the frequency of observations for every possible combination of symbols given the variables being compared (in our case symbols are *yes* and *no*). To explain this statistical test, we will use two nominal variables from the Tukutuku database—DOCPROC and PROIMPR—and data on 87 Web projects. DOCPROC measures if a Web project followed a defined and documented process, and PROIMPR measures if a project team was involved in a process improvement programme. Both can be either *yes* or *no*. Suppose we wish to investigate if there is an association between using a documented process and being part of a process improvement programme. If there is no association between using a documented process and being part of a process improvement programme, then one would expect that the proportion of projects that used a documented process and were involved in a process improvement programme to be similar to the proportion of projects that used a documented process and were not involved in a process improvement programme. Table 10 shows that this proportion is not the same.

The proportion of projects we would expect if the percentages were the same are calculated as follows (Maxwell, 2005).

The overall proportion of projects in our sample population that did not use a documented process is approximately 0.26 (23/87); the proportion that used a documented process is approximately 0.74 (64/87). This proportion can be used to obtain the

Table 10. Cross-tabulation; actual frequencies for documented process and process improvement

		Documented Process		Total
		no	yes	
Process Improvement	no	19	9	28
	yes	4	55	59
Total		23	64	87

Copyright © 2008, IGI Global. Copying or distributing in print or electronic forms without written permission of IGI Global is prohibited.

Table 11. Cross-tabulation: Expected frequencies for documented process and process improvement

		Documented Process		Total
		no	yes	
Process Improvement	no	7.4	20.6	28
	yes	15.6	43.4	59
Total		23	64	87

expected number of projects using a documented process for each process improvement category. Out of a total of 28 projects not involved in a process improvement programme, we would expect 28*(64/87) = 20.6 to use a documented process. Of a total of 59 projects involved in a process improvement programme, we would expect 59*(64/87) = 43.4 to use a documented process. The expected number of projects that did not use a documented process and was not involved in a process improvement programme is 7.4, and the expected number of projects that did not use a documented process but was involved in a process improvement programme is 15.6 (see Table 11). The expected frequencies differ from the actual frequencies; however, this does not immediately indicate that there is a relationship between using a documented process and being involved in a process improvement programme since these differences may be due to chance.

To obtain a cross-tabulation in SPSS, follow these steps:

- Select *Analyze* ⇨ *Descriptive Statistics* ⇨ *Crosstabs*.
- Select the variable from the list on the left that is to be displayed as a table row and click on the arrow button to have it moved to the box labeled *Row(s):*.
- Select the variable from the list on the left that is to be displayed as a table column and click on the arrow button to have it moved to the box labeled *Column(s):*.

Our next step is to use the Chi-square test to check if there is a relationship between using a documented process and being involved in a process improvement programme. This test can be applied to two nominal or ordinal variables. The output for the Chi-square test is shown in Figure 10.

Copyright © 2008, IGI Global. Copying or distributing in print or electronic forms without written permission of IGI Global is prohibited.

One of the ways to use the Chi-square test in SPSS is to follow these steps:

- Select *Analyze* ⇨ *Descriptive Statistics* ⇨ *Crosstabs*.
- Select the variable from the list on the left that is to be displayed as a table row and click on the arrow button to have it moved to the box labeled *Row(s):*.
- Select the variable from the list on the left that is to be displayed as a table column and click on the arrow button to have it moved to the box labeled *Column(s):*.
- Click on the button labeled *Statistics*.
- Tick the box *Chi-square*.

The most important piece of information in Figure 10 is the significance value (indicated by a dark arrow in Figure 10 with the label *Asymp. Sig.*) associated with the Chi-square statistic (Pearson Chi-square). Whenever this value is greater than 0.05, this means that the hypothesis that the use of documented process is independent from being involved in a process improvement programme, which represents the null hypothesis, cannot be rejected using a statistical significance α of 0.05. The Chi-square statistic shows a statistical significance of less than 0.05, thus indicating that there is a relationship between using a documented process and being involved in a process improvement programme.

It is important, however, to understand that although we found an association between using a documented process and being involved in a process improvement programme, this association does not necessarily imply causality.

Figure 10. Chi-square test output in SPSS assessing the association between using a documented process and being involved in a process improvement programme

Chi-Square Tests

	Value	df	Asymp. Sig. (2-sided)	Exact Sig. (2-sided)	Exact Sig. (1-sided)
Pearson Chi-Square	36.424[b]	1	.000		
Continuity Correction[a]	33.351	1	.000		
Likelihood Ratio	36.081	1	.000		
Fisher's Exact Test				.000	.000
N of Valid Cases	87				

a. Computed only for a 2x2 table

b. 0 cells (.0%) have expected count less than 5. The minimum expected count is 7.40.

Copyright © 2008, IGI Global. Copying or distributing in print or electronic forms without written permission of IGI Global is prohibited.

Pearson's Correlation Test

Pearson's correlation test is a parametric test that calculates the Pearson product moment correlation coefficient, r, to measure the strength and the direction of the relationship between two variables that were measured on an interval, ratio, or absolute scale. These variables are assumed to be normally distributed. If they are not, then the data sample used has to be large enough such that the population means can be assumed to be normally distributed (CLT). To explain how to calculate r, we will use as an example the data in Table 12. The equation that will be used to calculate r is as follows (Fielding & Gilbert, 2006):

$$r = \frac{\frac{\sum\limits_{i=1}^{N}(X_i - \bar{X})(Y_i - \bar{Y})}{N}}{\sqrt{\sum\limits_{i=1}^{N}\frac{(X_i - \bar{X})^2}{N}}\sqrt{\sum\limits_{i=1}^{N}\frac{(Y_i - \bar{Y})^2}{N}}} \qquad (1)$$

Table 12. Data sample example used to calculate r

Webpages	Effort
20	24
20	23
25	28
26	29
27	31
35	36
45	52
45	58
46	57
67	73
89	95
90	98
100	104
100	107
100	114
123	130

Copyright © 2008, IGI Global. Copying or distributing in print or electronic forms without written permission of IGI Global is prohibited.

where the following applies:

N is the number of observations in the data sample.

X_i is the ith's project value for the X variable.

$\overline{X}$ is the mean of variable X.

Y_i is the ith's project value for the Y variable.

$\overline{Y}$ is the mean of variable Y.

The mean of *Webpages* is 57.5 and the mean of *Effort* is 63.7. Table 13 details some of the steps used to calculate Pearson's r between *Webpages* and *Effort* for the 16 projects used in our sample data set.

Therefore:

$$r = \frac{\dfrac{83921.2}{16}}{\sqrt{4815.6}\sqrt{5726.7}} = 1 \qquad (2)$$

Table 13. Calculation of Pearson's r

X, Webpages	Y, Effort	$(X - \overline{X})(Y - \overline{Y})$	$\dfrac{(X - \overline{X})^2}{16}$	$\dfrac{(Y - \overline{Y})^2}{16}$
20	24	1682.2	99.4	111.2
20	23	460.0	25.0	33.1
25	28	700.0	39.1	49.0
26	29	754.0	42.3	52.6
27	31	837.0	45.6	60.1
35	36	1260.0	76.6	81.0
45	52	2340.0	126.6	169.0
45	58	2610.0	126.6	210.3
46	57	2622.0	132.3	203.1
67	73	4891.0	280.6	333.1
89	95	8455.0	495.1	564.1
90	98	8820.0	506.3	600.3
100	104	10400.0	625.0	676.0
100	107	10700.0	625.0	715.6
100	114	11400.0	625.0	812.3
123	130	15990.0	945.6	1056.3
	$\Sigma =$	83921.2	4815.6	5726.7

Copyright © 2008, IGI Global. Copying or distributing in print or electronic forms without written permission of IGI Global is prohibited.

It is not necessary to calculate Pearson's correlation coefficient manually since any statistical tool can provide this measure.

To obtain Pearson's correlation coefficient in SPSS, follow these steps:

- Select *Analyze* ⇨ *Correlate* ⇨ *Bivariate*.
- Select the two variables from the list on the left whose association you want to measure and click on the arrow button to have them moved to the box labeled *Variables*.
- Tick the option *Pearson* in the group labeled *Correlation Coefficients*.
- Tick the option *Two-tailed* in the group labeled *Test of Significance*.
- Optionally, tick the option *Flag significant correlations*.

The choice of a two-tailed test of significance depends on whether or not you know in advance the direction of the association. If you do not know the direction, you use a two-tailed test of significance; otherwise, you use a one-tailed test of significance.

The results obtained using SPSS for the sample data we used as an example is shown in Figure 11. It shows the correlation coefficients taking into account all the possible combinations of variables. Since we used two variables, results show 2x2 correlation coefficients. A correlation coefficient between a variable and itself is always equal to 1 since this represents a perfect linear association. SPSS provided a correlation coefficient slightly more precise than the one we obtained when performing the calculations manually. This is because it used data with higher precision (decimal places) than we did. The correlation between *Webpages* and *Effort* indicates a very strong significant linear and positive association, with a correlation coefficient

Figure 11. SPSS output for Pearson's correlation test

		Webpages	Effort
Webpages	Pearson Correlation	1	.996(**)
	Sig. (two-tailed)		.000
	N	16	16
Effort	Pearson Correlation	.996(**)	1
	Sig. (two-tailed)	.000	
	N	16	16

**Correlation is significant at the 0.01 level (two-tailed)*

Copyright © 2008, IGI Global. Copying or distributing in print or electronic forms without written permission of IGI Global is prohibited.

very close to 1. This correlation is statistically significant at 1%, which means that using this data set, there is a probability of only 1% that the null hypothesis can be rejected when in fact it is true.

The very strong linear relationship between *Webpages* and *Effort* is also shown in Figure 5 using a scatterplot.

Spearman's Correlation Test

Spearman's correlation test is the nonparametric test equivalent to Pearson's correlation test. It calculates Spearman's rho, r_s, to measure the strength and the direction of the relationship between two variables that were measured on an ordinal scale. It is also the technique of choice whenever interval, ratio, and absolute variables are not normally distributed and are part of a small data sample. To explain how to compute Spearman's rho, we will use as an example the data in Table 12. The equation that will be used to calculate r_s is as follows (Fielding & Gilbert, 2006):

$$r_s = 1 - \frac{6 \sum_{i=1}^{n} D_i^2}{n(n^2 - 1)},$$

(3)

where the following applies:

D is the difference between the ranks of the two variables whose association is being measured for the same project *i*.

n represents the number of observations in the data sample.

To compute Spearman's rho, projects are first ranked from high to low on each of the variables to have their associations measured; then the ranks (not the values) are employed to produce the correlation coefficient. Table 14 displays the original values and the rankings of the observations on both variables.

Therefore:

$$Effort = 3.686 + 1.04\angle$$

.

(4)

It is not necessary to calculate Spearman's correlation coefficient manually since any statistical tool can provide this measure.

Copyright © 2008, IGI Global. Copying or distributing in print or electronic forms without written permission of IGI Global is prohibited.

Table 14. Calculation of Spearman's rho

X, Webpages	Rank	Y, Effort	Rank	D	D^2
20	15.5	24	15	0.5	0.25
20	15.5	23	16	-0.5	0.25
25	14	28	14	0	0
26	13	29	13	0	0
27	12	31	12	0	0
35	11	36	11	0	0
45	9.5	52	10	-0.5	0.25
45	9.5	58	8	1.5	2.25
46	8	57	9	-1	1
67	7	73	7	0	0
89	6	95	6	0	0
90	5	98	5	0	0
100	3	104	4	-1	1
100	3	107	3	0	0
100	3	114	2	1	1
123	1	130	1	0	0
				$\sum D^2 =$	6

To obtain Pearson's correlation coefficient in SPSS, follow these steps:

- Select *Analyze* ⇨ *Correlate* ⇨ *Bivariate*.
- Select the two variables from the list on the left whose association you want to measure and click on the arrow button to have them moved to the box labeled *Variables*.
- Tick the option *Spearman* in the group labeled *Correlation Coefficients*.
- Tick the option *Two-tailed* in the group labeled *Test of Significance*.
- Optionally, tick the option *Flag significant correlations*.

Here again, the choice of a two-tailed test of significance depends on whether or not you know in advance the direction of the association. If you do not know the direction, you use a two-tailed test of significance; otherwise, you use a one-tailed test of significance.

The results obtained using SPSS for the sample data we used as an example is shown in Figure 12. Like Pearson's correlation test, Spearman's correlation test also

Copyright © 2008, IGI Global. Copying or distributing in print or electronic forms without written permission of IGI Global is prohibited.

Figure 12. SPSS output for Spearman's correlation test

			Webpages	Effort
Spearman's rho	Webpages	Correlation Coefficient	1.000	.991(**)
		Sig. (two-tailed)	.	.000
		N	16	16
	Effort	Correlation Coefficient	.991(**)	1.000
		Sig. (two-tailed)	.000	.
		N	16	16

**Correlation is significant at the 0.01 level (two-tailed)*

shows the correlation coefficients taking into account all the possible combinations of variables. Since we used two variables, results show 2x2 correlation coefficients. A correlation coefficient between a variable and itself is always equal to 1 since this represents a perfect linear association. SPSS provided the same value for the correlation coefficient as the one we obtained when performing the calculations manually. However, this coefficient is slightly different from the one obtained when computing the correlation coefficient using Pearson's correlation test. This is because some information is lost when we convert interval-, ratio-, or absolute-scale variables into rank orders (Maxwell, 2005). Similar to the results obtained using Pearson's correlation test, the correlation between *Webpages* and *Effort* indicates a very strong significant linear and positive association, with a correlation coefficient very close to 1. This correlation is statistically significant at 1%, which means that using this data set, there is a probability of only 1% that the null hypothesis can be rejected when in fact it is true.

Regression Analysis

Before explaining regression analysis, let us look again at the data we have used to explain correlation analysis; more specifically, let us look at the relationship between *Webpages* and *Effort*. This relationship is described using the scatterplot in Figure 13. This is the same scatterplot in Figure 5; however, it is repeated here to aid our explanation.

This scatterplot shows an upward trend in the data points, suggesting that the larger the size of a Web application, the higher the effort spent developing it. These data points are not perfectly aligned along the line, indicating that this is not a perfect

Copyright © 2008, IGI Global. Copying or distributing in print or electronic forms without written permission of IGI Global is prohibited.

Figure 13. Scatterplot showing the relationship between Webpages and Effort

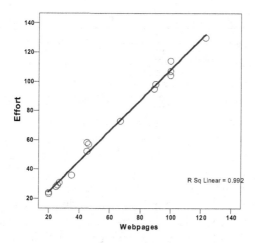

relationship. Suppose we wish to be able to estimate the amount of effort it takes to develop a Web application using as input the size of this application, measured as the total number of Web pages. Although it is not perfect, the relationship between *Effort* and *Webpages* can be expressed using equation 5.

$$Effort = 3.686 + 1.044 Webpages$$

(5)

This equation is called the regression equation and is used to describe the relationship between two or more variables measured at least on an interval scale (see Table 15).

Table 15. Types of variables to which regression analysis can be applied to

Variable Type	Independent Variable				
Dependent Variable	**Nominal**	**Ordinal**	**Interval**	**Ratio**	**Absolute**
Nominal					
Ordinal					
Interval			regression	regression	regression
Ratio			regression	regression	regression
Absolute			regression	regression	regression

Copyright © 2008, IGI Global. Copying or distributing in print or electronic forms without written permission of IGI Global is prohibited.

Table 16. Estimated effort using Equation 5

Estimated Effort	Web Pages
4.7	1
8.9	5
41.3	36
129.0	120
1360.9	1300

In our example, *Effort* is the dependent variable and *Webpages* is the independent variable. Whenever we have a single independent variable, the construction of a regression equation is called simple linear regression; if more than one independent variable is used, then it is called multiple linear regression. Using such an equation, we can predict effort for different Web applications, as presented in Table 16.

Table 6 indicates that, based on equation 5, a single Web page would take 4.7 person hours to create, and 1,300 Web pages would take 1,360.9 person hours to create. The general form of equations similar to equation 5 is given in equation 6:

$$Y = a + bX, \tag{6}$$

where *a* is called the intercept, which represents the value of *Y* where the regression line intercepts the *Y*-axis (and where $X = 0$), and *b* is the slope of the line, and represents the difference in *Y* for a unit difference in *X*. Both *a* and *b* can be either positive or negative (Fielding & Gilbert, 2006).

If we look back at the scatterplot presented in Figure 13, we will see that the fitted line does not go through all the points; however, there is still a clear linear trend in the relationship between *Webpages* and *Effort*. This fitted line was drawn using a method that enables it to be as close as possible to all the data points. This method aims to minimise the distances between the data points and the fitted line that represents the relationship between two or more variables, and is called ordinary least squares (OLS; Fielding & Gilbert, 2006). The distance between a data point and a fitted line is called error or residual (see Figure 14) and represents the difference between the original (actual) value of a data point (e.g., y3, y2, and y1 in Figure 14) and its estimated value (e.g., y'3, y'2, and y'1 in Figure 14). Estimated values are obtained using the equation that represents the fitted line (regression line). The fit of a regression line to the data is determined by how small the distances (residuals) are. The smaller the residuals, the better the fit of the regression line to the data.

Copyright © 2008, IGI Global. Copying or distributing in print or electronic forms without written permission of IGI Global is prohibited.

Figure 14. Regression line, intercept, slope, and residuals (errors)

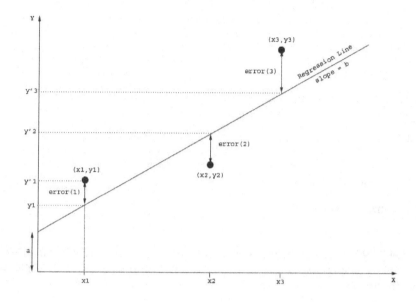

In order to obtain the best line according to the least squares regression method, two equations are used: one to obtain the slope *b* (equation 7), and another to obtain the intercept *a* (equation 8).

$$b = \frac{\sum_{i=1}^{n}(X_i - \overline{X})(Y_i - \overline{Y})}{\sum_{i=1}^{n}(X_i - \overline{X})^2} \quad , \tag{7}$$

where the following are true:

b is the slope.

n is the number of observations in the data sample.

X_i is the ith's project value for the *X* variable.

$\overline{X}$ is the mean of variable *X*.

Copyright © 2008, IGI Global. Copying or distributing in print or electronic forms without written permission of IGI Global is prohibited.

Y_i is the ith's project value for the Y variable.

$\overline{Y}$ is the mean of variable Y.

$$a = \overline{Y} - b\overline{X},\tag{8}$$

where the following are true:

a is the intercept.

b is the slope.

$\overline{X}$ is the mean of variable X.

$\overline{Y}$ is the mean of variable Y.

To explain how to obtain the regression line representing the relationship between *Effort* and *Webpages*, we will use as an example the same data previously employed, displayed in Table 17.

Table 17. Calculation of the regression line between Effort and Webpages

Y, Effort	X, Webpages	$X - \overline{X}$	$Y - \overline{Y}$	$(X - \overline{X})(Y - \overline{Y})$	$(X - \overline{X})^2$
24	20	-39.9	-42.2	1682.2	1590.0
23	20	-39.9	-43.2	1722.1	1590.0
28	25	-34.9	-38.2	1331.8	1216.3
29	26	-33.9	-37.2	1259.7	1147.5
31	27	-32.9	-35.2	1156.8	1080.8
36	35	-24.9	-30.2	750.9	618.8
52	45	-14.9	-14.2	211.0	221.3
58	45	-14.9	-8.2	121.8	221.3
57	46	-13.9	-9.2	127.5	192.5
73	67	7.1	6.8	48.5	50.8
95	89	29.1	28.8	839.2	848.3
98	90	30.1	31.8	958.4	907.5
104	100	40.1	37.8	1517.2	1610.0
107	100	40.1	40.8	1637.6	1610.0
114	100	40.1	47.8	1918.5	1610.0
130	123	63.1	63.8	4028.2	3984.8
$\overline{Y} = 66.2$	$\overline{X} = 59.9$			$\sum = 19311.4$	$\sum = 18499.8$

Copyright © 2008, IGI Global. Copying or distributing in print or electronic forms without written permission of IGI Global is prohibited.

Therefore:

$$b = \frac{19311.4}{18499.8} = 1 \tag{9}$$

and

$$a = 66.2 - (1 \cdot 59.9) = 3.7 \tag{10}$$

This makes the regression equation:

$$Y = 3.7 + 1X = 3.7 + X, \tag{11}$$

which we interpret as

$$Effort = 3.7 + Webpages. \tag{12}$$

Therefore, the estimated effort is equal to 3.7 + 1 times the estimated total number of Web pages that the Web application will have.

Once we have obtained the best regression line according to the ordinary least squares method, the next step is to measure how well the regression line fits the data. This measure, called the coefficient of determination (r^2) when there is a single independent variable, and multiple coefficient of determination (R^2) when there are two or more independent variables, represents the percentage of the variance in the dependent variable that is explained by the independent variable or variables (Fielding & Gilbert, 2006). So, let us assume that the coefficient of determination for the regression line represented by equation 12 is 75%. This means that 75% of the variance in *Effort* is explained by the variation in the total number of Web pages. That still leaves another 25% of unexplained variance, which may be related to other independent variables not related to *Webpages*, or due to random variation. For this reason, the general equation representing a regression line is commonly represented as:

$$Y = a + bX + \varepsilon, \tag{13}$$

Copyright © 2008, IGI Global. Copying or distributing in print or electronic forms without written permission of IGI Global is prohibited.

where ε represents an error term that represents all the other independent variables that may also have an effect on the dependent variable.

The coefficient of determination, which measures the proportion of the variance explained by the regression line, ranges from 0 to 1 and is calculated as:

$$r^2 = \frac{\exp lained \, var iance}{total \, var iance} \, .$$

(14)

Total variance is calculated as:

$$total \, var iance = \frac{\sum_{i=1}^{n}(Y_i - \bar{Y})^2}{n-1} \, ,$$

(15)

where the following applies:

n is the number of observations in the data sample.

Y_i is the ith's project value for the Y variable (dependent variable).

$\bar{Y}$ is the mean of variable Y.

Unexplained variance, that is, the variance of the residuals, is calculated as:

$$un \exp lained \, var iance = \frac{\sum_{i=1}^{n}(Y_i - Y'_i)^2}{n-1} \, ,$$

(16)

where the following is true:

n is the number of observations in the data sample.

Y_i is the ith's project value for the Y variable (dependent variable).

Y'_i is the predicted value for the Y_i value.

To explain how to obtain the coefficient of the determination for the regression line representing the relationship between *Effort* and *Webpages*, we will use as an example the same data previously employed, displayed in Table 18.

Copyright © 2008, IGI Global. Copying or distributing in print or electronic forms without written permission of IGI Global is prohibited.

Table 18. Calculation of the coefficient of determination for the regression line between Effort and Webpages

Y, Effort	Y'= 3.7 + Webpages	Y − Y'	(Y − Y')²	Y − Ȳ	(Y − Ȳ)²
24	23.7	0.3	0.09	-42.2	1779.8
23	23.7	-0.7	0.49	-43.2	1865.2
28	28.7	-0.7	0.49	-38.2	1458.3
29	29.7	-0.7	0.49	-37.2	1382.9
31	30.7	0.3	0.09	-35.2	1238.2
36	38.7	-2.7	7.29	-30.2	911.3
52	48.7	3.3	10.89	-14.2	201.3
58	48.7	9.3	86.49	-8.2	67.0
57	49.7	7.3	53.29	-9.2	84.4
73	70.7	2.3	5.29	6.8	46.4
95	92.7	2.3	5.29	28.8	830.2
98	93.7	4.3	18.49	31.8	1012.0
104	103.7	0.3	0.09	37.8	1429.8
107	103.7	3.3	10.89	40.8	1665.7
114	103.7	10.3	106.09	47.8	2286.0
130	126.7	3.3	10.89	63.8	4072.0
Ȳ = 66.2			Σ = 316.64		Σ = 20330.4

Therefore:

$$total\ var\,iance = \frac{20330.4}{15} = 1355.36 \tag{17}$$

and

$$un\exp lained\ var\,iance = \frac{316.64}{15} = 21.11 \tag{18}$$

This makes the explained variance:

$$\exp lained\ var\,iance = 1355.36 - 21.11 = 1334.25 \tag{19}$$

Copyright © 2008, IGI Global. Copying or distributing in print or electronic forms without written permission of IGI Global is prohibited.

Finally, the coefficient of determination can be obtained by:

$$r^2 = \frac{1334.25}{1355.36} = 0.984$$

(20)

A coefficient of determination of 0.984 means that 98.4% of the variance in effort can be explained by the variation in the total number of Web pages, which is exceptionally good. The interpretation of these results are that *Webpages* alone can explain 98.4% of the variation in *Effort* and, since this percentage is extremely high and very close to 1, it seems unlikely that there are any other necessary independent variables to be used that may also help explain the variance in estimated effort.

When more than one independent variable is used to construct a regression line, the measure of model fit changes from r^2 to R^2, which is the coefficient of multiple determination. The difference between r^2 and R^2 is that R^2 measures the percentage of variance in the dependent variable that can be explained by the variations in all the independent variables taken together (Fielding & Gilbert, 2006). However, a problem with using R^2 is that its value never decreases, but often increases when another independent variable is added to the regression. This means that we may end up getting a distorted view of which are the independent variables that really affect the value of the dependent variable. To circumvent this problem, it is common practice to use the adjusted R^2 instead, as this measure is adjusted for the number of independent variables used in the regression. As a rule of thumb, I tend to always use the adjusted R^2.

To use single or multiple regression analysis in SPSS, follow these steps:

- Select *Analyze* ⇨ *Regression* ⇨ *Linear*.
- Select from the list on the left the numerical variable that is the dependent variable, and click the right arrow such that this variable's name appears inside the box labeled *Dependent*.
- Select using the list on the left the numerical variables that are the independent variables, and click the right arrow such that these variables' names appear inside the box labeled *Independent(s)*.

The two pieces of information that are important for us are the model summary (see Figure 15) and the coefficients (see Figure 16).

The R^2 measure is 0.992, which is slightly different from the value we show in equation 20. This difference is due to SPSS using values with higher precision than those we employed. However, both values are still fairly high. The standard effort

Copyright © 2008, IGI Global. Copying or distributing in print or electronic forms without written permission of IGI Global is prohibited.

Figure 15. Model summary for regression line using Webpages to predict Effort

Model Summary

Model	R	R Square	Adjusted R Square	Std. Error of the Estimate
1	.996(a)	.992	.991	3.503

a Predictors: (Constant), Webpages

Figure 16. Coefficients for regression line using Webpages to predict Effort

Coefficients(a)

Model		Unstandardized Coefficients		Standardized Coefficients	t	Sig.
		B	Std. Error	Beta		
1	(Constant)	3.686	1.774		2.078	.057
	Webpages	1.044	.026	.996	40.527	.000

a Dependent Variable: Effort

(standard error) of the estimate measures the standard deviation of the residuals (actual - estimate).

Figure 16 shows the output table that is the kernel of the regression analysis. It provides the regression equation. The values for the intercept (constant) and slope are given in column B of the table, as correspond to equation 21.

$$Effort = 3.686 + 1.044 Webpages \qquad (21)$$

The standard error (standard error) represents the standard error of the regression coefficient B; *t* measures the relative importance of each variable and the constant in the regression. Significance values more than or equal to 0.05 mean that the variable or constant should be kept in the equation.

Copyright © 2008, IGI Global. Copying or distributing in print or electronic forms without written permission of IGI Global is prohibited.

When constructing a regression model (equation) using simple or multiple linear regressions, we need to ensure that the variables comply with the assumptions underlying regression analysis, which are as follow (Fielding & Gilbert, 2006).

1. The independent variables have been accurately measured, that is, measured without error. If this cannot be guaranteed, then these variables need to be normalised.

2. The relationship between dependent and independent variables is linear.

3. No important input variables have been omitted. This ensures that there is no specification error associated with the data set. The use of a prior theory-based model justifying the choice of input variables ensures this assumption is not violated.

4. The variance of the residuals is the same for all combinations of input variables (i.e., the residuals are homoscedastic rather than heteroscedastic).

5. The residuals must be normally distributed.

6. The residuals must be independent, that is, not correlated.

7. The independent variables are not linearly dependent; that is, there are no linear dependencies among the independent variables.

The tools to be used to verify Assumption 1 are boxplots, the K-S test, and histograms. Boxplots and histograms provide an indication of skewness, whether the variable is normally distributed or not, and the existence of outliers that may need to be removed from the analysis. The K-S test is a formal statistical test to check if a variable is normally distributed or not. It is often the case that variables need to be transformed as a result of this analysis, and the transformation most commonly used is the natural log.

The tools used to verify Assumption 2 are scatterplots and also Pearson correlation analysis. A scatterplot will visually show if there is a linear pattern in the relationship between two variables, and the Pearson's correlation test will formally measure the strength and direction of that relationship.

There are no tools to verify Assumption 3. The choice of independent variables should in theory be ruled by an organisation's needs; however, if this not the case, then the maximum that can happen is for the regression fit to be very poor, which may indicate that there are independent variables missing from the regression equation.

The tools to verify Assumption 4 are the scatterplot and a plot of the residuals against the predicted values. The latter is also used to verify Assumption 6. Let us look at the two scatterplots in Figure 17. These are two of the scatterplots used in Chapter 5. The scatterplot in Figure 17(a) shows that the dependent variable LTOTEFF exhibits

Copyright © 2008, IGI Global. Copying or distributing in print or electronic forms without written permission of IGI Global is prohibited.

fairly constant variability given the values for the independent variable LTOTWP, suggesting constant variance of the residuals. However, Figure 17(b) shows that the dependent variable LTOTEFF exhibits more variability at the zero point given the values for the independent variable LIMGNEW; that is, LTOTEFF varies more when the independent variable has a zero value, compared with nonzero values. This pattern suggests that the residuals do not present constant variance. In this case, even transforming the independent variable would not change this pattern and the best solution would be to remove LIMGNEW from the regression analysis.

The other tool that can be used to verify Assumption 4 is to obtain a plot of residuals against the predicted values. If residuals present a constant variance, they will be scattered all over the plot with no clear pattern (see Figure 18).

The tools that can be used to verify Assumption 5 are the histogram of the residuals (see Figure 19[a]) and the normal P-P plot (probability plots) for the residuals (see Figure 19[b]). Normal P-P plots are generally employed to verify if the distribution of a variable is consistent with the normal distribution. When the distribution is normal, the data points are close to linear.

Finally, the tools that can be used to verify Assumption 7 are Pearson's and Spearman's correlation tests as they measure the strength of the relationship between variables. If the variables identified are significantly correlated, this means that they are not independent and therefore should not be used together in the same regression equation.

Figure 17. Example of scatterplots showing constant and nonconstant variance of the residuals

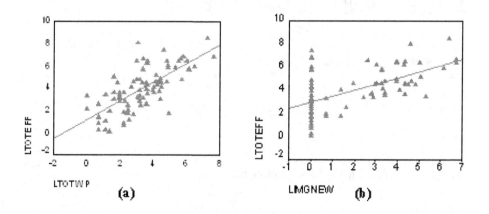

Copyright © 2008, IGI Global. Copying or distributing in print or electronic forms without written permission of IGI Global is prohibited.

Figure 18. Example of residual plot showing constant variance of the residuals (error term)

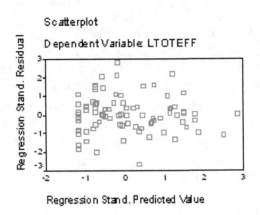

Figure 19. Example of histogram of residuals and P-P plot

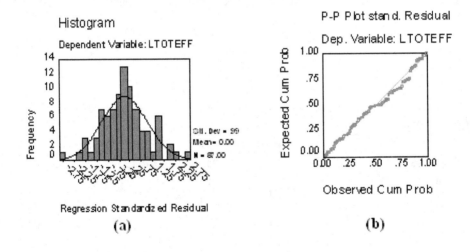

To obtain a residual plot in SPSS, follow these steps:

- Select *Analyze* ⇨ *Regression* ⇨ *Linear.*

Copyright © 2008, IGI Global. Copying or distributing in print or electronic forms without written permission of IGI Global is prohibited.

- Click on the button labeled *Plots*; select using the list on the left with the label *ZRESID* (standardized residuals) and click the right arrow such that this variable's name appears inside the box labeled *Y*. Select using the list on the left the label *ZPRED* (standardized predicted values) and click the right arrow such that this variable's name appears inside the box labeled *X* (see Figure 20[a]); click the button labeled *Continue*.

To obtain a normal P-P plot in SPSS, follow these steps:

- Select *Analyze* ⇨ *Regression* ⇨ *Linear*.
- Click on the button labeled *Plots*; tick the options *Histogram* and *Normal probability plot*. Click the button labeled *Continue* (see Figure 20[b]).

The last point that is important when conducting a regression analysis is to make sure that no individual observations have a very strong influence over the slope of the regression line. These observations are called outliers and their identification is very important to obtain an accurate regression line. Outliers can represent data points that are distant from the regression line and/or have an unusually large value on an independent variable (Fielding & Gilbert, 2006). Cook's *D* statistic can be used to identify such data points. Any data points exhibiting Cook's *D* greater than $4/n$, where *n* represents the total number of observations, are considered to have a high influence on the results. When there are high-influence data points, the stability of the model is tested by removing these points and observing the effect their removal has on the regression equation. If the coefficients remain stable and the adjusted

Figure 20. How to obtain some plots

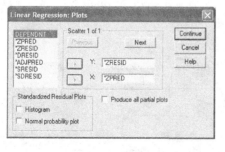
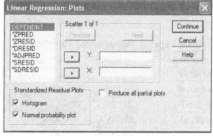

a   *b*

Copyright © 2008, IGI Global. Copying or distributing in print or electronic forms without written permission of IGI Global is prohibited.

R^2 increases, this indicates that the high-influence points are not destabilising the model and therefore do not need to be removed from the analysis.

To obtain Cook's D statistic in SPSS, follow these steps:

- Select Analyze ⇨ Regression ⇨ Linear.
- Click on the button labeled *Save*; tick the option *Cook's* under the group *Distances*. Click the button labeled *Continue*. A new variable will be created named COO_1.

One-Way Analysis of Variance

The one-way analysis of variance (ANOVA) technique enables one to measure the impact that categorical (measured on a nominal or ordinal scale) independent variables have on numerical dependent variables (see Table 19). In a way it corresponds to the regression analysis, however it uses categorical independent variables instead of numerical independent variables. It assumes that the sample is selected from a normally distributed population and that the data contains an equal number of observations on each category, which unfortunately is not always the case when the data represent real data sets of software or Web projects (Maxwell, 2005).

Let us assume that you wish to know if there is a difference in the amount of effort used to develop new Web projects vs. enhancing Web projects. The one-way ANOVA technique will check the hypothesis that the effort means of all the groups (e.g., new projects and enhancement projects) are equal, that is, that the populations from which new Web projects and enhancement projects are drawn have equal means.

The data we will use are presented in Table 20.

Table 19. Types of variables to which one-way ANOVA can be applied to

Variable Type	Independent Variable				
Dependent Variable	Nominal	Ordinal	Interval	Ratio	Absolute
Nominal					
Ordinal					
Interval	ANOVA	ANOVA			
Ratio	ANOVA	ANOVA			
Absolute	ANOVA	ANOVA			

Copyright © 2008, IGI Global. Copying or distributing in print or electronic forms without written permission of IGI Global is prohibited.

Table 20. Data sample to use with the one-way ANOVA technique

	Effort for New Web Projects	Effort for Enhancing Web Projects
	24	29
	23	36
	28	58
	31	57
	52	73
	104	95
	114	98
	130	107
Group Means (GM)	63.25	69.19
Group Variances	2037.36	847.27
Sample Mean (SM)	66.2	
Mean of Group Variances	1442.32	

The effort means for new Web projects and enhancing Web projects are 63.25 and 69.19, respectively. These values do not seem largely different from one another suggesting, at least at first glance, that there are no significant differences in the amount of effort used to develop new Web projects vs. enhancing Web projects. The group variance measures how much variance there is inside a single group. Thus, in our example, a small variance for a given group of projects (e.g., new projects) would represent effort values that would be very close to that group's mean (e.g., 63.25 for new projects). Table 20 shows that the effort variance for new projects is very large, and the effort variance for enhancement projects is also large, however, not as large as that observed for new projects. Although Table 20 is useful to give us an overview of the patterns in the data, further analysis is still necessary to assess whether the differences in effort between new and enhancement projects are statistically significant. What the one-way ANOVA statistical test does in order to check if the differences in the amount of effort used to develop new projects and enhancing projects are statistically significant is to calculate the ratio of the variance between groups, that is, between-groups variance, where groups are new projects and enhancement projects, to the variance within groups, that is, within-groups variance (Maxwell, 2005). This ratio is known as F. The larger the variance in the amount of effort between project types and the smaller the variance within each project type (group), the greater the likelihood that the difference in the amount of effort between project types represents a legitimate difference between the groups, as opposed to being caused due to chance.

Copyright © 2008, IGI Global. Copying or distributing in print or electronic forms without written permission of IGI Global is prohibited.

The between-groups variance (*BG*) calculates the total variation between each group's mean effort (63.25 and 69.19) and the total sample mean (66.2). The equation used to calculate *BG* is:

$$BG = n\frac{\sum_{j=1}^{k}(\overline{G}_j - \overline{S})^2}{k-1},$$ \hfill (22)

where the following applies:

n represents the number of observations in each group. Remember that when using ANOVA, this number is assumed to be the same for all groups. If this is not the case, the statistical tool being used will automatically include missing values such that the number of observations in each group becomes the same (Fielding & Gilbert, 2006).

k represents the number of groups being compared. In our example, $k = 2$ since we have two groups: new Web projects and enhancement Web projects.

$\overline{G}_j$ represents the mean effort for the jth group.

$\overline{S}$ represents the total sample's mean.

The within-groups variance (*WG*) calculates for a given group how much values vary within a single group. Using our example, *WG* measures, for each group, how close effort values are to the mean effort value for that group. Once *WG* is obtained for each group, the average *WG* is calculated and used to obtain *F*. The equation used to calculate *WG* and its average is shown below:

$$WG = \frac{\sum_{j=1}^{k}\dfrac{\sum_{i=1}^{n}(E_i - \overline{G}_j)^2}{n-1}}{k},$$ \hfill (23)

where the following apply:

n represents the number of observations in each group.

k represents the number of groups being compared. In our example, $k = 2$ since we have two groups: new Web projects and enhancement Web projects.

Copyright © 2008, IGI Global. Copying or distributing in print or electronic forms without written permission of IGI Global is prohibited.

$\overline{G}_j$ represents the mean effort for the jth group.

E_i represents the effort value E for the ith observation from the jth group.

To explain how to obtain the between-groups and within-groups variance, we will use as an example the same data previously employed, displayed in Table 20 (see Table 21).

Therefore:

$$BG = 8\frac{17.64}{1} = 141.14$$

(24)

and

Table 21. Calculation of the F ratio for the one-way ANOVA technique

	Effort for New Web projects (EN)	$(EN - \overline{G}_1)^2$	Effort for Enhancement Web projects (EE)	$(EE - \overline{G}_2)^2$
	24	1540.56	29	1615.24
	23	1620.06	36	1101.58
	28	1242.56	58	125.22
	31	1040.06	57	148.60
	52	126.56	73	14.52
	104	1660.56	95	666.16
	114	2575.56	98	830.02
	130	4455.56	107	1429.60
	$\Sigma=$	14261.50	$\Sigma=$	5930.91
Groups means $(\overline{G}_j)$	63.25		69.19	
Group variances	2037.36		847.27	
Sample mean $(\overline{S})$	66.2			
Mean of Group Variances	1442.32			
$(\overline{G}_j - \overline{S})^2$	8.70		8.94	

Copyright © 2008, IGI Global. Copying or distributing in print or electronic forms without written permission of IGI Global is prohibited.

$$WG = \frac{\dfrac{14161.50}{7} + \dfrac{5930.91}{7}}{2} = \frac{2884.63}{2} = 1441.31 \qquad (25)$$

This gives an F equal to:

$$F = \frac{BG}{WG} = \frac{141.14}{1441.31} = 0.097 \qquad (26)$$

Values of F smaller than 1 indicate that the within-groups variance is greater than the between-groups variance, which means that the groups' populations from which observations were drawn have equal means. When this occurs, we cannot reject the null hypothesis. In other words, a value of F equal to 0.097 indicates that the within-groups difference was much greater than the between-groups difference, which means that the differences in effort observed for the two different types of projects have occurred due to chance.

To obtain the one-way ANOVA in SPSS, follow the steps below:

- Select *Analyze* ⇨ *Compare Means* ⇨ *One-Way ANOVA*.
- Select using the list on the left the numerical variable that is the dependent variable, and click the right arrow such that this variable's name appears inside the box labeled *Dependent List*.
- Select using the list on the left the categorical variable that is the independent variable, and click the right arrow such that this variable's name appears inside the box labeled *Factor*.

The output generated in SPSS is shown in Table 22. The F measure is 0.096, which is slightly different from the value we show in Equation 26. This difference is due to SPSS using values with higher precision than those we employed. However, both are very similar. A significance value greater than 0.05 shows that the null hypothesis of equal group means cannot be rejected.

Copyright © 2008, IGI Global. Copying or distributing in print or electronic forms without written permission of IGI Global is prohibited.

Table 22. One-way ANOVA results in SPSS

	Sum of Squares	df	Mean Square	F	Sig.
Between Groups	138.063	1	138.063	.096	.762
Within Groups	20192.375	14	1442.313		
Total	20330.438	15			

How to Compare Distributions between Two or More Variables

In this subsection we are going to look at different types of analysis techniques to use when you wish to compare distributions between two or more variables. Table 23 provides a summary of which technique to use for each particular case as without a summary table it may be a little overwhelming trying to find out which one technique to use when. We have previously described the differences between parametric and nonparametric tests. However, before we carry on describing each individual statistical technique and how to use them in SPSS, we will explain the difference between paired and independent samples.

Suppose you have data on 20 Web projects in your validation set and you have obtained estimated effort for each of these 20 projects using two different effort estimation techniques, Technique A and Technique B. Thus, for each project in the validation set, you will have two values for estimated effort, each obtained using a different effort estimation technique, and two corresponding residuals (see Table

Table 23. Which technique to use when comparing two or more variables

	Two Samples		More than Two Samples	
	Paired Samples	Independent Samples	Paired Samples	Independent Samples
Parametric Tests	Paired-samples T-test	Independent-samples T-test	One-way ANOVA	
Nonparametric Tests	Wilcoxon test	Mann-Whitney U test	Friedman test	Kruskal-Wallis H test

Copyright © 2008, IGI Global. Copying or distributing in print or electronic forms without written permission of IGI Global is prohibited.

24). When we wish to compare the residuals obtained using Technique A to those obtained using Technique B, we cannot ignore the fact that both sets of residuals relate to the same original set of projects. Therefore, the statistical test we have to use in this situation is a paired test.

Now let us suppose you have data on 40 Web projects in your validation set and you have obtained estimated effort for each of these 20 projects using one particular effort estimation technique (Technique A), and have used a different effort estimation technique (Technique B) to obtain effort estimates for the remaining 20 projects in the validation set (see Table 25). Thus, for each project in the validation set, you will have a single value for estimated effort, obtained using either Technique A or Technique B. Since each technique has been applied to a separate set of projects,

Table 24. Example of when to use a paired technique

Project	Actual Effort	Estimated Effort Technique A	Estimated Effort Technique B	Residual Technique A	Residual Technique B
1	A1	EEA1	EEB1	ResA1	ResB1
2	A2	EEA2	EEB2	ResA2	ResB2
3	A3	EEA3	EEB3	ResA3	ResB3
4	A4	EEA4	EEB4	ResA4	ResB4

...

| 20 | A20 | EEA20 | EEB20 | ResA20 | ResB20 |

Table 25. Example of when not to use a paired technique

Project	Actual Effort	Estimated Effort Technique A	Residual Technique A	Project	Actual Effort	Estimated Effort Technique B	Residual Technique B
1	A1	EEA1	ResA1	21	A21	EEB21	ResB21
2	A2	EEA2	ResA2	22	A22	EEB22	ResB22
3	A3	EEA3	ResA3	23	A23	EEB23	ResB23
4	A4	EEA4	ResA4	24	A24	EEB24	ResB24

...

| 20 | A20 | EEA20 | ResA20 | 40 | A40 | EEB40 | ResB40 |

Copyright © 2008, IGI Global. Copying or distributing in print or electronic forms without written permission of IGI Global is prohibited.

if we were to compare the residuals obtained using Technique A to those obtained using Technique B, we would use an independent-samples statistical technique.

Comparing Two Variables

The sample data to be used with all the techniques to be presented below is described in Table 26. It displays the absolute residuals that have been obtained by subtracting estimated effort from actual effort. Two hypothetical effort estimation techniques have been used to obtain estimated effort: Technique A and Technique B. To explain some of the statistical techniques, we will sometimes assume that residuals have been obtained from the same set of original projects (paired samples), or that they have been obtained for independent sets of original projects (independent samples).

Table 26. Data sample to use

Absolute Residuals Technique A	Absolute Residuals Technique B
350.0	600.0
10.0	7.9
30.3	136.1
8.6	42.6
150.0	542.6
27.0	77.0
17.1	83.1
50.0	360.2
50.0	200.1
3.0	24.0
9950.0	85.5
10.0	7.6
4.3	10.9
8.3	53.3
6.2	52.1
40.0	17.6
8.0	15.0
30.0	0.1
20.0	135.5
1.0	8.8

Copyright © 2008, IGI Global. Copying or distributing in print or electronic forms without written permission of IGI Global is prohibited.

Paired-Samples T-Test

The paired-samples T-test is a statistical technique that assumes that the two attributes to be compared are not independent, and that the data are either normally distributed or come from a large sample (mean comes from a normal distribution). Here, the null hypothesis assumes that the average difference between the two sets of values is zero (Healey, 1993). This means that if we were to compute the difference between each pair of values, then add up all the differences and divide by the number of pairs, we would obtain zero. This is what would happen if the two sets of values were the same. The greater the overall difference between the two sets of values, the greater the chances that we will reject the null hypothesis. This test can only be used to compare two pairs of data at a time.

Table 27. Data sample to use for paired-samples T-test

Project	Absolute residuals Technique A	Absolute residuals Technique B	Difference (D)	D^2
1	350.0	600.0	-250.0	62500.0
2	10.0	7.9	2.1	4.4
3	30.3	136.1	-105.9	11209.8
4	8.6	42.6	-34.0	1155.3
5	150.0	542.6	-392.6	154098.1
6	27.0	77.0	-50.0	2495.5
7	17.1	83.1	-66.0	4353.8
8	50.0	360.2	-310.2	96253.5
9	50.0	200.1	-150.1	22542.9
10	3.0	24.0	-21.0	442.9
11	9950.0	85.5	9864.5	97307493.8
12	10.0	7.6	2.4	5.8
13	4.3	10.9	-6.6	43.6
14	8.3	53.3	-45.1	2031.7
15	6.2	52.1	-46.0	2111.9
16	40.0	17.6	22.4	502.4
17	8.0	15.0	-7.0	48.6
18	30.0	0.1	29.9	891.4
19	20.0	135.5	-115.5	13340.8
20	1.0	8.8	-7.8	60.1
	Σ 10773.6	Σ 2460.0	Σ 8313.6	Σ 97681586.5
			$\overline{X}_D$ 415.17	

Copyright © 2008, IGI Global. Copying or distributing in print or electronic forms without written permission of IGI Global is prohibited.

The sample data presented in Table 26 is also displayed in Table 27, where we have added extra columns for the computations.

The statistic to be obtained (t statistic) is computed as:

$$t = \frac{\overline{X}_D}{\frac{S_D}{\sqrt{N-1}}},$$
(27)

where

$\overline{X}_D$ is the mean of the differences (D) between the two sets of values.

S_D is the standard deviation of the differences, calculated as:

$$S_D = \sqrt{\frac{\sum D^2 - ((\sum D)^2 / N)}{N}} = \sqrt{\frac{97681586.5 - (69115856/20)}{20}} = \sqrt{\frac{94225794}{20}} = 2170.55,$$
(28)

where

$\sum D^2$ is the summation of the squared differences and

$\sum D$ is the summation of the differences.

Therefore:

$$t = \frac{415.17}{\frac{2170.55}{\sqrt{19}}} = 0.8337$$
(29)

This t value is not smaller than -2.093 or greater than 2.093, which represents the range of values for which the null hypotheses would be rejected. Therefore, what t tells us is that both ranges of residual values come from the same population; that is, they are not significantly different from one another. We obtain the values -2.093 and 2.093 by looking at a table with distribution of t that is available in many statistics books, for example, Healey (1993).

Copyright © 2008, IGI Global. Copying or distributing in print or electronic forms without written permission of IGI Global is prohibited.

Table 28. Paired-samples T-test results in SPSS

		Paired Differences					t	df	Sig. (2-tailed)
		Mean	Std. Deviation	Std. Error Mean	95% Confidence Interval of the Difference				
					Lower	Upper			
Pair 1	res1 - res2	415.69000	2226.94579	497.96022	-626.55271	1457.93271	.835	19	.414

To obtain the paired-samples T-test in SPSS, follow these steps:

- Select *Analyze* ⇨ *Compare Means* ⇨ *Paired-Samples T Test*.
- Select using the list on the left the two numerical variables that are to be compared, and click the right arrow such that these variables' names appear inside the box labeled *Paired Variables*.

The output generated in SPSS is shown in Table 28. The *t* statistic is 0.835, which is slightly different from the value we show in Equation 29. This difference is due to SPSS using values with higher precision than those we employed. However, both are very similar. A significance value greater than 0.05 indicates that the null hypothesis cannot be rejected, and that the differences between the two population means are equal.

Wilcoxon Signed-Rank Test

The Wilcoxon signed-rank test is a nonparametric test equivalent to the paired-samples T-test to be used when the data samples are small or not normally distributed, or not measured at least on an interval scale. This test uses the sign and rank of the absolute values of pair differences rather than means and standard deviations (Maxwell, 2005). Table 29 shows the same data used for the paired-samples T-test, also used to explain how to apply the Wilcoxon test.

The first step in this procedure is to obtain the differences between the paired values (column Original Difference). Once this is obtained, the next step is to remove the sign, and only use the absolute differences (column Absolute Difference). Next we

Copyright © 2008, IGI Global. Copying or distributing in print or electronic forms without written permission of IGI Global is prohibited.

Table 29. Wilcoxon signed-tank test results

Project	Absolute Residuals Technique A	Absolute Residuals Technique B	Original Difference	Absolute Difference	Rank of Absolute	Signed Rank
1	350.0	600.0	-250.0	250.0	17	-17
2	10.0	7.9	2.1	2.1	1	1
3	30.3	136.1	-105.9	105.9	14	-14
4	8.6	42.6	-34.0	34.0	9	-9
5	150.0	542.6	-392.6	392.6	19	-19
6	27.0	77.0	-50.0	50.0	12	-12
7	17.1	83.1	-66.0	66.0	13	-13
8	50.0	360.2	-310.2	310.2	18	-18
9	50.0	200.1	-150.1	150.1	16	-16
10	3.0	24.0	-21.0	21.0	6	-6
11	9950.0	85.5	9864.5	9864.5	20	20
12	10.0	7.6	2.4	2.4	2	2
13	4.3	10.9	-6.6	6.6	3	-3
14	8.3	53.3	-45.1	45.1	10	-10
15	6.2	52.1	-46.0	46.0	11	-11
16	40.0	17.6	22.4	22.4	7	7
17	8.0	15.0	-7.0	7.0	4	-4
18	30.0	0.1	29.9	29.9	8	8
19	20.0	135.5	-115.5	115.5	15	-15
20	1.0	8.8	-7.8	7.8	5	-5
					W	-134
					N	20

rank the absolute differences, where the smallest absolute difference is ranked 1, and so on. Once this step is finished, we attach to the rank the original sign (positive or negative), obtained from the column Original Difference. Once this final step has been completed, we can compute W, the sum of the signed ranks.

In this example, W equals -134. The range of possible values that W can take, using this example, varies from 210 to -210. 210 is the sum of the 20 unsigned ranks. Since W is negative, this suggests that the absolute residuals tend to be higher using Technique B.

Once we have W, we can calculate z, which is the statistic that will determine if the null hypothesis can be rejected or not (Lowry, 2006). The z statistic is calculated as:

Copyright © 2008, IGI Global. Copying or distributing in print or electronic forms without written permission of IGI Global is prohibited.

$$z = \frac{(W - \mu_w) \pm .5}{\sigma_w} \quad , \tag{30}$$

where

μ_w represents the mean of the sampling distribution W. In this instance, the assumption under the null hypothesis is that W will be close to 0, and therefore μ_w is equal to 0 (Lowry, 2006). When W is greater than μ_w, we use $-.5$; otherwise, we use $+.5$.

σ_w represents the standard deviation of the distribution of W, and is obtained using equation 30.

$$\sigma_w = \sqrt{\frac{N(N+1)(2N+1)}{6}} = \sqrt{\frac{20(21)(40+1)}{6}} = 53.57 \quad , \tag{31}$$

where

N represents the number of pairs being compared.

The z statistic is therefore:

$$z = \frac{(-134) + .5}{53.57} = -2.49 \quad . \tag{32}$$

If z is in the range ± 1.96, then this means that there are no differences between the two paired samples being compared. In our case, z is not within this range, therefore the residuals used in this example come from different populations; that is, they are statistically significantly different.

To obtain the Wilcoxon signed-rank test in SPSS, follow these steps:

- Select *Analyze* ⇨ *Nonparametric Tests* ⇨ *2 Related Samples*.
- Select using the list on the left the two variables that are to be compared, and click the right arrow such that these variables' names appear inside the box labeled *Test Pair(s) List*.
- Tick the test type *Wilcoxon*.

Copyright © 2008, IGI Global. Copying or distributing in print or electronic forms without written permission of IGI Global is prohibited.

Table 30. Wilcoxon signed-tank test results in SPSS

	res2 - res1
Z	-2.501(a)
Asymp. Sig. (2-tailed)	.012

a Based on negative ranks.
b Wilcoxon Signed Ranks Test

The output generated in SPSS is shown in Table 30. The Z statistic is -2.501, which is slightly different from the value we show in equation 32. This difference is due to SPSS using values with higher precision than those we employed. However, both are very similar. A significance value smaller than 0.05 indicates that the null hypothesis is to be rejected, and that the differences between the two samples are legitimate.

Independent-Samples T-Test

The independent-samples T-test is a statistical technique that assumes that the two attributes to be compared are not related to each other (independent), and that the data are either normally distributed, or come from a large sample (mean comes from a normal distribution). When the data sample is not large, the test requires that both samples present an equal variance in the population. This assumption is reasonable as long as the samples we use have similar size. Here the null hypothesis assumes that there are no differences in the sample means between the two samples being compared.

The sample data presented in Table 26 is also displayed in Table 31.

The statistic to be obtained (t statistic) is computed using an equation that is slightly different from the one employed for the paired-samples T-test:

$$t = \frac{\overline{X}_A - \overline{X}_B}{\sigma_{\overline{X}_A - \overline{X}_B}},$$

(33)

where

Copyright © 2008, IGI Global. Copying or distributing in print or electronic forms without written permission of IGI Global is prohibited.

Table 31. Data sample to use for the independent-samples T-test

Project	Absolute residuals Technique A	Project	Absolute residuals Technique B
1	350.0	21	600.0
2	10.0	22	7.9
3	30.3	23	136.1
4	8.6	24	42.6
5	150.0	25	542.6
6	27.0	26	77.0
7	17.1	27	83.1
8	50.0	28	360.2
9	50.0	29	200.1
10	3.0	30	24.0
11	9950.0	31	85.5
12	10.0	32	7.6
13	4.3	33	10.9
14	8.3	34	53.3
15	6.2	35	52.1
16	40.0	36	17.6
17	8.0	37	15.0
18	30.0	38	0.1
19	20.0	39	135.5
20	1.0	40	8.8
	$\overline{X}_A = 538.7$		$\overline{X}_B = 123$

$\overline{X}_A - \overline{X}_B$ is the difference in the sample means, and

$\sigma_{\overline{X}_A - \overline{X}_B}$ is the standard deviation of the sampling distribution of the differences in sample means, calculated as

$$\sigma_{\overline{X}_A - \overline{X}_B} = \sqrt{\frac{N_A s_A^2 + N_B s_B^2}{N_A + N_B - 2}} \sqrt{\frac{N_A + N_B}{N_A N_B}}, \qquad (34)$$

where

N_A and N_B are the sample sizes for samples A and B, respectively, and

s_A and s_B are the sample standard deviations for samples A and B, respectively.

Copyright © 2008, IGI Global. Copying or distributing in print or electronic forms without written permission of IGI Global is prohibited.

Therefore:

$$\sigma_{\bar{X}_A - \bar{X}_B} = \sqrt{\frac{(20)(2216.6)^2 + (20)(175.8)^2}{20 + 20 - 2}} \sqrt{\frac{20 + 20}{(20)(20)}} = (1613.15)(0.32) = 510.12 \tag{35}$$

and

$$t = \frac{538.7 - 123}{510.12} = 0.82 \tag{36}$$

This t value is not smaller than -2.093 or greater than 2.093, which represents the range of values for which the null hypotheses would be rejected. Therefore, what t tells us is that both ranges of residual values come from the same population; that is, they are not significantly different from one another. We obtain the values -2.093 and 2.093 by looking at a table with distribution of t that is available in many statistics books, for example, Healey (1993).

To obtain the independent-samples T-test in SPSS, you need first to prepare the data for analysis. This is shown in Figure 21.

The two original variables to be compared (res1 and res2) need to have their values aggregated into a new variable (both). It is also necessary to create another variable to be used to identify the two different groups each value belongs to. This is done using the new variable group.

Once this is done, we can use SPSS to compare samples by following these steps:

- Select *Analyze* ⇨ *Compare Means* ⇨ *Independent-Samples T Test*.
- Select using the list on the left the variable that aggregates the values for the two attributes to be compared. In our example, this variable is called *both*. Click the right arrow such that this variable's name appears inside the box labeled *Test Variable(s)*.
- Select using the list on the left the variable that is used to distinguish one sample from another. In our example, this variable is called *group*. Click the right arrow such that this variable's name appears inside the box labeled *Grouping Variable*. Click the button labeled *Define Groups*, and tick the option *Use specified values*. Enter in *Group 1* and *Group 2* the values to be used to distinguish both samples. In our example, these values are 1 and 2. Click the button labeled *Continue*.

Copyright © 2008, IGI Global. Copying or distributing in print or electronic forms without written permission of IGI Global is prohibited.

Figure 21. How to prepare the data for the independent-samples T-test

	res1	res2	both	group
1	350.00	600.00	350.00	1
2	10.00	7.90	10.00	1
3	30.30	136.10	30.30	1
4	8.60	42.80	8.60	1
5	160.00	542.80	160.00	1
6	27.00	77.00	27.00	1
7	17.10	83.10	17.10	1
8	60.00	360.20	60.00	1
9	50.00	200.10	50.00	1
10	3.00	24.00	3.00	1
11	9950.00	85.50	9950.00	1
12	10.00	7.60	10.00	1
13	4.30	10.90	4.30	1
14	8.30	63.30	8.30	1
15	6.20	52.10	6.20	1
16	40.00	17.60	40.00	1
17	8.00	15.00	8.00	1
18	30.00	.10	30.00	1
19	20.00	135.50	20.00	1
20	1.00	8.00	1.00	1
21			800.00	2
22			7.90	2
23			136.10	2
24			42.80	2
25			542.80	2
26			77.00	2
27			83.10	2
28			360.20	2
29			200.10	2
30			24.00	2
31			85.50	2
32			7.60	2
33			10.90	2
34			63.30	2
35			52.10	2
36			17.60	2
37			15.00	2
38			.10	2
39			135.50	2
40			8.00	2

The output generated in SPSS is shown in Table 32. The t statistic is 0.836, which is slightly different from the value we show in Equation 36. This difference is due to SPSS using values with higher precision than those we employed. However, both are very similar. The first point we need to consider when looking at Table 32 is whether the Levene's test for equal variances has shown significant differences in the variances between both samples. If it has, then the output for Sig. will show values less than or equal to 0.05. If Sig. has a value of more than 0.05, this means that the variances between the samples are not that different and therefore equal variances can be assumed. If this is the case, then we should consider the significance value associated with t (Sig., two-tailed), which is in the same row as *Equal Variances Assumed*. This is exactly the case in our example. Since the significance value as-

Copyright © 2008, IGI Global. Copying or distributing in print or electronic forms without written permission of IGI Global is prohibited.

Table 32. Independent-samples T-test results in SPSS

		Levene's Test for Equality of Variances		t-test for Equality of Means						
		F	Sig.	t	df	Sig. (2-tailed)	Mean Difference	Std. Error Difference	95% Confidence Interval of the Difference	
									Lower	Upper
Both	Equal variances assumed	3.345	.075	.836	38	.408	415.69000	497.20672	-590.85239	1422.23239
	Equal variances not assumed			.836	19.239	.413	415.69000	497.20672	-624.10093	1455.48093

sociated with *t* is greater than 0.05 (0.408), this indicates that the null hypothesis cannot be rejected, and that both samples of residuals have the similar population mean; that is, they have been drawn from the same population.

Mann-Whitney U Test

The Mann-Whitney U test is a nonparametric test equivalent to the independent-samples T-test to be used when the data samples are small or not normally distributed, or not measured at least on an interval scale. The U statistic, used in this test, is obtained by first pooling and ranking the values for each sample from highest to lowest. Once this step is finished, the ranks for the two samples are summed up and compared (Healey, 1993). Table 33 shows the same data that have been used throughout this section, with additional columns showing the ranking associated with each sample.

The U statistic is calculated as:

$$U = N_A N_B + \frac{N_A(N_A+1)}{2} - \sum R_A,$$

(37)

where

Copyright © 2008, IGI Global. Copying or distributing in print or electronic forms without written permission of IGI Global is prohibited.

Table 33. Mann-Whitney U test results

Project	Absolute residuals Technique A	Rank	Project	Absolute residuals Technique B	Rank
1	350.0	5	21	600.0	2
2	10.0	28.5	22	7.9	34
3	30.3	19	23	136.1	8
4	8.6	31	24	42.6	17
5	150.0	7	25	542.6	3
6	27.0	21	26	77.0	12
7	17.1	25	27	83.1	11
8	50.0	15.5	28	360.2	4
9	50.0	15.5	29	200.1	6
10	3.0	38	30	24.0	22
11	9950.0	1	31	85.5	10
12	10.0	28.5	32	7.6	35
13	4.3	37	33	10.9	27
14	8.3	32	34	53.3	13
15	6.2	36	35	52.1	14
16	40.0	18	36	17.6	24
17	8.0	33	37	15.0	26
18	30.0	20	38	0.1	40
19	20.0	23	39	135.5	9
20	1.0	39	40	8.8	30
		$\sum R_A = 473$			$\sum R_B = 347$

N_A and N_B are the sample sizes for samples A and B, respectively, and $\sum R_A$ is the sum of the ranks for sample A.

Therefore:

$$U = (20)(20) + \frac{(20)(21)}{2} - 473 = 400 + \frac{420}{2} - 473 = 137 \qquad (38)$$

In this example, we have computed U using data from sample A. Had we used data from sample B, U would be as follows:

Copyright © 2008, IGI Global. Copying or distributing in print or electronic forms without written permission of IGI Global is prohibited.

$$U' = (20)(20) + \frac{(20)(21)}{2} - 347 = 400 + \frac{420}{2} - 347 = 263 \qquad (39)$$

The smaller of the two values is the one taken as U.

Once we have obtained U, we still need to assess what this value of U indicates. When both samples are greater than 10, U's distribution approximates a normal distribution. The advantage this brings is that it enables us to use the Z-score tables in order to check the statistical significance associated with U (Healey, 1993). Thus, the only step left is to calculate the Z statistic associated with U, using the following equation:

$$Z = \frac{U - \mu_u}{\sigma_u}, \qquad (40)$$

where the following statements apply:

U is the sample statistic.

μ_u is the mean of the sampling distribution of sample U.

σ_u is the standard deviation of the sampling distribution of sample U.

μ_u is calculated as

$$\mu_u = \frac{N_A N_B}{2} = \frac{(20)(20)}{2} = \frac{400}{2} = 200, \qquad (41)$$

and σ_u is calculated as

$$\sigma_u = \sqrt{\frac{N_A N_B (N_A + N_B + 1)}{12}} = \sqrt{\frac{(20)(20)(41)}{12}} = \sqrt{\frac{16400}{12}} = \sqrt{1366.66} = 36.97. \qquad (42)$$

Therefore:

$$Z = \frac{137 - 200}{36.97} = -1.7. \qquad (43)$$

Copyright © 2008, IGI Global. Copying or distributing in print or electronic forms without written permission of IGI Global is prohibited.

A Z value of -1.7 is not considered to be in the critical region of ± 1.96. Therefore, we cannot reject the null hypothesis of no differences between the two samples.

To obtain the Mann-Whitney U test in SPSS, you need first to prepare the data for analysis, as has been shown in Figure 21.

The two original variables to be compared (res1 and res2) need to have their values aggregated into a new variable (*both*). It is also necessary to create another variable to be used to identify the two different groups each value belongs to. This is done using the new variable *group*.

Once this is done, then we can use SPSS to compare samples by following these steps:

- Select *Analyze* ⇨ *Nonparametric Tests* ⇨ *2 Independent-Samples*.
- Select using the list on the left the variable that aggregates the values for the two attributes to be compared. In our example, this variable is called *both*. Click the right arrow such that this variable's name appears inside the box labeled *Test Variable List*.
- Tick the *Test Type* Mann-Whitney U.
- Select using the list on the left the variable that is used to distinguish one sample from another. In our example, this variable is called *group*. Click the right arrow such that this variable's name appears inside the box labeled *Grouping Variable*. Click the button labeled *Define Groups*. Enter in *Group 1* and *Group 2* the values to be used to distinguish both samples. In our example, these values are 1 and 2. Click the button labeled *Continue*.

The output generated in SPSS is shown in Table 34.

Table 34. Mann-Whitney U test results in SPSS

	both
Mann-Whitney U	137.000
Wilcoxon W	347.000
Z	-1.704
Asymp. Sig. (2-tailed)	.088
Exact Sig. [2*(1-tailed Sig.)]	.091(a)

a Not corrected for ties.
b Grouping Variable: group

Copyright © 2008, IGI Global. Copying or distributing in print or electronic forms without written permission of IGI Global is prohibited.

The Z statistic is -1.704, which is slightly different from the value we show in equation 43. This difference is due to SPSS using values with higher precision than those we employed. However, both are very similar. If Asymp. Sig. (two-tailed) has a value smaller or equal to 0.05, this means that the two samples come from different populations and thus the null hypothesis can be rejected; otherwise, it means that both samples come from the same population and thus the null hypothesis cannot be rejected. In the context of our example, Asymp. Sig. (two-tailed) is equal to 0.088, which is greater than 0.05, therefore we cannot reject the null hypothesis.

Comparing More than Two Variables

The three tests that are commonly used to compare more than two samples (see Table 35) are the one-way ANOVA test (parametric test that has already been described in this chapter), Friedman's test (nonparametric test to be used with paired samples), and the Kruskal-Wallis H test (nonparametric test to be used with independent samples).

Friedman's Test

Friedman's test is a nonparametric test that allows the comparison of three or more paired samples to investigate if all samples could have been drawn from the same population (Hollander & Wolfe, 1973).

Procedure

Start with n rows and k columns. Within each row, rank the observations in ascending order. For example, looking at Table 36, the first row has four observations each corresponding to one of four absolute residuals: 350, 600, 9950, and 85.5. The value

Table 35. Tests used to compare more than two samples

	Two Samples		More than Two Samples	
	Paired Samples	Independent Samples	Paired Samples	Independent Samples
Parametric Tests	Paired-samples T-test	Independent-samples T-test	One-way ANOVA	
Nonparametric Tests	Wilcoxon test	Mann-Whitney U test	Friedman test	Kruskal-Wallis H test

Copyright © 2008, IGI Global. Copying or distributing in print or electronic forms without written permission of IGI Global is prohibited.

Table 36. Friedman's test results

ID	Residuals Tech. A	Rank	Residuals Tech. B	Rank	Residuals Tech. C	Rank	Residuals Tech. D	Rank
1	350	2	600	3	9950	4	85.50	1
2	10	3.5	7.90	2	10	3.5	7.60	1
3	30.30	3	136.10	4	4.30	1	10.90	2
4	8.60	2	42.60	3	8.30	1	53.30	4
5	150	3	542.60	4	6.20	1	52.10	2
6	27	2	77	4	40	3	17.60	1
7	17.10	3	83.10	4	8	1	15	2
8	50	3	360.20	4	30	2	0.10	1
9	50	2	200.10	4	20	1	135.50	3
10	3	2	24	4	1	1	8.80	3
		$\sum = 25.5$		$\sum = 36$		$\sum = 18.5$		$\sum = 20$

85.5 is the smallest of the group, therefore it is ranked 1. The second smallest value is 350, so it is ranked 2, and so on. Once all rows have been ranked, we sum the ranks for each column. When there are ties in the data, the statistic S is computed using the equation presented here:

$$S = \frac{12\sum\limits_{j=1}^{k}(R_j - nR..)^2}{nk(k+1) - \left[\frac{1}{(k-1)}\right]\sum\limits_{i=1}^{n}\{(\sum\limits_{j=1}^{g_i} t_{i,j}^3) - k\}}, \tag{44}$$

where

n is the number of observations (blocks, rows) in each sample,

k is the number of samples (treatments, columns) being compared, and

R_j is the sum (over the n observations) of ranks received by treatment j. Therefore, R_3 would represent the sum of the 10 ranks associated with Treatment 3 (Column 3), which is equal to 18.5 (see Table 36).

$R..$ is the number of treatments plus 1, divided by 2. Therefore, within the scope of our example, $R..$ is equal to $(4 + 1)/2 = 2.5$.

g_i represents the number of tied groups in row i. A tie is when there are two or more values that are equal. So, for example, Table 36 shows that two residuals have

Copyright © 2008, IGI Global. Copying or distributing in print or electronic forms without written permission of IGI Global is prohibited.

the same value, 10, so these are tied groups. This means that $g_2 = 2$; thus Row (or Group) 2 has two ties.

$t_{i,j}$ represents the size of the jth tied group in row i. Here, tied values within a row are each considered a tie of size 1.

When there are no ties, S is replaced by S' using the following equation (Hollander & Wolfe, 1973):

$$S' = [\frac{12}{nk(k+1)} \sum_{j=1}^{k} R_j^2] - 3n(k+1)$$
(45)

In our example, we have two ties, therefore we will explain the calculation of S using Equation 44. We have only one tie, which has occurred in Row 2. The term in curly brackets that is part of the denominator in equation 44 is zero for each row i in which there are no tied observations (Hollander & Wolfe, 1973). Therefore we only need to calculate that term for $i = 2$ since this is the row where ties exist. Row (Block) 2 has one tied group of size 2 (10, 10), and two tied groups each of size 1 (7.9, 7.6). Thus $t_{2,1} = 2$, $t_{2,2}=1$, $t_{2,4}=1$, $g_2 = 2$, and

$$\{(\sum_{j=1}^{g_2} t_{2,j}^3) - k\} = \{(2^3 + 1^3 + 1^3) - 3\} = 7$$

Therefore, applying all the parameters to equation 43 gives the following:

$$S = \frac{12[(25.5-25)^2 + (36-25)^2 + (18.5-25)^2 + (20-25)^2]}{10(4)(5) - \left[\frac{1}{3}\right](7)} = 11.44$$
(46)

An S value of 11.44 is considered to be in the critical region, using the Chi-square distribution, where the lowest level at which we should reject the null hypothesis is approximately 0.004. Therefore, there is a very strong indication that in the case of our example we should reject the null hypothesis that the residuals are equivalent with respect to their prediction accuracy.

To obtain the Friedman's test in SPSS, you follow these steps:

- Select *Analyze* ⇨ *Nonparametric Tests* ⇨ *K Related Samples.*

Copyright © 2008, IGI Global. Copying or distributing in print or electronic forms without written permission of IGI Global is prohibited.

Table 37. Friedman's test results in SPSS

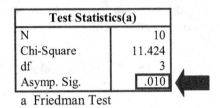

Test Statistics(a)	
N	10
Chi-Square	11.424
df	3
Asymp. Sig.	.010

a Friedman Test

- Select using the list on the left the variables that you wish to compare, and for each one click the right arrow such that this variable's name appears inside the box labeled *Test Variables*.

- Tick the test type *Friedman*.

The output generated in SPSS is shown in Table 37.

The S statistic (Chi-square) is 11.424, which is slightly different from the value we show in Equation 46. This difference is due to SPSS using values with higher precision than those we employed. However, both are very similar. If Asymp. Sig. has a value smaller or equal to 0.05, this means that the samples come from different populations and thus the null hypothesis can be rejected; otherwise, it means that samples come from the same population and thus the null hypothesis cannot be rejected. Within the context of our example, the Asymp. Sig. is equal to 0.010, which is smaller than 0.05, therefore we can reject the null hypothesis that the residuals are equivalent with respect to their prediction accuracy.

Kruskal-Wallis H Test

The Kruskal-Wallis H test is a nonparametric test that allows the comparison of three or more independent samples to investigate if all samples could have been drawn from the same population (Hollander & Wolfe, 1973). It uses the sum of the ranks of the samples being compared in order to compare their distributions. The H statistic used in this test is computed by first pooling and ranking the values for each sample from highest to lowest. Once this step is finished, the ranks for the S samples being compared are summed up and compared. Table 38 shows more sample data organised in a way where it provides three different and independent samples, and with additional columns showing the ranking associated with each sample.

Copyright © 2008, IGI Global. Copying or distributing in print or electronic forms without written permission of IGI Global is prohibited.

Table 38. Kruskal-Wallis H test results

Independent Sample 1		Independent Sample 2		Independent Sample 3	
Residuals Tech. A	Rank	Residuals Tech. B	Rank	Residuals Tech. C	Rank
350	27	600	30	950	31
10	9	7.9	5	15	10
30.3	16	136.1	24	4.3	3
8.6	8	42.6	19	8.3	7
150	25	542.6	29	6.2	4
27	14	77	22	40	18
17.1	11	83.1	23	8	6
50	20	360.2	28	30	15
51	21	200.1	26	20	12
3	2	24	13	1	1
		32	17		
$R_1 =$	153	$R_2 =$	219	$R_3 =$	107

The H statistic is calculated as (Hollander & Wolfe, 1973):

$$H = \frac{12}{N(N+1)} \sum_{j=1}^{k} \frac{R_j^2}{n_j} - 3(N+1)$$

(47)

where the following statements apply:

N represents the total number of observations aggregating all samples.

n_i represents the total number of observations in one treatment (column).

k represents the number of different treatments (columns).

R_j is the sum of all ranks received by treatment j. Therefore, R_3 would represent the sum of the 10 ranks associated with Treatment 3 (Column 3), which is equal to 107 (see Table 38).

Therefore:

Copyright © 2008, IGI Global. Copying or distributing in print or electronic forms without written permission of IGI Global is prohibited.

$$H = \frac{12}{31(32)}(\frac{(153)^2}{10} + \frac{(219)^2}{11} + \frac{(107)^2}{10}) - 3(32) = -1.09$$

$$(48)$$

An H value of -1.09 is considered to be in the critical region, using the Chi-square distribution, where the lowest level at which we should reject the null hypothesis is approximately ± 5.99. Therefore, there is strong indication that in the case of our example, we should reject the null hypothesis that the residuals are equivalent with respect to their prediction accuracy. When we look at Table 38, we can see that the sum of the residuals for Technique B is much larger than that for Techniques A and C, thus we already had an indication there that the null hypothesis was very likely to be rejected.

To obtain the Kruskal-Wallis H test in SPSS, you need to prepare the data first, similarly to what has been done for the Mann-Whitney U test.

The three original variables to be compared need to have their values aggregated into a new variable (*ThreeRes*). It is also necessary to create another variable to be used to identify the three different groups each value belongs to. This is done using the new variable *Group*. Once this is done, we can use SPSS to compare samples by following these steps:

- Select *Analyze* ⇨ *Nonparametric Tests* ⇨ *K Related Samples*.
- Select using the list on the left the variable that aggregates the values for the three attributes to be compared. In our example, this variable is called *Three-Res*. Click the right arrow such that this variable's name appears inside the box labeled *Test Variables*.
- Tick the test type *Kruskal-Wallis H*.

Table 39. Kruskal-Wallis test results in SPSS

Test Statistics(a,b)	
	ThreeRes
Chi-Square	7.416
df	2
Asymp. Sig.	.025

a Kruskal Wallis Test
b Grouping Variable: Group

Copyright © 2008, IGI Global. Copying or distributing in print or electronic forms without written permission of IGI Global is prohibited.

- Select using the list on the left the variable that is used to distinguish one sample from another. In our example, this variable is called *Group*. Click the right arrow such that this variable's name appears inside the box labeled *Grouping Variable*. Click the button labeled *Define Range*. Enter value 1 for *Minimum*, and value 3 for *Maximum*. Values 1 to 3 were used in our example to distinguish both samples. Click the button labeled *Continue*.

The output generated in SPSS is shown in Table 39.

When Asymp. Sig. has a value smaller or equal to 0.05, this means that the samples come from different populations and thus the null hypothesis can be rejected; otherwise, it means that samples come from the same population and thus the null hypothesis cannot be rejected. Within the context of our example, the Asymp. Sig. is equal to 0.025, which is smaller than 0.05, therefore we can reject the null hypothesis that the residuals are equivalent with respect to their prediction accuracy.

Conclusion

This chapter has provided an introduction to statistical techniques that are used when conducting empirical investigations, when obtaining effort estimation models using regression analysis, and when comparing different effort estimation techniques. The chapter was initiated by covered topics such as variable types and scales of measurement, descriptive statistics, normal distributions, and the distinction between parametric and nonparametric tests. Then it followed on to describing visual techniques used to understand the data we are about to analyse, followed by the use of techniques specific to identifying the existence or not of a strong relationship between variables. Finally, it looked at statistical techniques used to compare distributions between two or more variables.

This chapter is not exhaustive in the sense that there are many more statistical concepts and techniques that have not been presented here. We refer the reader to the references that have been used in this chapter as sources of further information in statistics.

References

Fenton, N. E., & Pfleeger, S. L. (1997). *Software metrics: A rigorous and practical approach* (2nd ed.). Boston: PWS Publishing Company.

Copyright © 2008, IGI Global. Copying or distributing in print or electronic forms without written permission of IGI Global is prohibited.

Fielding, J., & Gilbert, N. (2006). *Understanding social statistics* (2nd ed.). London: Sage Publications.

Healey, J. F. (1993). *Statistics: A tool for social research* (3rd ed.). CA: Wadsworth Publishing Company.

Hollander, M., & Wolfe, D. A. (1973). *Nonparametric statistical methods* (1st ed.). New York: John Wiley & Sons.

Kitchenham, B. A., MacDonell, S. G., Pickard, L. M., & Shepperd, M. J. (2001). What accuracy statistics really measure. *IEE Proceedings Software, 148*(3), 81-85.

Lowry, R. (2006). *Concepts and applications of inferential statistic*s. Retrieved July 2006 from http://faculty.vassar.edu/lowry/webtext.html

Maxwell, K. (2005). What you need to know about statistics. In E. Mendes & N. Mosley (Eds.), *Web engineering* (pp. 365-407). Germany: Springer-Verlag.

Sapsford, R., & Jupp, V. (Eds.). (2006). *Data collection and analysis.* London: Sage Publications.

Wild, J. C., & Seber, G. A. F. (2000). Chance encounters: A first course in data analysis and inference (1st ed.). New York: John Wiley & Sons.

Wohlin, C., Runeson, P., Host, M., Ohlsson, M. C., Regnell, B., & Wesslen, A. (2000). *Experimentation in software engineering: An introductio*n (1st ed.). MA: Kluwer Academic Publishers.

Copyright © 2008, IGI Global. Copying or distributing in print or electronic forms without written permission of IGI Global is prohibited.

Chapter XI

The Need for Empirical Web Engineering:
An Introduction

Abstract

The objective of this chapter is to motivate the need for empirical investigations in Web engineering, and additionally to describe the three main types of empirical investigations that can be used by Web companies to understand, control, and improve the products they develop and the processes they use. These three main types of empirical investigations are surveys, case studies, and formal experiments. Although all these three types are described in this chapter, we focused our attention on formal experiments as these are the most difficult type of investigation to plan and execute.

Copyright © 2008, IGI Global. Copying or distributing in print or electronic forms without written permission of IGI Global is prohibited.

Introduction

The World Wide Web (Web) was originally conceived in 1989 as an environment to allow for the sharing of information (e.g., research reports, databases, user manuals) amongst geographically dispersed individuals. The information itself was stored on different servers and was retrieved by means of a single user interface (Web browser). The information consisted primarily of text documents interlinked using a hypertext metaphor (Offutt, 2002).

Since its original inception, the Web has changed into an environment employed for the delivery of many different types of applications. Such applications range from small-scale information-dissemination-like applications, typically developed by writers and artists, to large-scale commercial, enterprise-planning and scheduling, collaborative-work applications. The latter are developed by multidisciplinary teams of people with diverse skills and backgrounds using cutting-edge technologies (Gellersen & Gaedke, 1999; Ginige & Murugesan, 2001; Offutt, 2002).

Numerous current Web applications are fully functional systems that provide business-to-customer and business-to-business e-commerce, and numerous services to a whole gamut of users (Offutt, 2002). The increase in the use of the Web to provide commercial applications has been motivated by several key factors, such as the possible increase of an organisation's competitive position, and the opportunity for small organisations to project their corporate presence in the same way as that of larger organisations (Taylor, McWilliam, Forsyth, & Wade, 2002).

Industries such as travel and hospitality, manufacturing, banking, education, and government utilised Web-based applications to improve and increase their operations (Ginige & Murugesan, 2001). In addition, the Web allows for the development of corporate intranet Web applications for use within the boundaries of organisations (*American Heritage Concise Dictionary*, 1994). The remarkable spread of Web applications into areas of communication and commerce makes it one of the leading and most important branches of the software industry (Offutt, 2002).

To date, the development of industrial Web applications has been in general ad hoc, resulting in poor-quality applications that are difficult to maintain (Murugesan & Deshpande, 2002). The main reasons for such problems are due to a lack of awareness of suitable design and development processes, and poor project management practices (Ginige, 2002). A survey on Web-based projects, published by the Cutter Consortium in 2000, revealed a number of problems with outsourced large Web-based projects (Ginige).

- 84% of surveyed delivered projects did not meet business needs
- 53% of surveyed delivered projects did not provide the required functionality

Copyright © 2008, IGI Global. Copying or distributing in print or electronic forms without written permission of IGI Global is prohibited.

- 79% of surveyed projects presented schedule delays
- 63% of surveyed projects exceeded their budget

As the reliance on larger and more complex Web applications increase, so does the need for using methodologies, standards, and best-practice guidelines to develop applications that are delivered on time and within budget, and that have a high level of quality and are easy to maintain (Lee & Shirani, 2004; Ricca & Tonella, 2001; Taylor et al., 2002). To develop such applications, Web development teams need to use sound methodologies; systematic techniques; quality assurance; rigorous, disciplined, and repeatable processes; better tools; and baselines. Web engineering aims to meet such needs (Ginige & Murugesan, 2001).

Web Engineering and How it Relates to a Scientific Process

The term Web engineering was first published in 1996 in a conference paper by Gellersen, Wicke, and Gaedke (1997). Since then, this term has been cited in numerous publications, and numerous activities devoted to discussing Web engineering have taken place (e.g., workshops, conference tracks, entire conferences).

Web engineering is described as "the use of scientific, engineering, and management principles and systematic approaches with the aim of successfully developing, deploying and maintaining high quality Web-based systems and applications" (Murugesan & Deshpande, 2001).

Engineering is widely taken as a disciplined application of scientific knowledge for the solution of practical problems. A few definitions taken from dictionaries support that.

Engineering is the application of science to the needs of humanity. This is accomplished through knowledge, mathematics, and practical experience applied to the design of useful objects or processes. (Wikipedia, n.d.)

Engineering is the application of scientific principles to practical ends, as the design, manufacture, and operation of structures and machines. (American Heritage Concise Dictionary, 1994)

The profession of applying scientific principles to the design, construction, and maintenance of engines, cars, machines, etc. (mechanical engineering), buildings, bridges, roads, etc. (civil engineering), electrical machines and communication

Copyright © 2008, IGI Global. Copying or distributing in print or electronic forms without written permission of IGI Global is prohibited.

systems (electrical engineering), chemical plant and machinery (chemical engineering), or aircraft (aeronautical engineering). (Collins English Dictionary, 2000)

In all of the above definitions, the need for "the application of scientific principles" has been stressed, where scientific principles are the result of applying a scientific process (Goldstein & Goldstein, 1978). A process in this context means that our current understanding—that is, our theory (hypothesis) of how best to develop, deploy, and maintain high-quality Web-based systems and applications—may be modified or replaced as new evidence is found through the accumulation of data and knowledge.

This process is illustrated in Figure 1 and described here (Goldstein & Goldstein, 1978):

- *Observation:* To observe or read about a phenomenon or set of facts. In most cases, the motivation for such observation is to identify cause and effect relationships between observed items since these entail predictable results. For example, we can observe that an increase in the development of new Web pages seems to increase the corresponding development effort.

- *Hypothesis:* To formulate a hypothesis represents an attempt to explain an observation. It is a tentative theory or assumption that is believed to explain the behaviour under investigation (Fenton & Pfleeger, 1997). The items that participate in the observation are represented by variables (e.g., number of new Web pages, development effort), and the hypothesis indicates what is expected to happen to these variables (e.g., there is a linear relationship between the number of Web pages and development effort, showing that as the number of new Web pages increases, so does the effort to develop these pages). These variables first need to be measured and to do so we need an underlying measurement theory.

- *Prediction:* To predict means to predict results that should be found if the rationale used in the hypothesis formulation is correct (e.g., Web applications with a larger number of new Web pages will use a larger development effort).

- *Validation:* To validate requires experimentation to provide evidence to either support or refute the initial hypothesis. If the evidence refutes the hypothesis, then the hypothesis should be revised or replaced. If the evidence is in support of the hypothesis, then many more replications of the experiment need to be carried out in order to build a better understanding of how variables relate to each other and their cause and effect relationships.

Note that we are not claiming that the phases presented here comprising a scientific method are exhaustive. In other words, there may be other literature in which the

Copyright © 2008, IGI Global. Copying or distributing in print or electronic forms without written permission of IGI Global is prohibited.

Figure 1. The scientific process

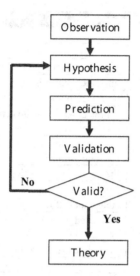

scientific method is introduced using a smaller or larger set of phases than those we have introduced in this chapter.

The scientific process supports knowledge building, which in turn involves the use of empirical studies to test hypotheses previously proposed, and to assess if current understanding of the discipline is correct. Experimentation in Web engineering is therefore essential (Basili, 1996; Basili, Shull, & Lanubile, 1999).

The extent to which scientific principles are applied to developing and maintaining Web applications varies among organisations. More mature organisations generally apply these principles to a larger extent than less mature organisations, where maturity reflects an organisation's use of sound development processes and practices (Fenton & Pfleeger, 1997). Some organisations have clearly defined processes that remain unchanged regardless of the people who work on the projects. For such organisations, success is dictated by following a well-defined process, where feedback is constantly obtained using product, process, and resource measures.

Other organisations have processes that are not so clearly defined (ad hoc) and therefore the success of a project is often determined by the expertise of the development team. In such a scenario, product, process, and resource measures are rarely used and each project represents a potential risk that may lead an organisation, if it gets it wrong, to go into bankruptcy (Pressman, 1998).

Copyright © 2008, IGI Global. Copying or distributing in print or electronic forms without written permission of IGI Global is prohibited.

Table 1. Classification of process, product, and resources for Tukutuku data set

ENTITY	ATTRIBUTE	DESCRIPTION
PROCESS ENTITIES		
PROJECT		
	TYPEPROJ	Type of project (new or enhancement)
	LANGS	Implementation languages used
	DOCPROC	If project followed defined and documented process
	PROIMPR	If project team was involved in a process improvement programme
	METRICS	If project team was part of a software metrics programme
	DEVTEAM	Size of project's development team
WEB DEVELOPMENT		
	TOTEFF	Actual total effort used to develop the Web application
	ESTEFF	Estimated total effort necessary to develop the Web application
	ACCURACY	Procedure used to record effort data
PRODUCT ENTITY		
WEB APPLICATION		
	TYPEAPP	Type of Web application developed
	TOTWP	Total number of Web pages (new and reused)
	NEWWP	Total number of new Web pages
	TOTIMG	Total number of images (new and reused)
	NEWIMG	Total number of new images your company created
	HEFFDEV	Minimum number of hours to develop a single function/feature by one experienced developer that is considered high (above average)
	HEFFADPT	Minimum number of hours to adapt a single function/feature by one experienced developer that is considered high (above average)
	HFOTS	Number of reused high-effort features/functions without adaptation
	HFOTSA	Number of adapted high-effort features/functions
	HNEW	Number of new high-effort features/functions
	FOTS	Number of low-effort features off the shelf
	FOTSA	Number of low-effort features off the shelf and adapted
	NEW	Number of new low-effort features/functions
RESOURCE ENTITY		
DEVELOPMENT TEAM		
	TEAMEXP	Average team experience with the development language(s) employed

Copyright © 2008, IGI Global. Copying or distributing in print or electronic forms without written permission of IGI Global is prohibited.

The variables used in the formulation of hypotheses represent the attributes of real-world entities that we observe. An entity represents a process, product, or resource. A process is defined as a software-related activity. Examples of processes are Web development, Web maintenance, Web design, Web testing, and Web projects. A product is defined as an artefact, deliverable, or document that results from a process activity. Examples of products are Web applications, design documents, testing scripts, and fault reports. Finally, a resource represents an entity required by a process activity. Examples of resources would be Web developers, development tools, and programming languages (Fenton & Pfleeger, 1997).

In addition, for each entity's attribute that is to be measured, it is also useful to identify if the attribute is internal or external. Internal attributes can be measured by examining the product, process, or resource on its own, separate from its behaviour. External attributes can only be measured with respect to how the product, process, or resource relates to its environment (Fenton & Pfleeger, 1997). For example, usability is in general an external attribute since its measurement often depends upon the interaction between user and application. An example of the classification of entities is presented in Table 1 using data definitions from the Tukutuku project. This project collects data on industrial Web projects for the development of effort estimation models and to benchmark productivity across and within Web companies (http://www.cs.auckland.ac.nz/tukutuku).

The measurement of an entity's attributes generates quantitative descriptions of key processes, products, and resources, enabling us to understand behaviour and result. This understanding lets us select better techniques and tools to control and improve our processes, products, and resources (Pfleeger, Jeffery, Curtis, & Kitchenham, 1997).

The measurement theory that has been adopted in this chapter is the representational theory of measurement (Fenton & Pfleeger, 1997). It drives the definition of measurement scales, presented later in this chapter.

Implementing Successful Measurement

If a Web company wishes to initiate or improve the use of measurement to their current products and processes, it first needs to establish a process that will help it achieve these goals. Here we will present a measurement process model proposed by McGarry et al. (2002) and outlined in Figure 2 (adapted from McGarry et al.). This process model has been successfully employed in a number of software projects worldwide and we believe it is also equally applicable to Web projects.

The measurement process model helps a company implement measurement on a project. It includes four main activities, which are as follows.

Copyright © 2008, IGI Global. Copying or distributing in print or electronic forms without written permission of IGI Global is prohibited.

Figure 2. Measurement process model

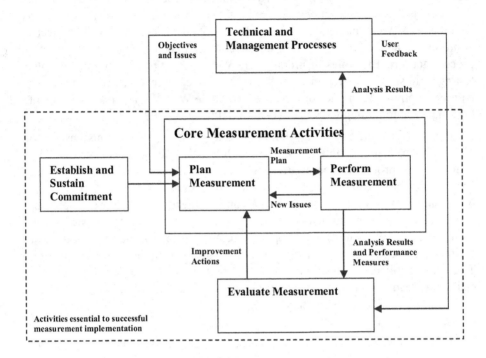

- Plan measurement
- Perform measurement
- Evaluate measurement
- Establish and sustain commitment

Each activity, detailed below, is fundamental to enable the implementation of measurement within an organisation successfully. In this chapter we are only briefly introducing each of the phases used to comprise the measurement process model. Further details are given in McGarry et al. (2002).

Copyright © 2008, IGI Global. Copying or distributing in print or electronic forms without written permission of IGI Global is prohibited.

Plan Measurement

This phase (see Figure 3) identifies the entities, corresponding attributes and measures relative to achieving a particular measurement goal, and is generally associated with one of the following categories that drive measurement goals: schedule and progress, resources and cost, product size and stability, product quality, process performance, technology effectiveness, and customer satisfaction.

Here the measures used to measure each of the attributes are also specified, as well as how the measurement will be carried out, the analysis that will be applied to the data gathered, the reporting mechanisms that will be used and their periodicity, when and how measurement will be carried out (or even if historical data from existing databases will be used as opposed to gathering data from scratch), who is to be involved in the measurement procedure(s), and how the organisation can ensure that the execution of this plan will be carried out without bias and with quality.

An example of a classification of entities and attributes is shown in Table 1, and a corresponding example of a measurement goal related to resources and cost is shown in Table 2.

Figure 3. Plan measurement phase (McGarry et al., 2002)

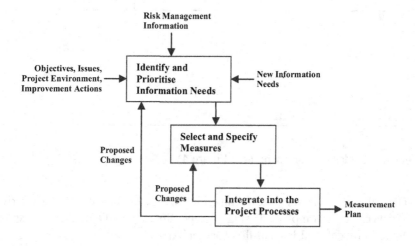

Copyright © 2008, IGI Global. Copying or distributing in print or electronic forms without written permission of IGI Global is prohibited.

Table 2. Measurement goal, questions, and measures

Goal	Question	Measure
Purpose: to measure Issue: Web development processes Object: development process Viewpoint: manager's viewpoint	What attributes can characterise the size of Web applications?	TYPEAPP TOTWP NEWWP TOTIMG NEWIMG HEFFDEV HEFFADPT HFOTS HFOTSA HNEW FOTS FOTSA NEW
	What Web project attributes are believed to have a bearing on Web development effort?	TYPEPROJ LANGS DOCPROC PROIMPR METRICS DEVTEAM
	What influence can developers have on the effort?	TEAMEXP
	How can development processes be measured?	TOTEFF
	How reliable is the effort data?	ACCURACY
	What influence can an authoring tool have on the effort required to author a Web application?	Type

Perform Measurement

This phase includes the following (see Figure 4).

1.   The gathering, analysing, and documenting of measurement data. The gathering of data can be accomplished using three possible types of empirical investigations, to be detailed later in this chapter. Analysis encompasses estimation, feasibility, and performance analysis. Estimation represents what we have seen throughout this book, that is, the use of past data to help estimate effort, to be

Copyright © 2008, IGI Global. Copying or distributing in print or electronic forms without written permission of IGI Global is prohibited.

Figure 4. Perform measurement phase (McGarry et al. 2002)

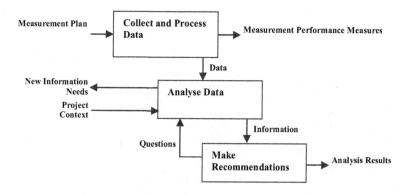

used to also estimate project costs and to allocate resources. This task should be carried out early on in a project's development life cycle. Feasibility analysis employs historical data, previous experience, and reliability checks to assess project plans. Finally, performance analysis assesses if a project is fulfilling a previously defined plan and targets (McGarry et al., 2002). This task aims to identify possible risks and problems and to suggest corrective actions.

2. To report to decision makers the results of the analysis and if any problems were identified. In addition, recommendations are also made outlining risks and problems identified during the data analysis that can affect a project's initial measurement goals. Examples of recommendations are as follows:

    a.   To extend a project's schedule to preserve quality

    b.   To add resources to a project in order to try to finish the project within time

    c.   To remove planned functionality in order to reduce project costs

Evaluate Measurement

This phase (see Figure 5) assesses both the measures and measurement process itself. The first step is to check if the entities, attributes, and measures used satisfy a project manager's information needs. The second step is to assess if the measurement process itself was carried out accordingly. The third step entails the documenting

Copyright © 2008, IGI Global. Copying or distributing in print or electronic forms without written permission of IGI Global is prohibited.

Figure 5. Evaluate measurement phase (McGarry et al. 2002)

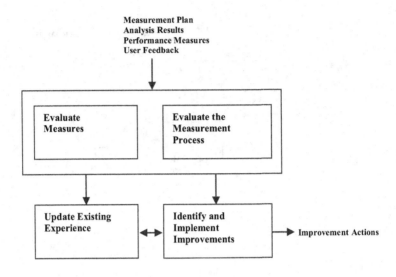

of the lessons learnt from evaluating measures and measurement processes, and finally the fourth details the actions that were carried out to improve the measures and measurement processes.

Establish and Sustain Commitment

This phase (see Figure 6) exists to ensure that a measurement programme is implemented effectively within an organisation; that is, it is supported at both the project and organisational levels. This means that the organisation's commitment to a measurement programme must be obtained, that responsibilities must be clearly defined and resources provided, and that the progress of this programme must also be reviewed.

The next section details three types of empirical investigations that can be used to gather data, with Chapter X detailing the types of analysis, within the context of effort estimation, which can be carried out using gathered data.

Copyright © 2008, IGI Global. Copying or distributing in print or electronic forms without written permission of IGI Global is prohibited.

Figure 6. Establish and sustain commitment phase (McGarry et al., 2002)

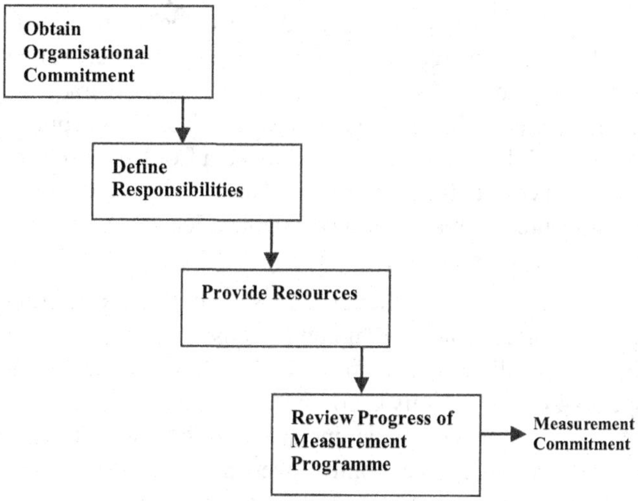

Overview of Empirical Assessments

Validating a hypothesis (research question), which is related to a measurement goal, encompasses experimentation, which is carried out using an empirical investigation. This section details the three different types of empirical investigation that can be carried out, which are the survey, case study, and formal experiment (Fenton & Pfleeger, 1997).

The concepts presented in this section can be used by a Web company to help carry out empirical investigation not only to help improve effort predictions, but also to help compare techniques, methodologies, languages, and so on.

- *Survey:* A retrospective investigation of an activity used to confirm relationships and outcomes (Fenton & Pfleeger, 1997). It is also known as "research in the large" as it often samples over large groups of projects. A survey should always be carried out after the activity under focus has occurred (Kitchenham et al., 2002). When performing a survey, a researcher has no control over the situation at hand; that is, the situation can be documented and compared to

Copyright © 2008, IGI Global. Copying or distributing in print or electronic forms without written permission of IGI Global is prohibited.

other similar situations, but none of the variables being investigated can be manipulated (Fenton & Pfleeger). Within the scope of software and Web engineering, surveys are often used to validate the response of organisations and developers to a new development method, tool, or technique, or to reveal trends or relationships between relevant variables (Fenton & Pfleeger). For example, a survey can be used to measure the effort prediction accuracy throughout an organisation between Web projects that used Sun's J2EE and projects that used Microsoft's ASP.NET because it can gather data from numerous projects. The downside of surveys is time. Gathering data can take many months or even years, and the outcome may only be available after several projects have been completed (Kitchenham et al.).

- *Case study:* An investigation that examines the trends and relationships using as its basis a typical project within an organisation. It is also known as "research in the typical" (Kitchenham et al., 2002). A case study can investigate a retrospective event, but this is not the usual trend. A case study is the type of investigation of choice to examine an event that has not yet occurred and for which there is little or no control over the variables. For example, if an organisation wants to investigate the effect of a programming framework on the accuracy of the effort estimates of the resulting Web application, but cannot develop the same project using numerous frameworks simultaneously, then the investigative choice is to use a case study. If the accuracy of the effort estimate for the resulting Web application is higher than the organisation's accuracy baseline, it may be due to many different reasons (e.g., chance, or perhaps bias from enthusiastic estimators or developers). Even if the programming framework had a legitimate effect on effort accuracy, no conclusions outside the boundaries of the case study can be drawn; that is, the results of a case study cannot be generalised to every possible situation. Had the same application been developed several times, each time using a different programming framework (as in a formal experiment), then it would be possible to have better understanding of the relationship between framework and effort prediction accuracy, given that these variables were controlled. Note that the values for all other attributes should remain the same (e.g., developers, programming experience, development tools, computing power, and type of application). A case study samples from the variables rather than over them. This means that, in relation to the variable programming framework, a value that represents the framework that is usually used on most projects will be the one chosen (e.g., J2EE). A case study is easier to plan than a formal experiment, but its results are harder to explain and, as previously mentioned, cannot be generalised outside the scope of the study (Kitchenham et al.).

- *Formal experiment:* Rigorous and controlled investigation of an event where important variables are identified and manipulated such that their effect on

Copyright © 2008, IGI Global. Copying or distributing in print or electronic forms without written permission of IGI Global is prohibited.

the outcome can be validated (Fenton & Pfleeger, 1997). It is also known as "research in the small" since it is very difficult to carry out formal experiments in software and Web engineering using numerous projects and resources. A formal experiment samples over the variable that is being manipulated, such that all possible variable values are validated; that is, there is a single case representing each possible situation. If we apply the same example used when explaining case studies above, this means that several projects would be developed, each using a different programming framework. If one aims to obtain results that are largely applicable across various types of projects and processes, then the choice of investigation is a formal experiment. This type of investigation is most suited to the Web engineering research community. However, despite the control that needs to be exerted when planning and running a formal experiment, its results cannot be generalised outside the experimental conditions. For example, if an experiment demonstrates that J2EE improves the effort prediction accuracy of e-commerce Web applications, one cannot guarantee that J2EE will also improve the effort prediction accuracy of educational Web applications (Kitchenham et al., 2002).

There are other concrete issues related to using a formal experiment or a case study that may impact the choice of study. It may be feasible to control the variables, but it may come at a very high cost or high degree of risk. If replicating a study is possible but comes at a prohibitive cost, then a case study should be used (Fenton & Pfleeger, 1997). A summary of the characteristics of each type of empirical investigation is given in Table 3.

There are a set of steps broadly common to all three types of investigations, and these are described below.

Table 3. Summary characteristics of the three types of empirical investigations

Characteristic	Survey	Case Study	Formal Experiment
Scale	Research in the Large	Research in the Typical	Research in the Small
Control	No control	Low level of control	High level of control
Replication	No	Low	High
Generalisation	Results representative of sampled population	Only applicable to other projects of similar type and size	Can be generalised within the experimental conditions

Copyright © 2008, IGI Global. Copying or distributing in print or electronic forms without written permission of IGI Global is prohibited.

Define the Goals of Your Investigation and Its Context

Goals are crucial for the success of all activities in an investigation. Thus, it is important to allow enough time to fully understand and set the goals so that each is clear and measurable. Goals represent the research questions (even when the goals are defined by an organisation and not a researcher), which may also be presented by a number of hypotheses. By setting the research questions or hypotheses it becomes easier to identify the dependent and independent variables for the investigation (Fenton & Pfleeger, 1997). A dependent variable is a variable whose behaviour we want to predict or explain. An independent variable is believed to have a causal relationship with, or have influence upon, the dependent variable (Wild & Seber, 2000). Goals also help determine what the investigation will do, and what data are to be collected. Finally, by understanding the goals, we can also confirm if the type of investigation chosen is the most suitable type to use (Fenton & Pfleeger). Each hypothesis of an investigation will later be either supported or rejected. An example of hypotheses is given below (Wild & Seber).

H_0 Using J2EE produces the same Web effort prediction accuracy as using ASP. NET.

H_1 Using J2EE produces a different Web effort prediction accuracy than using ASP. NET.

H_0 is called the null hypothesis and assumes the effort prediction accuracy of Web applications developed using J2EE is similar to that of Web applications developed using ASP.NET. In other words, it assumes that data samples for both groups of applications come from the same population. In this instance, we have two samples: one representing absolute residual values (actual effort - estimated effort) for Web applications developed using J2EE, and the other, absolute residual values for Web applications developed using ASP.NET. Here, the absolute residual is our dependent variable, and the choice of programming framework (e.g., J2EE or ASP.NET) is the independent variable.

H_1 is called the alternative or research hypothesis, and represents what is believed to be true if the null hypothesis is false. The alternative hypothesis assumes that samples do not come from the same sample population. Sometimes the direction of the relationship between dependent and independent variables is also presented as part of an alternative hypothesis. If H_1 also suggested a direction for the relationship, it could be described as follows.

H_1 Using J2EE produces better Web effort prediction accuracy than using ASP. NET.

Copyright © 2008, IGI Global. Copying or distributing in print or electronic forms without written permission of IGI Global is prohibited.

To confirm H_1, it is first necessary to reject the null hypothesis and, second, show that absolute residual values for Web applications developed using J2EE are significantly lower than absolute residual values for Web applications developed using ASP.NET.

We have presented both null and alternative hypotheses since they are both equally important when presenting the results of an investigation, and, as such, both should be documented.

To see if the data justify rejecting H_0, we need to perform a statistical analysis. Before carrying out a statistical analysis, it is important to decide the level of confidence we have that the data sample we gathered truly represents our population of interest.

If we have 95% confidence that the data sample we are using truly represents the general population, there still remains a 5% chance that H_0 will be rejected when in fact it truly represents the current situation. Rejecting H_0 incorrectly is called Type I error, and the probability of this occurring is called the significance level (α). Every statistical analysis test uses α when testing if H_0 should be rejected or not.

Issues to Consider with Empirical Assessments

In addition to defining the goals of an investigation, it is also important to document the context of the investigation (Kitchenham et al., 2002). One suggested way to achieve this is to provide a table, similar to Table 1, describing the entities, attributes, and measures that are the focus of the investigation.

Prepare the Investigation

It is important to prepare an investigation carefully to obtain results from which one can draw valid conclusions, even if these conclusions cannot be scaled up. For case studies and formal experiments, it is important to define the variables that can influence the results, and once defined, decide how much control one can have over them (Fenton & Pfleeger, 1997).

Consider the following case study that would represent a poorly prepared investigation.

The case study aims to investigate, within a given organisation, the effect of using the programming framework J2EE on the effort prediction accuracy of the resulting Web application. Most Web projects in this organisation are developed using ASP.NET, and consequently all of the development team and the project manager have experience with this language. The type of application representative of the

Copyright © 2008, IGI Global. Copying or distributing in print or electronic forms without written permission of IGI Global is prohibited.

majority of applications this organisation undertakes is in electronic commerce (e-commerce), and a typical development team has two developers, plus a project manager that oversees all projects. Therefore, as part of the case study, an e-commerce application is to be developed by two developers using J2EE, and managed by the same project manager that manages the other Web projects. Because we have stated this is a poorly executed case study, we will assume that no other variables have been considered or measured (e.g., developers' experience, project manager's experience, development environment).

The e-commerce application is developed, and the results of the case study show that the effort prediction accuracy of the delivered application is worse than that for the other similar Web applications developed using ASP.NET. When questioned as to why these were the results obtained, the investigator seemed puzzled and was without a clear explanation.

What is Missing?

The investigator should have anticipated that other variables can also have an effect on the results of an investigation, and should have taken these into account. Two such variables are the developers' programming experience and project manager's experience with managing J2EE projects. Without measuring experience prior to the case study, it is impossible to discern if the lower quality is due to J2EE or to the effects of learning J2EE as the investigation proceeds. It is possible that one or both developers and the project manager did not have experience with J2EE, and lack of experience has interfered with the benefits of its use.

Variables such as the developers' and project manager's experience should have been anticipated and if possible controlled; otherwise the investigator risks obtaining results that will be incorrect.

To control a variable is to determine a subset of values for use within the context of the investigation from the complete set of possible values for that variable. For example, using the same case study presented above, if the investigator had measured the developers' experience with J2EE (e.g., low, medium, high) and the project manager's experience with managing J2EE projects, and was able to control this variable, then he or she could have determined that two developers experienced with J2EE and a project manager with experience managing J2EE projects should participate in the case study. If there were no developers with experience in J2EE, and if the project manager also did not have experience managing J2EE projects, two developers and the project manager would be selected and trained.

If, when conducting a case study, it is not possible to control certain variables, they should still be measured and the results documented.

Copyright © 2008, IGI Global. Copying or distributing in print or electronic forms without written permission of IGI Global is prohibited.

If, on the other hand, all variables are controllable, then the type of investigation to use would be a formal experiment.

Another important issue is to identify the population being studied and the sampling technique used. For example, if a survey was designed to investigate the extent to which project managers use automatic project management tools, then a data sample of software programmers is not going to be representative of the population that has been initially specified.

With formal experiments, it is important to describe the process by which experimental participants and objects are selected and assigned to treatments (Kitchenham et al., 2002), where a treatment represents the new tool, programming language, or methodology you want to evaluate. The experimental object, also known as the experimental unit, represents the object to which the treatment is to be applied (e.g., development project, Web application, code). The control object does not use or is not affected by the treatment (Fenton & Pfleeger, 1997). In software and Web engineering it is difficult to have control in the same way as in, say, formal medical experiments.

For example, if you are investigating the effect of a programming framework on effort prediction accuracy, and your treatment is J2EE, you cannot have a control that is "no programming framework" (Kitchenham et al., 2002). Therefore, many formal experiments use as their control a baseline representing what is typical in an organisation. Using the example given previously, our control would be ASP. NET since it represents the typical programming framework used in the organisation. The experimental participant is the person applying the treatment (Fenton & Pfleeger, 1997). As part of the preparation of an investigation, we also include the preparation and validation of data collection instruments. Examples are questionnaires, automatic measurement tools, timing sheets, and so forth. Each has to be prepared carefully such that it clearly and unambiguously identifies what is to be measured. For each variable, it is also important to identify its measurement scale and measurement unit. So, if you are measuring effort, then you should also document its measurement unit (e.g., person hours, person months) or else obtain incorrect and conflicting data. It is also important to document at which stage during the investigation the data collection takes place. If an investigation gathers data on developers' programming experience (before they develop a Web application), size and effort used to design the application, and size and effort used to implement the application, then a diagram, such as the one in Figure 7, may be provided to all participants to help clarify what instrument to use and when to use it.

It is usual for instruments to be validated using pilot studies. A pilot study uses similar conditions to those planned for the real investigation, such that any possible problems can be anticipated. It is highly recommended that those conducting any empirical investigations use pilot studies as they can provide very useful feedback

Copyright © 2008, IGI Global. Copying or distributing in print or electronic forms without written permission of IGI Global is prohibited.

Figure 7. Plan detailing when to apply each instrument

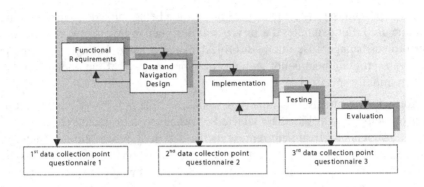

and reduce or remove any problems not previously anticipated. For example, it is often the case that those who designed a questionnaire believe it to be accurate and unambiguous. However, it is important to validate questionnaires to make sure that all questions are clearly stated and unambiguous, and that there is no bias embedded in these questions. Attention to the length of time it takes to answer a questionnaire is also one of the main points of a pilot study, since questionnaires that take too long to be answered reduce the likeliness of them being answered by a large number of people. If you have planned a formal experiment where participants will have to use two different applications, a pilot study will help make sure that the applications are easy to use, or, alternatively, if they require a certain amount of training before being used within the experiment.

Finally, it is also important to document the methods used to reduce any bias. This documentation will help when writing up the results of the investigation and also, as with formal experiments, help with future replications of the experiment.

Analysing the Data and Reporting the Results

The main aspect of this final step is to understand the data collected and to apply statistical techniques that are suitable for the research questions or hypotheses of the investigation. For example, if the data were measured using a nominal or ordinal scale, then statistical techniques that use the mean cannot be applied as this would violate the principles of the representational theory of measurement. If the data are not normally distributed and the sample is small, then it is possible to use nonpara-

Copyright © 2008, IGI Global. Copying or distributing in print or electronic forms without written permission of IGI Global is prohibited.

metric or robust techniques, or, in some cases, to transform the data to conform to the normal distribution (Fenton & Pfleeger, 1997). Further details on data analysis are presented later on in this chapter and also detailed further in Chapter X.

When interpreting and reporting the results of an empirical investigation, it is also important to consider and discuss the validity of the results obtained. There are three types of validity in empirical investigations that can be threatened (Kitchenham et al., 2002; Porter, Siy, Toman, & Votta, 1997): construct validity, interval validity, and external validity. Each is described below.

Construct validity: Represents the extent to which the measures you are using in your investigation really measure the attributes of the entities being investigated. For example, if you are measuring the size of a Web application using IFPUG function points, can you say that the use of IFPUG function points is really measuring the size of a Web application? How valid will the results of your investigation be if you use IFPUG function points to measure a Web application's size? Another example is if you want to measure the experience of Web developers developing Web applications and you use as a measure the number of years they worked for their current employer; it is unlikely that you are using an appropriate measure since your measure does not take into account as well their previous experience developing Web applications.

Internal validity: Represents the extent to which external factors not controlled by the researcher can affect the dependent variable. Suppose that, as part of an investigation, we observe that larger Web applications are related to more productive teams compared to smaller Web applications. We must make sure that team productivity is not being affected by using, for example, highly experienced developers to develop larger applications and less experienced developers to develop smaller applications. If the researcher is unaware of the developers' experience, it is impossible to discern whether the results are due to developers' experience or due to legitimate economies of scale. Typical factors that can affect the internal validity of investigations are variations in human performance, learning effects where participants' skills improve as the investigation progresses, and differences in treatments, data collection forms used, or other experimental materials.

External validity: Represents the extent to which we can generalise the results of our investigation to our population of interest. In most empirical investigations in Web engineering, the population of interest often represents industrial practice. Suppose you carried out a formal experiment with postgraduate students to compare J2EE to ASP.NET, using as the experimental object a small Web application. If this application is not representative of industrial practice, you cannot generalise the results of your investigation beyond the context in which it took place. Another possible problem with this investigation might

Copyright © 2008, IGI Global. Copying or distributing in print or electronic forms without written permission of IGI Global is prohibited.

be the use of students as the participant population. If you have not used Web development professionals, it will also be difficult to generalise the results to industrial practice. Within the context of this example, even if you had used Web development professionals in your investigation, if they did not represent a random sample of your population of interest, you would also be unable to generalise the results to your entire population of interest.

Detailing Formal Experiments

A formal experiment is considered the most difficult type of investigation to carry out since it has to be planned very carefully such that all the important factors are controlled and documented, enabling its further replication. Due to the amount of control that formal experiments use, they can be further replicated and, when replicated under identical conditions, if results are repeatable, they provide better basis for building theories that explain our current understanding of a phenomenon of interest. Another important point related to formal experiments is that the effects of uncontrolled variables upon the results must be minimised. The way to minimise such effect is to use randomisation. Randomisation represents the random assignment of treatments and experimental objects to experimental participants.

In this section we are going to discuss the typical experimental designs used with formal experiments (Wohlin, Host, & Henningsson, 2005), and for each typical design, we will discuss the types of statistical analysis tests that can be used to examine the data gathered from such experiments.

Typical Design 1

There is one independent variable (factor) with two values and one dependent variable. Suppose you are comparing the productivity between Web applications developed using J2EE (treatment) and Web applications developed using ASP.NET (control). Fifty people are participating in the experiment and the experimental object is the same for both groups. Assuming other variables are constant, participants are randomly assigned to J2EE or ASP.NET (see Figure 8).

Once productivity data are gathered for both groups, the next step is to compare the productivity data to check if productivity values for both development frameworks come from the same population (H_0) or from different populations (H_1). If the participants in this experiment represent a large random sample or the productivity data for each group are normally distributed, you can use the independent-samples t-test statistical technique to compare the productivity between both groups. This

Copyright © 2008, IGI Global. Copying or distributing in print or electronic forms without written permission of IGI Global is prohibited.

Figure 8. Example of one-factor design

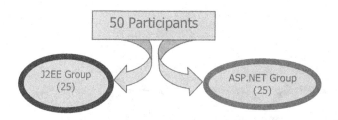

is a parametric test and as such it assumes that the data are normally distributed or the sample is large and random. Otherwise, the statistical technique to use would be the independent-samples Mann-Whitney test, a nonparametric equivalent to the t-test. Nonparametric tests make no assumptions related to the distribution of the data and that is why they are used if you cannot guarantee that your data are normally distributed or represent a large random sample.

Typical Design 1: One Factor and One Confounding Factor

There is one independent variable (factor) with two values and one dependent variable. Suppose you are comparing the productivity between Web applications developed using J2EE (treatment) and Web applications developed using ASP.NET (control). Fifty people are participating in the experiment and the experimental object is the same for both groups. A second factor (confounding factor), gender, is believed to have an effect on productivity; however, you are only interested in comparing different development frameworks and their effect on productivity, not the interaction between gender and framework type on productivity. The solution is to create two blocks (see Figure 9): one with all the female participants, and another with all the male participants, and then, within each block, randomly assign a similar number of participants to J2EE or ASP.NET (balancing).

Once productivity data are gathered for both groups, the next step is to compare the data to check if productivity values for both groups come from the same population (H_0) or come from different populations (H_1). The mechanism used to analyse the data would be the same one presented previously. Two sets of productivity values are compared: one containing productivity values for the 10 females and the 15 males who used J2EE, and the other containing productivity values for the 10 females and the 15 males who used ASP.NET. If the participants in this experiment represent a

Copyright © 2008, IGI Global. Copying or distributing in print or electronic forms without written permission of IGI Global is prohibited.

Figure 9. Example of blocking and balancing with one-factor design

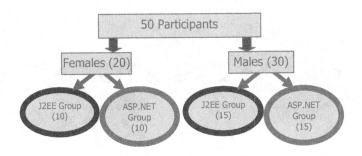

large random sample or the productivity data for each group are normally distributed, you can use the independent-samples t-test statistical technique to compare
the productivity between both groups. Otherwise, the statistical technique to use
would be the independent-samples Mann-Whitney test, a nonparametric equivalent
to the t-test.

Typical Design 2

There is one independent variable (factor) with two values and one dependent variable.
Suppose you are comparing the productivity between Web applications developed
using J2EE (treatment) and Web applications developed using ASP.NET (control).
Fifty people are participating in the experiment using the experimental object. You
also want every participant to be assigned to both the control and the treatment.
Assuming other variables are constant, participants are randomly assigned to the
control or the treatment, and then swapped around (see Figure 10).

Once productivity data are gathered for both groups, the next step is to compare the
productivity data to check if productivity values for both groups come from the same
population (H_0) or come from different populations (H_1). Two sets of productivity
values are compared: The first contains productivity values for 50 participants when
using J2EE; the second contains productivity values for the same 50 participants
when using ASP.NET. Given that each participant was exposed to both control and
treatment, you need to use a paired test. If the participants in this experiment represent a large random sample or the productivity data for each group are normally
distributed, you can use the paired-samples t-test statistical technique to compare
the productivity between both groups. Otherwise, the statistical technique to use

Copyright © 2008, IGI Global. Copying or distributing in print or electronic forms without written permission
of IGI Global is prohibited.

Figure 10. Example of Typical Design 2

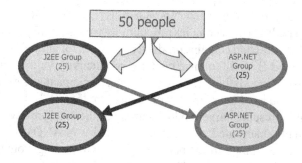

would be the two-related-samples Wilcoxon test, a nonparametric equivalent to the paired-samples t-test.

Typical Design 3

There is one independent variable (factor) with more than two values and one dependent variable. Suppose you are comparing the productivity amongst Web applications designed using Methods A, B, and C. Sixty people are participating in the experiment and the experimental object is the same for all groups. Assuming other variables are constant, participants are randomly assigned to one of the three groups (see Figure 11).

Figure 11. Example of Typical Design 3

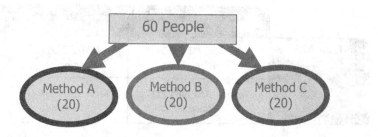

Copyright © 2008, IGI Global. Copying or distributing in print or electronic forms without written permission of IGI Global is prohibited.

Once productivity data are gathered for all three groups, the next step is to compare the productivity data to check if productivity values for all groups come from the same population (H_0) or come from different populations (H_1). Three sets of productivity values are compared: The first contains productivity values for 20 participants when using Method A, the second contains productivity values for another 20 participants when using Method B, and the third contains productivity values for another 20 participants when using Method C. Given that each participant was exposed to only a single method, you need to use an independent-samples test. If the participants in this experiment represent a large random sample or the productivity data for each group are normally distributed, you can use the one-way ANOVA (analysis over variance) statistical technique to compare the productivity among groups. Otherwise, the statistical technique to use would be the Kruskal-Wallis H test, a nonparametric equivalent to the one-way ANOVA.

Typical Design 4

There are at least two independent variables (factors) and one dependent variable. Suppose you are comparing the productivity between Web applications developed using J2EE (treatment) and Web applications developed using ASP.NET (control). Sixty people are participating in the experiment and the experimental object is the same for both groups. A second factor, gender, is believed to have an effect on productivity and you are interested in assessing the interaction between gender and framework type on productivity. The solution is to create four blocks (see Table 4) representing the total number of possible combinations. In this example, each factor has two values; therefore the total number of combinations would be given by multiplying the number of values in the first factor by the number of values in the second factor (2 multiplied by 2), which is equal to 4. Then, assuming that all participants have similar experience using both frameworks, within each gender

Table 4. Example of Typical Design 4

		Gender	
		Female	Male
Framework	**J2EE**	Female, J2EE (15) *Block 1*	Male, J2EE (15) *Block 2*
	ASP.NET	Female, ASP.NET (15) *Block 3*	Male, ASP.NET (15) *Block 4*

Copyright © 2008, IGI Global. Copying or distributing in print or electronic forms without written permission of IGI Global is prohibited.

Table 5. Examples of statistical tests for typical designs

Typical Design	Parametric Test	Nonparametric Test
Design 1: No explicit confounding factor	Independent-samples t-test	Independent-samples Mann-Whitney test
Design 1: Explicit confounding factor	Independent-samples t-test	Independent-samples Mann-Whitney test
Design 2	Paired-samples t-test	Two-related-samples Wilcoxon test
Design 3	One-way ANOVA	Kruskal-Wallis H test
Design 4	Independent-samples t-test	Mann-Whitney test

block, participants are randomly assigned to J2EE or ASP.NET (balancing). In this scenario, each block will provide 15 productivity values.

Once productivity data are gathered for all four blocks, the next step is to compare the productivity data to check if productivity values for males come from the same population (H_0) or come from different populations (H_1), and the same has to be done for females. Here productivity values for Blocks 2 and 4 are compared, and productivity values for Blocks 1 and 3 are compared. If the participants in this experiment represent a large random sample or the productivity data for each group are normally distributed, you can use the independent-samples t-test statistical technique to compare the productivity between groups. Otherwise, the statistical technique to use would be the Mann-Whitney test, a nonparametric equivalent to the independent-samples t-test.

Summary of Typical Designs

Table 5 summarises the statistical tests to be used with each of the typical designs previously introduced. Each of these tests is explained in detail in statistical books, such as Wild and Seber (2000).

Detailing Case Studies

It is often the case that case studies are used in industrial settings to compare two different technologies, tools, or development methodologies. One of the technolo-

Copyright © 2008, IGI Global. Copying or distributing in print or electronic forms without written permission of IGI Global is prohibited.

gies, tools, or development methodologies represents what is currently used by the company, and the other technology, tool, or development methodology represents what is being compared to the company's current situation. Three mechanisms are suggested to organise such comparisons to reduce bias and enforce internal validity (Wohlin et al., 2005).

To compare the results of using the new technology, tool, or development methodology to a company's baseline. A baseline generally represents an average over a set of finished projects. For example, a company may have established a productivity baseline against which to compare present and future projects. This means that productivity data have been gathered from past finished projects and used to obtain an average productivity (productivity baseline). If this is the case, then the productivity related to the project that used the new technology, tool, or development methodology is compared against the existing productivity baseline to assess if its productivity is very similar, higher, or lower than the baseline. Higher productivity would represent a productivity improvement and lower productivity would represent a productivity decline. In addition to productivity, other baselines may also be used by a company, for example, a usability baseline or defect-rate baseline. During such comparison, it is very important to be aware of larger differences between the current development environment (e.g., tools, languages) and that to which it is being compared. If both are very different, then any comparison will need to be interpreted taking these differences into account. Otherwise, any conclusions derived from the case study can be heavily biased.

- To compare the results of using the new technology, tool, or development methodology to a company's sister project, which is used as a baseline. This means that two similar and comparable projects will be carried out: one using the company's current technology, tool, or development methodology, and another using the new technology, tool, or development methodology. Both projects would need to be carried out by development teams with very similar characteristics (e.g., previous experience with the new technology, tool, or development methodology, and team size). In addition, the tools and development environments used should also be similar in order to reduce bias. For example, assume a Web company develops most of its Web applications using J2EE; however, it is interested in using a case study, with a sister project as the baseline, to compare productivity between J2EE and MS Web Designer. This comparison is only feasible if both development environments are similar as well. Once both projects are finished, measures such as productivity, usability, and actual effort can be used to compare the results.

- Whenever the technology, tool, or development methodology applies to individual application components, it is possible to apply at random the new technology, tool, or development methodology to some components and not

Copyright © 2008, IGI Global. Copying or distributing in print or electronic forms without written permission of IGI Global is prohibited.

to others. Later measures such as productivity and actual effort can be used to compare the results.

Detailing Surveys

There are three important points to stress here. The first is that, similar to formal experiments and case studies, it is very important to define beforehand what it is that we wish to investigate (hypotheses) and who the population of interest is. For example, if you plan to conduct a survey to understand how Web applications are currently developed, the best population to use would be one of the Web project managers as he or she has the complete understanding of the development process used. Interviewing Web developers may lead to misleading results as it is often the case that they do not have a broader understanding of the entire development process; if this is the case, their views will be biased. The sample of our population of interest should ideally represent a random sample. This means that each potential participant in the population has the same chance of being included in the sample as all the remaining potential participants from that population. Within the scope of Web and software engineering, to obtain a random sample is extremely difficult. In most cases, we have a self-selected sample, where participants agree to participate upon the receipt of an invitation. If, for example, you are surveying Web developers who have used a certain Web development methodology, it may be that those who agreed to participate in the survey are those developers that had a negative experience with using that methodology, which would lead to distorted results. Therefore, the results from nonrandom samples must be interpreted with caution.

The second point is related to piloting the survey. It is important to ask different users, preferably representative of the population of interest, to read the instrument(s) to be used for data collection to make sure questions are clear and no important questions are missing. It is also important to ask these users to actually answer the questionnaire in order to have a feel for how long it will take them to provide the data being asked for. This should be a similar procedure if you are using interviews.

Finally, the third point relates to the preparation of survey instruments. It is generally the case that instruments will be either questionnaires or interviews. In both cases, instruments should be prepared with care and be free of misleading questions that can bias the results. If you use ordinary mail to post questionnaires to users, make sure you also include a prepaid envelope addressed to yourself to be used to return the questionnaires. You can also alternatively have the same questionnaire available on the Web. Unfortunately, the use of electronic mail as means to broadcast a request to participate in a survey has been impaired by the advent of spam e-mail. Many of us nowadays use filters to stop the receipt of unsolicited junk e-mail, and therefore many survey invitation requests may end up being filtered and deleted. Whether you

Copyright © 2008, IGI Global. Copying or distributing in print or electronic forms without written permission of IGI Global is prohibited.

decide to use a questionnaire or to conduct an interview, it is important that they do not last too long as otherwise it will be difficult to find people willing to participate in your survey. For interviews, it is typical that they do not last more than 1 hour; in relation to questionnaires, they should last no longer than 20 minutes.

Conclusion

This chapter discussed the need for empirical investigations in Web engineering and introduced the three main types of empirical investigation: surveys, case studies, and formal experiments. Each type of investigation was described, although greater detail was given to formal experiments as they are the most difficult type of investigation to conduct.

References

American heritage concise dictionary (3rd ed.). (1994). Houghton Mifflin Company.

Basili, V. R. (1996). The role of experimentation in software engineering: Past, current, and future. *Proceedings of the 18th International Conference on Software Engineering*, 442-449.

Basili, V. R., Shull, F., & Lanubile, F. (1999). Building knowledge through families of experiments. *IEEE Transactions on Software Engineering, 25*(4), 456-473.

Collins English dictionary. (2000). Harper Collins Publishers.

Fenton, N. E., & Pfleeger, S. L. (1997). *Software metrics: A rigorous and practical approach* (2nd ed.). Boston: PWS Publishing Company.

Gellersen, H., & Gaedke, M. (1999). Object-oriented Web application development. *IEEE Internet Computing, 3*(1), 60-68.

Gellersen, H., Wicke, R., & Gaedke, M. (1997). WebComposition: An object-oriented support system for the Web engineering lifecycle. *Journal of Computer Networks and ISDN Systems, 29*(8-13), 865-1553.

Ginige, A. (2002, July). Workshop on Web engineering. Web engineering: Managing the complexity of Web systems development. *Proceedings of the 14th International Conference on Software Engineering and Knowledge Engineering* (pp. 72-729).

Ginige, A., & Murugesan, S. (2001). Web engineering: An introduction. *IEEE Multimedia, 8*(1), 14-18.

Copyright © 2008, IGI Global. Copying or distributing in print or electronic forms without written permission of IGI Global is prohibited.

Goldstein, M., & Goldstein, I. F. (1978). *How we know: An exploration of the scientific process.* New York: Plenum Press.

Kitchenham, B. A., Pfleeger, S. L., Pickard, L. M., Jones, P. W., Hoaglin, D. C., El Emam, K., et al. (2002). Preliminary guidelines for empirical research in software engineering. *IEEE Transactions on Software Engineering, 28*(8), 721-734.

Lee, S. C., & Shirani, A. I. (2004). A component based methodology for Web application development. *Journal of Systems and Software, 71*(1-2), 177-187.

McGarry, J., Card, D., Jones, C., Layman, B., Clark, E., Dean, J., & Hall, F. (2002). *Practical software measurement: Objective information for decision makers.* Addison-Wesley Professional.

Murugesan, S., & Deshpande, Y. (2001). Web engineering, managing diversity and complexity of Web application development. In *Lecture notes in computer science* (Vol. 2016). Heidelberg, Germany: Springer Verlag.

Murugesan, S., & Deshpande, Y. (2002). Meeting the challenges of Web application development: The Web engineering approach. *Proceedings of the 24th International Conference on Software Engineering* (pp. 687-688).

Offutt, J. (2002). Quality attributes of Web software applications. *IEEE Software, 19*(2), 25-32.

Pfleeger, S. L., Jeffery, R., Curtis, B., & Kitchenham, B. A. (1997). Status report on software measurement. *IEEE Software, 14*(2), 33-43.

Porter, A. A., Siy, H. P., Toman, C. A., & Votta, L. G. (1997). An experiment to assess the cost-benefits of code inspections in large scale software development. *Transactions on Software Engineering, 23*(6), 329-346.

Pressman, R. S. (1998). Can Internet-based applications be engineered? *IEEE Software, 15*(5), 104-110.

Ricca, F., & Tonella, P. (2001). Analysis and testing of Web applications. *Proceedings of the 23rd International Conference on Software Engineering* (pp. 25-34).

Taylor, M. J., McWilliam, J., Forsyth, H., & Wade, S. (2002). Methodologies and Website development: A survey of practice. *Information and Software Technology, 44*(6), 381-391.

Wikipedia. (n.d.). Retrieved October 25, 2004, from http://en.wikipedia.org/wiki/Main_Page

Wild, C., & Seber, G. (2000). *Chance encounters: A first course in data analysis and inference.* New York: John Wiley & Sons.

Wohlin, C., Host, M., & Henningsson, K. (2005). Empirical research methods in Web and software engineering. In E. Mendes & N. Mosley (Eds.), *Web engineering* (pp. 409-430). Heidelberg, Germany: Springer-Verlag.

Copyright © 2008, IGI Global. Copying or distributing in print or electronic forms without written permission of IGI Global is prohibited.

About the Author

Dr. Emilia Mendes is a senior lecturer in computer science at the University of Auckland (New Zealand), where she leads the WETA (Web Engineering, Technology and Applications) research group. She is the principal investigator in the Tukutuku research project (http://www.cs.auckland.ac.nz/tukutuku/), aimed at developing and comparing Web effort models using industrial Web project data, and benchmarking productivity within and across Web companies. She has active research interests in the areas of Web engineering, empirical software engineering, hypermedia, and computer science education. In particular, she focuses on Web quality and metrics; measurement, effort prediction, and productivity benchmarking for Web applications; object-oriented metrics and measurement; software and Web engineering education; evidence-based research; systematic literature reviews; and case-based reasoning, all areas in which she has published widely. Dr. Mendes has been on the programme committee of more than 70 conferences and workshops, and on the editorial boards of the *International Journal of Web Engineering and Technology*, the *Journal of Web Engineering*, and the *Journal of Software Measurement*. She has collaborated with Web companies in New Zealand and overseas on Web effort estimation and usability measurement. Dr. Mendes worked in the software industry for 10 years before obtaining her PhD in computer science from the University of Southampton (United Kingdom) and moving to Auckland. She is a member of the Australian and New Zealand Software Measurement Associations.

Copyright © 2008, IGI Global. Copying or distributing in print or electronic forms without written permission of IGI Global is prohibited.

Index

Copyright © 2008, IGI Global. Copying or distributing in print or electronic forms without written permission
of IGI Global is prohibited.

Copyright © 2008, IGI Global. Copying or distributing in print or electronic forms without written permission
of IGI Global is prohibited.

Copyright © 2008, IGI Global. Copying or distributing in print or electronic forms without written permission
of IGI Global is prohibited.

Copyright © 2008, IGI Global. Copying or distributing in print or electronic forms without written permission
of IGI Global is prohibited.

Copyright © 2008, IGI Global. Copying or distributing in print or electronic forms without written permission of IGI Global is prohibited.

Copyright © 2008, IGI Global. Copying or distributing in print or electronic forms without written permission of IGI Global is prohibited.